PENGUIN BOOKS

A DOUBLE LIFE

Sarah Burton's first book, *Imposters: Six Kinds of Liar*, was published by Penguin. She lives near Ely in Cambridgeshire.

A Double Life

A Biography of Charles and Mary Lamb

SARAH BURTON

PENGUIN BOOKS

PENGUIN BOOKS

Published by the Penguin Group
Penguin Books Ltd, 80 Strand, London WC2R 0RL, England
Penguin Group (USA) Inc., 375 Hudson Street, New York, New York 10014, USA
Penguin Books Australia Ltd, 250 Camberwell Road, Camberwell, Victoria 3124, Australia
Penguin Books Canada Ltd, 10 Alcorn Avenue, Toronto, Ontario, Canada M4V 3B2
Penguin Books India (P) Ltd, 11 Community Centre, Panchsheel Park, New Delhi – 110 017, India
Penguin Group (NZ), cnr Airborne and Rosedale Roads, Albany, Auckland 1310, New Zealand
Penguin Books (South Africa) (Pty) Ltd, 24 Sturdee Avenue, Rosebank 2196, South Africa

Penguin Books Ltd, Registered Offices: 80 Strand, London WC2R 0RL, England

www.penguin.com

Published by Viking 2003
Published in Penguin Books 2004
1

Printed in England by Clays Ltd, St Ives plc

For Leslie, with love

Contents

Acknowledgements

Warm thanks to my agent, David Miller, and my editors, Anya Waddington and Mary Mount, for their support and advice.

For helping the book along in various ways, thanks to Maxine Bailey, Margot Coates, Christine Cook, Tony Creasey, Angus Gannagé-Stewart, Jess Garrett, Gina Keene, Rob Laws, Annie Lee, Tahira Patwa, Miranda Pratt, Deborah Rogers, Dominic Sharp, Di Smart, Mary Stewart and Andrew Welfare. I would like to thank the Charles Lamb Society and, especially, Roger Pratt at Hereward Books. Anne and Reg Burton deserve special and loving thanks, as does my brother Matthew.

Prologue

Morning Chronicle

26 SEPTEMBER 1796

On Friday afternoon the Coroner and a respectable Jury sat on the body of a Lady in the neighbourhood of Holborn, who died in consequence of a wound from her daughter the preceding day. It appeared by the evidence adduced, that while the family were preparing for dinner, the young lady seized a case knife laying on the table, and in a menacing manner pursued a little girl, her apprentice, round the room; on the eager calls of her helpless infirm mother to forbear, she renounced her first object, and with loud shrieks approached her parent.

The child by her cries quickly brought up the land-lord of the house, but too late – the dreadful scene presented to him the mother lifeless, pierced to the heart, on a chair, her daughter yet wildly standing over her with the fatal knife, and the venerable old man, her father, weeping by her side, himself bleeding at the forehead from the effects of a severe blow he received from one of the forks she had been madly hurling about the room.

For a few days prior to this the family had observed some symptoms of insanity in her, which had so much increased on the Wednesday evening, that her brother early the next morning went in quest of Dr Pitcairn – had that gentleman been met with, the fatal catastrophe had, in all probability, been prevented.

It seems the young Lady had been once before, in her earlier years, deranged, from the harassing fatigues of too much business. – As her carriage towards her mother was ever affectionate in the extreme, it is believed that to the increased attentiveness, which her parents' infirmities called for by day and night, is to be attributed the present insanity of this ill-fated young woman.

The above unfortunate young person is a Miss Lamb, a mantua-maker, in Little Queen-Street, Lincoln's-inn-fields. She has been, since, removed to Islington mad-house.

The Jury of course brought in their Verdict, *Lunacy*.

Introduction

> We house together, old bachelor and maid, in a sort of
> double singleness.
>
> (Charles Lamb, on life with his sister Mary)

Tales from Shakespeare, the work that is today most associated
with the names of Charles and Mary Lamb, was an immediate
success on its publication in 1807. The *Critical Review* enthused:
'. . . we do not scruple to say, that unless perhaps we except
Robinson Crusoe, they [the 'Tales'] claim the first place, and
stand unique, without rival or competitor'.[1] Brisk sales of the
book ensured a second edition soon appeared and *Tales from
Shakespeare* has never been out of print since. Despite the fact
that it was a book for children, it has been described as forming
'one of the most conspicuous landmarks in the history of the
romantic movement'.[2]

The Lambs themselves were well placed at the hub of what
was to become recognized as the romantic movement and
knew – often intimately – anyone who was anyone, from
Samuel Taylor Coleridge and William Wordsworth to William
Hazlitt and Mary Shelley. They were in no sense hangers-on,
but on the contrary knew many of this circle long before they
became household names. The Lambs were not only highly
esteemed by many members of this group for their literary
abilities, but widely loved for their personal qualities. A degree
of the warmth their friends felt towards them was stimulated

by admiration and respect for the abiding love they bore each other.

The inseparability of Charles and Mary Lamb was a legend in their own lifetime. 'As, amongst certain classes of birds, if you have one you are sure of the other,' wrote Thomas De Quincey, 'so, with respect to the Lambs . . . seeing or hearing the brother, you knew that the sister could not be far off.' William Wordsworth imagined the couple as 'a double tree/ with two collateral stems sprung from one root', while Edward Moxon referred to 'their blended existence'.[3] Their cohabitation lasted for all of Charles's fifty-nine years of life, interrupted only by Mary's bouts of illness, when it was considered best for her to be under supervised care elsewhere. Even then, Charles visited his sister nearly every day, sometimes staying in the nursing-home with her. Although historians and critics have tended to portray Mary as the dependent partner in their relationship, from their correspondence it is clear that Charles needed his sister at least as much. During one of Mary's absences, Charles wrote to a friend:

I have every reason to suppose that this illness, like all her former ones, will be but temporary. But I cannot always feel so. Meantime she is DEAD to me, and I miss a prop. All my strength is gone, and I am like a fool, bereft of her co-operation. I dare not think, lest I should think wrong; so used am I to look up to her in the least & the biggest perplexity. To say all that I know of her would be more than I think anybody could believe or even understand; and when I hope to have her well again with me it would be sinning against her feelings to go about to praise her: for I can conceal nothing that I do from her. She is older, & wiser, & better than me, and all my wretched imperfections I cover to myself by resolutely thinking on her goodness. She would share life & death, heaven & hell with me. She lives but for me.[4]

Charles had many male correspondents, yet while he frequently praised his sister in those letters, he never unburdened himself in this vein. The friend to whom he wrote these words was Dorothy Wordsworth, sister of the poet, who was perhaps the one of their circle best able to comprehend that the sibling relationship could be an agonizing, as well as a companionable, kind of marriage. Lamenting his own shortcomings, Charles invoked connubial imagery when he wrote of his sister: 'I know that she has cleaved to me, FOR BETTER, FOR WORSE.'[5] Similarly, during one of her enforced absences he described himself as 'widowed'.[6]

Neither Charles nor Mary ever married, although both were very interested in children. Mary's ill health put marriage for her out of the question, while the financial and emotional strain of looking after his sister is the most usual explanation given for Charles's lifelong bachelorhood. It is possible that both were afraid of passing on the illness which had supposedly dogged the family through previous generations. Yet Charles was at least twice sufficiently in love to think of marrying, and Mary may be believed sincere when she wrote to a girlfriend who was having trouble with her sister-in-law: 'You will smile when I tell you I think myself the only woman in the world, who could live with a brother's wife, and make a real friend of her.'[7]

Instead the couple devoted themselves to each other, and to writing. Although he abandoned serious poetry early in his literary career, Charles's best-known poem ('The Old Familiar Faces') continues to appear in standard anthologies today and A. C. Bradley considered him the greatest critic of his century. There was a time when few middle-class homes would have been without a copy of either their collaborative effort, *Tales from Shakespeare*, or a collection of Charles's essays, penned under the pseudonym Elia. *The Essays of Elia* (1823) strongly influenced the essay form, while making a cult figure of their charming yet unreliable narrator.

Behind the amiable persona of Elia was the equally entertaining Charles; one has to go a long way to find him described by anyone of his acquaintance except in the most affectionate and admiring terms. Hazlitt's opinion is typical:

Mr Lamb excels in familiar conversation almost as much as in writing, when his modesty does not overpower his self-possession. He is as little of a proser as possible; but he *blurts* out the finest wit and sense in the world. [Charles's stammer made him a less eloquent speaker than writer.] . . . Mr Lamb is a general favourite with those who know him. His character is equally singular and amiable. He is endeared to his friends not less by his foibles than his virtues; he insures their esteem by the one, and does not wound their self-love by the other. He gains ground in the opinion of others by making no advances in his own.[8]

As for Mary, Hazlitt said that he had only ever met with one thoroughly reasonable woman, and she was Mary Lamb. Mary was known for 'the sweetness of her disposition, the clearness of her understanding, and the gentle wisdom of all her acts and words', and it was because of these qualities that many friends turned to her for advice and sympathy when they were experiencing all kinds of difficulties.[9] Though not a 'wit' like her brother, she was intelligent and insightful. While many of her friends waxed lyrical on the subject of her virtues as a confidante and adviser, Henry Crabb Robinson's economic praise serves as well as any: 'With her I can unbosom myself cordially.'

The Lambs lived extremely modestly, mostly in rented lodgings, although their hospitality was famous. The London literary scene of the time has been characterized as 'inbred', as the same set of acquaintances moved from one drawing-room to the next, although it is more justly characterized as a loose grouping of like minds who, finding each other's company stimulating, framed the week in order to enjoy it often. Sunday lunch saw the gathering of writers and artists at the studio of Benjamin Haydon; on Tuesdays Thomas Alspaper was 'at home' for music and whist; on other occasions the composer Vincent Novello offered music, cheese and beer; but it was the Lambs' suppers, usually held on a Wednesday or Thursday, which were the high point of the week, comprising feasts less for the palate than for the mind and soul. 'How oft did we cut into the haunch of letters, while we discussed the haunch of mutton on the table! How we skimmed the dream of criticism! How we got into the heart of controversy! How we picked out the marrow of authors!' recalled Hazlitt. 'What I would not give for another Thursday evening,' wrote the radical writer and publisher Leigh Hunt, while the lawyer Crabb Robinson remembered, 'In Lamb's humble apartment I spent many happy hours and saw a greater number of excellent persons than I have ever seen collected together in one room.'[10]

Charles and Mary also counted among their close friends and regular correspondents the Wordsworths and Coleridge (Charles's closest friend from his schooldays at Christ's Hospital to the day Coleridge died), as well as William Godwin, Mary Shelley, Thomas De Quincey, Robert Southey and a host of other now less familiar literary figures. However, gatherings at the Lambs' were not solely a forum for serious talk, and literature was often not the principal topic of conversation: also numbered among the Lambs' friends were actors, artists and musicians, as well as a disparate collection of people who appealed to the Lambs' idiosyncratic taste, from sea captains to eccentric academics. While their home was often an intellectual hotbed, it was also the scene of a good deal of hilarity and drinking; as Hazlitt put it: 'wit and good fellowship was the motto inscribed over the door'.[11]

At the centre of this most glittering circle in the opening years of the nineteenth century were Charles Lamb and the quieter, more reserved, much-loved figure of his sister Mary. Certainly a reason for the particular regard in which the couple were held by some of their many friends was the knowledge that the Lambs woke up every morning to a private nightmare, a phantom which haunted their past, their present and their future. Only a handful of the habitués of the Lambs' convivial weekly gatherings were aware that the couple were living with the consequences of a calamitous event which had taken place in their family, leaving Charles dependent on alcohol, and Mary suffering periodic attacks of insanity.

1. Polly and Charley

Her memory is unnaturally strong; and from ages past, if we may so call the earliest records of our poor life, she fetches thousands of names and things that never would have dawned on me again, and thousands from the ten years she lived before me. What took place from early girlhood to her coming of age principally lives again (every important thing and every trifle) in her brain with the vividness of real presence. For twelve hours incessantly she will pour out without intermission all her past life, forgetting nothing, pouring out name after name to the Waldens as if in a dream; sense and nonsense; truths and errors all huddled together; a medley between inspiration and possession.

(Letter from Charles Lamb to Miss Fryer, 14 February 1834)

When Charles and Mary's father, John Lamb, was a boy growing up in Lincoln in the 1730s, he and his schoolfellows defined themselves as either 'Above Boys' or 'Below Boys', depending on whether they lived or boarded in the part of town which was on the hill or in the valley. This accident of geography was seized upon by the Lincoln schoolboys as an adequate rationale for hostility between the two tribes. In his essay 'Poor Relations' Charles recalled his sensations of anxiety as a child during the regular visits of one of his father's old schoolfriends, whom his father would unfailingly bait with the old controversy, continuing to insist on 'the general superiority, in skill and hardihood, of the *Above Boys* (his own faction) over the *Below Boys*'. While Charles's account is amusing, it conveys no note of jocularity in the exchanges between the two old rivals, which were so heated that the child Charles feared they would end in blows. Perhaps the reason that John Lamb (otherwise known for his characteristic good humour and love of quips) stood so emphatically upon this apparently trivial piece of history was that he would never be an 'Above Boy', in any sense, again.

Lincoln School had been a going concern since the dawn of the eleventh century and its curriculum (Latin and Greek, English reading and writing and accountancy) fitted its pupils for a range of respectable and secure professions. A large number of alumni went into posts as rural parsons, although the school also produced a number of senior academics and civil servants. In common with most contemporary schools, all the boys – about sixty in number, ranging in age from seven to eighteen – were taught in one room, organized in 'forms' (literally, benches). Boy who lived in the many villages dotting the fens around Lincoln boarded in the town; this was in all probability John Lamb's situation.

John Lamb's father was a cobbler, but a number of poor boys gained places by becoming cathedral choristers or by an arrangement with Lincoln Christ's Hospital – one of the famous 'Bluecoat' schools providing free education – which annually sent one or two of its most promising students to Lincoln School in the hope of securing a university place. John Lamb may have entered the school by either of these routes. In any event, John was not destined for university, let alone the church. A change in the family's fortunes is the most likely explanation for the discontinuation of his education. While still a boy he was sent to Bath to go into domestic service as a footman. The 'Above Boy' was to remain a servant, and acutely conscious of his status as such, until the day he died.

By the time Mary was born in 1764 John Lamb had moved to London and was in the post he was to occupy for the rest of his life: that of general factotum to the lawyer Samuel Salt. John also assisted, in the capacity of butler, at the dining arrangements in the Inner Temple Hall. In 'The Old Benchers of the Inner Temple' Charles painted this telling portrait of Salt and his servant (whom he here calls 'Lovel'):

S. had the reputation of being a very clever man, and of excellent discernment in the chamber practice of the law. I suspect his knowledge did not amount to much. When a case of difficult disposition of money, testamentary or otherwise, came before him, he ordinarily handed it over with a few instructions to his man Lovel, who was a quick little fellow, and would dispatch it out of hand by the light of natural understanding, of which he had an uncommon share. It was incredible what reputes for talents S. enjoyed by the mere trick of gravity. He was a shy man; a child might pose him in a minute – indolent and procrastinating to the last degree. Yet men would give him credit for vast application in spite of himself. He was not to be trusted with himself with impunity. He never dressed for a dinner party but he forgot his sword – they wore swords then – or some other necessary part of his equipage. Lovel had his eye upon him on all these occasions, and ordinarily gave him his cue. If there was anything which he [Salt] could speak unseasonably, he was sure to do it . . . Yet S. was thought by some of the greatest men of his time a fit person to be consulted, not alone in matters pertaining to the law, but in the ordinary niceties and embarrassments of conduct – from force of manner entirely . . .

Salt . . . never knew what he was worth in the world; and having but a competency for his rank, which his indolent habits were little calculated to improve, might have suffered severely if he had not had honest people about him. Lovel took care of everything. He was at once his clerk, his good servant, his dresser, his friend, his 'flapper', his guide, stop-watch, auditor, treasurer. He [Salt] did nothing without consulting Lovel, or failed in anything without expecting and fearing his admonishing. He put himself almost too much in his hands, had they not been the purest in the world. He resigned his title almost to respect as a master, if L. could ever have forgotten for a moment that he was a servant.*

Professionally a man of many parts, John Lamb also turned his 'natural genius' to sculpture, intricate carpentry and humorous poetry, some of which was published, although Charles's claim that his father was 'next to Swift and Prior' in this field may display more of filial admiration than judgement. His most valuable bequest to his children was his considerable intelligence. Doubtless he was in some part responsible for the poetic facility of both Charles and Mary, and while Mary inherited his diplomatic skills, to Charles fell an addiction to puns and wordplay. John Lamb also engendered in Charles and Mary a lifelong passion for card-games.

It has been reasonably suggested that all three of the Lamb children absorbed from their father a liberal and benevolent outlook on life derived from the twin currents of Reform in politics and Dissent in religion.[1] Both Charles and Mary would continue to have an unshakeable religious faith throughout their lives, though neither were great church-goers; similarly they were not strongly party-political, but could become exercised over single-issue politics. An inbred tolerance and respect for those who held views different from their own did not, however, prevent them from challenging those views.

* In Charles's play Mr H— (1806) the hero's valet, John, also seems based on Mr Lamb, knowing his master's 'foibles', anticipating his lapses, and cautioning him against unseasonable speech.

Regarding his father's character, Charles always emphasized his honesty, which he at one point interestingly refined to 'an incorrigible and losing honesty'. That John Lamb was trusting, as well as trustworthy, may explain why the family appears to have been cheated out of a legacy which could have made their life more comfortable.[2] John Lamb was not the sort to make a fuss about money, and by example taught his children the same handicapping virtue. Charles provides a clue to this in a letter to William Wordsworth, in which he apologizes for not having bought some books Wordsworth had asked him to procure for him, explaining:

I have been waiting for the liquidation of a debt to enable myself to set about your commission handsomely, for it is a scurvy thing to cry GIVE ME the money first, & I am the first of the family of the Lambs that have done it for many centuries: but the debt remains as it was, and my old friend that I accommodated has generously forgot it![3]

'Scurvy' behaviour, it seems, was to be avoided, at all costs.

John Lamb also impressed on his children the notion that it was a man's values and conduct rather than the conditions of his birth which made him a gentleman (or not); by the same token, social rank did not exempt any man from censure for 'scurvy' behaviour. According to his son:

In the cause of the oppressed he never considered inequalities, or calculated the number of his opponents. He once wrested the sword out of the hand of a man of quality that had drawn upon him; and pommelled him severely with the hilt of it. The swordsman had offered insult to a female – an occasion upon which no odds against him could have prevented the interference of Lovel. He would stand next day bare-headed to the same person, modestly to excuse his interference – for L. never forgot rank, where something better was not concerned.

Charles, for one, took his father's example to heart, and as a writer was to return many times to the lack of consonance between inherited gentility (which conferred value on the 'men of quality') and what he had been brought up to appreciate as 'true' gentility (which conferred value on everyone else, even and especially the poor and the merely female).

Social status was a ticklish subject for the Lambs. Elizabeth Field, Charles and Mary's mother, may well have considered herself a cut above her husband's family, although she too was from the servant class. Her father, Edward Field, and grandfather had been gardeners and her widowed mother, Mary, was housekeeper to a substantial property near Widford in Hertfordshire, the owners of which, the Plumer family, rarely visited. On William Plumer's death in 1767, his son retained Mary Field as a companion-cum-housekeeper for his elderly mother. Following Mrs Plumer's death, Mrs Field stayed on to look after the usually empty house. Consequently, as Charles wrote, 'though she was not indeed the mistress of this great house, but had only the charge of it . . . still she lived in it in a manner as if it had been her own, and kept up the dignity of the great house in a sort while she lived'.[4] Mary Field's sister (Elizabeth's aunt), Ann Gladman, had also done well in her way, marrying 'a substantial yeoman'; she too lived in Hertfordshire, near Wheathampstead (about twenty miles from Widford).

Plumer the elder and the younger – they were both Whig MPs – were great friends of Samuel Salt and it would have been during Salt's visits to Blakesware that a relationship between Salt's 'man' and the daughter of Plumer's housekeeper would have developed below stairs. John Lamb and

Elizabeth Field were married at St Dunstan's-in-the-Field, London, on 29 March 1761. John was about thirty-six, his wife about twenty-four. Elizabeth was, according to her daughter Mary, 'a perfect gentlewoman', but unfortunately there exists no detailed description of her in any of Charles or Mary's writing. This was possibly a subject too painful to be considered, even from behind the mask of 'Elia', Charles's essayist alter-ego.

John and Elizabeth Lamb's first child, Elizabeth, was born in 1762 and died in infancy. A healthy baby, John, was born the following year and was to prove the apple of his mother's eye. A year later Mary arrived, who also thrived. The next year Samuel was born and soon died. After four confinements in as many years there was perhaps a welcome interval before, in 1768, another little girl, also named Elizabeth, was born. She too died in childhood and Mary was evidently old enough to feel the loss. As an adult she was to write to a friend who had recently lost her own child:

Together with the recollection of your dear baby, the image of a little sister I once had comes as fresh into my mind as if I had seen her lately. A little cap with white satin ribbon, grown yellow with long keeping, and a lock of light hair, were the only relics left of her. The sight of them always brought her pretty, fair face to my view, that to this day I seem to have a perfect recollection of her features.[5]

Mary does not mention another child, Edward, born two years later, which suggests that he may have died almost immediately, and thus she never knew him. Of the first six little Lambs, John and Mary were the only ones to survive infancy.*

* There was possibly a further child, William, who died in 1772.

There is good reason to believe that Mary's childhood was a difficult one. As Charles was to write in a letter to Samuel Taylor Coleridge many years later:

Poor Mary, my mother indeed *never understood* her right. She loved her, as she loved us all with a MOTHER'S LOVE, but in opinion, in feeling, & sentiment, & disposition, bore so distant a resemblance to her daughter, that she never understood her right. Never could believe how much *she* loved her – but met her caresses, her prot-estations of filial affection, too frequently with coldness and REPULSE, – Still she was a good mother, God forbid I should think of her but *most* respectfully, MOST affectionately. Yet she would always love my brother above Mary, who was not worthy of one tenth of that affection, which Mary had a right to claim.[6]

When the last of the Lambs was born, in 1775, Mary was eleven years old, and finally found in her baby brother Charles a repository for the affection her mother rejected.* Although Charles was not emotionally neglected to the same extent as his sister, his descriptions of Elizabeth's brand of 'Mother's love' rarely rose above 'fondness' for him, concern for his 'welfare', and pride in 'her *school-boy*'. Like Mary, little Charles was acutely aware that not only in his mother's but in his grandmother's eyes their brother John was 'a king to the rest of us'.[7]

Although there is no record that Mary ever complained in later life of her mother's coldness towards her, as an adult she advised a young woman who was suffering from some unspecified unhappiness 'to devote herself to a younger brother she had, in the same way that she had attended to her own brother Charles in his infancy, as the wholsomest and

* Charles Lamb was born on 10 February 1775.

surest means for all cure'.[8] If Charles was Mary's cure, Mary was Charles's nurse, teacher, companion and example. 'She is older, & wiser, & better than me' was the belief he held until the end of his life. As an adult female – and a spinster – socially inferior to her much younger brother who had 'now become my lord & master', she recalled with some relish the absolute dominion she had enjoyed over him as a child, 'whom I could controul and correct at my own pleasure'.[9]

Mary was a gentle tyrant, and the influence she had over Charles contrasted sharply with her relationship with her older brother. While her letters give no indication of her feelings, her definition of a typical elder brother as one who had unlimited right 'to domineer over you, to be the inspector of all your actions, & to direct, & govern you with a stern voice & a high hand' seems likely to have found its model in her own elder brother.[10] Charles was mercifully preserved from direct competition with his brother by their age gap – he was twelve years younger than John, whereas only eighteen months separated John and Mary. (Charles and Mary's diminutive stature and dark colouring also contrasted with tall blond John.) Charles suffered an illness as a small child which was probably poliomyelitis, leaving him with rather spindly legs and a 'plantigrade' step as an adult. During his recuperation, while he was still lame, it was his handsome elder brother who carried him on his back; Charles was to follow in his big brother's footsteps, attending the same school and later working in the same office, but it was his bond with his sister which was to become a legendary example of interdependence.

At about the time that Charles joined the Lamb family, its number was swelled by another addition: his aunt, Sarah Lamb, came to live with them. Sarah, although a well-meaning individual, was a stranger to tact. It was she who, during one of the tense visits of the 'Below Boy' – whom the family knew to be living in greatly reduced circumstances – sent a *frisson* round the table by pressing an extra portion on him with the searing words: 'Do take another slice, Mr Billet, for you do not get pudding every day.'[11]★

Charles wrote about his aunt in the most affectionate terms. A woman of few words (for which, given the above example, the family may well have been grateful), she spent most of her time reading an eclectic range of religious works and attending a variety of churches. Born and bred on the Lincolnshire Fens, unlike her brother Sarah Lamb had not lost her plain country manner. 'Andsome is as andsome duzz,' she used to tell her nephew.[12] As Charles summed up his recollections of her, despite her clumsy manner, 'she was a steadfast, friendly being, and a fine *old Christian*. She was a woman of strong sense, and a shrewd mind – extraordinary at a *repartee*; one of the few occasions of her breaking silence – else she did not much value wit.' If the plan had been that Aunt Sarah would help out with domestic chores in the expanding household, this seems to have been unlikely in the event. The only 'secular employment' Charles recalled seeing her engaged in was 'the splitting of French beans, and dropping them into a China basin of fair water'.[13] However, it is Mary's pen, in a letter to her friend Sarah Stoddart (later to marry William Hazlitt), that most

★ Biographers of the Lambs universally conflate the name of Sarah Lamb with that of Aunt Hetty (the aunt of the Elia essays, a character based on Sarah Lamb), often referring to Sarah Lamb as Aunt Hetty. However, there is no evidence that the family ever called Sarah Hetty, Charles referring to her in letters uniformly as 'my Aunt' and Mary using 'Aunt' and also 'Aunty'. Hetty is not a diminutive of Sarah, but of Harriet, Henrietta or Elizabeth. Elizabeth was a Field family name and Charles and Mary later had a maid called Hetty. It is likely that Charles drew his Elian aunt's name from either of these sources.

vividly evokes the tensions in the Lamb household obtained by Sarah Lamb's presence:

My father had a sister lived with us, of course lived with my Mother her sister-in-law, they were in their different ways the best creatures in the world – but they set out wrong at first. They made each other miserable for full twenty years of their lives – my Mother was a perfect gentlewoman, my Aunty as unlike a gentlewoman as you can possibly imagine a good old woman to be, so that my dear Mother (who though you do not know it, is always in my poor head and heart) used to distress and weary her with incessant & unceasing attentions, and politeness to gain her affection, The OLD WOMAN could not return this in kind, and did not know what to make of it – thought it all deceit, and used to hate my Mother with a bitter hatred, which of course was soon returned with interest . . .[14]

The effect of this domestic atmosphere on John, Mary and Charles can only be imagined. Like her niece, Sarah Lamb devoted herself to little Charles; he was not merely her favourite: she would often tell him he was the *only* thing in the world she loved. When Charles nearly died of smallpox at the age of five, it was his aunt, not his mother, he remembered at his bedside crying 'with mother's tears'.[15]

John had his mother's and grandmother's virtually undivided love, and Charles was the sole interest of his old aunt's heart, but it seemed that all three women were, at best, largely indifferent to Mary. Before the arrival of the little brother she was to dote on, Mary had discovered the consolation of reading and was often to be found (if, indeed, anyone looked) with her head in a book. As Charles recalled, 'reading was her daily bread'.[16] While – thanks to the patronage of Samuel Salt – John and Charles were to set off for school in the distinctive blue coats of Christ's Hospital, most of what Mary knew she taught herself. As Charles was to record:

Her education in youth was not much attended to; and she happily missed all that train of female garniture, which passeth by the name of accomplishments. She was tumbled early, by accident or design, into a spacious closet of good old English reading, without much selection or prohibition, and browsed at will upon that fair and wholesome pasturage . . .[17]

Mary's love of books was perhaps the most significant example she set her brother. To the end of Charles's life, the ageing couple could be discovered poring over an old book together, their pleasure in the text doubled in the sharing of it. Books were to become to them emblems of humanity in an often hard world; like their recollections of childhood (to which they often had recourse in later life), literature represented a safe place to which they could retreat.

Mary had taught Charles to read and evidently took every opportunity to improve his literacy. It was at this time that when the children were wandering in a churchyard, Mary spelling out the inscriptions on the tombstones to little Charles, he – impressed by the unceasing litany of virtuous characters – looked up at his big sister and asked whether *naughty* people were buried somewhere else. Apart from 'graveyard poetry', which was to remain a favourite source of amusement to them, Charles and Mary had more opportunities for reading than most servants' children. Their taste for reading was probably inspired by their father, who bought books when he could afford them and both read and wrote poetry, some of which was published. Aunt Sarah was also a voracious reader, although of religious works. In addition to their father's modest collection they had access to Samuel Salt's private library and Charles was permitted to frequent the extensive collection held in the Temple library. Before he entered school, Charles's choice of reading matter, like Mary's, was guided only by his own curiosity, and he too devoured an eclectic range of titles, albeit 'with child-like apprehensions, that dived not below the surface of the matter'.[18] Consequently, when Charles read the Parables, rather than drawing the conventional moral conclusions, he automatically empathized with the underdogs in the stories: his heart went out to the man who built his house on sand; he felt indignant at the censure heaped on the man who kept his talent; and he harboured a tender pity for the foolish virgins.

He was soon to come across a book which would put an end to such idiosyncratic interpretations, and which would question the hitherto undoubted authority of his texts. Initially attracted to Thomas Stackhouse's *New History of the Holy Bible* (1737) by its illustrations, little Charles began to read it, and in the process prematurely awakened and began to exercise his critical faculty. The *New History* consisted of Bible stories followed by *objections* – aspects of the tales which threatened to render them incredible – which were in turn followed by reassuring explanations or *solutions*.

The habit of expecting objections to every passage, set me upon starting more objections, for the glory of finding a solution of my own for them. I became staggered and perplexed, a sceptic in long coats. The pretty Bible stories which I had read, or heard read in church, lost their purity and sincerity of impression, and were turned into so many historic or chronologic theses to be defended against whatever impugners. I was not to disbelieve them, but – the next thing to that – I was to be quite sure that some one or other would or had disbelieved them. Next to making a child an infidel, is the letting him know that there are infidels at all. Credulity is the man's weakness, but the child's strength. O, how ugly sound scriptural doubts from the mouth of a babe and a suckling![19]

Existing side by side with Charles's precocious theological puzzling was the more conventional childish appetite for tales of ghosts and witches. Sarah Lamb, nicely styled his 'legendary aunt', had an ample fund of folklore and fantastic tales. As an adult Charles was to prize this tradition as much as his more highbrow reading, as he despaired at the fashion of 'improving' literature for children, peddled by the likes of Anna Letitia Barbauld and Sarah Trimmer. Such writers subscribed to the view that every children's story should double up as a lesson and their stories were consequently moralistic and pedestrian, strenuously avoiding the fanciful and the romantic. For Charles the development of the imagination and the intellect went hand in hand; as he wrote to Coleridge:

Knowledge insignificant & vapid as Mrs. B's books convey, it seems, must come to a child in the *shape of knowledge*, & his empty noddle must be turned with conceit of his own powers, when he has learnt, that a Horse is an Animal, & Billy is better than a Horse, & such like: instead of that beautiful Interest in wild tales, which made the child a man, while all the time he suspected himself to be no bigger than a child. Science has succeeded to Poetry no less in the little walks of Children than with Men. – : Is there no possibility of averting this sore evil? Think what you would have been now, if instead of being fed with Tales and old wives 'fables in childhood, you had been crammed with Geography & Natural History.? DAMN THEM. I mean the cursed Barbauld Crew, those BLIGHTS & BLASTS of all that is HUMAN in man & child.[20]

Even the didact Stackhouse, with his objections and solutions, furnished material for Charles's more typically childish interests: the depiction of 'the Witch raising up Samuel' in the book both fascinated and repelled him: 'It was he [Stackhouse] who dressed up for me a hag that nightly sate upon my pillow . . . I durst not, even in the day-light, once enter the chamber where I slept, without my face turned to the window, aversely from the bed where my witch-ridden pillow was.'[21]

Charles did not ascribe the *cause* of his 'midnight terrors, the hell of my infancy' to Stackhouse, however. 'That detestable picture' merely made concrete and more horrifying the nightmares he regularly experienced as a child.

I was dreadfully alive to nervous terrors. The night-time solitude, and the dark, were my hell. The sufferings I endured in this nature would justify the expression. I never laid my head on my pillow, I suppose, from the fourth to the seventh or eighth year of my life – so far as memory serves in things so long ago – without an assurance, which realized its own prophecy, of seeing some frightful spectre.[22]

Whether Charles suffered more than most children from nightmares is difficult to gauge; what is clear is that as an adult he retained an unusually vivid impression of the power of dreams to terrify. In fact, the demons never completely left his pillow, assailing him, in one form or another, for ever.

An appreciation of the contrasting pleasures of town and country formed a significant portion of Charles and Mary's informal education. Both were born and brought up in the Inner Temple, which, at that time, had the atmosphere of a separate, cloistered world within the great bustling city of London. 'What a transition for a countryman visiting London for the first time – the passing from the crowded Strand or Fleet-street, by unexpected avenues, into its magnificent ample squares, its classic green recesses! . . . Indeed, it is the most elegant spot in the metropolis,' Charles wrote later.²³ The Temple was the legal centre not just of London, but of the whole country, housing the four great Inns of Court. Lawyers both lived and worked here, and due to Samuel Salt having recognized the indispensability of John Lamb's comprehensive services (Elizabeth Lamb also almost certainly assisted in the household), the Lamb family occupied the ground floor of Salt's substantial chambers at 2 Crown Office Row. The squares and gardens of the Temple were Charles and Mary's playground; its statuary, sundials and fountains their first friends. The architectural decorations of the Temple also afforded the children their first glimpse of classical allusion: the winged horse which stood over the entrance to the Inner Temple and the frescoes of the Virtues adorning the Paper-buildings provided young Charles with 'my first hint of allegory!'

The characters who peopled this enchanted island were equally fascinating and awe-inspiring to the young Charles and his older sister, who gave the lawyers who walked the 'terrace' a wide berth. ('The old benchers had it almost sacred to themselves, in the forepart of the day at least. They might not be sided or jostled. Their air and dress asserted the parade. You left wide spaces betwixt you, when you passed them.') While the majority of the 'old benchers' gravely paraded 'with both hands folded behind them for state, or with one at least behind, the other carrying a cane', it was of course the eccentric and unusual among them who captured the young Lambs' imaginations. One Wharry, for example, had a peculiar way of walking, 'which was performed by three steps and a jump regularly succeeding. The steps were little efforts, like that of a child beginning to walk; the jump comparatively vigorous, as a foot to an inch.' Charles and Mary never discovered the cause of this peculiarity; equally mystifying was how one Mingay, who had an iron hand, had lost his real one.

Charles later recalled: 'I detected the substitute, before I was old enough to reason whether it were artificial or not. I remember the astonishment it raised in me. He was a blustering, loud-talking person; and I reconciled the phenomenon to my ideas as an emblem of power.' Skipping Wharry and the man with the iron hand had their place alongside Pegasus and the Virtues in 'the mythology of the Temple', and Charles and Mary regarded the former as much as the latter with 'superstitious veneration'.[24]

The Lamb children were something of a rarity in the Temple; of the eleven benchers mentioned by Charles only one had children.[25] John, Mary and Charles had warmer, closer relationships with the men of the Temple who were of their father's class. One of these, Randal Norris, remained a friend until his death in 1827. Although Charles was then in his early fifties, Norris would always call him 'Charley': 'in his eyes I was still the child he first knew me'. Norris was in charge of the Temple library, and despite the fact that he was not an educated man, 'there was a pride of literature about him from being amongst books . . . and from some scraps of doubtful Latin which he had picked up in his office of entering students, that gave him very diverting airs of pedantry.'[26] Charles found Norris in the library one day attempting to decipher one of Chaucer's works. On the boy's approach Norris laid down the book and with an 'erudite look' stated, 'in those old books, Charley, there is sometimes a deal of very indifferent spelling'. The anecdote illustrates not only the enduring relationships which bound Charles and Mary to the Temple – causing Mary to state, 'I wish to live and die in the Temple where I was born,' and Charles to declare, 'We never can strike root so deep in any other ground,' but also the sense in which they were already growing up and away from their roots intellectually.[27]

The tranquillity of the Temple represented the young Lambs' 'native soil', but they also fed hungrily on the sights and sounds of the city which surrounded them. One third of the country's business was then conducted in London. The sprawling metropolis was the scene of continual traffic, producing a perpetual roar which one contemporary American visitor described as reminiscent of the noise produced by Niagara Falls. London provided a rolling programme of uninterrupted entertainment. As an adult Charles wrote extensively of his enduring pleasure in urban scenes, in this case to Wordsworth:

The Lighted shops of the Strand and Fleet Street, the innumerable trades, tradesmen and customers, coaches, waggons, play houses, all the bustle and wickedness round about Covent Garden, the very women of the Town, the Watchmen, drunken scenes, rattles; – life awake, if you awake, at all hours of the night, the impossibility of being dull in Fleet Street, the crowds, the very dirt & mud, the Sun shining upon houses and pavements, the print shops, the OLD BOOK stalls, parsons cheap'ning books, coffee houses, steams of soups from kitchens, the pantomimes, London itself, a pantomime and a masquerade, all these things work themselves into my mind and feed me without a power of satiating me. The wonder of these sights impells me into night-walks about her crowded streets, and I often shed tears in the motley Strand from fullness of joy at so much LIFE . . .[28]

While this is a man's perspective, it grew out of a boy's. As Charles explained to his country-loving friend Robert Lloyd:

I have lent out my heart with usury to such scenes from my childhood up . . . depend upon it that a man of any feeling will have given his heart and his love in childhood & in boyhood to ANY

scenes where he has been bred, as we[l]l to DIRTY STREETS (&
smoky walls as they are called) as to green Lanes 'where live nibbling
sheep' & to the everlasting hills and the Lakes & ocean.[29]

Nevertheless, Charles doubted that countryphiles Wordsworth and Lloyd could comprehend his 'low Urban Taste',
or understand that it was not mere familiarity that made him
love the city, but that it remained the place of wonders that it
had seemed to him as a boy.

Sobering sights sometimes detained the Lamb children in
London's streets, such as the hired men (unrespectfully in
coloured coats) shouldering a pauper's corpse to burial in a
coffin made of rough planks, or the fraudsters in the pillory
outside the Royal Exchange being pelted with bad eggs and
bricks. Then there were metropolitan charms, such as the
caged squirrels, the 'Live Signs', outside Tinmen's shops
(where Charles couldn't resist sticking his fingers through the
bars, and was rewarded with bites) and the intriguing clock
on St Dunstan's church. Above the clock face, set into a niche,
were two life-size painted wooden carvings of 'savages or wild
men', who struck the quarter hours with great clubs, their arms
and heads moving with each blow. (As an adult, when the
figures were removed and the old church demolished, it is
reported that Charles wept.[30]) The 'professional notes' of the
little chimney-sweeps, whose mysterious trade fascinated him
as a boy, furnished Charles's dawn chorus; even the city's
beggars 'were so many of her sights, her lions . . . They were the
standing morals, emblems, mementos, dial-mottos, the spital
sermons, the books for children, the salutary checks and pauses
to the high and rushing tide of greasy citizenry . . .'[31] The
sights of London ('and what else but an accumulation of sights
– endless sights – *is* a great city; or for what else is it desirable?')
were, to Charles and Mary, their lakes and mountains.

This is not to say that the countryside held no charms for the Lamb children. Their mother's family connections enabled the three of them to spend several happy holidays with their great-aunt and grandmother in their respective Hertfordshire homes while their parents remained in London. From about the age of five or six until she was about fifteen, Mary often visited Mackery End, her great-aunt's farm, near Wheathampstead in Hertfordshire. The company of her numerous cousins and the free range of farmyard, garden, orchard and meadows must have been a welcome and much-anticipated treat for Mary, who at home only failed to please her mother and succeeded only in being outshone by her older brother.

Mary's first visit to Mackery End in the early 1770s is evoked in her story 'Louisa Manners'. Mary never forgot the almost overwhelming impact of the countryside on a town child who had never 'seen a bit of green grass, except in the Drapers' garden' nor ever seen 'so much as a cabbage growing out of the ground before'. From her first glimpse on the road of the fields 'full, quite full, of bright shining yellow flowers', a sequence of unfamiliar and charming spectacles unfolded before her: horses, sheep, cows, hens, chicks and ducklings; pear-blossom, apple-blossom, cherry-blossom, buttercups, cowslips, daffodils, bluebells and violets; rows of cabbages, radishes, peas and beans . . . Mary's first visit appears to have stretched from spring through to summer (it is possible that on this occasion Mary was sent away from London to leave her mother free to deal with the birth, then sickness and death of one of her siblings), the strong sense of benevolence of her aunt's household infusing the whole farm, from the cream syllabub her aunt made for Louisa in the story, explaining it as 'a present from the red cow', to the eggs Louisa collected: 'A hen', her aunt informed her, 'was a hospital bird, and always laid more eggs than she wanted, on purpose to give her mistress to make puddings and custards with'. Louisa also made friends. There were her cousins, one of whom took upon herself the task of educating Louisa in matters of rural taste: 'Every day I used to fill my basket with flowers, and for a long time I liked one pretty flower as well as another pretty flower, but Sarah was much wiser than me, and she taught me which to prefer.' She also befriended one of the farm-hands, whose black beard had initially scared her, who picked her up so that she could see into the bees' hives, fascinated 'to see them make honey in their own homes', and who brought Louisa 'a bird's nest, full of speckled eggs'. Lastly there was Louisa's most docile companion, 'the good-natured pied cow, that would let me stroke her, while the dairy maid was milking her'. There is every reason to suppose (especially in view of the consonance in the description of the farm with those in Charles's essay 'Mackery End') that these vivid images were Mary's own experiences.

Her annual visits to Mackery End appear to have been among the happiest in Mary's youth. Her narrator Louisa says that the time she spent there 'is always in my mind'. On Mary's final visit she had the 'care and sole management of my little brother Charles then an urchin of three or four years'. This must have been in 1778 or 1779, and was probably Charles's only childhood visit there, as he only recalled going in the company of his sister. 'The oldest thing I remember,' he later wrote, 'is Mackery End.' (The sudden death of their Aunt Ann in July 1779 put an end to their childhood visits. However, the couple returned to visit the farm as adults in 1815, when Charles declared that he had never seen Mary 'look so happy in his life'.[32])

Pleasant as Mackery End was for Mary, vivid in both their recollections were their holidays at their grandmother's home at Blakesware, near Widford. In the summer of 1815, when in her early fifties, Mary retraced the first part of the route to Blakesware from London, recalling with pleasure her childhood journeys in the Ware stagecoach 'in the days of other times', and both she and Charles drew on their recollections of the house in their writing.

By the time Charles was old enough to visit their grandmother, Mrs Field lived almost alone in the great house, which was hardly ever visited by its owners. When Mary was a child, however, its elderly mistress, Mrs Plumer, was still alive. It appears that her story 'Margaret Green' describes Mary's own experiences at Blakesware. Mrs Beresford in the story (Mrs Plumer) received no visitors and used only a few rooms in the house, spending most of her time, now that her eyesight was too poor for her to sew herself, superintending Margaret's mother's (Mary's grandmother's) progress on whatever project was currently in hand. Mrs Beresford would greet little Margaret in the morning and, apart from complimenting her on her psalm reading, refrained from further conversation with the child for the rest of the day. Perhaps following her employer's example, or perhaps believing that children (or girls, at any rate) should be seen and not heard, Margaret's mother also

. . . almost wholly discontinued talking to her. I scarcely ever heard a word addressed to me from morning to night. If it were not for the old servants saying 'Good morning to you, miss Margaret,' as they passed me in the long passages, I should have been the greatest part of the day in as perfect a solitude as Robinson Crusoe.

Mary had free range of the old house, its cavernous rooms and shrouded furnishings. Her visits to Blakesware contrasted sharply with those to Mackery End. Here were no cousins to play with, no sweet-tempered cow to stroke:

An old broken battledore, and some shuttlecocks with most of the feathers missing, were on a marble slab in one corner of the hall, which constantly reminded me that there had once been younger inhabitants here than the old lady and her gray-headed servants. In another corner stood a marble figure of a satyr: every day I laid my hand on his shoulder to feel how cold he was.

The solitary child used to frequent the gallery of family portraits, wishing 'to have a fairy's power to call the children down from their frames to play with me'. There can be little doubt but that Mary was left to her own devices far too much. The central narrative of the story 'Margaret Green' is so extremely peculiar for a children's story that it seems unlikely it could have come from anywhere other than life.

Compared with Charles's accounts of his holidays later at Blakesware – all after the death of old Mrs Plumer – where he romped confidently through the place imagining himself its heir, Mary's have the flavour of semi-secrecy and suggest illegitimate pleasures. 'It must have been because I was never spoken to at all,' reflects Margaret Green, 'that I forgot what was right and what was wrong.' Forbidden more than half an hour's reading a day, she would wait until the family Bible was unattended before daring 'softly to lift up the leaves and peep into it'. Similarly, in the shuttered best suite of rooms, where the beautiful hand-worked upholstery was covered with dust-sheets, she would again peep under the covers, 'for I constantly lifted up a corner of the envious cloth, that hid these highly-prized rarities from my view'. Margaret in the story is intrigued by a locked door, which she has attempted many times to open, when one day it allows her in. Her precious discovery proves to be a large library. After a fruitless search, over several visits, for something 'entertaining', Margaret at last finds a book called *Mahometism Explained*.

Obsessive and unmediated absorption in the book results, in the story, in Margaret concluding that 'I must be a Mahometan, for I believed every word I read.'

At length I met with something which I also believed, though I trembled as I read it: – this was, that after we are dead, we are to pass over a narrow bridge, which crosses a bottomless gulf. The bridge was described to be no wider than a silken thread; and it said, that all who were not Mahometans would slip on one side of this bridge, and drop into the tremendous gulf that had no bottom. I considered myself as a Mahometan, yet I was perfectly giddy whenever I thought of myself passing over this bridge.

One day, seeing the old lady totter across the room, a sudden terror seized me, for I thought, how would she ever be able to get over the bridge. Then too it was, that I first recollected that my mother would also be in imminent danger; for I imagined she had never heard the name of Mahomet, because I foolishly conjectured this book had been locked up for ages in the library, and was utterly unknown to the rest of the world.

All my desire was how to tell them the discovery I had made; for I thought, when they knew of the existence of 'Mahometism Explained,' they would read it, and become Mahometans, to ensure themselves a safe passage over the silken bridge. But it wanted more courage than I possessed, to break the matter to my intended converts; I must acknowledge that I had been reading without leave; and the habit of never speaking, or being spoken to, considerably increased the difficulty.

My anxiety on this subject threw me into a fever. I was so ill, that my mother thought it necessary to sleep in the same room with me. In the middle of the night I could not resist the strong desire I felt to tell her what preyed so much on my mind.

I awoke her out of a sound sleep, and begged she would be so kind as to be a Mahometan. She was very much alarmed, for she thought I was delirious, which I believe I was; for I tried to explain the reason of my request, but it was in such an incoherent manner that she could not at all comprehend what I was talking about.

The next day a physician was sent for, and he discovered, by several questions that he put to me, that I had read myself into a fever.

The doctor prescribes drugs and rest but after a few days decides to remove Margaret from the environment and takes her to stay with him and his wife. (It was not unusual, at this time, for individuals suffering from mental illness to be taken into the families of doctors — and also clergymen — in the reasonable belief that a change of scene plus a little benevolent objective care might effect an improvement.)

The doctor's wife prescribes a ride to Harlow fair, and during the journey learns not only about Margaret's experiment with Mahometism, but also 'the solitary manner in which I had spent my time'. The story ends happily, with Margaret returning from the fair with a basket full of presents and a head empty of Mahomet. Over the next few days the doctor's wife plays with Margaret, invites other children to play, and generally entertains and diverts her, while also finding time to have a serious talk about 'the error' into which Margaret had fallen. Margaret returns home 'perfectly cured'.

Several elements combine to suggest that the narrative, as well as the setting and characters, is at least based on a real experience. Firstly, the subject-matter is highly unusual for contemporary juvenile fiction (as far as could be from 'a Horse is an Animal, & Billy is better than a Horse, & such like'). The extremely evocative style of its telling also speaks of an authentic experience, vividly remembered. The story appeals to both the adult's and the child's point of view in a manner which suggests a real episode in childhood reflected upon in adulthood. Finally, it is known that Mary suffered at least one episode of psychological disturbance early in her life, although it has never been possible to establish its nature or its occasion.★

The baby of the family, Charles, had rather different experiences at Blakesware. Mrs Plumer being now dead, Mrs Field lived almost alone in the great house and the Lamb children enjoyed greater freedoms during their visits. While Mary taught Charles to marvel at the marble busts of the twelve Caesars in the mosaic-floored hall, the Hogarths and family portraits which hung around the walls, and the tapestries depicting biblical and classical scenes in the bedrooms, their brother John (whom their grandmother loved best, 'because he was so handsome and spirited a youth'), would, 'instead of moping about in solitary corners like some of us . . . mount the most mettlesome horse he could get, when but an imp no bigger than themselves, and make it carry him half over the county in a morning, and join the hunters when there were any out'. While Charles never tired of 'roaming about that huge mansion, with its vast empty rooms, with their worn-out hangings, fluttering tapestry, and carved oaken pannels, with the gilding almost rubbed out', or wandering in the grounds, collecting berries and fir cones, or 'basking in the orangery, till I could almost fancy myself ripening too along with the oranges and the limes in that grateful warmth', John, while fond of the old house and its gardens, 'had too much spirit to be always pent up within their boundaries . . .'[34]

Considering that robust and adventurous John was Mrs Field's prototype 'ideal' grandchild, it is not surprising that she found Mary, the thoughtful bookworm, lacking. 'Polly, what are those poor crazy moyther'd brains of yours think of

★ An earlier illness is mentioned in the newspaper account reprinted in the Prologue and also by Charles in a letter to Coleridge.[33]

always?' she would ask, discomfited by her grand-daughter's awkward questions and original observations.³⁵ This much-quoted and significant statement – the only piece of direct speech either Mary or Charles reported of their grandmother – makes much more sense if the *Mahometism Explained* episode is countenanced as having been grounded in truth. However, given that Mary had sole charge of her little brother a great deal of the time, it seems unlikely that there were serious concerns about her general state of mind when she was in her teens. What seems more likely is that Mary was repeatedly given to understand that she was not all she should be.

Apart from the fatal insensitivity Mrs Field shared with her daughter – that she made no attempt to disguise her infinite preference for John over his brother and sister and largely ignored the latter – the children's grandmother was a good, religious and widely respected woman. Her 'tall, graceful, upright' figure became bowed down in later life with breast cancer, which she endured for many years in great pain, yet this too 'she bore with true Christian patience'. She continued to work, and by the time she died (in 1792) had been house-keeper at Blakesware, according to Charles, for upwards of fifty years. Like John Lamb senior, old Mrs Field was a devoted and diligent servant; also as in the case of John Lamb, her extreme deference to social rank made Charles slightly un-comfortable. 'If she had a failing,' he observed, ' 'twas that she respected her master's family too much, not reverenced her Maker too little.'³⁶

Social status reared its problematic head at Blakesware more, perhaps, than anywhere else in the landscape of Charles and Mary's childhood. When Charles (aged twenty-one) wrote to Coleridge in 1796 he explained his grandmother's role at Blakesware, but it is noticeable that in another letter alluding to the house (to Robert Southey in 1799), he neglects to explain his actual relationship with Blakesware, perhaps allowing his correspondent to infer that his family's background was rather more exalted than it really was.[37]

Whether or not this was the case, in his much later essay on Blakesware (which, in the persona of Elia, he styled Blakesmoor), Charles explained the actual impact and impression which this uninhabited mansion had on the grandson of its housekeeper. On the one hand, it gave him an insight into a world outside his own:

I was here as in a lonely temple. Snug firesides – the low-built roof – parlours ten feet by ten – frugal boards, and all the homeliness of home – these were the condition of my birth – the wholesome soil which I was planted in. Yet, without impeachment to their tenderest lessons, I am not sorry to have had glances of something beyond; and to have taken, if but a peep, in childhood, at the contrasting accidents of a great fortune.[38]

But on the other, it made him yearn to be part of its lineage. He went on to explain that one does not have to be born noble to experience the 'feeling of gentility', and to describe how, as a child, he used to stand poring over the absent residents' coat of arms, absorbing the heraldic images, until 'I received into myself Very Gentility'. While the house's actual owners had long ago deserted their ancestral home, Charles felt 'I was the true descendent of those old W—s; and not the present family of that name, who had fled the old waste places.' Surveying the gallery of old family portraits, Charles would give them 'in fancy my own family name'. This was more than early evidence of Charles's ability to empathize completely with an environment; it also spoke of his childhood understanding of his father's tenet that those who had advantage and privilege were not necessarily deserving, and those born under the low rooves and who dined at modest tables were disadvantaged for no good reason. The indifference of the Plumers to their old family seat subverted, in the young boy's mind, the rationale for the status quo. It is also deeply informing to compare Charles's reflections on the Plumer family portraits – Charles who was the darling of his aunt and his sister – with Mary's, who simply yearned for their younger subjects to step down from their frames and play with her.

Poor little Charles did not leave his nightmares in London. His grandmother, insulated from superstitious anxieties by the fact that she was 'so good and religious', quite possibly did not calculate the effect of her ghost stories on the infant Charles. She told the children how, as she slept alone in the empty house, 'she believed that an apparition of two infants was to be seen at midnight gliding up and down the great staircase near where she slept', but was sure they would do her no harm. Similarly, she told them of the haunted bedroom, where the dowager had died, and which Charles tentatively entered only in daylight, 'with a passion of fear; and a sneaking curiosity, terror-tainted, to hold communication with the past'. His own bedroom was no less of a challenge:

Why, every plank and pannel of that house for me had magic in it. The tapestried bedrooms – tapestry so much better than painting – at which childhood ever and anon would steal a look, shifting its coverlid (replaced as quickly) to exercise its tender courage in a momentary eye-encounter with those stern bright visages, staring reciprocally . . .[39]

Blakesware was, for both Charles and Mary, both a treat and a challenge, like its most welcome treasure, its library. The library does not seem to have been out-of-bounds for Charles; from its shelves he might take down a volume of

Cowley's poetry and retreat to a sunny windowseat, over-looking the lawn, with his booty. Here, again, the Lambs were exceptional for children of their class in having access (legitimate or otherwise) to a wide range of literature.

Charles and Mary's cultural opportunities were also compara-tively privileged in another direction: the theatre. Again, it was a family connection that was the key. Their godfather Francis Fielde kept a shop in Holborn which supplied oil to light Drury Lane Theatre, which in turn provided him with free tickets to some of the shows. Just as Randal Norris had been memorable to Charles for his erudite air (displayed in his disapproval of Chaucer's indifferent spelling and his own doubtful Latin), the Lambs' godfather was distinctive for his gentlemanly and imposing manner, which was enhanced by his regular use of the term *vice versa*, which he pronounced *verse verse*. As a small boy, Charles acknowledged, these words 'impressed me with more awe than they would do now, read aright from Seneca or Varro'. His godfather evidently also approved of young Charles, and was, many years later, to make him the bequest of a cottage at Button Snap in Hertfordshire.

'There is nothing in the world so charming as going to a play,' declares the narrator of Mary's story 'Emily Barton'; the extent to which this was Charles and Mary's opinion as chil-dren is evident in their detailed recollections of their first theatrical experiences. Mary's first play was Congreve's *The Mourning Bride*; Charles's was the opera *Artaxerxes* – both were double bills, followed by Harlequin pantomimes. The crowds of people, the lighted candles and lamps, the air of expectation on those first occasions – all remained fresh in their minds for many years, and a trip to the theatre remained a special treat throughout their adult lives. Unable to bear the suspense, and overwhelmed by the promise signified by 'the green curtain that veiled a heaven to my imagination', five-year-old Charles hungrily took in every detail of the auditorium, which appeared to him to be constructed entirely out of sugar candy, before, 'incapable of the anticipation', capitulating to the unbearable wait: 'I reposed my shut eyes in a sort of resignation upon the maternal lap.' Then it began.

The curtain drew up . . . here was the court of Persia. It was being admitted to a sight of the past. I took no proper interest in the action going on, for I understood not its import . . . All feeling was absorbed in vision. Gorgeous vests, gardens, palaces, princesses, passed before me. I knew not players. I was in Persepolis for the time; and the burning idol of their devotion almost converted me into a worshipper. I was awe-struck, and believed those significations to be something more than elemental fires. It was all enchantment and a dream. No such pleasure has since visited me but in dreams.[40]

It was to be the beginning of a lifelong love affair with the theatre, with all the highs and lows, the pleasures and disappointments that such attachments entail. Charles sat soberly through the comedy which followed, as he did, the next year, when he was taken to see *Lady of the Manor* and *Lun's Ghost*. Harlequin again appeared in the second piece, and the effect of him rising from the dead enormously impressed the serious little boy: 'I saw the primeval Motley come from his silent tomb in a ghastly vest of white patch-work, like the apparition of a dead rainbow.' The following year (Charles was now seven) he saw Congreve's *The Way of the World*, and as yet had no sense of the comedic element: 'I think I must have sat at it as grave as a judge; for, I remember, the hysteric affectations of good Lady Wishfort affected me like some solemn tragic passion.'

Charles was not to visit a playhouse again for six years. When he did, it would appear to him that the theatre had lost something of its indefinable magic. But it was not the theatre that had changed:

I had left the temple a devotee, and was returned a rationalist. The same things were there materially; but the emblem, the reference, was gone! – The green curtain was no longer a veil, drawn between two worlds, the unfolding of which was to bring back past ages, to present 'a royal ghost,' – but a certain quantity of green baize, which was to separate the audience for a given time from certain of their fellow-men who were to come forward and pretend those parts. The lights – the orchestra lights – came up a clumsy machinery. The first ring, and the second ring, was now but a trick of the prompter's bell – which had been, like the note of the cuckoo, a phantom of a voice, no hand seen or guessed at which ministered to its warning. The actors were men and women painted. I thought the fault was in them; but it was in myself, and the alteration which those many centuries – of six short twelve-months – had wrought in me.[41]

The intervening six years had extended the scope of Charles's knowledge and taught him to discipline his responses. In short, he had been to school.

2. The Schoolboy and the Mantua-maker

The Christ's Hospital or Blue-Coat boy, has a distinctive character
of his own, as far removed from the abject qualities of a common
charity-boy as it is from the disgusting forwardness of a lad
brought up at some other of the public schools. There is *pride* in it
. . . differencing him from the former; and there is a *restraining
modesty*, from a sense of obligation and dependence, which must
ever keep his deportment from assimilating to that of the latter.

(Charles Lamb, 'Recollections of Christ's Hospital')

Mary's formal education did not extend beyond a few years
at William Bird's Academy, a local day school in Fetter Lane,
Holborn, where she learnt Arithmetic and English composition. Discipline was not a strong point, the young Assistant
having frequently to shout at the girls: 'Ladies, if you will not
hold your peace, not all the powers in heaven can make you!'[1]
(Her family did not have the resources to pursue further
education, especially for a girl, had they seen the propriety of
doing so.) After that she began her apprenticeship, probably
at the age of about fourteen, as a dressmaker. By the time
Charles left Christ's, she was a fully-fledged mantua-maker,
and soon had a young apprentice of her own.

Dressmaking was labour-intensive and often tedious work,
mantua-making more so, and her additional domestic duties
(as the only daughter of the house) left Mary little time to call
her own. Charles gives us a hint of this in his essay on the

pleasures of reading. In it he considers books as physical objects, and writes of the pleasingly grubby condition of the volumes in circulating libraries:

How they speak of the thousand thumbs, that have turned over their pages with delight! – of the lone sempstress, whom they may have cheered (milliner, or harder working mantua-maker) after her long day's needle-toil, running far into midnight, when she has snatched an hour, ill spared from sleep, to steep her cares, as in some Lethean cup, in spelling out their enchanting contents![2]

Mary was to take a less romantic view of this situation, writing: 'Needle-work and intellectual improvement are naturally in a state of warfare.'

While we know hardly anything about Mary's life during the period that her younger brother was at school, the only piece of non-fiction she ever published – also the only project she undertook entirely without her brother's collaboration – gives us an unparalleled opportunity to understand an aspect of Mary's intellectual and political life that is elsewhere barely hinted at. Mary wrote the essay 'On Needle-work' under the nom-de-plume 'Sempronia' for the *British Lady's Magazine*, in 1814 at the age of fifty, when she was in more comfortable circumstances, but it was confessedly informed by her years as a young professional sempstress. The eminently reasonable tone of the essay went some way towards disguising the radical nature of its proposal. Her argument was that needlework was an instrument of oppression.

'On Needle-work' questioned the almost universal practice of middle-class women occupying their 'idle' moments in sewing. Sewing had long been a favoured pursuit for women of this class for many reasons: principally, it demonstrated industry (the devil being ever ready to make work for idle hands) yet was a peculiarly feminine form of industry, much more work often being entailed in the decoration of the article than in making the thing itself. It was therefore not 'real work' but a kind of physical manifestation – almost a 'sign' – of domestic femininity.

Mary's closely argued case devolved on two premises. Firstly, there was no economic imperative for middle-class women to make their family's clothes: sewing was time-consuming and garments could be cheaply bought ready-made:

'A penny saved is a penny earned,' is a maxim not true unless the penny be saved in the same time in which it might have been earned. I, who have known what it is to work for *money earned*, have since had much experience in working for *money saved*; and I consider, from the closest calculation I can make, that a *penny saved* in that way bears about a true proportion to a *farthing earned*.

Moreover, women who did not *need* to produce their own linen were taking the bread from the mouths of the vast class of women who could *only* earn their living by their needle – this being at the time one of the very few respectable professions open to women who had to support themselves. The amateur needlewomen not only contracted the market for professional sempstresses, but also pushed down the prices they were able to charge, as people are generally not prepared to pay the true price for work that they could do themselves 'for nothing'.

Secondly, Mary insisted, middle-class women not only economically deprived the professional needlewomen, but also culturally disadvantaged themselves. By imposing upon themselves the quite unnecessary burden of endless needle-work – turning to embroidery and elaborate patchwork when there was no essential sewing to be done – they conspired to reduce their own opportunities to improve their minds through reading, conversation and other 'leisure' pursuits to which men readily resorted. Female 'accomplishments' such as embroidery actively inhibited women from accomplishing anything more meaningful. Men, Mary reasoned, did not feel the same obligation to fill up their day with a variety of self-imposed and inconsequential tasks.

'They can do what they like,' we say. Do not these words generally mean they have time to seek out whatever amusements suit their tastes? We dare not tell them we have no time to do this; for if they should ask in what manner we dispose of our time we should blush to enter upon a detail of the minutiae which compose the sum of a woman's daily employment. Nay, many a lady who allows not herself one quarter of an hour's positive leisure during her waking hours, considers her husband as the most industrious of men if he steadily pursues his occupation till the hour of dinner, and will be perpetually lamenting her own idleness.

Real business and *real leisure* make up the portion of men's time: – two sources of happiness which we certainly partake of in a very inferior degree.

Mary concluded that, in order to further the interests of both classes of women, needlework should *only* be undertaken as paid work. This essay has been neglected by – if it is not unknown to – modern feminists, although Jane Aaron has justly observed: 'It boldly stands out today as one of the earliest expositions in British literature of what would later be called feminism.'[3]

While Mary was pursuing her occupation as a lowly semp-stress her younger brother was taking full advantage of the educational opportunities denied her sex. Mary had been Charles's first teacher; he then attended a school run by a Mrs

Reynolds before entering, at the age of seven, Christ's Hospital (then in Newgate Street), popularly known as the Bluecoat School, after the uniform the pupils wore.

Charles's elder brother John, who had also been a Bluecoat boy, had left the school and begun his forty years' service as an accountant in the South Sea House by the time Charles arrived at Christ's, in October, 1782.* John Lamb senior could never have afforded the standard of education his sons received free of charge at Christ's; his employer, Samuel Salt, used his influence to secure the Lamb boys places at this unique establishment. It is impossible to know whether Salt saw something in the boys worth developing, or whether this was an opportunity for him to demonstrate to John Lamb the extent to which he appreciated his stewardship.

The essence of Christ's is here described by Leigh Hunt, who entered the school the year after Charles left:

Perhaps there is not a foundation in the country so truly English, taking that word to mean what Englishmen wish it to mean; – something solid, unpretending, of good character, and free to all. More boys are to be found in it, who issue from a greater variety of ranks, than in any other school in the kingdom; and as it is the most various, so it is the largest, of all the free-schools. Nobility do not go there, except as boarders. Now and then, a boy of a noble family may be met with, and he is reckoned an interloper, and against the charter; but the sons of poor gentry and London citizens abound; and with them, an equal share is given to the sons of tradesmen of the very humblest description, not omitting servants.[4]

Leigh Hunt recalled, with characteristic pride in his old school's democratic ethos, two pupils who would go home

* John Lamb attended Christ's Hospital from 1770 to 1778.

43

together, parting at the door, the one to go up to his father (the master of the house) in the drawing-room, the other to go down to *his* father (the coachman) in the kitchen. At school, however, all boys were treated – and treated each other – as equals: 'The cleverest boy was the noblest, let his father be who he might.'

In short, Christ-Hospital is well known and respected by thousands, as a nursery of tradesmen, of merchants, of naval officers, of scholars, of some of the most eminent persons of the day; and the feeling among the boys themselves is, that it is a medium, far apart indeed, but equally so, between the patrician pretension of such schools as Eton and Westminster, and the plebeian submission of the charity schools.[5]

However, the school did not perceive its role as catering for the lowest of the low; while it was true, in the words of another of Charles's contemporaries, that there 'rigid justice holds impartial rule;/ Where no rich dunce can rise on bags of gold,/ Nor meed of merit can be bought or sold',[6] the school's purpose was not to educate the poorest children, but

. . . to preserve, in the same rank of life in which they were born, the children of reputable persons of the middle class, who either by the death or overwhelming calamities of their parents must otherwise have sunk down to a state, which to *them* would be penury and heart-breaking, because alike unfitted to their bodily and their mental habits.

Christ's Hospital existed, in Samuel Taylor Coleridge's phrase, 'to catch the falling, not to lift up the standing from their natural and native rank'.[7] Again this suggests that the Lambs – either through the lost legacy, or through some earlier 'fall' – had at some point had some claim to a more genteel. lifestyle than that which they now endured.

The distinctiveness of the school's character and the special status of its otherwise often underprivileged students was reflected in certain special rights extending far back in time, such as the boys' ancient privilege of free admission to the Tower of London to see the bears, wolves, lions and other big cats then kept there. More immediately impressive was their striking uniform, which had not changed since the school had been first established, in 1552 by Edward VI, for 'the maintenance of a certain number of poor orphan children, born of citizens of London'. Their costume was a standardized version of the sort of clothes worn by children 'in humble life' in Tudor times, consisting of 'a blue drugget gown, or body, with ample coats to it; a yellow vest underneath in winter-time; small-clothes of Russia duck; yellow stockings; a leathern girdle; and a little black worsted cap, usually carried in the hand'.[8] The girdle, of red leather, was stamped with stars and roses, a full-length figure of a Christ's Hospital boy and the head of the founder. (If these emblems served to remind the boys of the school's noble tradition, the yellow component of their costume had a less glorious genesis, having been introduced in 1638 'to avoid vermin, by reason the white cotten is held to breed the same'.[9])

This costume, although a 'badge of dependence', was worn with great pride. Both Lamb and Hunt record that the quaintly dressed yellow and blue figures were unfailingly shown respect and kindness outside the school's walls, and their conspicu-ousness heightened the boys' sense of their special corporate status. Charles was to meet with, correspond with, and go out of his way to help his old schoolfriends for the rest of his life; the old school tie was, in the Bluecoats' case, of particular significance, as for most of them Christ's had offered them an escape route from economically reduced and culturally restricted circumstances.

This is not to say that life at Christ's was either exceptionally comfortable nor that the education it offered was of a consistently excellent standard. Many of the boys probably ate better at home. Their day began at 6a.m. in the summer (an hour later in the winter) with a breakfast of bread and water (beer was provided but it was apparently too disgusting to drink). Lessons would follow until 11a.m. when there was an hour's playtime before dinner, which consisted of more bread and, every other day, a tiny piece of meat, which nevertheless was often left half-eaten, due to its extreme toughness. 'On the other days, we had a milk-porridge, ludicrously thin; or rice-milk, which was better.' More play, followed by more lessons, ensued, until 5p.m. in summer (an hour earlier in winter). Supper was at 6p.m., and followed immediately by bed in winter, but in summer the boys played until 8p.m. Once a month the boys could look forward to roast beef, and twice a year they were treated to roast or boiled pork. Coleridge remembered, 'Our food was portioned; and, excepting on Wednesdays [a rice-milk day], I never had a bellyfull. Our appetites were damp, never satisfied; and we had no vegetables.'[10] Here Charles had an enviable advantage over many of his classmates; the proximity of his home and the kindliness of his aunt meant that he was often the grateful recipient of all manner of treats with which to supplement the meagre diet provided by the school.

I remember the good old relative (in whom love forbade pride) squatting down upon some odd stone in a by-nook of the cloisters, disclosing the viands . . . ; and the contending passions of L. at the unfolding. There was love for the bringer; shame for the thing brought, and the manner of its bringing; sympathy for those who were too many to share in it; and, at top of all, hunger (eldest, strongest of passions!) predominant, breaking down the stony fences of shame, and awkwardness, and a troubling over-consciousness.[11]

(The above account was written by Charles, although the point-of-view is not his own, but Elia's, whom he makes Charles's schoolfellow.) The 'shame' to which he alludes as one of the competing emotions which the appearance of his aunt would inspire is more fully and precisely acknowledged in a letter he wrote to Coleridge, several years after they had left school. In the letter Charles admitted that when his aged aunt used to 'toddle' to school 'with some nice thing she had caused to be saved for me': I school-boy like only despised her for it, & used to be ashamed to see her come & sit herself down on the old coal hole steps as you went into the old grammar school, & opend her apron & brought out her bason . . .'[12] For all its egalitarian principles, or perhaps because of them, one influence of school-life was that it taught Charles to be embarrassed by his aunt, whose plain-dealing and plain-speaking seemed to the special little Bluecoat merely vulgar.

For taciturn Aunt Sarah food was a medium of love, and giving food to her favourite nephew was an expression of her affection for him. Charles was later to write of the moment that he recognized this fact. The boys had two half-holidays in the week and Charles was unusual in being able to go home on these occasions. As he prepared to return to school in the evening, his aunt would always give him some treat to take back with him. On this particular evening she gave him a plum-cake, still hot from the oven.

In my way to school (it was over London Bridge) a grey-headed old beggar saluted me (I have no doubt at this time of day that he was a counterfeit). I had no pence to console him with, and in the vanity of self-denial, and the very coxcombry of charity, schoolboy-like, I made him a present of – the whole cake! I walked on a little, buoyed up, as one is on such occasions, with a sweet soothing of self-satisfaction; but before I had got to the end of the bridge, my better feelings returned, and I burst into tears, thinking how ungrateful I had been to my good aunt, to go and give her good gift away to a stranger, that I had never seen before, and who might be a bad man for aught I knew; and then I thought of the pleasure my aunt would be taking in thinking that I – I myself, and not another – would eat her nice cake – and what should I say to her the next time I saw her – how naughty I was to part with her pretty present – and the odour of that spicy cake came back upon my recollection, and the pleasure and the curiosity I had taken in seeing her make it, and her joy when she sent it to the oven, and how disappointed she would feel that I had never had a bit of it in my mouth at last – and I blamed my impertinent spirit of alms-giving, and out-of-place hypocrisy of goodness, and above all I wished never to see the face again of that insidious, good-for-nothing, old grey impostor.[13]

Like many of the other ideas and recollections Charles used in the Elia essays, this story was first related in a letter, again to Coleridge. However, there is a subtle difference between the two accounts: whereas Elia's aunt had baked the cake for him, Charles's aunt had bought it, indeed 'had strained her pocket-strings to bestow a sixpenny whole plum-cake upon me'. Of all the things that the fictional Elia agonized over, none concerned the cost – in money – of the cake, whereas the real Charles realized, with shame, 'the sum it was to her'. The same sense of shame felt by Charles the schoolboy when his aunt toddled up to school in her apron can be detected in Charles the writer, when he deliberately omits references such as these to his family's straitened financial circumstances. Mary, too, was delicate about such matters.

Coleridge's description of the school's organization gives a sense of the grim efficiency with which boys were sifted, assessed and propelled through its various sub-schools until they emerged suitably qualified for designated occupations:

There are five schools – mathematical, grammar, drawing, reading, and writing – all very large buildings. When a boy is admitted, if he reads very badly, he is either sent to Hertford, or to the Reading School. Boys are admissible from seven to twelve years of age. If he learns to read tolerably well before nine, he is drafted into the Lower Grammar School, if not, into the Writing School, as having given proof of unfitness for classical studies. If, before he is eleven, he climbs up to the first form of the Lower Grammar School, he is drafted into the Head Grammar School. If not, at eleven years of age, he is sent into the Writing School, where he continues till fourteen or fifteen, and is then either apprenticed or articled as a clerk, or whatever else his turn of mind or of fortune shall have provided for him. Two or three times a year the Mathematical Master beats up for recruits for the King's boys, as they are called; and all who like the navy are drafted into the Mathematical and Drawing Schools, where they continue till sixteen or seventeen years of age, and go out as midshipmen, and school-masters in the navy. The boys who are drafted into the Head Grammar School, remain there till thirteen; and then, if not chosen for the University, go into the Writing School.[14]

While an interest in the visual arts was not particularly encouraged by the curriculum, the Great Hall where the boys took their meals contained a portrait of Henry VIII by Holbein, and the 130-foot-long inner wall was almost covered by an enormous Antonio Verrio depicting James II receiving King's boys. Such scenes imbued the boys with a due sense of the school's august history, as well as introducing them to the kind of art which hung on richer family's walls.

On the quality and style of education on offer at Christ's, Hunt asserted that 'Few of us cared for any of the books that were taught; and no pains were taken to make us do so.'

[The master] would not help us with a word, till he had ascertained that we had done all we could to learn the meaning of it ourselves. This discipline was useful; and, in this and every other respect, we had all the advantages which a mechanical sense of right, and a rigid exaction of duty, could afford us; but no farther.[15]

However, the school encouraged the writing of poetry. While the school's approach to the subject was bound up in what Hunt calls 'the trammels of . . . regular imitative poetry and versification' and Charles thought the Reverend James Boyer 'a rabid pedant' whose 'English style was crampt to barbarism',[16] Coleridge was to go on to commend the master for his formative influence. 'In the truly great poets, he would say, there is a reason assignable, not only for every word, but for the position of every word.' He would make the boys demonstrate the unique aptness of the vocabulary in the classics they studied, and defend it in their own writing.

In our own compositions, (at least for the last three years of our school education,) he showed no mercy to phrase, metaphor, or image, unsupported by a sound sense, or where the same sense might have been conveyed with equal force and dignity in plainer words. *Lute*, *harp*, and *lyre*, *Muse*, *Muses*, and *inspirations*, *Pegasus*, *Parnassus* and *Hippocrene* were all an abomination to him. In fancy I can almost hear him now, exclaiming 'Harp? Harp? Lyre? Pen and ink, boy, you mean! Muse, boy, Muse? Your nurse's daughter, you mean! Pierian spring? Oh aye! The cloister-pump, I suppose!' Nay, certain introductions, similes, and examples, were placed by him on a list of interdiction.[17]

Boyer's training must take some credit for the development of both Charles's and Coleridge's writing styles and the specific use of a precise and unpretentious vocabulary was to be the hallmark of many of the Romantic poets. As at the libraries of Blakesware, Samuel Salt and the Temple, Charles enjoyed un-restricted reading at school, where an interest in a wide range of literature was encouraged. Boyer, however, was chiefly memorable – indeed was infamous – among all Bluecoat boys for his cruelty rather than his poetry.

Charles had, by the age of seven when he entered Christ's in 1782, developed his most characteristic mannerism, a severe stammer. C. V. Le Grice, a contemporary of Charles's at Christ's, recalled that, far from rendering Charles an object of ridicule, he was 'indulged by his school-fellows and by his master on account of his infirmity of speech'. Charles's appear-ance also made him stand out from the crowd: his eyes were of different colours; 'one was hazel, the other had specks of grey in the iris, mingled as we see red spots in the blood-stone'. Dark-skinned, slightly built and with a distinctive gait, prob-ably the legacy of polio, young Charles had a monk-like and contemplative air which Le Grice attributed to the conjunc-tion of the unusual circumstances of his upbringing in the Temple and the distinctive character of the school. Just as the Temple had a cloistered atmosphere, Christ's also formed a world within a world, *in* but not *of* the city. As Leigh Hunt wrote: 'Thousands, indeed, have gone through the City and never suspected that in the heart of it lies an old cloistered foundation, where a boy may grow up, as I did, among six hundred others, and know as little of the very neighbourhood as the world does of him.'[18] So, as Le Grice put it, Charles 'passed from cloister to cloister, and this was all the change his young mind ever knew'. Unlike the boys whose families lived further afield, on the twice-weekly half-holidays, within ten minutes Charles could be 'in the gardens, on the terrace, or at the fountain of the Temple; here was his home, here his recreation'. Le Grice believed that this doubly-cloistered existence enormously influenced the development of Charles's character and that this physical context 'mixed itself with all his habits and enjoyments, and gave a bias to the whole'.

Charles was, Le Grice remembered, 'an amiable, gentle boy, very sensible and keenly observing', with a 'mild' countenance. Just as his classmates and teachers responded kindly to, rather than mocked, the vulnerability his stammer suggested, his gentle personality brought out gentleness in others. Unusually, Le Grice noted, 'I never heard his name mentioned without the addition of Charles, although, as there were no other boys of the name of Lamb, the addition was unnecessary; but there was an implied kindness in it, and it was a proof that his gentle manners excited that kindness.'[19]

While the regime at Christ's was often uncomfortable, and its discipline often harsh, Charles was to confess that he had never been happier than during his seven years there; this happiness was derived as much from the fellowship of other boys as anything. Apart from general companionship, the pleasure of sharing an 'in' joke with a friend was immeasurably multiplied when that joke was shared with 600 other boys. Leigh Hunt describes the interminable Sundays, most of which the boys spent in church: 'We did not dare go to sleep. We were not allowed to read. The great boys used to get those who sat behind them to play with their hair. Some whispered to their neighbours, and the others thought of their lessons and tops.' The boys were watched over, and kept in order, by the steward, and they could only revenge themselves on him by ascribing a special shared meaning to one passage of the Bible whenever it was read during the service. 'This was the parable of the Unjust Steward. The boys waited anxiously till the passage commenced; and then, as if by a general conspiracy, at the words "thou unjust steward," the whole school turned their eyes upon this unfortunate officer . . .' The steward studiously avoided showing a flicker of acknowledgement that he was the object of the glaring gaze of 600 boys, but this only persuaded them that 'the more unconscious he looked, the more he was acting'.[20]

Their collective suffering at the brutish hand of the Reverend Boyer also bound the boys together. Boyer not only routinely flogged, but slapped, punched and kicked his pupils indiscriminately. Leigh Hunt recalled that the master once 'knocked out one of my teeth with the back of a Homer, in a fit of impatience at my stammering', while another Old Blue remembered seeing him 'take a little boy by the ears, and pinch him till the poor fellow roared and shrieked with the agony'.[21] (Bleeding ears were a not uncommon sight in Boyer's classes.) Boyer was hated and feared in equal measure and it is perhaps unsurprising that at least one boy was caught 'putting the inside of the master's desk to a use for which the architect had clearly not designed it'. Many years later, learning that Boyer was on his deathbed, Coleridge exclaimed: 'Poor J.B.! – may all his faults be forgiven; and may he be wafted to bliss by little cherub boys, all head and wings, with no *bottoms* to reproach his sublunary infirmities.'[22] Yet Coleridge was prepared to admit that Boyer visited him in nightmares even as an adult.

Their shared fears and pleasures, their very isolation from the rest of the world, strengthened the boys' sense of community. An Old Blue himself, the school's historian G. A. T. Allen (writing in 1937) reflected on the effect of the unique circumstances of the school on the boys during Charles's period there:

It will be seen that the outlook of the boys on life must have been extremely restricted – literally cloistered. Cabin'd, cribb'd, confin'd amid the massive buildings, shut in by stout walls and iron railings, guarded by beadles watchful and greedy as Cerberus at the gates, they could not but feel that C.H. was their microcosm, that the outer world was an alien country which would not concern them until they left school.[23]

Indeed, access to the outside world was strictly controlled, and loyalty to and respect and affection for the school were encouraged at the expense of home ties. Early in his school career, returning unhappily to Christ's after the holidays, Coleridge was discovered in tears by Boyer, who delivered this rebuke: 'Boy! The school is your father! Boy! The school is your mother! Boy! The school is your brother! The school is your sister! The school is your first-cousin, and your second cousin, and all the rest of your relations! Let's have no more crying!'[24]

The identification with school as family-substitute led to extremely deep and often lifelong friendships. Of the relation-ships Charles formed at Christ's the most significant was with Samuel Taylor Coleridge. Coleridge was the youngest of ten children, and like Charles was born to mature parents. (His father, a vicar, was fifty-three when Coleridge was born, his mother forty-five; Mr and Mrs Lamb were approximately fifty and forty years old when Charles was born.) Although two years older than Charles, Coleridge started at Christ's in the same year, his father having died suddenly. Retreating from family tensions, Coleridge, like Mary and Charles, had become a voracious reader early in childhood, and also like them suffered bouts of trauma as a result of obsessive and unmediated exposure to a wide range of literature. He reflected in later life on the effect a tale from *The Arabian Nights* had had on him as a child; the story made such a deep impression on him 'that I was haunted by spectres, whenever I was in the dark – and I distinctly remember the anxious & fearful eagerness, with which I used to watch the window, in which the books lay – & whenever the Sun lay upon them, I would seize it, carry it by the wall, & bask, & read.'[25] Both the powerful and haunting over-identification with the fiction, and the relationship to the book itself as a concrete yet magical object, resonate strongly with Mary and Charles's childhood experiences as readers. Coleridge was also to develop similar views to those held by Charles on the value of unorthodox literature – in particular that which treated of the supernatural – in stimulating the development of children's critical and creative faculties.

Should children be permitted to read Romances, & Relations of Giants & Magicians, & Genii? – I know all that has been said against it; but I have formed my faith in the affirmative. I know no other way of giving the mind a love of 'the Great', & 'the Whole' . . . I have known some who have been *rationally* educated, as it is styled. They were marked by a microscopic acuteness; but when they looked at great things, all became a blank & they saw nothing . . . and uniformly put the negation of a power for the possession of a power – & called the want of imagination Judgment, & the never being moved to Rapture Philosophy![26]

This chimes with Charles's grievance against 'the cursed Barbauld crew' who promulgated the superiority of Billy over his Horse, rather than encouraging 'that beautiful Interest in wild tales, which made the child a man'. Less significant, but nonetheless noteworthy, is the similarity between Coleridge's relationship with his older brother Frank and those between Mary and Charles and their brother John. Frank, Coleridge wrote, regarded his younger brother 'with a strange mixture of admiration and contempt – strange it was not –: for he hated books, and loved climbing, flighting, playing, & robbing orchards, to distraction', whereas Coleridge himself 'took no pleasure in boyish sports – but read incessantly'.[27] These similarities of early experience meant Coleridge and the Lambs instinctively understood each other.

Whereas Charles and Mary's home lay only a short walk from school, Coleridge was far from his family in Devon and horribly homesick. (Richard Holmes has calculated that Coleridge returned to his family home only three or four times over his nine years at school.) It is unsurprising that the two boys were instantly mutually attracted, sharing the same interests and sense of humour, possibly instinctively recognizing in each other the heart of a nascent poet. From this schoolboy affection grew their lifelong friendship.

Unlike Coleridge and some of his other friends, there was no question of Charles going to university. Every year a handful of the top scholars at Christ's Hospital were selected for university – usually Cambridge – where their fees would be paid by endowments from Christ's. During their final year at school these boys enjoyed the title of 'Grecians'. Charles would have been a prime candidate for a School Exhibition, but Grecians were expected, on the whole, ultimately to proceed to careers in the church and therefore had to be strong orators (indeed, speech-making formed part of their school training). Both Charles Lamb's and Leigh Hunt's speech impediments inhibited their progress to that rank: both were unable to rise above the rank of Deputy Grecian and consequently missed out on university. Charles was later to admit having felt 'defrauded' of 'the sweet food' of higher education, but appears to have submitted stoically to his loss.[28] When he left Christ's in November 1789, aged fourteen, the practical plan was for Charles to follow his brother in a career in accountancy.

Much as his father had taken pride – and perhaps consolation – in having been an 'Above Boy', Charles was to write, even in his mid-fifties, to his old friend George Dyer – another ex-Bluecoat – 'I don't know how it is, but I keep my rank in fancy still since school-days. I can never forget I was a Deputy Grecian! And writing to you, or Coleridge, besides affectation, I feel a reverential deference as to Grecians still. I keep my soaring way above the Great Erasmians, yet far beneath the other.'* Also in common with his father, his status as a schoolboy was never quite matched – in his eyes at least – by his station in life thereafter. He continued, to Dyer, not entirely tongue-in-cheek: 'Alas! What am I now? What is a Leadenhall clerk or India pensioner to a deputy Grecian?'[29]

In the short space between being Deputy Grecian and lowly clerk, however, Charles was permitted one last treat: probably in the summer or late autumn of 1789 he and Mary (then aged fourteen and twenty-five respectively) took a holiday in Margate, Kent. Neither Charles nor Mary had ever seen the sea, and they had never been away from home together for such a long period. The journey to Margate (by sailing-boat from London) was almost as rewarding as the visit itself, despite

---

* Great Erasmians were below Lower Grecians but above Little Erasmians.

the 'not very savoury, not very inviting, little cabin', and Mary and Charles drew as much amusement from their fellow passengers as they did from the scenery. One of their companions, to their great entertainment, proved to be an astonishing liar, whose 'wild fablings' whiled away several hours on board.

He had been Aid-de-camp (among other rare accidents and fortunes) to a Persian prince, and at one blow had stricken off the head of the King of Carimania on horseback. He, of course, married the Prince's daughter . . . There was some story of a Princess – Elizabeth, if I remember – having intrusted to his care an extraordinary casket of jewels, upon some extraordinary occasion . . .[30]

Travelling in Egypt their fellow passenger had seen a phoenix, and 'had actually sailed through the legs of the Colossus at Rhodes'. At this point another passenger made so bold as to assert that he must be mistaken, as the Colossus had been destroyed centuries before, 'to whose opinion, delivered with all modesty, our hero was obliging enough to concede thus much, that "the figure was indeed a little damaged"'. This teller of tall tales, and other circumstances, as Charles later wrote, 'combined to make it the most agreeable holyday of my life'. It was also to be the last Charles made as a 'free man', as on his return to London, the counting-house beckoned.

The Margate trip also produced Charles's first sonnet. While it is very much a product of its period (styled after Charles's darling W. L. Bowles), 'Written at Midnight, by the Seaside, After a Voyage' does preserve the intensity of romantic feelings produced by a recognition of the 'sublime' in the heart of the young poet:

O! I could laugh to hear the midnight wind,
That, rushing on its way with careless sweep,
Scatters the ocean waves. And I could weep
Like to a child. For now to my raised mind
On wings of winds comes wild-eyed Phantasy,
And her rude visions give severe delight.
O winged bark! How swift along the night
Pass'd thy proud keel! Nor shall I let go by
Lightly of that drear hour the memory,
When wet and chilly on thy deck I stood,
Unbonnetted, and gazed upon the flood,
Even till it seemed a pleasing thing to die, –
To be resolv'd into th'elemental wave,
Or take my portion with the winds that rave.

(Coleridge thought the sonnet 'divine' and consequently declared Charles 'a man of uncommon Genius' to Robert Southey.[31])

It is a measure of Samuel Salt's regard for his employee, Mr Lamb, that Charles's place at Joseph Paice's counting-house (27 Bread Street Hill, a street off Cheapside), like his place at Christ's, had been secured with Salt's assistance. Nothing is known of Charles's period working there, but he has left us a portrait of Paice. Charles later wrote of the merchant: 'He took me under his shelter at an early age, and bestowed some pains upon me. I owe to his precepts and example whatever there is of the man of business (and that is not much) in my composition. It was not his fault that I did not profit more.'[32] Paice was also a literary man, who had known the novelist Samuel Richardson and could repeat by heart passages from Shakespeare and his contemporaries, whom he particularly revered. Charles's (at the time unfashionable) interest in Renaissance writers probably owed much to Paice's influence.

Charles was impressed by Paice's even-handed courtesy towards women, no matter how lowly their social status; he was 'the only pattern of consistent gallantry I have ever met with'.

He had not *one* system of attention to females in the drawing-room, and *another* in the shop, or at the stall. I do not mean that he made no distinction. But he never lost sight of sex, or overlooked it in the casualties of a disadvantagous situation. I have seen him stand bare-headed – smile if you please – to a poor servant girl, while she had been inquiring of him the way to some street – in such a posture of unforced civility, as neither to embarrass her in the acceptance, nor himself in the offer, of it. He was no dangler, in the common acceptation of the word, after women: but he reverenced and upheld, in every form in which it came before him, *womanhood*.[33]

John Lamb senior's inculcation in his children of the value and dignity of the individual person, regardless of class, and their right to decent treatment, can again be detected in Charles's approval of Paice's attitude to women.

If Mary's views on the oppressed condition of women were striking for their modernity, Charles's appreciation of the double-standard grew to be impressive in its fervour. 'Elia', in a rare moment of uncompromising political earnestness, was to express Charles's disgust thus:

In comparing modern with ancient manners, we are pleased to compliment ourselves upon the point of gallantry; a certain obsequiousness, or deferential respect, which we are supposed to pay to females, as females.

I shall believe that this principle actuates our conduct, when I can forget, that in the nineteenth century of the era from which we date our civility, we are but just beginning to leave off the very frequent practice of whipping females in public, in common with the coarsest male offenders.

I shall believe it to be influential, when I can shut my eyes to the fact, that in England women are still occasionally – hanged.

I shall believe in it, when actresses are no longer subject to be hissed off a stage by gentlemen.[34]

Growing up with Mary as his guide and example, it is not surprising that Charles's view of society's treatment of women was infused with a sense of outrage. In his eyes, Joseph Paice represented a rare and memorable model of a man who genuinely respected the female sex.

Either Joseph Paice or Samuel Salt was soon to forward Charles's career by procuring for him the position of clerk in a much larger institution, the South Sea Company, of which both men were directors. Charles's brother John had been at the South Sea House for several years already (he was now Deputy Accountant) and was to spend the rest of his working life within its walls, but Charles's period there, in the office for Pacific Trade, was to be much briefer, lasting for only five months from 1 September 1791.

Charles went on to immortalize the South Sea House and his colleagues there in one of his Elia essays. Mostly middle-aged or elderly bachelors (for the pay was poor), confirmed in their peculiar and sometimes eccentric ways, the clerks contributed to a monastic atmosphere (here was another of Charles's cloisters), seeming to him to have the air of 'domestic retainers in a great house, kept more for show than use'. While Charles could entertain himself in contemplating melancholy Evans, who was notable for wearing his hair in the old-fashioned style, powdered and frizzed, or Thomas Tame, whose nobleman's stoop ('which, in great men, must be supposed to be the effect of an habitual condescending attention to the application of their inferiors') belied not only his actual poverty, but an intellect 'of the shallowest order', such company compared poorly with the bright young men Charles had left on quitting Christ's, and did little to compensate for the dull work in which he was engaged.

Once a fortnight, John Tipp, who 'thought an accountant the greatest thing in the world, and himself the greatest accountant in it', would hold open house which Charles sometimes attended. There Tipp would accompany musicians (who only came for the food) on his inexpertly managed fiddle: 'He did, indeed, scream and scrape most abominably.'[35] However, it was away from his office and colleagues that Charles recreated in earnest. The family's straitened financial circumstances proved something of a check on one of Charles and Mary's favourite activities – theatre-going – but they managed to increase the number of occasions on which they could go by always occupying the cheapest seats. In later life Mary recalled how 'we squeezed out our shillings a-piece to sit three or four times in a season in the one-shilling gallery', although Charles had qualms about subjecting his sister to the 'rough' company with which they shared their vantage point, reservations, however, to which his sister did not subscribe:

. . . you felt all the time that you ought not to have brought me – and more strongly I felt obligation to you for having brought me – and the pleasure was the better for a little shame – and when the curtain drew up, what cared we for our place in the house, or what mattered it where we were sitting, when our thoughts were with Rosalind in Arden, or with Viola at the court of Illyria?[36]*

★ This is not actually Mary's authentic voice, but Charles's recollection of it, in the guise of a conversation between Elia and his cousin Bridget.

Thinking back on those days, while Mary reasoned that she was not treated any worse in the gallery than she had since been treated in the pit, she reminded Charles of how he used to rationalize their situation, in an attempt to assuage his doubts:

You used to say, that the gallery was the best place of all for enjoying a play socially – that the relish of such exhibitions must be in proportion to the infrequency of going – that the company we met there, not being in general readers of plays, were obliged to attend the more, and did attend, to what was going on, on the stage – because a word lost would have been a chasm, which it was imposs-ible for them to fill up. With such reflections we consoled our pride . . .

This is perhaps an appropriate point at which to consider how Charles and Mary's relationship was weathering their separate lives. While Charles was at school he had boarded (as was the blanket policy regardless of the proximity of a student's home), going home only during the holidays (the longest of which was three weeks in the summer) and on two half-days each week. Rather than relish school as his private, exclusive realm, he shared his experiences with his sister and it seems unlikely that he would not also have shared a great deal of his learning with her too, like the characters in Mary's poem, 'The Sister's Expostulation on the Brother's Learning Latin and the Brother's Reply'. Evidence of their entrenched habit of shar-ing their thoughts and feelings on every subject and event can be found in letters written by both of them. In 1800, when Charles was in his mid-twenties, he wrote to Robert Lloyd about a visit he had made to his landlord's family in Oxford, adding some incidental and revealing thoughts on the nature of sibling relationships in general:

Gutch's family is a very fine one, consisting of well grown sons & daughters, and all likely & well favor'd. What is called a HAPPY family – that is, according to my interpretation, a NUMEROUS assemblage of young men & women, all fond of each other to a certain degree, & all happy together, but where the very number forbids any two of them to get close enough to each other to share secrets & BE FRIENDS. That close intercourse can only exist, (commonly, I think) in a family of two or three – I do not envy large families. The fraternal affection by diffusion & multi-participation is ordinarily thin & weak –. They dont get near enough to each other.[37]

While Charles clearly believed that his and Mary's closeness had a great deal to do with the fact that they were two of only three children (a small family at that time), he does not say that small families inevitably breed this intimacy – it clearly did not have the same effect on either Charles's or Mary's relationship with their brother John – but that it makes such relationships more possible or more likely. His key phrase 'to share secrets & BE FRIENDS' is echoed in a letter Mary wrote to her friend Sarah Stoddart in 1803:

Secresy, though you appear all frankness, is certainly a grand failing of yours, it is likewise your *brothers* and therefore a family failing – by secresy I mean you both want the habit of telling each other at the moment everything that happens, – where you go – and what you do – that free communication of letters and opinions, just as they arise, as Charles and I do, and which is after all the only groundwork of [any(?)] friendship . . .[38]

This habit of mutual disclosure – which came to Charles and Mary as naturally as breathing – not only bound them closely together, but increased the distance between them and their brother John. He neither shared in their 'secrets', nor shared his own with them.

In the essay 'My Relations', Charles (as Elia) attempted to delineate what still to him remained largely hidden: the personality of his brother John (here in the persona of Elia's cousin James). The 'fiery, glowing, tempestuous' James of childhood had no more in common with Elia and Bridget (Mary) as a young man: 'James is an inexplicable cousin,' Elia begins.

With great love for *you*, J.E. hath but a limited sympathy with what you feel or do. He lives in a world of his own, and makes slender guesses at what passes in your mind. He never pierces the marrow of your habits . . . He has not much respect for that class of feelings which goes by the name of sentimental.

John appears to have left home while Charles was still at school, and was the only one of the three to marry. Thereafter he had little to do with his brother and sister, and at the time when he could have played the big brother by giving the family support – physical, emotional or financial – he actively backed away from his responsibilities.

If their position in a small family drew Charles and Mary closer together, and their mother's undisguised preference for John had the same effect, the fact that the family's financial situation was always precarious was also attributed (by them at least) as a factor which united rather than divided them. As Elia addressed Bridget, in the essay 'Old China', looking back on their youth from the relative comfort of middle age:

It is true we were happier when we were poorer, but we were also younger, my cousin . . . That we had much to struggle with, as we grew up together, we have reason to be most thankful. It strengthened, and knit our compact closer. We could never have been what we have been to each other, if we had always had the sufficiency which you now complain of.

Again John is excluded from the picture, not only because he cut himself loose, at the first opportunity, from sharing in and helping to ameliorate the family's privations, but because he himself represented one of the factors which Charles and Mary had to 'struggle with'. John was ever part of the problem, not the solution.

Charles and Mary's holiday in Margate and their trips to the theatre therefore represented real highlights in the context of a family life which was to become increasingly troubled. For Mary they also constituted her only opportunities, apart from reading, for any kind of escape from the daily grind of needlework and housework. While Charles also worked he was, due to the privilege afforded to his sex, able to have a social life outside the home. He regularly met up with many of his old schoolfriends, his genial personality combining with his always sharp wit to make him an ideal drinking companion.

This was the situation of Charles and Mary in 1791; both adults embarked on their working lives, making the best of the little they had. In fact, this period marked the end of an age of innocence, as the next year was to prove a turning point. The fortunes of the Lamb family were to take a sharp downturn, and Charles was to fall in love.

3. The Salutation and Cat

Coleridge, I know not what suffering scenes you have gone through at Bristol, – my life has been somewhat diversified of late. The 6 weeks that finished last year & began this your very humble servant spent very agreeably in a MAD HOUSE AT HOXTON –. I am got somewhat rational now, & DON'T BITE ANY ONE. But MAD I was – & many a vagary my imagination played with ME, enough to make a VOLUME if all told . . .

(Letter from Charles Lamb to Samuel Taylor Coleridge
[27 May 1796])

In the winter of 1795/6 Charles Lamb was to suffer an episode of psychiatric illness so severe that he had to be removed to a lunatic asylum. Just as Charles believed his brother made 'slender guesses' at what went on in his mind, there are little more than slender clues about the cause and nature of this breakdown. What is certain is that the year 1792 marked the beginning of a period of creeping crisis for the whole family, and that Charles's personal relationships added to his particular burden to a point where the demands of everyday life became intolerable.

On 8 February that year, two days before his seventeenth birthday, Charles left his employment at the South Sea House. Shortly afterwards he went on a solo visit to Blakesware to stay with his grandmother. She was now suffering terribly with breast cancer, and 'bowed down' by almost constant pain. While he was there Charles met – or perhaps renewed an acquaintance with – and fell in love with a local girl. He was to refer to her in the Elia essays as 'Alice W—n' and in poetry as 'Anna'; research suggests she was Ann Simmons, from the nearby village of Widford.

Tantalizingly little information exists about this liaison; Charles refers in the Elia essays to the relationship on only three occasions, and then briefly. He was – naturally – a novice in love. As a small boy 'Elia' had a crush on a neighbour at the Temple 'who had power to thrill the soul of Elia, small imp as he was, even in his long coats; and to make him glow, tremble, and blush with a passion . . .' The sound of her singing at her harpsichord moved young Elia's heart 'strangely'; the effect that she had on him 'not faintly indicated the day-spring of that absorbing sentiment, which was afterwards destined to overwhelm and subdue his nature quite, for Alice W—n'.[1]

In another essay Elia has a dream in which he imagines that he married Alice; that she died; that he is telling their two children about their mother: 'I told how for seven long years, in hope sometimes, sometimes in despair, yet persisting ever, I courted the fair Alice W—n . . . I explained to them what coyness, and difficulty, and denial meant in maidens . . .'[2] Although in this fantasy Elia eventually secured Alice (albeit only to be prematurely widowed) and, significantly, father-hood, in reality Charles did not, as he mentions in a third essay. In 'New Year's Eve' Elia meditates on the value of unhappy experiences, reasoning that, for example, 'It was better that our family should have missed that legacy, which old Dorrell cheated us of, than that I should have at this moment two thousand pounds *in banco*, and be without the idea of that specious old rogue.' In the same vein: 'Methinks, it is better that I should have pined away seven of my goldenest years, when I was thrall to the fair hair, and fairer eyes, of

Alice W——n, than that so passionate a love-adventure should be lost.' It was better, Charles consoled himself, to have loved and lost than never to have loved at all.

There is widely cited belief that his grandmother warned him away from pursuing a serious relationship with Ann because of the history of hereditary insanity in the Lamb family. This rather breathtaking intervention is curious for two reasons. First, it is the only reference to the idea that there *was* a history of insanity in the family: neither John nor Sarah Lamb appears to have suffered in this department, and this reservation was not to stop Charles and Mary's brother John from marrying (although he married a widow with a daughter and had no children of his own). Second, Mary Field must have had this conversation with Charles during this visit or soon after, as she was to die later in the year, which suggests that Charles fell immediately, seriously and obviously in love and was already contemplating marriage. The fact that he energetically pursued the relationship suggests that he, for one, disregarded this impediment, if impediment it was.

Were these threats of a genetic predisposition to insanity the bitter ramblings of an elderly, very sick woman who possibly never approved of her daughter's marriage? Or was this the family secret which explained Mary Field's anxiety over Mary's preoccupations, occasioning her reference to Mary's 'poor crazy moyther'd brains'? The third possibility is that this anecdote is a myth, and that the idea of insanity being hereditary in the family was later built into the mythology of the Lambs, in an attempt to make sense of subsequent events.

Shortly after Charles returned to London, in April 1792, aged seventeen, he began his career as a clerk in the Accountants' Office of the East India House. He was to remain there for the next thirty-three years. The East India Company was a unique organization. Having been granted a monopoly on trade with the Eastern hemisphere by charter from Parliament in 1600, by the time Charles joined the ranks of the Company's servants it was the *de facto* ruler of substantial portions of India. Thomas Macaulay spoke for many when he doubted the fitness of a commercial enterprise for such a role:

A society [i.e. the Company] which judging a priori from its constitution was as little suited for the imperial function as the Merchant Taylors' Co. or the New River Co., was exercising sovereignty over more people, with a larger revenue and a larger army than that under the direct control of the executive government of the United Kingdom.[3]

The sheer scale of the Company's operation required the support of a massive infrastructure in London. The Company not only built its own ships (comprising the largest private fleet in Britain), but supplied everything required to fit them out, from nails and anchors, made in its own foundry, to cordage and sails, made in its own spinning shed – the Company even manufactured its own gunpowder. The East India Dock Company was established in order to provide a state-of-the-art dock for its exclusive use. Elsewhere in the city the Company made its mark, building its own chapel in Poplar, beside its own hospital. Its warehouses in Cutler Street in the City covered five acres and employed 4,000 warehousemen and 400 clerks. A further thirty acres of warehouses were devoted to the storage of tea alone. To this day, the key roads into London from the East End remain those built by the company, at a cost of £10,000 in 1801: East India Dock Road and Commercial Road, facilitating easy access between the East India Dock and the City. In order to ensure a steady supply of suitable staff for its Presidencies (administrative bases) and 'factories' (trading posts) abroad, the Company established its own college, Haileybury, in 1809, to train future bureaucrats for service in India, instructing them for two years in Asian languages and culture as well as economics and accountancy.

As impressive, in their own way, as the miles of warehousing and the fleet of EastIndiamen (as the Company's ships were known) anchored at Blackwall were the headquarters of the Company's vast organization: the elegant and imposing, pillared, porticoed and pedimented East India House in Leadenhall Street, to which Charles reported on 5 April 1792. Above the main entrance stood Britannia, presiding over Europe on horseback on one side and Asia on a camel on the other. Traffic in and out of the building was constant as it was conveniently sited close both to its City investors and to the wharves and warehouses servicing its operations. As well as providing the administrative base for the Company, the building housed its library, its own museum and a Sale Room, where Charles would later attend the all-important auctions of imported goods. The 'howling and yelling' on auction days were often sufficient to penetrate the august structure's stone walls.

The volume of paperwork generated by the Company's activities, all of which passed through East India House, was vast. The Company not only had a monopoly on the import of oriental products, but an export monopoly too. EastIndiamen arriving in India and China from London sold their cargoes and bought tea, coffee, cocoa, silk, cotton, porcelain, and so on, both for home consumption and for re-export to Europe and America. The Company also had the right to enforce the monopoly, should it be challenged, as it was by the equally expansionist-minded French. Following the campaigns of 1745–61, the East India Company's own Robert Clive had helped establish the Company as not only the dominant economic and military power in India (by 1805 the Company employed 500,000 troops in Bengal, Madras and Bombay) but its dominant political power too. While it was supervised by the British government, and collected taxes on its behalf (providing the exchequer in London with half a million pounds a year from land revenues in Bengal alone, at the time that Charles joined the Company), what had begun as a trading company had become an imperial power in its own right.

The fact of the monopoly on eastern trade assisted the East India Company's success, but could not, on its own, ensure it. Like all import-export ventures, the Company depended on investment. The financial organization of the Company pioneered the joint-stock concept. Previously, a small number of large investors would combine forces to invest in one specific voyage. Whether the project succeeded or failed the effects on the investors were extreme – vast fortunes were made by some, while others lost everything. Joint stock, which involved a large number of small investors financing longer-term schemes, encompassing a number of expeditions, avoided the boom or bust effect, sharing both the risk and the spoils over a wider investment base. By the middle of the seventeenth century the East India Company had attracted sufficient confidence to operate on the basis of continuous investment, with stocks being valued and traded.

A further contributory factor to the success of the East India Company lay in its administrative structure, which was designed to process policy and information speedily, efficiently, and with close attention to detail. This was where the army of clerks at East India House came into the equation. The huge accountants' office on the first floor was divided into a number of compartments, each of which housed six desk-bound clerks. Assisting Charles Lamb and his peers in their work was the highly efficient postal system operated by the Company. At that time postage was paid not by the sender but by the recipient. Not only Charles and Mary but a number of their friends were to make good use of this 'free' service by asking their correspondents to address mail to them to Charles at the office (his name spelt 'Lambe' being the code). Much important correspondence between this circle (for example, between Wordsworth and Coleridge) may well not even have existed had it not been for Charles's East India connection, which relieved the writers the considerable, and sometimes prohibitive, expense of postage.

At the time that Charles became a servant of the East India Company, a certain amount of excitement surrounded the institution. The recent loss of the great war for America was ascribed by some to what became known as a 'swing to the East' – that is, an unprecedented popular interest in all things oriental. As Philip Lawson has observed: 'Between 1784 and 1813 public knowledge of Company affairs and British activities in India generally increased markedly. Every aspect of the Company's operations was openly debated in Parliament and the press.'[4]

While the general impression given by biographers of Charles's service at the East India House has tended to be one of unremitting gloom and tedium (on bad days he would feel he and his desk were merging into one: 'the wood has entered my soul' he would groan), in fact he had a good deal of face-to-face business with merchants, sea captains and other interested parties who visited the accountants' office. There is little doubt but that at the time he joined the Company it was a bustling and successful concern, conducted with vigour and confidence – a hub of news, certainly – a much-talked-about and not unglamorous place in which a promising young man might set out in his professional life. It was true that Charles would have vastly preferred the life of a Cambridge undergraduate, but given that this was not an option, all things considered, things were looking up for him: he was in love; he was on the first rung of a career ladder which would lead to lifelong financial security; he could think in terms of becoming independent from his family – and even of marrying. But barely three months later disaster struck: on 27 July Samuel Salt died.

Samuel Salt not only provided the family with its principal income (through John Lamb senior's wages) but also with the roof over its head, as they occupied half of his double set of chambers. John Lamb was now himself in poor health and in his late sixties: while he had for many years been indispensable to Salt, as a commodity in the wider work market he was by this time virtually unemployable. All he had left were his duties as butler at Inner Temple Hall, and by the end of January of the following year he was unable to fulfil even these, having almost completely lost the use of his left hand and being 'otherwise very infirm'. While it might seem fortuitous that Charles had just commenced his permanent post at the East India House, this was in fact no help at all: his father and brother had each put up bonds of £500 for Charles on entering the Company and Charles received only a £30 gratuity for his three-year probationary period as a clerk. This left only John and Mary's wages; John had either left home already, or was on the point of departing, although he probably contributed something to his parents, and Mary had only the income from her needlework which, if her pay was typical, was barely enough to support a single person, let alone five adults.

In another cruel blow, only four days after Salt's death, Mary Field died. While Charles and Mary's grandmother was elderly and ill and her death must have been expected, it came at a bad time; with her passing all the comforts of Blakesware also vanished from the Lambs' landscape. There were to be no more holidays in the big house, no more wandering through its empty halls or feasting their senses in its gardens. There was to be no more idleness, no more day-dreaming.

By the end of the winter 1792/3, when Salt's property was sold, John Lamb senior was unemployed and never to work again. Salt had left him £500 of South Sea stock, on which the family was largely to depend for the next three years.[5] In February 1793 Charles and Mary moved house for the first time in their lives. With their mother and father and Aunt Sarah they travelled only a few streets away, to 7 Little Queen Street, Holborn, which they shared initially with a newly married couple, Mr and Mrs Weight, who were due to move to Manchester. There is only one anecdote surviving from this period of adjustment. Mary, like her tactless Aunt Sarah, Charles noted, 'would sometimes press civility out of season' and the Weights were to recall Mary one day remarking that she, as a professional dressmaker, should be permitted 'to improve Mrs. Weight's caps'.[6]

No record survives ascertaining whether poor Mrs Weight suffered her caps to undergo such alterations, and no more is known of the Lamb family until the winter of 1794/5 when Coleridge, on vacation from Jesus College, Cambridge, was spending time with Charles. It was at this time that Coleridge introduced his free-thinking friend and fellow poet, Robert Southey, to Charles. Southey remembered visiting the Lambs at Little Queen Street one evening during this period, and finding them 'evidently in uncomfortable circumstances'. He recollected Elizabeth Lamb's 'invalid appearance' (as if matters could have got any worse, she too had been smitten by some kind of creeping paralysis, possibly caused by a stroke) and noted that 'the father's senses had failed him before this time'.[7]

If Charles was feeling the strain of a senile father, an invalid mother, cramped lodgings and financial problems, he could at least escape to the East India House during the day and go out occasionally in the evenings. Mary had all the same pressures – and more – but was tied to the house, endeavouring to do as much work as possible in order to help support the family in the face of continual interruptions due to her being at the beck and call of three elderly and infirm relations. While Charles had the added burden of his unrequited – or unresolved – long-distance involvement with Ann Simmons now drawing to a close, it was Mary who, as Charles acknowledged in a poem addressed to her, 'woulds oftimes lend/An ear to the desponding, love sick Lay,/Weeping my sorrows with me . . .' Mary was the first person to whom Charles would turn in his anguish, to whom he would pour out his troubles, and this represented yet another responsibility she was to bear alone.

It is not surprising to learn that Mary became seriously ill during that winter. It is not known for certain whether this illness was of a physical or mental nature, but two years later it was reported that she had at some point previously 'been deranged, from the harassing fatigues of too much business'. Whatever the nature of the illness, it was considered extremely serious. Coleridge, also apparently unaware of the nature of Mary's complaint, wrote to Southey that she had been confined to her bed, 'dangerously' ill. Coleridge, who had lost his own much-loved sister on whose 'soft bosom I reposed my cares' (much like Charles), deeply sympathized with his friend and wrote him a poem in which he imagined Charles watching over his sister during her crisis:

> In fancy (well I know)
> Thou creepest round a dear-loved Sister's bed,
> With noiseless step, and watchest the faint look,
> Soothing each pang with fond solicitude,
> And tenderest tones medicinal of love.

Coleridge informed Southey that Mary's illness 'preyed a good deal on his [Charles's] spirits', explaining that 'She is all his comfort, he hers. They dote on each other.'[8]

By now Coleridge knew Mary well and had an extremely high opinion of both her intellect and her character. 'Her mind is elegantly stored; her heart feeling,' he told Southey, and to Charles, again in poetic strain, he wrote of

> Her Soul affectionate yet wise,
> Her polish'd wit as mild as lambent glories
> That play around a holy infant's head.[9]

(Mary, no doubt, would have been thoroughly embarrassed by this simile, but it was designed to appeal to her less squeamish, more poetically minded, brother.) To Charles's great relief Mary recovered and conscientiously and diligently resumed her duties.

Later in life Charles was to observe that 'the home of the very poor is no home' and to suggest that men living in such circumstances sometimes resorted to the ale house in search of 'an image of the home, which he cannot find at home'.[10] While poverty and illness stalked the Lamb household it is perhaps not altogether surprising to find the nineteen-year-old Charles taking refuge, on occasion, in convivial friends and welcoming inns over that difficult winter. He spent an undetermined but apparently significant portion of his time in the company of a number of Blues (as the ex-Bluecoat boys were styled). First among these was James (familiarly known as Jem) White. After finishing at Christ's White had also become a clerk, in his case at the treasurer's office at their old school (it was a policy at Christ's only to employ old boys). Charles, Jem White, and another Blue, John Mathew Gutch, frequently met up at the Three Feathers in Hand Court, Holborn, to drink Burton ale. Charles found White incomparable company. Many years later, only a few months before his own death, on meeting another old schoolfriend Charles was to exclaim: 'Jem White! There never was his like! We never shall see such days as those in which Jem flourished!' As far as Charles was concerned, Jem White represented 'half the fun of the world', adding 'of my world at least'. While Gutch characterized White as 'a remarkably open-hearted, joyous companion, very intimate with the Lamb family', he also recalled the particular bent of White's wit. According to Thomas Noon Talfourd, Charles 'always insisted that for hearty joyous humour, tinged with Shakespearean fancy, Jem never had an equal'. This Shakespearean fancy led to White being given the nickname among his intimates of Sir John (after Falstaff). Apparently White's improvisations, based on Shakespeare's character, 'excited great mirth'. Some flavour of this has been preserved in his playful skit 'The Original Letters of Sir John Falstaff and his Companions' (1796), which Charles aided and abetted.

Other Blues with whom Charles socialized included the Le Grice brothers. Both had been Grecians, both had gone to Cambridge, and both shared a love of, and facility at, sharp and disarming repartee. The elder Le Grice, Charles Valentine, was 'full of puns and jokes, very genial' but his younger brother Samuel was, according to Leigh Hunt, 'the maddest of all the great boys in my time; clever, full of address, and not hampered with modesty'. His reputation at school, due to his diligent pursuit of the matron's daughters, led Hunt to dub him 'our Lord Rochester'. (Sammy was indeed to turn out a rake.) Charles himself remembered the twinkling-eyed younger Le Grice as 'sanguine, volatile, sweet-natured'.[11]

Beautiful Robert Allen was also of their number. Another Grecian, Allen had gone from Christ's to Oxford, where his friendship with the revolutionary Southey had confirmed him a radical. Although Charles remembered his 'cordial smile, and still more cordial laugh', he was more legendary for his stunning good looks. In an incident cited by both Charles and Leigh Hunt, he pinched a woman's bottom in the street; unsurprisingly, the woman rounded on him, 'tigress-like', her half-formed curse – 'Bl—' – still on her lips when she was 'suddenly converted' by Allen's angelic features. 'Bl—ess thy handsome face!' she exclaimed.[12] Marmaduke Thompson, another Grecian, was also one of Charles and Allen's cohort. The schoolboy friendship which was then blossoming into the most significant of Charles's life, however, was with Coleridge.

Like many of his generation, Coleridge's political development was accelerated and shaped by the egalitarian ideas of the French revolution. His rooms at Jesus College were a hive of political activity and discussion; a further distraction from his studies (and strain on his pocket) came in the shape of bouts of unregulated drinking and whoring. His initially distinguished academic record began to show the strain and his debts mounted – neither result endearing him to his family. At the end of the first term of his second year Coleridge took the dramatic step – the first of several attempts at redemption which became blurred with escapism – of volunteering for the army, under the name Silas Tomkyn Comberbache. The experiment proved to be one of the many 'wild Schemes of impossible extrication' which Coleridge typically undertook with abandoned enthusiasm, but which sooner or later lost their appeal, leaving only debts and broken promises in their wake.[13] After four months in the 15th Light Dragoons, his family achieved the 'impossible extrication' and got him discharged on the grounds of insanity.

Before returning to his academic studies, Coleridge undertook the first of his epic walks, accompanied by college friend Joseph Hucks. It was while visiting Robert Allen at Oxford that Coleridge had first met Robert Southey, with whom he began to develop 'Pantisocracy': the proposal of a small-scale rural commune based on democratic and egalitarian principles. Southey introduced Coleridge to the Fricker family (who also became enthusiasts for Pantisocracy) and encouraged Coleridge's relationship with Sara Fricker, sister of Edith, whom Southey was to marry. (Coleridge had left unresolved – like so many things in his life – a relationship he had begun while still at school with Mary Evans, significantly also the sister of a schoolfriend's sweetheart.) The Pantisocratic project was to consist of twelve couples, including Coleridge and Southey and Sara and Edith Fricker, who would build their Utopian community in America. (Women and men, incidentally, were to have equal democratic and economic rights.) Having returned to Cambridge in autumn 1794 (the Pantisocrats planned to set sail the following spring), Coleridge spent a month of the winter in London, agonizing over whether to abandon his education, disappoint his family, and finally draw a line under his relationship with Mary Evans, or to abandon his Pantisocratic vision, disappoint Southey, and reconsider his commitment to Sara Fricker.

During this period in London, Coleridge visited Charles and Mary on several occasions, when even brother John found him fascinating and thought-provoking company. Coleridge was staying at the Salutation and Cat in Newgate Market, where he and Charles spent many long evenings feasting on Welsh rarebit and poetry, lubricated with punch and eggnog, wreathed in tobacco-smoke and metaphysics. During his schooldays Coleridge had been a pleasure to listen to; as a young man be became positively spell-binding. As William Hazlitt recorded:

His genius at that time had angelic wings and fed on manna. He talked on forever; and you wished him to talk on for ever. His thoughts did not seem to come with labour and effort; but as if borne on the gusts of genius . . . His voice rolled on the ear like the pealing organ, and its sound alone was the music of thought.[14]

William Wordsworth was to comment in a similar vein: 'He talks as a bird sings, as if he could not help it: it is his nature.'[15]

The ingredient which lent a particular piquancy to Charles and Coleridge's heart-to-hearts at the Salutation and Cat was the fact that both these creative, sensitive and original young men were frustrated in love. As Charles wrote to Coleridge some time later:

You came to Town, & I saw you at a time when your heart was yet bleeding with recent wounds. Like yourself, I was sore galled with disappointed HOPE. You had 'many an holy lay, that mourning soothed the mourner on his way.' I had ears of sympathy to drink them in . . .[16]

When Coleridge left, however, Charles abruptly awoke from this consoling reverie and suddenly and keenly felt 'a dismal VOID in my heart'. 'I have never met with any one, never shall meet with any ONE, who could or can compensate me for the top of your SOCIETY . . .' he later wrote to his friend. Even Jem White (that 'WIT of the first magnitude'), of whom Charles was so fond, and who had 'many a social & good quality', was nevertheless 'a man to whom I have never been accustomed to impart my <u>DEAREST FEELINGS</u>'; 'White has *all kindness*, but not *sympathy* . . .'[17]

Coleridge's company had charmed him temporarily, but not cured him of his malady: 'In your conversation you had blended so many pleasant fancies, that they cheated me of my grief. But in your absence, the tide of melancholy rushd in again, & did its worst MISCHIEF by overwhelming my Reason.'[18] Charles's descent into serious mental trouble is not charted. The material which would have given us clues – the poetry he was writing and a journal of 'my foolish passion' for Ann Simmons 'which I had a long time kept' – he consigned to the fire at about this time, presumably in an attempt to acknowledge concretely the vanity of both ambitions. He similarly destroyed a book he had kept up for years, into which he had copied significant passages from Beaumont and Fletcher and other Renaissance playwrights from 'a thousand sources', and also burned letters from Coleridge as soon as he had read them. Even though this material was lost, the nature of what Charles selected for destruction is illuminating, pointing to there being more than one cause – from his point of view at least – for his state of mind. The destruction of the journal and the poetry, which were probably two manifestations of the same obsession, indicates the death of hope in the relationship with Ann Simmons certainly being one of these causes. The destruction of the book of extracts may represent a less obvious realization: quite possibly the reality of Charles's future – a lifetime of slavery to a desk at the East India House and to ailing parents at home – was sinking in, dashing any hope he had entertained of becoming a serious writer. Why he burned Coleridge's letters is initially more puzzling, but perhaps as revealing.

Following his recovery and discharge from the madhouse at Hoxton, still in a state of depression, he wrote a number of letters to Coleridge which fortunately have survived, and which allude to this period. Repeated reference to the many nights the two young men spent in the smoky little room at the Salutation and Cat indicate that, as Charles acknowledged, that scene was 'continually presenting itself to my recollection'. Even a year later Charles recalled his intense pleasure at listening to Coleridge

. . . when you were repeating one of Bowles's sweetest sonnets in your sweet manner, while we two were indulging sympathy, a solitary luxury, by the fireside at the Salutation. Yet I have no higher ideas of heaven. Your company was one 'cordial in this melancholy vale' – the remembrance of it is a blessing partly, and partly a curse.[19]

It may have been this passionate ambivalence towards Coleridge's influence on him that led him to enjoy and then destroy his friend's letters. Coleridge had gone away and was to be married: it must have seemed to Charles that the Salutation and Cat period, and the mutual intimacy and sympathy that attended it, were gone for ever. Coleridge's letters therefore summoned an idea that was immensely attractive to Charles, but at the same time beyond reach.

Significantly, Charles did not destroy all of Coleridge's letters, just the ones he received in the period immediately leading up to his 'derangement'. He had thought of burning them all, but for a quite different and infinitely illuminating reason. As he later confessed to Coleridge:

I almost burned all your letters, – I did as bad, I lent 'em to a friend to keep out of my brother's sight, should he come and make inquisition into our papers, for, much as he dwelt upon your conversation while you were among us, and delighted to be with you, it has been his fashion ever since to depreciate and cry you down, – you were the cause of my madness – you and your damned foolish sensibility and melancholy – and he lamented with a true brotherly feeling that we ever met . . .[20]*

While the idea that John might 'make inquisition' into Charles's private letters again suggests the domineering and insensitive nature of his brothering, John's opinion cannot be dismissed, raising the possibility that, far from keeping Charles sane during the Salutation and Cat period, Coleridge might have been helping drive him mad. Much later in life John was to express the view that 'wit' – here in the sense of acutely intelligent and imaginative thought – 'whose brilliant, fiery, delectable particles, when used as a will o' th' wisp to mislead, [is] dazzling and most dangerous'.[21] Whatever John's failings and personal prejudices were, as Charles himself acknowledged, despite his inquisitorial and judgemental elder-brother manner, John was on this occasion motivated by a genuine fraternal concern.

The idea that Coleridge might have contributed to Charles's problems rather than their solutions – although it comes from a rather different angle to John's objections – during this period has also been suggested by the academic F. V. Morley, who in 1932 published an account of Charles's early literary endeavours. Morley suggests that, at this particular time, Coleridge's company had a dangerous effect 'on the unsettled and unstable Lamb, at the eager age of nineteen'. Coleridge was indeed two years older than Charles – two years which at that time of life are significant – and was undoubtedly a genius in search of a focus for his life (a goal which was ever to prove elusive to him). Coleridge was characteristically an engaging

---

* He may as well have burned them as he was never able to retrieve the letters from this 'friend'.

and inspiring conversationalist on whatever his current project or preoccupation happened to be, but equally characteristically dropped it and moved on – leaving a terrible mess in his wake – when a more attractive idea captured his imagination. Morley's point is that Coleridge's temperament was adapted to – and in some senses insulated against the effect of – experimenting with ideas and feelings. He could afford, in this case, to take the idea of thwarted love to its most painful and idealized limits, because he was entirely capable of walking away from it unscathed. But, Morley thinks, Charles was a much more tender plant. She argues that the passion in both young men's early poems was artificial, but that Charles grew to believe in its reality, to the point of its becoming a fixed delusion.[22] Rather than helping Charles get over Ann Simmons, in this analysis, Coleridge may have encouraged him into an unrealistic and ultimately damaging preoccupation with it. It is certainly noticeable that when Charles recalled the Widford romance, he would frequently quote from his love poems rather than from life.

While Morley emphasizes Coleridge treating Charles's feelings and emotions irresponsibly, there is evidence that Coleridge was also exerting an unsettling influence on Charles's intellect. Immediately prior to his confinement at Hoxton, Charles wrote a letter – substantially the same letter – to a number of his friends earnestly recommending them to read David Hartley's *Observations on Man* (1749). (Hartley's doctrine of 'Necessity' was a theory of the intellectual and moral development of the individual which emphasized the importance of childhood experiences. It was to have considerable impact on the romantics.) No copies of the letter have been found, but Valentine Le Grice recalled it was 'very well written' and perfectly remembered one phrase in it: 'Hartley appears to me to have had as clear an insight into all the [secrets] of the human mind as I have into the items of a Ledger – as an Accountant has – a good counting-Housical Simile you'll say, and apropos from a clerk in the India House.'[23]

The following day the friends who had received the letter received a second, this time from Elizabeth Lamb, explaining that Charles had written the letter in a state of madness and had subsequently had to be confined. She concluded by asking them not to reply to it. Hartley was currently dominating Coleridge's thinking (indeed, he was to name his first son after the philosopher) and had been a substantial subject of his intercourse with Charles. While Coleridge could not be accused of making his friend mad, he was clearly the strongest influence on Charles's thinking in the immediate lead-up to his breakdown.

In short, putting Charles in the company of a box of fireworks like Coleridge at a time when he was emotionally and psychologically vulnerable was inviting disaster. There are many testaments to Coleridge's genius and charisma; that Charles later developed an awareness of the dangerous and destructive capacity of his friend is evident less than a year after these events, when he was still recovering from the worst experience of his life. While Coleridge was the first person he wrote to, and while he solicited his comfort in the shape of correspondence, Charles knew he had not the resources to cope with Coleridge's company: 'I have my reason and strength left . . . I charge you don't think of coming to see me. Write. I will not see you if you come.'[24]

So, there was not one but a collection of unresolved problems pressing on Charles, added to which was the blessing/curse of Coleridge's influence, and then Coleridge's withdrawal, to Bristol and marriage with Sara Fricker, just at a point when Charles may have become emotionally dependent on his brilliant friend. There is also an admissible further factor: drink. At the time that Charles became ill, alcohol abuse was widely held as a major cause of mental illness. Although nowadays the relationship tends to be represented as rather more complex, the link is certainly one which Charles himself recognized. (One of his fictional characters was observed to be 'ravished' by wine, which together with vanity 'engenders madness'. The same character also drinks to excess because he is unhappy.*) This period marks the beginning of an uneasy relationship with alcohol which was to dog Charles for the rest of his life and, according to some, hastened its end.

All of these factors may help explain the lead-up to the complete breakdown of rationality which led him to the Hoxton madhouse in December 1795. Following his recovery, Charles promised to 'amuse' Coleridge 'with an account as full as my memory will permit of the strange turn my PHRENSY took'. No letter survives with this account but Southey recalled: 'I have heard Coleridge say that, in a fit of derangement, Lamb fancied himself to be Young Norval.'[25] Young Norval was the hero of the romantic tragedy *Douglas* by John Home. Charles seems to have found madness in a manner liberating: 'I look back upon it AT TIMES with a gloomy kind of ENVY. For while it lasted I had many many hours of pure happiness. Dream not Coleridge, of having tasted all the grandeur & wildness of FANCY, till you have GONE MAD.'[26]

In the spring of 1796 four of Charles's sonnets (including the Margate poem) were published in Coleridge's *Poems on Various Subjects*. The *Critical Review* declared Charles's 'effusions' 'very beautiful'. Yet any satisfaction Charles derived from this was fleeting and insubstantial; overall, since his

* The eponymous hero of *John Woodvil*.

madness had subsided, he was left feeling flat and dejected: 'All now seems to me VAPID; comparatively so.' He wrote of feeling in 'a stupor that makes me indifferent to the hopes & fears of this life'. In his depression Charles also felt lonely, 'cast as I am "on life's wide plain, friendless"'.[27] He was not, of course, literally friendless, but the Blues he drank with could not compensate for the loss of Coleridge's company, as this example of tipsy *tendresse* in a letter to Coleridge shows:

I have been drinking egg-hot and smoking Oronooko (associated circumstances, which ever forcibly recall to my mind our evenings and nights at the Salutation); my eyes and brain are heavy and asleep, but my heart is awake; and if words came as ready as ideas, and ideas as feelings, I could say ten hundred kind things. Coleridge, you know not my supreme happiness at having one on earth (though counties separate us) whom I can call a friend.[28]

Charles was about to discover just how many friends he did have, following the catastrophe which was to shape the rest of his life.

By the end of the summer of 1796 Charles had pretty much regained his equilibrium. Mary, however, was feeling the strain of her circumstances. Their mother was now almost completely paralysed and totally dependent on Mary, who cared for her, washed her, fed her and slept with her. Their father was now senile to the point of imbecility and also required a good deal of looking after. Aunt Sarah was apparently in good health, but now in her mid-eighties and unable to assist much with domestic chores. Mary also had her work and was training a girl apprentice. As well as her domestic and professional cares, it was Mary who bore the brunt of stretching the family's tight budget to accommodate its needs. To make matters worse, her elder brother John had come home, not to help but to be nursed himself. A serious accident – a piece of masonry had fallen on his foot – had led to an infection which made him delirious and amputation was a strong possibility. John was no less demanding a patient than his parents (Charles wrote 'we are necessarily confined with him the afternoon & evening till very late') and it was again Mary who bore the brunt of the nursing.[29]

Merely imagining a day in Mary's life at this time reveals that she was carrying out duties alone which would have kept several people busy. Burning the candle at both ends and sharing a bed with her paralysed mother, she was getting hardly any sleep. A dutiful and loving daughter, she was not complaining: Mary never complained. However, something was going to snap. By mid-September, Mary was beginning to display symptoms of mental illness. On the evening of 21 September her behaviour was becoming so disturbing that Charles set out first thing the following morning to fetch the doctor. The doctor was out and after a protracted and fruitless search Charles returned home alone. When he arrived at Little Queen Street a scene of unmitigated horror met his eyes.

He may have heard the apprentice girl's screams as he approached the house. Perhaps he collided with the child in the hallway as she fled, speechless with terror. Charles pushed the parlour-door open warily. The only sound was that of a man sobbing. As the door swung open, inch by inch the scale of the disaster was revealed. Furniture was overturned; the floor was littered with food, broken crockery, and cutlery. His mother, father and sister were covered in blood. His mother lay dead in her armchair. His father, bleeding from his head, was weeping. His aunt, white with shock, seemed rooted to the spot and apparently lifeless. Presiding over this shocking tableau was its author. Mary, her face and clothes spattered with blood, stood over their mother's body, a carving-knife in her hand.

4. Friend-confessor, Brother-confessor

Your letter, my friend, struck me with a mighty horror. It rushed
upon me and stupefied my feelings . . . Your poor father is, I
hope, almost senseless of the calamity; the unconscious instrument
of Divine Providence knows it not, and your mother is in heaven.

(Letter from Samuel Taylor Coleridge to Charles Lamb,
28 September 1797)

In 1786 Margaret Nicholson attempted to attack King George
III with a dessert knife. As soon as she was discovered to be
deranged she was confined in the Bethlehem Hospital (usually
called Bethlem or Bedlam). She was not committed for trial,
nor was there any talk of her hanging. This was the usual way
of dealing with the criminally insane. The same discretion was
widely applied and Mary Lamb was one such beneficiary: she
was not treated as a criminal but as a lunatic. She did not stand
trial, and was declared insane only at the coroner's court which
sat to establish the cause of her mother's death.

Mary was even more fortunate than Margaret Nicholson,
as she was not sent to Bethlem. At the time Mary killed her
mother an insane person charged with a criminal offence could
be 'liberated on security being given that he should properly
be taken care of as a lunatic'. At this time it was the family,
rather than the state, in cases like Mary's, who took responsibility for arranging care for the mentally ill. Had Mary committed

the same crime three years later than she did, it would have been a different story.

In 1800 the King was again the victim of a deranged would-be assassin, when James Hadfield shot and wounded him. Because of the seriousness of the crime, Hadfield did stand trial, but was acquitted on the grounds of insanity. The verdict was significant on two counts. First, it demonstrated the triumph of a humane approach to a mentally ill individual over what might have been a more politically expedient response (Hadfield was, after all, an ex-soldier, and attacked the King during a period when revolutionary war and radical insurgence were at their height). Second, it exposed a legal loophole, because the law made no provision for Hadfield's future safe-keeping. An *Act for the Safe Keeping of Insane Persons Charged with Offences* (1800) was consequently rushed through Parliament, which provided that anyone charged with treason, murder, or felony who was acquitted on the grounds of insanity was to be kept in strict custody 'during His Majesty's pleasure'. Under this Act, Mary would not only have stood trial for her offence, but would have been committed to Bethlem, probably for the rest of her life.

The cases of Margaret Nicholson and James Hadfield were of course high-profile and well-documented due to the eminence of their victim, but George III made a more significant contribution to the history of mental illness: his own derangement caused the subject of madness to figure on the public opinion agenda. (His first mental disturbance occurred in 1788 and he suffered repeated bouts of illness before sinking into senility from about 1810.) His case was widely discussed at the time, from places such as the smoky rooms of the Salutation and Cat to the floor of the House of Commons. While to those like Percy Bysshe Shelley the King's physical and mental deficiencies only compounded his political failings (*vis-à-vis*

Shelley's 'old, mad, blind, despised king'), more generally this factor may have contributed to the sense in which the mentally ill were objects of pity rather than of contempt.[1] The press report of the Lamb murder conveys this same sense of pity for the whole family as victims, including the deranged perpetrator of the terrible crime.

To be able to put Mary's situation in a meaningful context it is first necessary to understand how mental illness was viewed and managed during this period. First, there are myths to debunk. The idea that the ill-treatment of inmates in lunatic asylums was both universal and seen as legitimate is wholly misleading. Similarly, the notion that the mentally ill were officially perceived as somehow less than human (which simultaneously justified their inhumane treatment) is also untrue. There were many, too many, instances of barbaric abuse of such people at this time; what is important is that such practices went against the prevailing values of the time, rather than being in line with them. Throughout the eighteenth century advertisements for madhouses promised 'gentleness and kindness', 'the greatest tenderness and humanity' towards those in their care and an abhorrence of 'any violence to any patient'. Benjamin Faulkner, a madhouse keeper in the 1780s, was not untypical in arguing for the treatment of lunatics as 'rational creatures . . . with attention and humanity'. Private madhouses also often touted the pleasant environments they offered, the clean air and the good food. How often such standards were maintained is another matter; the point here is that such advertisements demonstrate that these were appealing ideas of how the mentally ill should be cared for, and that their ill-treatment was far from socially sanctioned. (Even the rules of the Bethlem Hospital as early as 1677 expressly forbade the beating or abuse of the inmates, in fact no force was to be used except 'upon absolute Necessity').[2]

Neither were the insane perceived as a race apart; indeed, as Roy Porter has observed, 'insanity might be widely seen as a hazard of humanity, a fate which, under desperate circumstances, could seize anyone and everyone, for a galaxy of reasons, from the bite of a rabid dog to oppressive weather (especially during the "dog days" of Midsummer Madness) to earwigs in the head (according to Cornish folklore) or overwhelming grief, pride, love or joy'. He also notes (which we know to have been recognized in Mary's case) that mad people were by no means necessarily mad all the time: 'insanity was a blow afflicting by degrees, in fits, coming and going with remissions, oscillating in intensity'.[3]

Setting aside the extent of sympathy felt for Mary, there remained the practical problem of what was to be done with her. Her father was barely aware of what was going on and had for some time before the murder been in no state to make decisions. Brother John proving characteristically unhelpful, the burden of responsibility fell to Charles, then only twenty-one years old. Immediately after the murder, probably at Charles's suggestion, Mary was taken to a private madhouse in Islington.

The use of private madhouses was far from unusual, as there was no state provision for the care of the mentally ill. Even following the Act of 1800 (prompted by Hadfield's case) Parliament built no asylums, nor authorized any to be built, and it was to be another forty-five years before it required local authorities to provide them. The infamous Bethlem Hospital was a charity and theoretically existed only to cater for paupers; it also discouraged 'incurables'. Moreover, up until the eighteenth century it serviced not just the capital city but the whole country, and was consequently always oversubscribed. From the pauper whose parish was prepared to pay to the aristocrat who could not be managed at home, private care was the only solution.

Private madhouses were usually much smaller than is generally imagined, catering perhaps for a dozen inmates. Care, in this large unregulated industry, varied from the exemplary to the appalling. The Revd Dr Francis Willis ran a private madhouse in Greatford, Lincolnshire, where the regime astonished one visitor (Frederick Reynolds), who noticed, on his approach to the town, 'almost all the surrounding ploughmen, gardeners, threshers, thatchers, and other labourers, attired in black coats, white waistcoats, black silk breeches and stockings, and the head of each *bien poudrée, frisée et arrangée*. These were the doctor's patients: and dress, neatness of person and exercise being the principal features of his admirable system, health and cheerfulness conjoined towards the recovery of every person attached to that most valuable asylum.' (Dr Willis also treated George III.) Dr Edward Long Fox's madhouse, near Bristol, catered for the kind of patient who could not be suffered to wander in the surrounding fields; its yards were surrounded by twelve-foot-high walls, but Dr Fox had thoughtfully provided 'large mounds of earth . . . raised in the centre, which allow the patients to enjoy the view without danger of getting over the wall'. At Dr Fox's the visitor found each patient had an airy, clean, separate bedroom, and that occupational therapies were employed, as well as music, board-games and a bowling-green for recreation. The doctor also kept 'silver pheasants', doves and greyhounds for his patients' amusement. While two or three patients were in straitjackets, none were in chains or in bed. Twenty-eight servants serviced seventy patients in premises 'delightfully and cheerfully situated'.[4]

Unfortunately, many private madhouses fell short of these

high standards. Although many abuses were successfully covered up for the benefit of patients' friends and relations who visited, those on the inside – both fellow inmates and visiting doctors – testified to a catalogue of gross neglect, routine beatings, rape, torture and even murder occurring within the walls of the worst of these establishments. Corruption was *de rigueur* in such places. On the petty level, it was common practice to steal and sell new clothes brought for patients and then inform relatives that the patient had ripped them to shreds and needed more, as it was to charge exorbitant sums for drugs which were never bought, let alone administered. More serious corruption also abused both the individual and the law. All manner of troublesome and tiresome people could conveniently be removed to the private madhouse, be they perfectly sane, for a sizeable fee to the keeper, who could even arrange to come and drag the person from their bed, at home in the middle of the night.[5] This is exactly what happened to the Revd George Chawner, aged sixty, whose adulterous wife paid to have him taken out of the way. He was incarcerated for seven years before he managed to escape. (His subsequent prosecution of the madhouse failed on a technicality.[6]) On the other hand, the madhouse also provided asylum for sane criminals – again at a price. Lord de Dunstanville paid £1,200 per annum to a private madhouse to keep his brother in the luxury to which he was accustomed in order to evade legal action for presumably unmentionable crimes. 'These houses are, in a hundred cases,' asserted one ex-inmate, 'mere cloaks to avoid punishment of the law.'[7] Although madhouses had to submit to official inspections, contemporary accounts show that it was an easy matter to hide potentially embarrassing patients, as it was to render others incapable of conversation by drugging or intimidating them beforehand. More staggeringly audacious was the substitution of a patient who had complained to the authorities with a raving maniac (in no position to question his or her ascribed identity) for questioning when the authorities investigated.

Due to the difficulty in properly regulating madhouses, they often attracted the worst kind of entrepreneur; a number of proprietors were drunkards, while others were themselves psychologically disturbed. Dr James Pownall became the proprietor of a Wiltshire madhouse in 1853, even though he was known to have suffered several attacks of mania, during which he was extremely violent and had been confined. Within a year of opening his establishment he had shot one of his own patients and he subsequently murdered a servant girl, slitting her throat with a razor.[8]

The practice of 'boarding out' patients was also widespread. Those who ran private madhouses would, when the madhouse was filled to capacity, commonly pay their keepers (as employees were called) or ex-keepers to maintain individuals in their own homes, or premises rented especially for this purpose; many doctors and clergymen also took in single patients. Again, the standards of care varied enormously. The advantage for the individual boarded with a caring keeper was obvious: the patient benefited from one-to-one attention, a more normal physical environment and better quality social interaction – at its best this sort of care represented a kind of foster-home for adults, an ideal of 'care in the community'. However, there was unfortunately an enormous advantage for the unscrupulous keeper: the law offered no protection, no system of inspection, and no standards of care governing the treatment of individually boarded-out patients. Worse, with no witness but the four walls around them, abuse could occur in utter secrecy.

Mary was later to experience 'boarding out' and also spent long periods in the Hoxton madhouses. The large private asylum was at this time highly exceptional. At the time of Mary's crime there were probably only three in the whole country, all within a few hundred yards of each other, at Hoxton. Hoxton (or Hogsdon) had a history of association with care for the mentally ill. A century before Mary first entered there, Hoxton was already the destination of the majority of London's private mental patients. So synonymous was the place with madness that, just as Bethlem has given us the term 'bedlam', one of Hoxton's institutions, Balmes House (also spelt Bammes and Baumes), is believed to have given birth to the expression 'balmy' or 'barmy'. Over the ensuing years Mary was to spend time both at Balmes House (by that time renamed Whitmore House) and at Hoxton House, where Charles had also been voluntarily confined. The third institution, Holly House, catered principally for paupers, the cost of whose care was met by their parishes.

Given the extent to which these places featured in their lives, Charles and Mary's surviving writings are deafeningly silent on the quality of care and living conditions in the Hoxton madhouses. It is quite likely that anything they may have written on the subject was subsequently lost (if not destroyed) as part of the veil that was drawn over Mary's history of mental illness by their closest friends. This absence of material has made it easy for biographers to skim over the subject, probably also having considered the fact that Mary returned repeatedly to their custody, sometimes voluntarily, but always with Charles's consent, and consequently not unreasonably assuming that this pointed to the Lambs finding the Hoxton madhouses satisfactory. All the extraneous evidence tells quite a different story.

The evening following the murder, after Mary had been removed to the Islington madhouse, Charles quickly discovered what it was to have 'the whole weight of the family thrown on me'. Brother John had evidently absented himself; always unwilling to become involved with caring for his parents and aunt, he now had the excuse of his bad leg to exempt him from such duties. (The family appears to have kept no maid at this time, Mary presumably having run the household single-handed.) Charles's charges, John and Sarah Lamb, presented a pathetic sight: the senile father, more disorientated than ever, his wounded head wrapped in bandages, and the aged aunt, who was in a state of shock, lying 'insensible, to all appearance like one dying'. In the next room lay the corpse of Elizabeth Lamb. His father and aunt settled for the night, Charles retreated to his room, where he lay awake all night but 'without terrors and without despair'.[9]

His emotional response that first night was significant. In the days that followed Charles continually surprised himself by his ability to hold things together, rather than collapsing under the weight of the 'terrible calamities' which had fallen on the family. That first night of wakefulness was the last. Charles found he could eat, sleep and generally function much better than he – or anyone – expected. He suffered only one moment of emotional turmoil, which he described in a letter to Coleridge:

Within a day or 2 after the fatal ONE, we drest for dinner a tongue, which we had had salted for some weeks in the house. As I sat down a feeling like REMORSE struck me, – this tongue poo[r] Mary got for ME, & can I partake of it NOW, when she is far AWAY – a thought occurrd & relieve[d] me, – if I give into this way of feeling, there is not a chair, a room, an object in our rooms, that will not awaken the keenest griefs, I must arise above such weaknesses –. I hope this was not want of true feeling. I did not let this carry me tho' too far. On the very 2d day (I date from the day of HORRORS) as is usual in such cases there were a matter of 20 people I do think supping in our ROOM –. They prevailed on me to eat *with them* (for to eat I never refused) they were all making merry! In the room, – some had come from friendship, some from busy curiosity, & some from INTEREST; I was going to partake with THEM, when my recollection came that my poor dead mother was lying in the next room, the very next room, a mother who thro' life wished nothing but her children's welfare – indignation, the rage of grief, something like remorse, rushed upon my mind in an agony of emotion, – I found my way mechanically to the adjoing (*sic*) room, & fell on my knees by the SIDE of her coffin, asking forgiveness of heaven, & sometimes of her, for forgetting her SO SOON. Tranquillity returned, & it was the only violent emotion that master'd me, & I think it did me good. –[10]

Ironically, in one way at least the 'terrible calamities that have fallen on our family' had a positive effect – with immediate and very real demands being made on Charles, he was able at last to let go of his preoccupation with Ann Simmons ('Thank God, the folly has left me for ever,' he reflected), and simply had no time for the introspection and self-pity which had recently characterized his state of mind.[11] In the letter in which he broke the news of the family tragedy to Coleridge he begged a reply: 'Write, – as religious a letter as possible – but no mention of what is gone and done with – with me the former things are passed away, and I have something more to do than to feel –.'[12] 'Mention nothing of poetry,' he added. As in previous periods of crisis, Charles destroyed all his writing, now viewing his aspirations as a poet as a positive impediment to his ability to deal with the realities pressing upon him. He was surprised to find himself feeling calm and composed 'and able to do the rest that remains to do'.[13] In this letter and those that followed, Charles repeatedly thanked

God for preserving his senses; that someone who had himself recently been so mentally unbalanced could cope so admirably with the distressing and demanding circumstances in which Charles found himself, seemed almost miraculous. Having turned away from introspection, Charles was now to depend heavily on his faith and his friends.

To his great credit Coleridge, whose own life was often characterized by turmoil, was evidently a rock during this period. Respecting Charles's injunction against visiting him, Coleridge dutifully delivered the 'religious' letter, in which he also approved Charles's abandonment of 'what you justly call vanities' – i.e. his poetry. He also invited Charles to go and stay with him – an arrangement which would have been inconvenient to both households (Coleridge's wife having very recently given birth to their first child, Hartley, and Charles's father and aunt not able to cope alone), the proposal was nonetheless cheering. This letter, which Charles re-read many times subsequently, proved an 'inestimable treasure' to him.[14]

Other old Blues came to the rescue, most notably Samuel Le Grice, who fulfilled the role of a brother to Charles for the first few days after the tragedy – his real brother continuing to maintain his distance – and was in constant attendance on the family, entertaining Charles's most demanding and 'teasing' charge – old John Lamb – by reading to him, chatting and playing cards with him, 'meal-times excepted, literally all day long'. (Six years later, on learning of Samuel's premature death, Charles reflected to Coleridge that 'there was more of kindness and warmth in him than almost any other of our school-fellows'.[15]) There was help from other quarters: Philip Norris, who worked at Christ's Hospital, acted 'as a father' to Charles, and his wife 'as a Mother'. One distant relation sent the family £20, while another offered to take in Aunt Sarah.

Initially, Mary's disorder seemed to Charles 'frightful & hopeless', but visiting her a week after the murder he reported he found her 'calm & serene' ('far very very far', he added hastily, 'from an indecent forgetful serenity'). Charles had evidently harboured great fears about this moment, particularly about whether the guilt induced by realization of what she had done would prevent her ever being able to come to terms with it. The key to her slow recovery lay in her acceptance – shared by the courts, the press, Charles and his friends – that at the time of the murder she had been entirely unconscious of her actions. This she appeared to do. Charles wrote to Coleridge of the good news:

My poor dear dearest sister, the unhappy & unconscious instrument of the Almighty's judjments [sic] to our house, is restored to her senses; to a dreadful sense & recollection of what has past, awful to her mind & impressive (as it must be to the end of life) but temper'd with religious resignation, & the reasonings of a sound judgment, which in this early stage knows how to distinguish between a deed committed in a transcient fit of frenzy, & the terrible guilt of a MOTHER's murther.[16]

Charles was naturally anxious, however, not to make it appear that either Mary or himself were coping *too* well. 'She has a most tender and affectionate concern for what has happened,' he assured Coleridge, just as he was concerned that his own 'tranquillity' should not be interpreted as indifference.

The problem with the murder, which neither Mary nor Charles was probably willing to contemplate, was that it represented a resolution of sorts (albeit a horrific one) of tensions in the household. If Elizabeth Lamb's parenting was the most significant factor in the origins of Mary's psychological instability, the strain her illness exerted on Mary was also the most significant factor (in Charles's view) in the sheer physical exhaustion which precipitated Mary's complete breakdown. Viewed dispassionately, Mary's act removed the primary obstacle to her peace of mind and body. And if she did not consciously know what she was doing when she murdered her mother, the circumstances of the killing suggest that on some level she did. Four other people were at risk during the critical moments: the little apprentice, whom Mary threatened but did not harm; John and Sarah Lamb, both present in the room when Mary was hurling cutlery around, slightly injuring the former; and Charles, who arrived moments after the murder, while Mary was still armed, and who got close enough to take the knife out of her hand. While the apprentice was the initial focus of Mary's rage – whatever she had done proving the final straw which broke Mary's over-burdened mind – it was her mother, and her mother's intervention, that transformed a violent and menacing outburst into a murder. Elizabeth Lamb was not the accidental victim of a flying fork – Mary stabbed her, possibly repeatedly, through the heart.

Furthermore, Mary's action served to remove her from an environment which was physically and emotionally demanding (and where there seemed little prospect of things getting any better) to a place where nothing was expected of her at all. In the madhouse she was not expected to cook her own food or wash her own clothes, let alone do it for five other adults. While it would be going too far to make a case for Mary's murder of her mother as a calculated strategy, it seems likely that she at least subconsciously selected her mother as the focus of her rage, and also that madness was perhaps her only route out of the household. (It must not be forgotten that Mary had recently witnessed her brother escape his cares and responsibilities both at home and at work by taking himself off to one of the Hoxton madhouses for a few weeks.) Setting aside the circumstances of their mother's death, the guilt which both Charles and Mary shouldered was that – objectively – it represented something of a relief.

In modern child psychotherapy it is widely recognized that the child presenting the problem is often expressing a stress within the family: he or she is the symptom rather than the cause. Such a child, at one end of the scale, may wet the bed, or bite other children, signalling that something is wrong – investigation often reveals that the child is sinned against rather than sinning. At the other end of the scale, the child or young adult may express the problem in a far more violent way, through self-injury, or an appalling attack on another person or child. It is recognized that most family homicides occur as the result of stresses within the family which become unmanageable. Some application of modern psychology to the Lamb phenomenon may be useful in opening areas which so far have been obscured from view.

A case could be made, for example, for Mary being the expression of all the (largely) *un*expressed aggression in the Lamb family for years prior to the matricide. These might include the simmering feud between Elizabeth and Sarah Lamb; Elizabeth's preference of John over her other children; the precariousness of the family finances – which could produce its own problems between John and Elizabeth Lamb. Unlike her brothers Mary had no life outside the home and she would have been most damaged by problems within the family. She could easily have been made to feel that it was she who was at fault (as sometimes children of divorcing parents feel culpable). There could of course have been other problems which history has rendered invisible, such as child abuse or domestic violence, which it is impossible to make a case either for or against. When these family tensions find expression through an individual, they are often a crude attempt to 'cure' the whole family. By her act, in this analysis, Mary attempted, in a rush of unreasoning emotion, to resolve an intolerable situation: mother was eliminated, father was silenced, aunt was sent away, brother John departed, brother Charles took charge and she was relieved of all responsibility. Above all, a kind of peace descended – at an enormous cost, but peace nevertheless. Whether or not such an analysis is admissible, it is significant that both Charles and Mary separately acknowledged experiencing a sense of resigned calm following the attack.

The offer of a home for Sarah Lamb enabled Charles to begin to shape the family's future life. Aunt Sarah was keen to take it up, and generously transferred her meagre income (interest on a small lump sum) to help with Mary's expenses. Charles calculated that with this, the £20 gift plus a £100 legacy his father was due at Christmas, there would be just enough money to support him and his father, plus an 'old maid' to look after him while Charles was at work, while keeping Mary in private care at Islington. This last arrangement was crucial, because ever since the murder John had been putting pressure on his brother to have Mary put in a public asylum, as was the fate of those lunatics whose families could not afford to maintain them in the private madhouses. Mary was only too well aware of the debate going on between her brothers and had told her keepers at Islington that 'she knew she must go to BETHLEM for life; that one of her brother's would have it so, but the other would wish it Not, but be obliged to go with the stream . . .'[17] It is a sign of Mary's doubts about her psychological stability that long before the catastrophe she had secretly feared incarceration in Bethlem; her only hope of avoiding this lay in her younger brother's ability to resist her older brother's arguments. Fortunately, Charles was absolutely determined to keep Mary at Islington. ('I know John will make speeches about it,' he wrote to Coleridge, 'but she shall not go into an HOSPITAL.') John, having moved out and disengaged himself from the troubles of the family, failed to see why Charles did not do the same. Despite the fact that John (who as elder brother should really have been shouldering the greater part of the burden of responsibility) was less use than no brother at all, Charles was anxious that Coleridge should not gain too bad an opinion of him. The complex John, who otherwise barely features in the surviving correspondence, is tantalizingly glimpsed in Charles's *apologia*:

Let me not leave one unfavorable impression on your MIND respecting my Brother. Since this has happened he has been very kind & brotherly; but I fear for his mind, – he has taken his ease in the world, & is not fit himself to struggle with difficulties, nor has much accustomed himself to throw himself into their way, – & I know his language is already, 'Charles, you must take care of yourself, you must not abridge yourself of a single pleasure you have been used to' &c &c. & in that style of talking. But you, a necessarian, can respect a difference of mind, & love what is *amiable* in a character not perfect. He has been very good, but I fear for his mind. Thank God, I can unconnect myself with him, & shall manage all my father's monies in future MYSELF, if I take charge of Daddy, which POOR John has not even hinted a wish, at any future time even, to share with ME –[18]

It is interesting that Charles expresses fears for his brother's mind here. While it is possible that he is projecting his own anxieties on to John (there is no other evidence of John having any kind of psychological problem, but this should be seen in a general context of absence of information about him) – or perhaps soliciting Coleridge's sympathy for his brother, rather than his censure – it does seem a peculiar emphasis. It is known that in later life at least, John felt extremely uncomfortable about anything that seemed like abnormal or eccentric behaviour. Again, this may allude to the possibility that madness ran in the family, rendering all three of the Lamb offspring paranoid, in varying degrees, about succumbing to it. Mary, according to her keepers, confessed that during the years before the murder she could not walk past Bethlem Hospital without being assailed by the fear that 'here it may be my fate to end my days'. At the close of the letter under discussion Charles resolves to be 'serious, circumspect, & deeply religious thro' life' by which means he hopes 'may *both* of us escape madness in future'. There but for the grace of God, go I, he suggests. John's response was quite different, recoiling as he did from Mary's madness; his anxiety to get his sister put away may well have been an expression of the psychoanalytical concept of projection. In this analysis, John perceived in Mary, in Shelley's words, 'the shade from his own soul upthrown'. At the very least it seems safe to say that both brothers saw something of themselves in Mary. John's willingness to wash his hands of her, however, freed Charles to make the practical arrangements. He duly came to an arrangement with the Islington madhouse, where Mary would have a room and a nurse to herself for under £60 a year. There was to be no more talk of Bethlem.

Charles visited Mary almost daily, but due to the fact that there were nearly always other people present, they committed their more private thoughts to paper. Unfortunately none of this correspondence has survived but a scrap of a letter from Mary which Charles quoted from memory in a letter to Coleridge. In it Mary wrote:

I have no bad terrifying dreams. At midnight when I happen to awake, the nurse sleeping by the side of ME, with the noise of the poor mad people around me, I have no fear. The spirit of my mother seems to descend, & smile upon me, & bid me LIVE to enjoy the life & reason which the Almighty has given me −. I shall see her again in heaven; she will then understand me better, my Grandmother too will understand me better, & will then say no more as she used to Do, 'Polly, what are those poor crazy moyther'd brains of yours thinkg. of always?'[19]

Mary's condition continued to improve. It is sadly ironic that Mary appears to have experienced at the Islington mad-house a greater portion of female friendship and affection than had fallen to her share at home. Charles wrote that the women who looked after her had taken to Mary 'very EXTRAORDI-NARYLY', making her 'one of the family, rather than one of the patients': 'They love her, and she loves them.'

A month after the 'day of horrors' Charles was pleased to inform Coleridge of Mary's 'continued reason and com-posedness of mind'. He visited her frequently and was pleased to continue to find her keepers 'vastly indulgent to her'. Mary, who had the knack of making herself agreeable to anybody, further endeared herself to her keepers by making herself useful with her needle. Both her skill and her willingness to employ it, Charles hinted to Coleridge, hugely influenced Mary's treatment at Islington, and she was consequently 'as comfortably situated in all respects as those who pay twice or thrice the sum'.[20]

Having allowed a decent period to elapse since the murder, Coleridge was now encouraging his friend to renew his literary interests. He duly wrote to Charles asking for any revisions he wanted to make before he included a selection of Charles's poems in an anthology he was compiling (*Sonnets from Various Authors*). Charles's reply reveals his ambivalence about the propriety of devoting his attention to 'the idle trade of versi-

fying' which he declared 'I long to leave off, for it is unprofit-
able to my soul' and distracted him 'from the proper business
of *my* life'. Yet despite his claim that he was 'sick to death' of
the subject of his sonnets, he *did* answer Coleridge's editorial
queries and, claiming he only wanted them printed 'to get rid
of 'em', he enclosed some more poems with the letter. He
also enjoined Coleridge to remove the title he had originally
given some of the poems (or 'my *things*', as he disparaged
them): 'Love Sonnets'. ' 'Twill only make me look little in my
own eyes,' he explained, 'for it is a passion of which I retain
nothing.' Again, his evident sensitivity to how the poems would
appear in print militated against his stated wish to have nothing
more to do with them. ('Take my sonnets once for all, and do
not propose any re-amendments, or mention them again in
any shape to me, I charge you. I blush that my mind can
consider them as things of any worth.'[21]) If this letter reveals
Charles's struggle to find a comfortable attitude to his writing
it may also indicate – more simply – a young writer's nervous-
ness at the prospect of publication.

Indeed, Charles was not destined to be remembered as a
poet, but the sense in which he *understood* or was creatively
attuned to poetry is also evident in this interesting and so far
feverish letter. The first child of Coleridge's marriage had just
been born and Coleridge had sent Charles a poem, entitled
'To a Friend Who Asked, How I Felt When the Nurse
Presented My Infant To Me'. The sonnet detailed the transition from his intellectual response to scanning 'that face of
feeble infancy' in its cradle to the feeling of love which flooded
him when he first saw his wife nursing the baby. Charles was
particularly touched by the end of the poem, which reflected
on how witnessing the love of the mother for the child
increased the father's love for them both. Charles was evidently
responding to Coleridge's letter late at night and by the time

he signed off was tired. He returned to it with an afterthought, treating Coleridge to what subsequently has become some of the most widely-quoted advice ever given to any poet:

I will keep my eyes open reluctantly a minute longer to tell you, that I love you for those simple, tender, heart-flowing lines with which you conclude your last, and in my eyes best, sonnet (so you call 'em),

> So, for the mother's sake, the child was dear,
> And dearer was the mother for the child.

Cultivate simplicity, Coleridge, or rather, I should say, banish elaborateness; for simplicity springs spontaneous from the heart, and carried into daylight its own modest buds and genuine, sweet, and clear flowers of expression. I allow no hot-beds in the gardens of Parnassus . . .[22]

Gone is the fever, the self-doubt, the struggle between pride and piety; here in a mere postscript Charles unguardedly reveals a calm certainty in his own poetic judgement, if not his poetic powers. (Coleridge's biographer Richard Holmes acknowledges Coleridge's debt to Charles's 'natural taste and perception' in the development of his verse at this time. He writes of the paragraph beginning '*Cultivate simplicity*': 'This, both in imagery and argument, must count as an early declaration of the Romantic sensibility in poetry.'[23])

Despite his aspiration to indifference over the fate of his poems, Charles picked up his pen a few days later to give Coleridge further editorial instructions. First he sought Coleridge's opinion on his proposed dedication:

I mean to inscribe them to my sister. It will be unexpected, and it will give her pleasure; or do you think it will look whimsical at all?

As I have not spoke to her about it, I can easily reject the idea. But there is a monotony in the affections, which people living together or, as we do now, very frequently seeing each other, are apt to give in to: a sort of indifference in the expression of kindness for each other, which demands that we should sometimes call to our aid the trickery of surprise.[24]

The dedication was to run:

> The few following poems,
> Creatures of the fancy and the feeling
> In life's more vacant hours,
> Produced, for the most part, by
> Love in idleness,
> Are,
> With all a brother's fondness,
> Inscribed to
> MARY ANN LAMB,
> The author's best friend and sister.

The dedication was only natural: Mary was to be the first sharer in all Charles's literary achievements (and failures); what is more interesting is Charles's desire to assure his sister of his active friendship, over and above the passive 'monotony' of sibling ties.

He had come to another decision, and wanted Coleridge ('whether you like it or no') to preface his poems with some lines from Philip Massinger's play *A Very Woman*. The verse runs:

> This beauty, in the blossom of my youth,
> When my first fire knew no adulterate incense,
> Nor I no way to flatter but my fondness,

In the best language my true tongue could tell me,
And all the broken sighs my sick heart lend me,
I sued and served. Long did I love this lady.

The verse was a perfect choice for Charles's purposes. Having contextualized the 'Anna' poems firmly in the past (freeing him to reinstate the title 'Love Sonnets'), Charles simultaneously dissipated their claim to his present emotions and (rather neatly) disarmed the potential critic by suggesting that the poet had already moved on from 'the best language' his youth had been able to supply. Satisfied with this presentation of his poetry, Charles remained determined that it would be his last. He closed his instructions to Coleridge with these remarks, on his abandonment of both 'Anna' and poetry:

This is the pomp and paraphernalia of parting, with which I take my leave of a passion which has reigned so royally (so long) within me; thus, with its trappings of laureatship, I fling it off, pleased and satisfied with myself that the weakness troubles me no longer. I am wedded, Coleridge, to the fortunes of my sister and my poor old father. Oh! my friend, I think sometimes, could I recall the days that are past, which among them should I choose? not those 'merrier days,' not the 'pleasant days of hope,' not 'those wanderings with a fair hair'd maid,' which I have so often and so feelingly regretted, but the days, Coleridge, of a *mother*'s fondness for her *school-boy*. What would I give to call her back to earth for *one* day, on my knees to ask her pardon for all those little asperities of temper which, from time to time, have given her gentle spirit pain; and the day, my friend, I trust will come; there will be 'time enough' for kind offices of love, if 'Heaven's eternal year' be ours. Hereafter, her meek spirit shall not reproach me. Oh, my friend, cultivate the filial feelings! and let no man think himself released from the kind 'charities' of relationship: these shall give him peace at the last; these are the best foundation for every species of benevolence. I rejoice to hear, by certain channels, that you, my friend, are reconciled with all your relations. 'Tis the most kindly and natural species of love, and we have all the associated train of early feelings to secure its strength and perpetuity.[25]

Still less than two months after the murder, it is not surprising to find nostalgia, regret, guilt and grief invading Charles's thoughts, nor to find his consolation in religion and 'the most kindly and natural species of love' – his family, and principally his sister.

While Coleridge's family relationships were characteristically stormy, a strict observance of filial duty was wearing Charles out. Life having settled into a reformed normality, with Mary at Islington, John conspicuously absent, Aunt Sarah away with relations, and Mother dead, Charles had only his father at home, but the old man's demands were sorely trying. Charles often did not get home from work until after seven o'clock and was then harried by his senile father ('who will not let me enjoy a meal in peace') until he played cards with him. Having been used to the company of his wife and accommodating daughter while Charles was at work, John Lamb was doubtless now bored during the daytime, with only an elderly maid for company, and looked forward to Charles's return each evening as much as Charles dreaded his father's childlike perpetual badgering for entertainment. One evening when, after repeated games of cribbage, Charles expressed a wish to write a letter, his father replied: 'If you won't play with me, you might as well not come home at all!' 'The argument was unanswerable,' Charles concluded, and he took up the cards again.[26]

John Lamb was not the only one feeling lonely. After the initial period of re-adjustment Charles found himself increasingly feeling isolated and unstimulated. Having to look after his father in the evenings, Charles had no social life during this period, and his only contact outside the family was with his colleagues at the East India House, with whom he had little in common. 'Not a soul loves Bowles here; scarce one has heard of Burns; few but laugh at me for reading my Testament –,' he complained to Coleridge, 'they talk a language I understand not: I conceal sentiments that would be a puzzle to them. I can only converse with you by letter and with the dead in their books.'[27] Reading satisfied some of Charles's longing for stimulation, affording 'a kind of Communion, a kind of friendship even, with the great & good'. As during his lonely holidays as a child, 'Books are to me instead of friends.'[28] But books, like friends, he observed, were scarce: both Charles and Mary (for whom 'reading was her daily bread') had exhausted their supply and were hungry for new material. And while Charles acknowledged that his sister was 'all I can wish in a companion', her experience of life was as limited as Charles's.

. . . our spirits are alike poorly, our reading and knowledge from the self-same sources, our communication with the scenes of the world alike narrow: never having kept separate company, or any 'company' 'together' – never having read separate books, and few books together – what knowledge have we to convey to each other?[29]

The continuing correspondence with Coleridge represented a lifeline, Charles's letters providing an outlet for his emotions and thoughts and the return traffic bringing welcome news of a world (both of realities and ideas) outside the narrow path he now trod. 'I love to write to you. I take a pride in it –,' Charles explained. 'It makes me think less meanly of myself. It makes me think myself not totally disconnected from the better part of Mankind.'[30] Charles was not only a good listener, full of sound (if not sometimes rather pious) advice (understandable given his recent experiences and the comfort he had found in reflections of a religious nature), but his morale benefited from the fact that a man he admired as much as Coleridge should confide his fears and hopes in him. Charles said he loved Coleridge's letters and Rousseau's *Confessions* in the same way, 'and for the same reason: the same frankness, the same openness of heart, the same disclosure of all the most hidden and delicate affections of the mind'. Coleridge's letters spoke straight to Charles's heart: 'they make me proud to be thus esteemed worthy of the place of friend-confessor, brother-confessor, to a man like Coleridge.'[31]

However, having access to Coleridge only by mail was also frustrating. 'I have no one to talk all these matters about to,' he complained.

Pray, pray, write to me: if you knew with what an anxiety of joy I open such a long packet as you last sent me, you would not grudge giving a few minutes now & then to this intercourse (the ONLY intercourse, I fear we two shall ever have) this conversation with your friend – such I boast to be called –[32]

It has been stated that Charles hero-worshipped Coleridge, and his letters do indeed demonstrate his depth of feeling for his friend and pride in their association. However, although Charles esteemed Coleridge highly, he in no sense considered him infallible: his letters to Coleridge of this period are full of editorial advice, in which he dishes out praise and criticism with equal candour.

Early in December 1796, barely six weeks after the murder, Mary was considered sufficiently well to leave the madhouse. What treatment – if any – she had been receiving is impossible to ascertain. The emphasis at the time was more on securing society from the hazards posed by the violent mentally ill than on curing them; however, various treatments were widely employed. These included traditional remedies such as bleeding and purging, as well as drugs. As a 'maniac' it is likely that Mary was given digitalis and/or opium. Both hot and cold baths were widely used and women's hair was often cut short literally to cool the head. It is of course possible that Mary's insanity subsided of its own accord. Though she had recovered, coming home was of course an impossibility during her father's lifetime, Charles being convinced that it would be damaging for both of them to be together. He was also aware that whenever Mary did come home they would have to endure gossip and possibly hostility. Brother John was not the only person who had put pressure on Charles to keep Mary locked up; several others (Charles did not say who – possibly neighbours) had expressed the opinion that Mary 'should be in perpetual confinement'. 'What she hath done to deserve, or the necessity of such an hardship I see not; do you?' he asked Coleridge, who perhaps found the suggestion slightly less baffling.[33] However, someone else *was* coming home, to Charles's mixed emotions. The wealthy relation who had taken in Sarah Lamb now reported her to be 'indolent and mulish' and wished to be rid of her again. It appeared that Aunt Sarah had made repeated and tactless reference to her former life among her brother's family to the extent that her hostess was unable to enjoy 'ease and tranquillity' while Sarah remained under her roof. While Charles naturally wished to rescue his aunt from 'the chilling air of such patronage', her return would upset the very finely balanced finances of the Lamb household – there was already no contingency for extraordinary payments such as might be incurred if a member of the family required medical treatment.[34] The thought of supporting himself and two aged relations on a shoestring filled Charles with gloom and apprehension.

Christmas 1796 was trying for both Charles and Mary. The miseries of confinement were made worse for Mary by catching scarlet fever, which at first looked like a mild case but soon made her seriously ill. However difficult that Christmas must have been for Charles, the first without Mary or Elizabeth Lamb, by the time it was over he had begun to resolve his feelings about his own poetry. It was perhaps not surprising that Charles suffered mixed feelings about the validity of his own writing in the face of a close personal relationship with a poetic genius such as Coleridge. In early December Charles sent Coleridge some more new poems, again claiming that he had finally 'done with verse-making'. Coleridge, however, refused to take no for an answer and continued to coax and flatter Charles into picking up his pen again. 'Poets have sometimes a disingenuous way of forswearing their occupation,' Charles admitted. 'This though is not my case.'[35] Yet in January 1797 he sent Coleridge another poem, dedicated to Mary, which seems to suggest he had resolved his ambivalence towards poetic activity. Having established the metaphor of himself and Mary as fellow travellers 'thro' life's unequal ways', he reasoned:

> It were unwisely done, should we refuse
> To cheer our path, as featly as we may,
> Our lonely path to cheer, as trav'ellers use
> With merry song, quaint tale, or roundelay.

Perhaps it was appreciating the relationship between the reunited older siblings (like Charles and Mary, John Lamb was a decade younger than his sister Sarah) which suggested to Charles that life was too short to deny oneself a little cheer, or perhaps time had begun to do its healing work, but in any case by January 1797 Charles had determined, it seems, to allow himself the comfort and distraction of the odd 'song' and embraced poetry, once again, as a poet.

The new year brought both grief and hope. On 9 February Sarah Lamb, Charles's aunt and 'cherisher of infancy', died. She had never recovered from the shock of witnessing the murder the previous September, and being uprooted during her brief, chilly sojourn away from her brother and her favourite nephew had probably not helped matters. Charles was consoled by her statement during her final days that she was glad she had come home to die with him. By the time she died she was in 'a deplorable state', her robust frame having diminished to 'a mere skeleton'. Her death came as a release for both Sarah and her nephew.

Grief soon turned to optimism. Having fully recovered from scarlet fever, Mary had been both physically and mentally fit for some time, but remained exiled from the family home. She was stoical: 'She bears her situation as one who has no right to complain,' Charles told Coleridge.[36] In early spring she began to be rehabilitated, moving out of the Islington madhouse and into lodgings in Hackney. The brother and sister were now able to spend all Charles's days off together, in a more relaxed and private environment, and Charles's feelings of isolation receded somewhat. 'Congratulate me on an ever-present and never-alienable friend like her,' Charles commanded Coleridge.[37]

By the summer, however, Charles's spirits had begun to sink again.

I see nobody, and sit, and read or walk, alone, and hear nothing. I am quite lost to conversation from disuse; and out of the sphere of my little family, who, I am thankful, are dearer and dearer to me every day, I see no face that brightens up at my approach. My friends are at a distance; worldly hopes are at a low ebb with me, and unworldly thoughts are not yet familiarised to me, though I occasionally indulge in them. Still I feel a calm not unlike content.[38]

From immediately after the murder onwards, Coleridge had issued repeated invitations for Charles to visit him. At the end of June Charles was almost childishly excited at the prospect of finally being able to accept. During the short trip to Nether Stowey in Somerset that followed he was not only able to renew his acquaintance with his old friend, but to meet many of Coleridge's circle, among whom he found a brother and sister who were to become among Charles and Mary's closest friends: the poet William Wordsworth and his sister Dorothy. Although Charles was not yet aware of the fact, it was the dawning of a new era of his life.

5. Lloyd and Southey

She gave me eyes, she gave me ears;
And humble cares, and delicate fears;
A heart, the fountain of sweet tears;
And love, and thought, and joy.

(William Wordsworth, 'The Sparrow's Nest', II, 17–20)

This was how William Wordsworth paid homage to his sister Dorothy. Although nearly two years younger than him, William recognized that his sister had shaped his view of the world. She had been a sensitive observer of nature and of human life since she was a small child, and has been described as 'probably . . . the most distinguished of English writers who never wrote a line for the general public'.[1] Although Dorothy and William's relationship differed in character from Mary and Charles's, there are distinct points of connection. William Wordsworth's biographer, Juliet Barker, has acknowledged the inestimable contribution made by his sister to his literary output: 'Their natural empathy makes it impossible to separate out what may or may not have been contributed by Dorothy: their reactions were the same and they drew on, and assimilated, each other's responses, so that these became indivisible.' While the journals Dorothy kept – on which her brother drew extensively – posthumously 'indisputably established her as a literary figure in her own right', Mary *did* see her own work published during her lifetime, though not with her name attached to it.² Both couples' 'natural empathy' is widely attested; William, like Charles, described his sister as 'my dearest Friend'. As Mary was to support and encourage her brother's literary endeavours, Dorothy was William's standard-bearer; in the moments of his gravest doubts: 'She, in the midst of all, preserved me still/ A poet, made me seek beneath that name/ My office upon earth.'³ In recognition of this crucial role, significantly, both Charles and William dedicated their first collections of published poetry to their sisters.

While the emotional bond between Charles and Mary was unusually strong, the relationship between William and Dorothy was characterized on both sides by feelings which can only be described as passionate; indeed the intensity of their love for one another sometimes makes for quite uncomfortable reading. These – almost transgressive – emotions were perhaps a result of having been orphaned and separated when young. Born into a loving family at Cockermouth in Cumberland (William in 1770, Dorothy in 1771), following the premature death of their mother, when Dorothy was six and William eight, Dorothy (the only girl among five children) was sent to live with a relation seventy miles away in Halifax, Yorkshire. The Wordsworth children were not to be reunited for nine years. Dorothy and William had been parted as small children and returned to each other as sexually mature young adults.

Like Coleridge and the Lambs, William's childhood reading was unsupervised and consequently wide-ranging; also like them, as an adult he maintained the importance of works of the imagination such as *The Arabian Nights* ('The child whose love is here, at least does reap/ One precious gain – that he forgets himself'⁴) over the likes of Billy and his everlasting Horse. His famous assertion that 'The Child is Father of the Man' also chimed with Charles and Coleridge's belief in the primacy of the role of childhood experience in forming the adult's world-view.

Initially Dorothy did her best to educate herself, and later benefited from the benevolence of an uncle with whom she studied for two hours daily. William went on to study at St John's College, Cambridge, on a school scholarship. Despite disillusionment and politicization, William took his exams and secured his B.A. (fellow radicals Coleridge and Southey, whom William met in Bristol in 1795, both left university without degrees). Sharing Charles and Coleridge's sense of the value of feeling and the imagination in literature, the three were also politically empathetic. Like Charles, William refused to acknowledge the notion that virtue could be inherited along with a title and was consequently against primogeniture, the class system and the crown. A less contentious taste Charles and William also shared was a lifelong passion for the theatre. While sympathetic to each other, however, William and Charles were not alike in experience. Five years older than Charles, at the time of their meeting at Nether Stowey William had twice visited revolutionary France, on the second occasion leaving his French mistress pregnant.

Charles and William knew of each other, and each other's work, through Coleridge (the second edition of Coleridge's *Poems on Various Subjects*, which included all Charles's poems to date, had been published the month prior to their meeting in 1797). Charles was also acquainted with a brother and cousin of William and Dorothy's through the East India House. The process of acquaintance at Nether Stowey was accelerated by a domestic accident: Sarah Coleridge had accidentally spilt a pan of boiling milk over her husband's foot, leaving him housebound, so Charles, William and Dorothy were obliged to explore the surrounding countryside (all three, like Coleridge, were great walkers) without their loquacious host. It was while his friends were on one such expedition that Coleridge wrote the poem 'This Lime-Tree Bower My Prison', addressed to 'my gentle-hearted Charles' . . .

> . . . for thou hast pined
> And hunger'd after Nature, many a year,
> In the great City pent, winning thy way
> With sad yet patient soul, through evil and pain
> And strange calamity!

The evenings were spent in conversation and reading poetry aloud; Wordsworth's 'Lines Left Upon a Seat in a Yew-Tree' left a particularly deep impression on a rather subdued Charles. Political conversation was also stimulating, the company being joined, for part of Charles's visit, by local democrats Tom Poole and John Cruikshank.

Pitched head first into the intellectually bracing pool of political and literary luminaries to whom Coleridge introduced him, Charles found he had been so out of the habit of sustained and challenging conversation that he was often reduced to silence during his visit to Nether Stowey. Having thirsted for so long after the *idea* of the company of like minds – and better minds – he was overwhelmed by its reality and so disorientated that on his leaving, in an 'oblivious' state of mind, he forgot his only overcoat. However, the visit did him good: not only did the many and varied conversations give him much food for thought, but the kindness of Coleridge's wife and friends (who perhaps knew some, though not all, of Charles's story) touched him deeply.

On his return to London towards the end of July 1797, Charles and his father moved house, to 45 Chapel Street, Pentonville. The reason for this removal is not known, but Charles may have aimed at being out of the house at Little

Queen Street, the scene of 'our EVIL day', before its anniversary. Pentonville was also closer to Mary (still in Hackney). The following month Charles allowed himself another short trip away from home, visiting Robert and Edith Southey at Burton, with the poet Charles Lloyd. Coleridge was again the common connection. Lloyd had first met Coleridge in 1795, falling so completely under his spell that he moved into the Coleridges' house shortly after the birth of their son, David Hartley. Some flavour of Lloyd's passionate admiration for the poet is preserved in these lines addressed to Coleridge:

> My Coleridge! Take the wanderer to thy breast,
> The youth who loves thee, and who, faint, would rest
> (Oft rack'd by hopes that frenzy and expire)
> In the long sabbath of subdued desire![5]

Coleridge was to be both Lloyd's tutor and landlord for the sum of £80 per year. However, by the end of 1796 Coleridge had ended Lloyd's tutelage, although Lloyd remained his friend, lodger, and sometimes patient, suffering as he did from epilepsy and occasional bouts of derangement, during which Coleridge would nurse and restrain him. Having heard a great deal about Charles from Coleridge, when Lloyd was in London in January 1797, he introduced himself, and the two became close friends, collaborating on a collection of poetry which would be published as *Blank Verse*. Only two days separated Charles and Lloyd in age, but their backgrounds could not have been more different, Lloyd coming from a wealthy Quaker family. When Charles joined Lloyd and Southey at Burton, all three owed their mutual acquaintance to Coleridge. Within a matter of months all three would become alienated from him.

Back in London, Charles was keenly aware of the approaching anniversary and was at his desk at the East India House when he felt moved to write about the feelings its recollection evoked. The resulting lines ('Written a twelvemonth after the Events') came to him 'with unusual celerity'. On its swiftly accomplished completion, Charles immediately recognized it as the best piece of writing he had yet produced. Lloyd agreed with him, and Charles sent the poem to Coleridge, saying confidently, 'I expect you to like it better than any thing of mine.'[6]

In order to understand the significance of the poem, it is necessary to consider the poetry Charles had produced before this turning point. There had been the 'Anna' poems, pretty but unexceptional expressions of unrequited – or frustrated – romantic love. He had also written personal verses of homage to his grandmother, of apology to his sister, of thanks to Charles Lloyd and of disappointment to Samuel and Sara Coleridge as well as a collection of miscellaneous and competent verses on a variety of themes, such as the allegorical 'Vision of Repentance', which treated of crushing guilt and unending sorrow. The anniversary piece, however, was the first directly to confront his own specific grief. Although he had written about his mother and his sister individually in verse before, this was the first poem – again significantly – which he allowed both his mother and his sister to inhabit simultaneously.

The lines are also significant in that they demonstrate a pattern which was to become a feature of Charles's confessional writing: the poem works up material from his private letters, and hence from his authentic innermost feelings. In this case thoughts and phrases which first appeared in his letters to Coleridge of October and November the previous year are organized into a consoling meditation. An equally important aspect of this poem is that Charles adapts not just his own, but one of Mary's letters. Charles had previously quoted the letter as well as he could from memory in a letter to Coleridge, and in the poem he gives it almost verbatim:

> Thou and I, dear friend,
> With filial recognition sweet, shall know
> One day the face of our dear mother in heaven,
> And her remember'd looks of love shall greet
> With answering looks of love, her placid smiles
> Meet with a smile as placid, and her hand
> With drops of fondness wet, nor FEAR REPULSE. –

(The desire to achieve a kind of reconciliation with their mother simultaneously obliviates not only Mary's sin, but by the inference in the last line quoted – underlined in the original version – Elizabeth Lamb's failings as a mother.) The adoption and appropriation of Mary's ideas and expressions in his own work was a natural activity of Charles's writing, but compared with the retrospective recognition of Dorothy Wordsworth's contribution to her brother's work, Mary's yet remains largely unacknowledged.

From a biographical standpoint the poem is also important. It implies a distressing circumstance which subsequent letters confirm: in the lead up to the anniversary of the murder Mary was overwhelmed once again by 'the sorest malady of all' – insanity. All the progress she had made – a return, in fact, to complete normality – was swiftly reversed, as she descended into the unreachable depths of madness. Both Charles and Mary had clearly hoped that she was totally cured; the return of her illness came as a severe blow to them both. Not for the last time, Charles compared her plight – unfavourably – with death:

> Thou didst not keep
> Her soul in death. O keep not now, my Lord,
> Thy servants in far worse, in spiritual death,
> And darkness blacker than those feared shadows
> O' the Valley, all must tread.

At the end of the poem Charles returns to the image of madness as a 'darkness' which has overshadowed his early adulthood:

> I only am left, with unavailing grief
> One Parent dead to mourn, & see one live
> Of all life's joys bereft, & desolate: –
> Am left, with a few friends, & one above
> The rest, found faithful in a length of years,
> Contented as I may, to bear me on
> T' the not unpeaceful Evening of a Day
> MADE BLACK BY MORNING STORMS. –

It was perhaps the circumstance that Charles was already able to anticipate a 'not unpeaceful Evening' – just as earlier he had observed in a letter to Coleridge that amid all his troubles he felt 'a calm not unlike content' – that enabled him to write of his unresolved situation. Rather than feeling he had nothing concrete to hold on to, he – crucially – recognized that he had to accept and embrace uncertainty in order to find peace. This was *his* test, *his* trial of faith.

On Christmas Day Charles felt Mary's absence especially keenly and again unburdened himself in verse, describing himself as 'a widow'd thing', utterly estranged from Mary, whose mind was then 'a fearful blank,/ Her senses lock'd up'; but again the poem ends on a not unhopeful note.[7] Writing on these occasions, when both memories of his mother and his sister's recurrence of madness must have tested his own emotional stability, seemed to unlock something in Charles. His advice to Coleridge to 'cultivate simplicity' he now appeared to apply with even greater austerity to some of his own work. 'The Old Familiar Faces', which he wrote after spending a convivial evening with Lloyd, White and others, again represents a completely new departure for Charles, in terms of the urgency of his need to express his feelings triumphing over his conventional poetic style. In the middle of this convivial company, as Lloyd was playing the piano, Charles suddenly felt a rush of emotion and, breaking away from his friends, ran into the street, soon finding himself at the Temple, the scene of his and Mary's childhood. Here he composed a poem, a *cri de cœur* remarkable as much for its bare and dogged directness as for the keen sense of loss and separation it conveys.

> Where are they gone, the old familiar faces?
>
> I had a mother, but she died, and left me,
> Died prematurely in a day of horrors –
> All, all are gone, the old familiar faces.
>
> I have been laughing, I have been carousing,
> Drinking late, sitting late, with my bosom cronies,
> All, all are gone, the old familiar faces.
>
> I loved a love once, fairest among women;
> Closed are her doors on me, I must not see her –
> All, all are gone, the old familiar faces.
>
> I have a friend, a kinder friend has no man;
> Like an ingrate, I left my friend abruptly;
> Left him, to muse on the old familiar faces.

Ghost-like, I paced round the haunts of my childhood.
Earth seems a desert I was bound to traverse,
Seeking to find the old familiar faces.

Friend of my bosom, thou more than a brother,
Why wert not thou born in my father's dwelling?
So might we talk of the old familiar faces —

How some they have died, and some they have left me;
And some are taken from me; all are departed;
All, all are gone, the old familiar faces.*

As winter progressed with no sign of Mary's recovery, this sense of social disengagement became more profound, Charles becoming increasingly withdrawn and depressed. Lloyd was now living in London with Charles's old schoolfriend Jem White, and went out of his way to draw Charles out of himself. Lloyd's well-meaning attempts to distract him only irritated Charles, who felt not only unable to enjoy himself but guilty at even trying. 'I seem to breathe more freely, to thin[k] more collectledly [sic], to feel more properly & calmly, when alone,' he wrote to Coleridge.[8] However, he relented and continued his collaboration with Lloyd on *Blank Verse* and also worked on his own prose narrative, *The Tale of Rosamund Gray*.

By late January 1798 Mary was at last beginning to improve, to the extent that Charles was thinking about finding some kind of situation for her. Light employment within a household would have been ideal, but how many families were

* Ann Simmons is the love of the fourth stanza; Lloyd the friend of the fifth, Coleridge of the seventh. In the original text the line 'And some are taken from me' was italicized — this referred of course to Mary. In the published version of 1818 the first stanza was omitted.

likely to throw open their doors to a murderer? Coleridge had offered to have Mary with his family, but just as Charles had avoided seeing Coleridge when he felt on the edge of sanity, he believed Mary could easily be overset by such stimulating company. As Charles put it:

. . . your invitation went to my very heart – but you have a power of exciting interest, [of] leading all hearts captive, too forcible [to] admit of Mary's being with you –. I consider her as perpetually on the brink of madness –. I think, you would almost make her dance within an inch of the precipice – she must be with duller fancies, & cooler intellects . . . I know a young man of this description, who has suited her these twenty years, & may live to do so still – if we are one day restor'd to each other.[9]

In his heart of hearts Charles knew that the only person he could feel secure would provide Mary with the kind of environment she needed was him.

At some undetermined point during the Pentonville years Charles conceived a romantic interest in a neighbour, a young Quaker woman called Hester Savory. To describe this attachment as a relationship would be misleading, as during the time that he was in love with her, he never once spoke to her. The duration of his undeclared passion is unknown, as is whether the object of his affection was aware of – let alone returned – his sentiments. Charles was to express the view that 'Every Quakeress is a lily'[10] and indeed it seems likely that Charles's interest in Hester Savory was more to do with her as a symbol of beauty, tranquillity and simplicity (there were no uncomplicated women in Charles's life) than anything deeper. He was ever to admire the calmness and 'silent grace' which characterized Quakers' deportment.[11] The pleasant sight of

Hester going about her business in her neat and simple dress, surmounted by her sunny countenance, daily buoyed up Charles with an image of cheerful and graceful femininity. He did not desire her so much as treasured her image in his landscape.

The fact that Charles and Hester never spoke, but smiled at each other across the street, was in its way a kind of communication. Charles was always to be interested in the Society of Friends, and found their taciturnity particularly appealing. (He likened the silence enjoyed between old friends, when the absence of speech is comfortable and actively expressive of intimacy, to the peace and quiet of a Quakers' meeting, when one enjoys 'at once solitude and society'.[12]) It is extremely tempting to attribute an event Charles described in his essay on 'Valentine's Day' to this period. In the essay Elia's friend, 'E.B.', lives opposite a young woman, whom he often observes, himself unseen, from his parlour window. 'E.B. meditated how he could repay this young maiden for many a favour which she had done him unknown; for when a kindly face greets us, though but passing by, and never knows us again, nor we it, we should feel it as an obligation; and E.B. did.' E.B., who is an artist, designs a beautiful Valentine's card and posts it to her, just for the pleasure of seeing her receive it. The postman duly delivers the envelope . . .

[E.B.] saw, unseen, the happy girl unfold the Valentine, dance about, clap her hands, as one after one the pretty emblems unfolded themselves. She danced about, not with light love, or foolish expectations, for she had no lover; or, if she had, none she knew that could have created those bright images which delighted her. It was more like some fairy present; a God-send, as our familiarly pious ancestors termed a benefit received, where the benefactor was unknown. It would do her no harm. It would do her good for ever after. It is good to love the unknown.

Whether the anecdote was based in truth or imagination, it is consistent with the idea of Hester Savory.

Much of Charles's poetry had been frank autobiography. The short story *Rosamund Gray* was a fictional tale inhabited by characters based on real people and re-opens the question of the character of Charles's first romance and the reasons for its demise. Set in Widford, the scene of Charles's romance with Ann Simmons, the eponymous heroine is in love with Allan Clare, who has 'sighed for her' since he was a boy of fourteen and she twelve. Allan and Rosamund, like Charles and 'Anna', spend most of their time together wandering around the countryside. On one of these occasions Allan flings his arms around Rosamund and kisses her, with unexpected results:

Allan had indulged before in these little freedoms, and Rosamund had thought no harm in them – but from this time the girl grew timid and reserved – distant in her manner, and careful of her behaviour, in Allan's presence – not seeking his society as before, but rather shunning it – delighting more to feed upon his idea in absence.

The description of Rosamund's reaction resonates strongly with the Anna/Alice Charles describes in the love sonnets and Elia essays – modest to the point of disdain – and raises the possibility (impossible to settle) that Charles pushed his suit a little too intensely for her liking. Back to the story: Allan's wealthy parents died when he was little and he was brought up by his sister, Elinor, ten years his senior – clearly a portrait of Mary Lamb:

Elinor Clare was an excellent young lady – discreet, intelligent, and affectionate. Allan revered her as a parent, while he loved her as his own familiar friend. He told all the little secrets of his heart to her . . . Elinor Clare was the best good creature – the least selfish human being I ever knew – always at work for other people's good, planning other people's happiness – continually forgetful to consult for her own personal gratifications, except indirectly, in the welfare of another – while her parents lived, the most attentive of daughters – since they died, the kindest of sisters – I never knew but *one* like her.

Strong elements of autobiography have been recognized in the story;[13] extracts from Elinor's letters in the story also appear to offer glimpses into the real past, from the detail of her recollection of their invalid mother 'in her old elbow chair – her arms folded upon her lap' to the regret and guilt of the bereaved child: 'My heart ached with the remembrance of infirmities, that made her closing years of life so sore a trial for her. I was concerned to think, that our family differences have been one source of disquiet to her.'

The plot is strangely disturbing: Rosamund goes out for a walk one night and is raped by a character called Matravis. Her helpless grandmother, then Rosamund, then Elinor, all die, leaving Allan alone in the world. Many years later Allan happens to be with a friend, the narrator of the tale, who is a surgeon, when he is treating a dying man. The patient turns out to be Matravis: Allan weeps over his deathbed.

The story appears to be about forgiveness, but is also about the knock-on effect of an apparently random evil deed. The parallels with the Lamb tragedy are clear; the rape signifying the murder, the deaths of Rosamund and her grandmother suggesting the deaths of Elizabeth and Sarah Lamb, Elinor's death signifying Mary 'in far worse, in spiritual death' – both leave the younger brother unsupported and alone – and Allan weeping over the dying perpetrator of the crime signifies Charles's bootless grief. The tale also represents a kind of wish-fulfilment: Allan, unlike Charles, achieves closure: the story is now resolved for him, whereas it is an ongoing saga for Charles. The fact that Charles wrote this decidedly odd story at all suggests it had some significant meaning for him, or even a therapeutic value.

There is one further aspect of *Rosamund Gray* which nags at anyone considering it biographically: the narrator mentions in passing – and to no purpose in the tale – that an ugly and unfounded rumour had circulated regarding Allan and Elinor's father. Could this be another of those elusive hints at madness in the family? Ugly rumours and tale-telling were about to feature prominently in Charles's own life and to lead, ultimately, to a period of estrangement from Coleridge. Missing correspondence between the two writers contributes to further muddy what are already rather murky waters surrounding the affair, into which Charles appears to have been drawn by Lloyd and, to a lesser extent, Southey.

Relations between Southey and Coleridge had deteriorated before this time, since the indefinite postponement (for which, read abandonment) of establishing a Pantisocracy. Southey held Coleridge responsible for the collapse of the scheme, while Coleridge felt he had been pressured into an unsatisfactory marriage by Southey. It has been suggested that Coleridge became somewhat jealous of Charles and Lloyd's closeness – both as friends and collaborators – and may have felt put out by their growing independence from him. (Lloyd was now working on his novel *Edmund Oliver*, without reference to his one-time mentor.)

In December 1797 the radical *Monthly Magazine* (in which

four of Charles's poems had previously appeared) printed 'Sonnets Attempted in the Manner of Contemporary Writers' by Nehemiah Higginbottom. Higginbottom claimed that by exposing the 'infantine simplicity, vulgar colloquialisms, and lady-like Friendships' of those whose poetry he burlesqued, he aimed to 'do good to our young Bards'. He aimed to achieve this by ridiculing 'that affectation of unaffectedness, jumping and misplaced accent in common-place epithets, flat lines forced into poetry by italics (signifying how mouthis[h]ly the Author would read them) puny pathos: &c &c . . .'[14] The first sonnet ran:

> Pensive at eve, on the *hard* world I mused,
> And *my poor* heart was sad; so at the Moon
> I gazed, and sighed, and sighed: for ah how soon
> Eve saddens into night! Mine eyes perused
> With tearful vacancy the *dampy* grass
> That wept and glittered in the *paly* ray:
> And I *did pause me* on my lonely way
> And *mused me* on the *wretched ones* that pass
> O'er the bleak heath of sorrow. But alas!
> Most of *myself* I thought! When it befel,
> That the *soothe* spirit of the *breezy* wood
> Breath'd in mine ear: 'All this is very well,
> But much of *one* thing is for *no* thing good.'
> Oh *my poor heart's* Inexplicable Swell!

The self-centred, self-pitying tone and the archaisms and exclamations are designed to raise a knowing smile in the reader, while the anthropomorphisms taken just too far (evening 'saddening' into night is rather fine; grass 'weeping' dew, however, is an irresistibly bad idea) and the invented adjectives ('*dampy* grass', '*paly* ray') demonstrate the satirist's keen awareness of the narrow path the new poetry trod between the sublime and the ridiculous.

Charles and Lloyd instantly identified Coleridge as the actual author, and themselves as the lampooned poets. Quite what possessed Coleridge to attack his friends whom he knew to be emotionally vulnerable (Lloyd had also recently paid a visit to a madhouse) is unfathomable. No one appeared mollified by the crucial fact that Coleridge had also parodied his *own* poetry in the Higginbottom piece. To further confuse the issue, Southey also detected − or imagined − himself pilloried in one of the sonnets. Had Coleridge merely shown his friends the skit prior to publication, he might well have avoided the trouble which followed.

Southey had the most reason to leap at the opportunity of a scrap with Coleridge, having been let down by him once too often (Coleridge was, as Hazlitt later observed laconically, 'a past master of the prospectus') and, in the guise of Abel Shufflebottom, gained some satisfaction by publishing his own parodies of four of Coleridge's sonnets. Lloyd also took the slight to heart, although his grievance against Coleridge was less easy to define; it was perhaps a symptom of his psychological problems which left him spoiling for a fight with his one-time nurse and mentor; or perhaps, having lived in such close quarters with his idol (he and Coleridge had shared a bed while Sara was nursing baby Hartley), he had, like Southey, become disillusioned with Coleridge the *man*. The publication of Lloyd's novel *Edmund Oliver*, based on an outline supplied by Southey, marked a further sharp deterioration in relations: the eponymous hero bore an unmistakable resemblance to Coleridge and unflatteringly retailed his love-life and his episode as a dragoon. Possibly worse, the book described Coleridge's dependence on opium and his bouts of heavy drinking.

All in all it represented a gross abuse of Coleridge's trust and confidence. He took offence; worse, Charles was drawn in on Lloyd's side by implication: Lloyd had dedicated the book to him.

Dorothy Wordsworth was also sucked into the fray as Lloyd used her as a conduit through which to conduct his argument with Coleridge. Lloyd informed Coleridge (through Dorothy) that Charles was on his side and had determined to end his correspondence with Coleridge. Lloyd also repeated to Dorothy, Charles and Southey things Coleridge had said about them – confidentially – to him, in Charles's case showing him a letter Coleridge had written to Lloyd, comparing the opposing proportions of genius and talent in Coleridge and Charles. They were all to realize, too late, that Lloyd was a 'sad Tattler'. Coleridge, however, who probably knew Lloyd better than anyone, detected his influence in the deterioration of all these relationships, and wrote to Charles in early May 1798 charging him with naïvety in trusting and siding with Lloyd. Coleridge wrote:

Both you and Lloyd became acquainted with me at a season when your minds were far from being in a composed or natural state & you clothed my image with a suit of notions & feelings which could belong to nothing human. *You* are restored to comparative saneness, & are merely wondering what is become of the Coleridge with whom you were so passionately in love. *Charles Lloyd's* mind has only changed its disease.[15]

Charles's own awareness of the sometimes overwhelming effect of Coleridge's attentions would have allowed him to admit the truth of much of what Coleridge had said. However, had Charles wished to remain relatively uninvolved with the whole sorry affair, and give Coleridge the benefit of the doubt, a repeated remark of Coleridge's tipped the scales.

'Poor Lamb,' Coleridge was supposed to have said; 'if he wants any *knowledge*, he may apply to me.' The repeater (or inventor) of this line was presumably also Lloyd, with whom Charles was staying in Birmingham at the time. Hurt and angry, while still with Lloyd, Charles composed a stinging rejoinder. Having learnt that Coleridge's interest in German philosophy was leading to a visit with the Wordsworths to German universities, he fired off a list of taunting 'Theological Propositions' to which he attached the following letter:

Learned Sir, my Friend,

Presuming on our long habits of friendship, & emboldened further by your late liberal permission to avail myself of your correspondence, in case I want any knowledge, (which I intend to do when I have no Encyclopaedia, or Lady's Maga-zine at hand to refer to in any matter of science,) I now submit to your enquiries the above Theological Propositions, to be by you defended, or oppugned, or both, in the Schools of Germany, whither I am told you are departing, to the utter dissatisfaction of your native Devonshire, & regret of universal England; but to my own individual consolation, if thro the channel of your wished return, Learned Sir, my Friend, may be transmitted to this our Island, from those famous Theologi-cal Wits of Leipsic & Gottingen, any rays of illumination, in vain to be derived from the home growth of our English Halls and Colleges. Finally, wishing Learned Sir, that you may see Schiller, & swing in a wood (*vide* Poems), & sit upon a Tun, & eat fat hams of Westphalia,

I remain
Your friend and docile Pupil to instruct
Charles Lamb[16]

Although Charles vented his spleen in a humorous fashion (even in great pain he could not help pulling his punches to Coleridge), Coleridge took the point as seriously as he knew it was intended. Immediately recognizing Lloyd's hand in the affair, Coleridge showed the letter to his publisher, Joseph Cottle, remarking that Lloyd and Charles would 'do each other no good'. Coleridge did not reply to the letter from Charles. Nearly two years were to pass before he received another.

May 1798 saw the publication of Charles and Lloyd's collection of poetry *Blank Verse*. An anonymous review in the *Analytical Review* panned it:

We may be very deficient in taste: but the whining monotonous melancholy of these pages is to us extremely tiresome. Mr. Lloyd and Mr. Lamb shed a sepulchral gloom over every object, and their poetry is such an unvaried murmur, that, so far from sympathizing in their poetical sorrows, we feel a much stronger propensity to smile, than we do to weep.[17]

The faults the reviewer identifies irresistibly conjure the memory of 'Nehemiah Higginbottom' and his *black heath* of Sorrow'. (Significantly, the reviewer goes on to be harder on Lloyd than on Charles, a proportionality also evident in Coleridge's parody.) The *Anti-Jacobin Review* in August characterized the young poets' style as 'a kind of baby language which they are pleased to term *blank-verse*'. The following month *Blank Verse* was at last favourably reviewed in the *Critical Review*, noting that Charles's contributions now eschewed 'Vain loves and wanderings with a fair hair'd maid'. 'His present pieces,' the reviewer observed, 'imply past sufferings and present resignation.' Although the review appeared anonymously, it is not altogether surprising to learn that this sympathetic critic was Southey.

Having, for the meantime, lost Coleridge's friendship, in August Lloyd also disappeared from Charles's immediate family of friends, taking up his place at Caius College, Cambridge. Possibly due to the approach of the second anniversary of the 'day of horrors', Mary suffered another relapse, jeopardizing both her and Charles's hopes that she would ever be able to return home. However, it proved short-lived, and Charles was soon able to write to Robert Lloyd, Charles Lloyd's younger brother, that 'I trust that she will yet be restored to me'.[18] Charles had become very fond of Robert, and considered him 'the flower of their family'.[19] At this time Robert was an apprentice draper in Saffron Walden, Essex, and appears to have been suffering the feelings of frustration and boredom Charles Lamb had had to learn to live with as a clerk at the East India Company, possibly made keener in Robert's case by his beloved brother's departure for university. Despite the fact that Charles was pre-occupied with Mary's illness, he found the time to write Robert a thoughtful and illuminating letter on the subject of friendship.

I hope you get reconciled to your situation. The worst in it is that you have no *friend* to talk to – but wait in patience, and you will in good time make friends. The having a friend is not indispensibly necessary to virtue or happiness – religion removes those barriers of sentiment which partition us from the disinterested love of our brethren –. we are commanded to love our enemies, to do good to those that hate us; how much more is it our duty then to cultivate a forbearance and complacence towards those who only differ from us in dispositions and ways of thinking –. there is always, without very unusual care there must always be, something of SELF in friendship, we love our friend because he is like ourselves, can consequences altogether unmix'd and pure be reasonably expected from such a source – do not even the publicans & sinners the same –? . . . Robert, friends fall off, friends mistake us, they change, they grow unlike us, they go away, they die, but God is everlasting & incapable of change, and to him we may look with chearful, unpresumptuous HOPE, while we discharge the duties of LIFE in situations more untowardly than yours. You complain of the impossibility of improving yourself, but be assurd that the opportunity of improvement lies more in the mind than the situation −. humble yourself before God, cast out the selfish principle, wait in patience, do good in every way you can to all sorts of people, never be easy to neglect a duty tho' a small one, praise God for all, & see his hand in all things, & he will in time raise you up *many friends* − or be himself in stead an unchanging friend −. God bless you.

C Lamb[20]

While a good deal of reflection on his friendships with Coleridge, Southey and Charles Lloyd informs this letter, it also provides a reminder that in periods of stress and alienation (physical separation from Mary; emotional estrangement from Coleridge) Charles, like his sister, looks to God − the only steadfast and immutable 'friend' − for comfort and security. The letter also shows Charles's capacity for a new elder-brotherly role which came to characterize his relationship with Robert: mature, reflective, objective, simultaneously reassuring and gently admonishing. However, the quality of Charles's advice always depended on his own state of mind, as is demonstrated by a letter written three months later, also in response to a complaining one from Robert: 'One passage in your Letter a little displeas'd me ... You say that "this World to you seems drain'd of all its SWEETS!"' (This, of course, is a complaint in exactly the same vein as Charles himself had made to Coleridge not so very long before.)

At first I had hoped you only meant to insinuate the high price of Sugar! but I am afraid you meant more −. O Robert, I do'nt know what you call sweet, – – Honey & the honey comb, roses & violets, are yet in the earth. The sun & moon yet reign in Heaven, & the lesser lights keep up their pretty twinklings – – meat & drinks, sweet sights & sweet smells, a country walk, spring & autumn, follies & repe[ntan]ce, quarrels & reconcilements, have all a sweetness by turns – . . . good humor & good nature, friends at home that love you, & friends abroad that miss you, you possess all these things, & more innumerable, & these are all sweet things – – –. You may extract honey from every thing; do not go a gathering after gall –. the bees are wiser in their generation than the race of sonnet writers & complainers, Bowless & Charlotte Smiths, & all that tribe, who can see no joys but what are past, and fill peoples' heads with notions of the Unsatisfying nature of Earthly comforts –. I assure you I find this world a very pretty place – –.[21]

(It will be remembered that the author of 'The Old Familiar Faces', only too recently, could 'see no joys but what are past'.) Charles continued a regular correspondence with both Southey and Robert Lloyd during Charles Lloyd's first term at Cambridge, often enclosing extracts of his latest literary enterprise; he had embarked on a stage tragedy entitled *John Woodvil*.*

In September 1798 Coleridge and Wordsworth's ground-breaking collection of poetry *Lyrical Ballads* appeared, contain-ing, of course, Coleridge's extraordinary 'Rime of the Ancient Mariner'. Perhaps still blinded by their feelings for Coleridge the man, Charles Lloyd chose to dislike the poem, while Southey, reviewing it for the *Critical Review*, declared it 'a poem of little merit' and in parts 'absurd or unintelligible',[22] while privately expressing the view that the poem was 'non-sense'. Charles Lamb was alone among Coleridge's disaffected

* Originally entitled *Pride's Cure*.

friends in acknowledging Coleridge's success in the poem, appreciating its 'miraculous' effects and celebrating its ability to play 'tricks with the mind'.[23] Charles also showed greater prescience than his friends in asserting Wordsworth's 'Tintern Abbey' one of the finest poems ever written.

It is worth considering what Charles's own stature as a poet was at this time. He had had individual poems published in various periodicals, and his poems had appeared in collections with those of both Coleridge and Lloyd. The same edition of *Critical Review* in which Southey panned 'The Rime of the Ancient Mariner' contained a very encouraging review of Charles and Lloyd's *Blank Verse*. The publisher Joseph Cottle had commissioned engravings of Charles, Wordsworth, Southey and Coleridge; these same four names would shortly be classed as 'the modern school of poets'. If lampoon is a measure of anything Charles might also have been secretly gratified to see his name appear alongside those of Coleridge, Southey and Lloyd – albeit as the subjects of barbed verse – in the first issue of the *Anti-Jacobin* in July 1798, and may indeed have derived a degree of satisfaction from Gillray's cartoon, appearing the following month, which represented Coleridge and Southey as philosophical donkeys and Lloyd and Lamb as a toad and a frog.

The summer of 1798 also saw the publication of *Rosamund Gray*. It was later to be highly regarded in some quarters; Percy Bysshe Shelley, for example, wrote:

What a lovely thing is *Rosamund Gray*! How much knowledge of the sweetest, and deepest parts of our nature is in it! When I think of such a mind as Lamb's – when I see how unnoticed remain things of such exquisite and complete perfection – what should I hope for myself, if I had not higher objects in view than fame?[24]

At the time of its appearance, as Shelley suggests, the story excited little attention. Having attempted poetry and prose, Charles had already turned to drama. Now closer to Southey than either man was to Coleridge, it was to him that he outlined his aspirations for *John Woodvil*. They were not unambitious: 'My Tragedy will be a medley (or I intend it to be a medley) of laughter & tears, prose & verse & in some places rhime, songs, wit, pathos, humour, & if possible sublimity, – at least, tis not a fault in my intention, if it does not comprehend most of these discordant atoms . . .'[25] Restoration theatre had a strong appeal for both Charles and Mary (Congreve's plays had been among the first they saw as children) and it was the early Restoration period in which Charles set *John Woodvil*. The plot turns on the eponymous hero's revelation – while drunk – of his exiled father's whereabouts, leading to his father's discovery and murder.

The hero's situation – feeling guilt and responsibility for the death of a parent – of course resonates with the Lambs' own story; the drunken state in which he makes his blunder forms a kind of double-bind: does it ameliorate his guilt (as Mary's madness did) or make him more culpable? The theme of sharing information which should not be shared also echoes more recent events – Lloyd's 'tattling' had had far-reaching and unhappy consequences. A further autobiographical element of the play lies in the nature of its conclusion. As Winifred Courtney has observed: 'The optimism of its ending – that through Calamity one may come to one's own best self – is his own emergence from the struggle, his determination to leave bitterness to others.'[26] Most striking, though, is the part played by alcohol in the play; there are several debates and soliloquys devoted to the pleasures and pitfalls of drinking, prefiguring what would be Charles's most fascinating and controversial work, 'Confessions of a Drunkard'. With the benefit of hindsight, it is clear that *John Woodvil* gives the first hints of Charles's tendencies to addiction.

Interestingly, it is at the same period that Charles was writing *John Woodvil* that it is possible to detect in a letter to Southey the germ of 'Elia', the persona in which he was to pen his most celebrated works.

My Taylor has brought me home a [ne]w coat Lappel'd with a VELVET collar. HE assures me every body wears velvet collars now – – Some are born fashionable, some achieve fashion, & others, like your humble servant, have fashion thrust upon them –. The rogue has been making inroads hitherto by modest degrees, foisting upon me an additional Button, recommending GAYTERS, but to come upon me thus FULL TIDE OF LUXURY, neither becomes him as a Taylor or the ninth of a man –.[27]

The evident relish with which Charles considers his new coat reminds the reader forcibly that he often trod a narrow path in an uneventful life; the nature of his work, his lack of money and his onerous family responsibilities formed in Charles a characteristic which was to make Elia so popular: the recognition of the *event* in the everyday.

Over the autumn and winter Charles had continued to act as Robert Lloyd's confessor and adviser as Robert's relationship with his father deteriorated. Over Christmas, his sister Priscilla had received a proposal of marriage from Christopher Words-worth (one of William and Dorothy's brothers), which she very much wanted to accept. Her father, however, opposed the match, making her unhappy and 'alarmingly ill', simul-taneously putting her brother Charles in an uncomfortable situation, as Christopher Wordsworth was his tutor at Caius. Robert crossed swords with his father at around the same time due to his wish to discontinue attending Quaker meetings.

(Mrs Lloyd also disapproved of her son's *fantastical* trousers'.) These stresses exacerbated by the fact that he was suffering from financial problems, Charles Lloyd senior over-reacted to both his refractory offspring. Although Charles Lamb did his best to reconcile Robert to his father's wishes, the strain of being under the same roof as his irrational father proved too much for Robert, and he fled to London, taking sanctuary with Charles. Although Charles was later on very good terms with Robert's father (who, like his friend Thomas Clarkson, was an abolitionist), at this time the Lloyds were not at all sure he was a good influence on the impressionable Robert. His sister Priscilla wrote to Robert:

Lamb would not I think by any means be a person to take up your abode with. He is too much like yourself – he would encourage those feelings which it certainly is your duty to suppress. Your station in life – the duties which are pointed out by that rank in society which you are destined to fulfill – differ widely from his . . .[28]

Although Robert had, in Charles's opinion, 'the sweetness of an angel in his heart', it was combined with 'admirable firmness of purpose' and he refused to budge from Pentonville without certain guarantees from his father.[29] The first week of February 1799 brought his brother Charles with the news that their father had consented to Priscilla's marriage. Both brothers remained with Charles for two weeks before returning to their family home in Birmingham.

Mary's health continued to be an unpredictable quantity. While her early periods of illness had lasted several months, the attack in the summer lasted only a few weeks, and she was evidently subject to much shorter 'fits', which would come and go within the space of a few days or even hours. (Charles wrote to Southey in October that Mary was 'quite well – she had a slight attack the other day, which frighten'd me a good deal, but it went off unaccountably – '.[30]) It is not clear exactly what shape these 'fits' took. Later evidence shows that the death of someone close to her was often the catalyst for a return of her derangement, and on at least one occasion the unexpected mention of her mother tipped her over the edge. Coleridge described one attack which declared its onset by her beginning to smile strangely, and he knew her well enough immediately to send for help. In January 1799 Charles was able to report that 'my sister Mary was never in better health or spirits than now'.[31] However, her improved health made no difference to her prospects for returning home. She had not seen her father since the 'day of horrors' and indeed was never to see him again.

The surviving letters of this period make no mention of old John Lamb, now sunk into a pathetic semi-stupor. Charles found the contrast between his father's present state and his memories of his former vibrant self almost too painful to dwell on. He had written:

> One parent yet is left – a wretched thing.
> A sad survivor of his buried wife,
> A palsy-smitten, old, old man,
> A semblance most forlorn of what he was,
> A merry cheerful man. A merrier man,
> A man more apt to frame matter for mirth,
> Mad jokes, and anticks for a Christmas eve;
> Making life social, and the laggard time
> To move on nimbly, never yet did cheer
> The little circle of domestic friends.[32]

In April 1799 the 'sad survivor' died. Charles reproved Robert Lloyd, who still complained of his own parents' expectation that he would attend Quaker meetings, 'I know that if my parents were to live again, I would do more things to please them, than merely sitting still six hours in a week.'[33] Immediately following his father's death, Charles moved to new lodgings in the same road (from 45 to 36 Chapel Street). It was to be a new beginning. Mary was coming home.

6. Toad and Frog

So saying, she departed,
Leaving Sir Francis like a man, beneath
Whose feet a scaffolding was suddenly falling . . .

(Charles Lamb, *The Witch*)

The circumstances under which it was possible for Mary, a murderer, who continued to be subject to bouts of insanity during which she became violent, to be discharged into the community, are unclear. Brother John opposed her release and the local authorities warned that they might be obliged to have her legally committed for life. It is possible that Charles made an application directly to the Home Secretary, guaranteeing that Mary would pose no threat to public safety – Lloyd certainly later believed this to have been the case. In any event, permission was granted for her to return to Charles's custody and after two and a half years of separation, Charles and Mary began a new life in a new home.

For the first time in their lives (he was now twenty-four and she thirty-five) they lived alone together, with only an aged servant, Hetty, and were masters of their own destiny. Mary did not return to mantua-making but subsidized the household economy on the 'a penny saved is a penny earned' principle, buying only what she could not make herself and even then haggling with local traders to stretch Charles's meagre income as far as possible. Their spare time was spent in long walks together, or at home reading and – in Charles's case, at least – writing. The circumstances of their life together were more free from stresses and more conducive to health and happiness than they had ever been before.

Although Charles in particular was always to remain cautious about subjecting Mary to too much excitement, they could at last entertain friends comfortably. Whereas Charles had been able to seek company outside the home, Mary's principal companions had been her keepers before living quietly alone in Hackney. Sharing a home with her brother made available to Mary social opportunities inaccessible even to respectable spinsters who lived alone. The year 1799 therefore not only brought Charles and Mary together again but gave them a home which was to play a central role in London literary social life. The warmth and generosity with which they received even casual acquaintances is widely testified, Thomas De Quincey remarking that Charles 'was, with his limited income . . . positively the most hospitable man I have known in this world'.[1] That first year introduced three very important additions to their growing circle of acquaintances: George Dyer, Thomas Manning and William Godwin – all, in their different ways, eccentrics.

These three exemplify the staggering diversity of the Lambs' circle. While Godwin, as a publisher, was to advance Charles and Mary's literary careers, Manning is believed by some to have been next in importance to Coleridge in Charles's literary development.[2] While both Charles and Mary were stimulated by people of outstanding intellectual and creative abilities, De Quincey noted that they also welcomed 'numerous dull people, stupid people, asinine people, for no other reason upon earth than because [Charles] believed them to have been used or oppressed . . .'[3] By Charles's own assessment, their friends were indeed 'for the most part, persons of an uncertain fortune' and 'in the world's eye a ragged regiment'[4] but to the Lambs friendship was not a matter of charity; highly valuing personality itself, their friends were selected 'for some individuality of character which they manifested'. This individuality was not necessarily a strength; they often loved people not just regardless of their flaws, but precisely because of them. As 'Elia' Charles was to write: 'I love a *Fool* – as naturally, as if I were of kith and kin to him . . . I have never made an acquaintance since, that lasted; or a friendship, that answered; with any that had not some tincture of the absurd in their characters.'[5] Such was the case with George Dyer.

Dyer was a poet, a radical and a respected Classicist. Another ex-pupil of Christ's Hospital, he was twenty years older than Charles, had left school a Grecian and had studied at Emmanuel College, Cambridge. His vast fund of learning was the result of wide and constant reading and he was always to be found 'busy as a moth over some rotten archive'; whereas Charles sometimes claimed to fear he was being assimilated into his desk at the East India House, Dyer was 'grown almost into a book' as the result of hours of poring over old volumes.[6] Dyer was gifted, but as one writer has gently observed, 'rather over-estimated his place in the poetic firmament'.[7] Charles's affection for Dyer lay in part in their shared affection for books, but also in Dyer's essential absurdity. A famously absent-minded eccentric, Dyer had been known to mistake a coal-scuttle for his hat, and once managed to arrive home after dinner at Leigh Hunt's before realizing he had left one of his shoes under his host's table. Although he lived in great disorder with scant regard for personal hygiene (as Charles subtly described Dyer's preference for the university cities, 'He cares not much for Bath'), Dyer was a good and generous soul. The blend of humanity and folly in his character made him irresistible to Charles and Mary.

A month after Mary joined Charles at Pentonville, he accepted an invitation to dine with John Bartram, a silversmith and pawnbroker, and his wife. Mrs Bartram was an old friend of Charles's, now living in London. Southey wrote to his wife:

I went to the India house. Among other things Lamb told me he dined last week twice with his Anna – who is married, and he laughed and said she was a stupid girl. There is something quite unnatural in Lambs levity. If he never loved her why did he publish those sonnets? If he did why talk of it with bravado laughter, or why talk of it at all?[8]

Was Charles laughing at Anna or at his own folly? He was shortly to write a piece in the style of one of his favourite authors, Robert Burton, which may shed some light on his feelings at this time. The author describes a melancholic patient who has come to him for relief:

My fine Sir is a lover, an *innamorato*, a Pyramus, a Romeo; he walks seven years disconsolate, moping, because he cannot enjoy his miss, *insanus amor* is his melancholy, the man is mad; *delirat*, he dotes; all this while his Glycera is rude, spiteful, not to be entreated, churlish, spits at him, yet exceeding fair, gentle eyes (which is a beauty), hair lustrous and *smiling* . . .

The girl marries our lover's rival, a boorish ignoramus, and many years later our lover meets her again, but is surprised by his feelings, finding her

. . . forward, coming, *amantissima, ready to jump at once into his mouth*, her he hateth, feels disgust when she is but mentioned, thinks her ugly . . . that which he affecteth so much, that which drives him mad, distracted, phrenetic, beside himself, is no beauty which lives

. . . but something *which is not*, can never be, a certain *fantastic opinion* or *notional image* of his mistresse . . .⁹

Rosamund Gray hints at similar self-knowledge where the narrator observes 'There is a *mysterious character* . . . which true lovers have ever imputed to the object of their affections' and describes Rosamund as rather even than seeing her loved one, 'delighting more to feed upon *his idea* in absence'.*

Mary's first extant poem, 'Helen Repentant Too Late', written a few months later, can also be read as an allegory of the relationship's character and resolution. The narrator of the poem has nursed an unrequited passion for haughty, beautiful, high-born Helen for twenty years ('On sighs I've fed,/ Your scorn my bread'). 'Helen grown old,/ No longer cold' eventually relents, telling her admirer 'You to all men I prefer'. However, the poet demurs:

> Can I, who loved
> My Beloved
> But for the 'scorn was in her eye,'
> Can I be moved
> For my Beloved,
> When she returns me 'sigh for sigh'?

The answer is no: again, when the rejecting, unattainable mistress becomes compliant, the lover loses interest. It seems that Charles had finally shaken off his passion for Ann Simmons: his 'notional image' of her evaporated when confronted by this London housewife, stripped of the beauties with which the woody glades of Hertfordshire and his own youthful romanticism had imbued her.

* Italics in last phrase mine.

Now completely 'cured' of his passion for Ann, in October Charles returned to Widford, scene of their relationship, and looked over Blakesware, the old house where his grandmother had been housekeeper. He wrote to Southey of the tapestry-hung bedrooms and the marble hall lined with the heads of the twelve Caesars, but not of the emotions the trip evoked: 'there are feelings which refuse to be translated, sulky aborigines, which will not be naturalized in another soil. Of this nature are old family faces and scenes of infancy.'[10] The triumph of 'Elia' was to be the translation of these feelings so that the reader, too, felt them; but Charles as yet lacked both the confidence to address his 'sulky aborigines' and the ability to detect the universal in his own subjective experience. Southey's first *Annual Anthology* had been published in September and included a poem by Charles ('Living Without God in the World') but for the time being his sights remained fixed on writing for the stage. Despite having written to Manning only a few days before that 'My scribbling days are past',[11] almost Charles's last act of the year was to send a copy of his play *John Woodvil* to his hero, the actor John Philip Kemble, who was to pass it directly to the management at Drury Lane Theatre.

By the winter of 1799 the breach with Coleridge had been healed and Charles was on good terms both with him and Charles Lloyd. The latter had married Sophia Pemberton in the summer and settled in Cambridge, to which he now invited Charles for the first week of December. It does not appear that Mary was invited to Cambridge. She and Charles were to become accustomed to there being a very limited number of homes willing to welcome her (Sophia Lloyd was now pregnant and may have felt particularly uncomfortable about having someone of Mary's history in the house). Mary appears to have borne this and other indignities 'as one who has no right to complain' and did not deter Charles from making his solo excursions. Nevertheless, Charles's pleasure on such occasions was tinged with guilt.

Despite Mary's absence, Cambridge charmed Charles. All the things he loved – but of which he never had a sufficiency – were united in his experience of the university city: books and cloisters, classical learning and new ideas – and the leisure to enjoy them. Here he could participate – in his mind if not in fact – in the idealized continuation of his life after Christ's Hospital; he could imagine himself, who had been 'defrauded in his young years of the sweet food of academic institution', as partaking in the pleasures and privileges of the more fortunate Grecians. 'I can here play the gentleman, enact the student,' he later wrote.

Here I can take my walks unmolested, and fancy myself of what degree or standing I please . . . I can rise at the chapel-bell, and dream that it rings for *me*. In moods of humility I can be a Sizar, or a Servitor. When the peacock vein rises, I strut a Gentleman Commoner. In graver moments, I proceed Master of Arts.

In other words, 'I fetch up past opportunities'.[12]

Of all Cambridge's treasures, Thomas Manning was Charles's greatest find. Manning was Lloyd's mathematics tutor. Like Lloyd, raised a Quaker, he was a man of extraordinary talents (he was fluent in fifteen languages) and, like Coleridge, a spell-binding speaker. Temperamentally he suited Charles: he was an armchair radical, was interested in poetry and ideas, enjoyed drinking and humour. The two young men instantly warmed to one another and recognized each other as kindred spirits. It was to be the beginning of a long and rewarding friendship. Charles's enthusiasm for Manning's company is evident as he anticipates a New Year trip to Cambridge to 'crush a cup to the infant century' in January 1801 with Manning:

Embark at six oClock in the morning, with a fresh gale, on a Cambridge one-decker, very cold till eight at night, Land at St. Mary's light house, Muffins and Coffee upon Table (or any other curious production of Turkey or both INDIES) –. Snipes exactly at nine. Punch to commence at ten, *with argument*; difference of opinion is expected to take place about eleven, perfect unanimity, with some haziness and dimness, before twelve –.[13]

Disappointed that Manning had not come to see him on another occasion, he railed: 'Pray what maps do you use, when you travel? Perhaps you have hit upon one that leaves London *out*.'[14] Manning was now Charles's prime correspondent and confidant.

The tone of Charles's relationship with Coleridge – now staying in London – correspondingly shows a less dependent Charles than previously, quite capable of teasing the great man. In a letter of January 1800 he congratulated Coleridge on a piece in the *Morning Post* and invited him to meet Manning ('He is a man of a thousand'), who was visiting Charles and Mary at Pentonville. Charles added with mild sarcasm, 'I am afraid if I did not at intervals call upon you, I should *never see you*. But I forget, the affairs of the nation engross your time and your mind.'[15] Charles succeeded in bringing Manning and Coleridge together, to all parties' great satisfaction. If Lloyd, of whom Manning held the highest opinion, had prejudiced him against Coleridge, the meeting in the event 'dazzled' Manning.

It appears that Lloyd had been up to his old tattling tricks again, but on this occasion the butt of his tales was the more vulnerable character of a woman, the writer Mary Hays. Hays had entertained, in the past, strong feelings for both Godwin and William Frend and it was through Dyer that she had entered the Lambs' circle. Some misunderstanding had arisen between her and Charles Lloyd, resulting in both showing each other's letters to friends (Lloyd to make her an object of ridicule, Hays to expose his calumny). This public exposure of dirty laundry was unsavoury enough, but once more Lloyd's machinations threatened to lose Charles a friend: while not admiring Hays's conduct, he, Southey and Coleridge thought Lloyd had behaved appallingly (Charles said he could not have sent the letter Lloyd wrote Hays – supposedly of apology – 'to my ENEMY's BITCH'[16]); Manning, however, took Lloyd's side. Charles, anxious this time not to alienate anyone, resolved to write no more to Manning on the matter. In any case he had a welcome diversion from the sordid affair: he had met the notorious William Godwin.

Godwin was probably most infamous as an atheist, and Charles affected relief that 'he has neither horns nor claws' and was 'quite a tame creature'.[17] Highly politicized, Godwin was not obviously Charles's cup of tea ('Public affairs – except as they touch upon me, & so turn into private – I cannot whip my mind up to feel any interest in,' he confessed to Manning[18]), and the marriage Godwin was soon to make would further complicate many of his relationships. Godwin's first wife, Mary Wollstonecraft, had died two years earlier in 1797, leaving her child by an earlier relationship, Fanny Imlay (aged five in 1799) and her child by Godwin, the future Mary Shelley (now a toddler of two). Although very fond of children, Godwin was something of an authoritarian, Coleridge comparing the girls' 'cadaverous silence' with his own boisterous Hartley (who, incidentally, did not endear Godwin to Coleridge's brand of parenting by smacking 'Mr Gobwin' on the shin with a skittle). Godwin and his second wife were to be responsible for Charles and Mary's substantial body of work for children, one of which (*Tales from Shakespeare*) became a classic. However, Charles enjoyed the company of 'that good-natured heathen', not least because of the high opinion both men shared of Coleridge.[19]

At the beginning of March 1800, while his wife and son were in the West Country visiting friends, Coleridge came to stay with Charles and Mary, remaining until the first week of April. Mary remained 'in fine health' and Charles declared Coleridge's company was like 'living in a continuous feast'. Living under one roof revived all the old kindred feelings between the one-time schoolmates. 'The more I see of him in the quotidian undress and relaxation of his mind, the more cause I see to love him and believe him a *very* GOOD *man*, and all those foolish impressions to the contrary fly off like morning slumbers,' wrote Charles.[20] Coleridge teasingly alluded to Charles and Mary as 'The Agnus Dei & the Virgin Mary' during his stay.[21]

Doubtless Mary had all along cautioned Charles against judging Coleridge too harshly, although we do not know what opinion she held of Charles Lloyd's role (it may be significant that her brother never sends Mary's love to Charles Lloyd at the end of his letters, which he often does in those to Robert Lloyd and to Manning). We know that Mary was particularly tolerant of friends' vagaries and also that her opinion carried a great deal of weight with her brother. Although Mary gave advice freely when consulted, she did not tend to judge people by the standards she applied to herself. Her strategy, she explained to her close friend Sarah Stoddart, was 'looking into peoples real characters, and never expecting them to act out of it – never expecting another to do as I would do in the same case'. When she evidently found Sarah's conduct with an admirer left a great deal to be desired, she added, 'as I cannot enter into your feelings, I can certainly have nothing to say to it, only th[a]t I sincerely wish you happy in your own way, however odd that way may appear to me to be'. When Sarah expected her behaviour to draw censure from Mary, Mary explained, 'all this gives me no offence, because it is your nature, and your temper, and I do not expect or want you to be otherwise than you are, I love you for the good that is in you, and look for no change'.[22]

Charles took a similarly pragmatic view of the human race and was shortly to write: 'I am determined to lead a merry Life in the midst of Sinners. I try to consider all men as such, and to pitch my expectations from human nature as low as possible. In this view, all unexpected Virtues are Godsends and beautiful exceptions.'[23]

However, while Mary took people as she found them, she had strong objective views of right and wrong. As Charles observed in a portrait of Elia's cousin Bridget (clearly based on Mary):

We are both of us inclined to be a little too positive; and I have observed the result of our disputes to be almost uniformly this – that in matters of fact, dates, and circumstances, it turns out, that I was in the right, and my cousin in the wrong. But where we have differed upon moral points; upon something proper to be done, or let alone; whatever heat of opposition, or steadiness of conviction, I set out with, I am sure always, in the long run, to be brought over to her way of thinking.[24]

Charles was the exception to Mary's rule of not attempting to change people – having been taught right from wrong as a child by his big sister he was accustomed to look to her for guidance just as she felt not only entitled, but duty bound, to remonstrate with him when she deemed it necessary.

Perhaps Mary's reluctance to judge people was related to her own psychological instability: not that she doubted her own judgement (when she was well) but that she was keenly aware that others could all too easily misjudge *her*. In any event, the fact that she and Charles remained loyal in their friendships with people who often managed to alienate their other friends (Coleridge and Hazlitt are two typical examples) is testament to their ability to love the person while strongly disliking some of the person's characteristics. As Charles wrote to Coleridge, in defence of the selfish behaviour of Charles and Mary's brother John: 'But you, a necessarian, can respect a difference of mind, & love what is *amiable* in a character not perfect.'[25]

There was of course much in Coleridge himself that was amiable in a character far from perfect and this protracted visit probably did much to cement the friendship between him and Mary, as Coleridge remained with her at Pentonville busy with his translations of Schiller during the day (wearing an odd dressing-gown which made him look, Charles opined, 'like a conjuror'), while Charles was at the East India House.[26] Coleridge had always encouraged Charles to write and now Charles reported to Manning, 'He ferrets me day and night to *do something*,' having 'lugg'd me to the brink of engaging to a Newspaper' and suggesting an imitation of Robert Burton.[27] However, typically, Coleridge left 'on a visit to his God, Wordsworth' before making the necessary introduction.[28] Following Coleridge's departure 'a tribe of authoresses' who admired him continued to call at Pentonville 'and, in defect of you, hive and cluster upon us'. Charles came home from work one evening to find one of these authoresses closeted with Mary: 'I just came in time enough, I believe, luckily to prevent them exchanging vows of undying friendship.' Nevertheless Mary and Charles became temporarily sucked in by a largely female coterie of Coleridge's London admirers.

Pressured into accepting an invitation from the writer Elizabeth Benger, Charles and Mary found themselves feeling disappointing substitutes for the man himself, as a bemused Charles described to Coleridge:

Her lodgings are up two pairs of stairs in East Street. Tea and coffee, and macaroons – a kind of cake I much love. We sat down. Presently Miss Benje broke the silence, by declaring herself of a quite different opinion from D'Israeli, who supposes the differences of human intellect to be the mere effect of organization. She begged to know my opinion. I attempted to carry it off with a pun upon organ; but that went off very flat. She immediately conceived a very low opinion of my metaphysics; and, turning round to Mary, put some question to her in French, – possibly having heard that neither Mary nor I understood French.

Benger proceeded to assert Saxon the purest dialect in Germany before moving to the subject of poetry, to Charles's relief, where he felt he 'might now put in a word to some advantage, seeing that it was my own trade in a manner'.

But I was stopped by a round assertion, that no good poetry had appeared since Dr. Johnson's time. It seems the Doctor has suppressed many hopeful geniuses that way by the severity of his critical strictures in his 'Lives of the Poets'. I have ventured to question the fact, and was beginning to appeal to *names*, but I was assured 'it was certainly the case.' Then we discussed Miss More's book on education, which I had never read.

Further discussions followed on the use of mixed metaphors, whether Pope was a poet, and the relative merits of the ten translations of 'Pizarro' – Mary declining the kind offer of the loan of examples for comparison. The Lambs survived more macaroons before beating a retreat, but not before their hostess had extracted a promise to return the following week 'and meet the Miss Porters, who, it seems, have heard much of Mr. Coleridge, and wish to meet *us*, because we are *his* friends'. Charles assured Coleridge he was already preparing himself: 'I read all the reviews and magazines of the past month against the dreadful meeting, and I hope by these means to cut a tolerable second-rate figure.'[29] (Elizabeth Benger was, incidentally, of 'the cursed Barbauld Crew', which included Anna Letitia Barbauld and Elizabeth Inchbald – whom Charles called the two bald women – champions of Billy and his infamous Horse.)

By early May 1800 Charles and Mary's elderly maid, Hetty, had fallen seriously ill. Mary devoted herself to the old lady's care, nursing her day and night, but after a week Hetty died. The death of someone close to her was always to have a particularly profound effect on Mary, recalling as it did the awful circumstances of the death of her mother. The loss of Hetty, added to Mary's fatigue, sent her over the precipice. Within two days of the death she was so dangerously violent that Charles was obliged to have her confined. Her relapse shook Charles to the very core. The night before Hetty's funeral, alone in the house except for her corpse and with no one but the cat for company, Charles wrote miserably to Coleridge:

My heart is quite sunk, and I dont know where to look for relief –. Mary will get better again, but her constantly being liable to such relapses is dreadful, – nor is it the least of our Evils, that her case & all our story is so well known around us. We are in a manner *marked*.

Unable to sleep properly away from home and unable 'to endure the change and the stillness' in his own house, Charles felt utterly inconsolable. 'I am completely shipwreck'd,' he told Coleridge. The choice of word is telling, for Charles considered himself not only isolated and without resources, but trapped. He made the awful admission to Coleridge: 'I almost wish that Mary were dead.'[30]

Charles tried to reconcile himself to the silent house, but after a week gave up the lease and moved in with his old schoolmate Jem White while he looked for new lodgings. Although he still felt at times 'my daily & hourly prop has fallen from me.. I totter and stagger with weakness, for nobody can supply her place to me . . .',[31] he was cheered by the offer of John Mathew Gutch, another old school-friend, to be his landlord, leasing him a set of rooms at 27 Southampton Buildings, Chancery Lane. (The arrangement was particularly helpful to the Lambs as Gutch was well acquainted with the history of Mary's condition.) The anonymity inner-city life afforded had a strong appeal for Charles, as he told Manning:

It is a great object to me to live in town, where we shall be much more *private*; and to quit a house & a neighbourhood where poor Mary's disorder, so frequently recurring, has made us a sort of marked people.. We can be no where private except in the midst of London.[32]

Landlords' and neighbours' understandable sensitivity to Mary's condition was a recurring problem for the Lambs; between 1799 and 1823 they moved house eight times.

Charles's depression peaked on the last day of May ('I never in my life have been more wretched than I was all day yesterday') and on 1 June he took himself to Widford for a few days of solitary recuperation.[33] Mary was yet 'very bad' and he was unable to see her before going into the country, but on his return to London, himself feeling much better, he was delighted to find his sister 'perfectly recover'd' and ready to come home. 'So soon hath this terrifying tempest passed over,' Charles reflected with some relief.[34] Both Charles and Mary must have harboured the hope that the new life they had built together might cure Mary of her malady. However, the relapse strongly suggested that she might never expect to be free of it. As it happened, Mary was about to embark on the longest period of uninterrupted health she was ever to enjoy, extending from June 1800 to March 1803; however, thereafter her psychosis was to seize her almost every year for the rest of her life and the bouts of madness to extend in length. Charles and Mary were to learn to live with madness as a kind of third partner in their lives, and to be alert to the early signs of its reawakening. As well as being emotionally prepared for recurrences of Mary's psychosis, there were practical preparations; Charles and Mary bought a straitjacket which became their perpetual companion.

The idea that the Lambs were 'in a manner *marked*' no doubt increased their co-dependence: while their closest friends knew the whole sad story, other friends were aware of Mary's illness but did not know about the murder. Although madness was at this time viewed with some sympathy, it was nonetheless frightening and some people (including her older brother) were clearly frightened of Mary. Yet it is clear that when Mary was well, no aspect of her behaviour or demeanour betrayed her. Thomas Noon Talfourd, Charles's first biographer, became a close friend of the couple in later life and left this important observation:

Miss Lamb would have been remarkable for the sweetness of her disposition, the clearness of her understanding, and the gentle wisdom of all her acts and words, even if these qualities had not been presented in marvellous contrast with the distraction under which she suffered for weeks, latterly for months, in every year. There was no tinge of insanity discernible in her manner to the most observant eye; not even in those distressful periods when the premonitory symptoms had apprised her of its approach, and she was making preparations for seclusion.

In all its essential sweetness, her character was like her brother's; while, by a temper more placid, a spirit of enjoyment more serene, she was enabled to guide, to counsel, to cheer him; and to protect him on the verge of the mysterious calamity, from the depths of which she rose so often unruffled to his side. To a friend in any difficulty she was the most comfortable of advisers, the wisest of consolers. Hazlitt used to say, that he never met with a woman who could reason, and had met with only one thoroughly reasonable – the sole exception being Mary Lamb.[35]

Although both Talfourd and Hazlitt do not enter the Lambs' story for some years yet, when compared with other accounts this description emerges as a fair representation of Mary's character throughout her life: kind, calm, intelligent and wise. Thomas Moore, Henry Crabb Robinson and Walter Savage Landor respectively considered Mary 'a woman of singular good sense', 'one of the most amiable and admirable of women' and 'the finest genius that ever descended on the heart of women'.[36] Most never knew of, let alone witnessed, the other Mary – a nightmarish reversal of all these qualities. The wild, violent, irrational, incapable, mad Mary was utterly undetectable in her normal state.

As Charles freely admitted, he had little interest in current affairs in the abstract or general sense, and was more likely to become exercised over specific issues rather than subscribe to an over-arching political philosophy; nonetheless he was perceived as a 'Jacobin'. His writing had appeared in print alongside Coleridge's and Lloyd's and *Blank Verse* had been dedicated to Southey: in a nest of known radicals, Charles was guilty by association – hence his inclusion in Gillray's cartoon for the *Anti-Jacobin*. While Charles considered himself a necessarian this was a philosophical, rather than a political, system.

Jacobinism had originally referred to the political faction who had controlled the French Revolution from 1792 to 1794, and who had formulated the 'Declaration of the Rights of Man and of the Citizen' in 1793. The Declaration asserted equality and freedom for all (social rank to be defined not by birth but by public service); property rights; the supremacy of the law; the law to be democratically formulated and its servants to be accountable; freedom of speech and religious belief; and just and proportional taxation. Rational and attractive, in England Jacobinism appealed to many of the Lambs' circle, while back in France it had become linked with extremism and associated with 'the Terror'. Napoleon's devastating progress through Europe and then Egypt also fanned the flames of anti-Jacobinism in Britain.

Charles Lamb therefore found himself tarred with the same brush as his more radical friends; on seeing the Gillray cartoon Southey wrote to a friend, 'I know not what poor Lamb has done to be croaking there.'[37] Similarly, Lloyd in his 'Letter to the Anti-Jacobin Reviewers' defended Charles against 'infamy' and the charge of being a 'Democrat', adding, 'Whenever he has thrown his ideas together, it has been from the irresistible impulse of the moment, never from any intention to propagate a system, much less any of "folly and wickedness".'

★

When Charles had embarked on *John Woodvil* it was less the result of a strong desire to write for the stage than the result of a strong desire to earn some extra money. Theatre-writing could be lucrative, but Charles had already experienced the vagaries of the profession when he enquired of his script a year after it had been submitted to Kemble and was informed it had been lost. He sent another copy, but was 'in weekly expectation of the TOLLING BELL & death warrant'.[38] The play was – eventually – rejected. As it became plain that Mary's illness and the costs it incurred were likely to become a permanent feature of their life together, Charles looked about him for various means by which he could augment his modest salary from the East India Company. By June 1801, through his 'radical' friends, he found himself attached to the ailing Jacobin *Albion*. The *Albion* was based in a recently vacated museum, the grim, cramped quarters of which yet seemed redolent of 'the occupation of dead monsters'. The proprietor and editor, John Fenwick, had spent his last guinea (and, Charles maintained, the last guineas of several of his friends) buying the title (a 'hopeless concern') and now 'resolutely determined upon pulling down the Government in the first instance, and making both our fortunes by way of corollary . . . Our occupation was now to write treason.' Once again, it was more by luck than judgement that Charles found himself 'radicalized':

Recollections of feelings – which were all that now remained from our first boyish heats kindled by the French Revolution, when if we were misled, we erred in the company of some, who are accounted very good men now – rather than any tendency at this time to Republican doctrines – assisted us in assuming a style of writing, while the paper lasted, consonant in no very under tone to the right earnest fanaticism of F[enwick].[39]

'There were times, indeed, when we sighed for . . . more gentleman-like occupation,' Charles acknowledged, but he worked hard at giving Fenwick what he wanted.

If Charles was an able student, duly producing his daily quota of political intrigue, insinuation and character assassination, he proved in the end rather too adept. It was his pen that produced the piece which finally got the *Albion* closed down. (In attacking James Mackintosh, an opponent of Godwin's, Charles had suggested that having behaved like Judas, he should now emulate his prototype in hanging himself: 'This thou may do at last; yet much I doubt,/If thou hast any Bowels to gush out!'[40])

'The Albion is dead, dead as nail in door,' he wrote to Manning at the end of August, 'and my revenues have died with it.' Although he had needed the money, Charles was not a little ashamed of having stooped so low for the *Albion*, as he admitted to Manning: 'to confess the truth, I had arrived to an abominable pitch, I spared neither age nor sex, when my cue was given me.'[41] While some of his puns especially were truly awful, and some of his imagery distasteful if striking (such as his suggestion that the government's spin-doctors were so adept at twisting the truth that should they swallow a nail, they would excrete a corkscrew), he also wrote a deal of impassioned but rational argument, such as his piece 'What Is Jacobinism?' in which he castigated the knee-jerk habit of government supporters of labelling all opposition, of all kinds, as 'Jacobinism' rather like a parrot that knows only one word which it utters indiscriminately. 'These men have set up an universal *idol*, or *idea*, under that name, to which they find it convenient to refer *all evil* . . .' When faced with any argument which disturbed their own views, 'these men had neither the mind to *grasp*, nor the soul to *embrace* [these ideas]; their only alternative was to *depreciate*'.[42] For all Charles's high-mindedness expressed here, depreciation was very much the *Albion's* currency.

Charles had been in the *Albion's* employ for perhaps only three months, during June, July and August 1801, when he hastened its demise. As soon as it sank, due to the influence of his friend Dyer he got himself attached to the *Morning Chronicle*, the most powerful Whig daily, edited by the Scot James Perry. However, the extremity of the alteration was too great; three-quarters of what he submitted was rejected by Perry and Charles reflected that 'I soon found that it was a different thing writing for the Lordly Editor of a Great Whig Paper to what it was scribbling for the poor Albion.'[43] His stint with the *Chronicle* lasted only two weeks, from early to mid-September 1801, at which point Charles considered abandoning journalism altogether.

Aware of his friend's financial situation, Coleridge had eventually got round to recommending Charles to Daniel Stuart of the *Morning Post*, for whom Coleridge had been supplying political pieces, on and off, since Stuart had taken over the editorship in 1795. Charles was shortly summoned to its handsome offices, where, in contrast to the dark 'den' occupied by the *Albion*, silver inkwells sat on polished rosewood desks. Charles was not to write about current affairs *per se*; despite his facility at 'depreciation' he was not a political animal. Stuart noted (as Charles himself had confessed to Manning): 'Of politics he knew nothing; they were out of his line of reading, and thought.'[44] Neither was he to write the literary imitations he had favoured since the days when he had assisted White in his *Original Letters &c. of Sir John Falstaff and His Friends* (1796) – Stuart rejected his first offering (the piece of *homage* to Burton suggested by Coleridge). Charles's role in Stuart's eyes lay at the lighter end of the journalistic spectrum, where he was to come up with a quantity of witty paragraphs and verse lampooning the latest ladies' fashions, or mercilessly mocking the celebrities of the day at the then handsome price of sixpence a joke. His friend John Rickman observed: 'I think [the *Post*] will have an interest in paying him very handsomely. When daily papers run against one another in peace, in times of no intelligence, where can such an aid be found as Lamb? I have heard wit from him in an evening to feed a paper for a week.'[45] This kind of writing was hard work, but did have its perks. As Coleridge expressed it, during his stint at the *Morning Post*:

We Newspaper scribes are truly Galley-Slaves ... Yet it is not unflattering to a man's Vanity to reflect that what he writes at 12 at night will before 12 hours is over have perhaps 5 or 6000 Readers! To trace a happy phrase, good image, or new argument running thro' the Town, & sliding into all the papers! Few Wine merchants can boast of creating more sensation ...[46]

While initially it must have seemed like easy money to a young man as clever and as naturally inclined to humour and wordplay as Charles, jesting to order soon revealed itself to be a serious business, as full of stress and tedium as the most earnest literary endeavour. 'Somebody has said,' he later wrote, 'that to swallow six cross-buns daily consecutively for a fortnight would surfeit the stoutest digestion. But to have to furnish as many jokes daily, and that not for a fortnight, but for a long twelvemonth, as we were constrained to do, was a little harder execution.'[47] Furthermore, Charles did not have all day to dream up his witticisms. He was at work at the East India House during the day and could then have spent his evenings composing piquant passages. However, he did not; 'as our evening hours, at that time of life, had generally to do with any thing rather than business'. Writing for newspapers happily involved heavy drinking with newspapermen and he was often rolling into bed after midnight and getting up at 5a.m. in order to attempt to drag finely honed wit out of a hangover.

'O those headaches at dawn of day,' he recalled, 'to be necessitated to rouse ourselves at the detestable rap of an old hag of a domestic, who seemed to take a diabolical pleasure in her announcement that it was "time to rise;" and whose chappy knuckles we have often yearned to amputate, and string them up at our chamber door, to be a terror to all such unseasonable rest-breakers in future . . .' Coming up with half a dozen jokes 'with malice prepended' before the day's proper work began soon became exquisite torture. He hoped, however, to gain sufficient confidence from Stuart to be let loose on theatrical reviews. The first of these appeared in January 1802. The following month his best essay to date (and the earliest herald in print of the eventual arrival of 'Elia') appeared: 'The Londoner'.

What could or should have been the beginning of Charles's writing career in earnest, however, came to nothing. Charles admitted that he could not cope with writing theatre reviews the same night as the performance, as Stuart preferred ('I tried it once, & found myself non compos. I ca'nt *do* a thing against time'), and Stuart did not want more in the same vein as 'The Londoner'. Charles was extremely frustrated, as he wrote to Rickman: 'My Editor uniformly rejects all that I do considerable in length . . . my poor paragraphs do only get in, when there are none of any body else's. Most of them are rejected; all, almost, that are *personal*, where my forte lies.'[48] Not above one in five of Charles's submissions got into the *Post*, an even lower ratio than on the *Chronicle*, and apart from anything Charles found the whole process degrading. No amount of money could compensate for 'the drudgery of going every day to an Editor with my scraps, like a Pedlar, for him to pick out & tumble about my ribbands & posies, and to wait in his lobby &c.'[49] After Charles's death Stuart defended his rejection of Lamb's early attempts, explaining that 'his drollery was vapid, when given in short paragraphs for a newspaper'.[50] This may well have been true, but in any case Charles was not temperamentally suited to what he called 'task work', as he told Godwin, he was 'an author by fits'; 'Any work which I take upon myself as an engagement, will act upon me to torment.'[51]

Bearing in mind the difficulties Charles imposed on himself by burning the candle at both ends, it is reasonable to ask how serious he was about his journalism. Was he, as one editor claimed, simply lazy? Examples from later in his life demonstrate that he was indeed a great procrastinator, and that he often approached his work in a negative frame of mind. We are aware of this primarily through Mary's observations. 'Charles often plans but never begins,' she complained to Dorothy Wordsworth in 1804, and when she had brought him in to collaborate on *Tales from Shakespeare* she told Sarah Stoddart how Charles was 'groaning all the while & saying he can make nothing of it, which he always says till he has finished . . .'[52] He claimed never to work well under pressure, and his letters show deadlines pressing down on him like a physical weight. (In retrospect, it seems possible that the cocktail of pressures which led him to the madhouse in the winter of 1795/6 may have been exacerbated by the stresses of office work to which he was not then accustomed. Even much later in life during periods of hectic business at the East India House he would suffer nightmares, imagining he had made critical mathematical errors.)

It is also worth tackling head-on Stuart's charge that Charles's humour was 'vapid' – at least in the form of pithy paragraphs. Although it is difficult to judge the contemporary effectiveness of wit at the distance of two centuries, some of his verbal puns were found at the time to be excruciating (as Keats discovered) whereas others were highly successful. Charles himself held that the worst puns were the best ('so exquisitely good, and so deplorably bad, at the same time'). His own favourite example was one of Jonathan Swift's: An Oxford scholar meets a porter who is carrying a hare through the streets. The scholar asks the porter: 'Prithee, friend, is that thy own hare, or a wig?' Charles commented that 'There is no excusing this, and no resisting it.'[53] The best jokes, he believed, were those which bore the least analysis. A joke in print is, of course, a subtly different matter from a verbally delivered pun, but it is difficult to find any of Charles's which would raise a smile today. To give but one example from his *Albion* days, it seems unlikely that a pun on the name Vansittart being derived from 'Fancy a tart' could ever have raised more than a groan, and it can only be guessed that many of these were indeed the desperate products of early morning hangovers.

It is likely that there were things which Charles alone (with the possible exception of Mary) found funny, but it is important to recognize that his best jokes were made spontaneously, whether verbally in company or committed to paper. The social pressure to be amusing (probably exacerbated by his essential shyness) and the pressure of the editor's deadline equally deadened his humorous faculty. 'My Spirits absolutely require freedom & leisure,' he acknowledged.[54] In addition to this, the percentage of the work he did which was accepted – at the *Post* and the *Chronicle* at least – was vastly outweighed by the quantity he produced which never saw the light of day and the effort exerted in its production. While Charles took a natural pride in seeing his work in print, the adventure was ultimately demoralizing.

Charles's humour required more space to develop than Stuart's pithy paragraphs allowed. In his Elia essay on 'Valentine's

Day', for example, he would have the leisure to muse on the design of Valentine cards and question why the particular organ of the heart – 'that little three-cornered exponent of all our hopes and fears' – had been fixed on as the symbol of love, and how it would have been if another 'anatomical seat' had been chosen, leading lovers to declare: 'Madam, my *liver* and fortune are entirely at your disposal' or to ask the delicate question, 'Amanda, have you a *midriff* to bestow?' Although, as here, he was adept at exposing the absurd in the everyday, some of his best humour has an element of cruelty in it, such as his meditation on the popular fallacy 'That handsome is as handsome does'. 'Those who use this proverb can never have seen Mrs Conrady,' he begins.

The soul, if we may believe Plotinus, is a ray from the celestial beauty. As she partakes more or less of this heavenly light, she informs, with corresponding characters, the fleshly tenement which she chooses, and frames to herself a suitable mansion.

All which only proves that the soul of Mrs Conrady, in her pre-existent state, was no great judge of architecture.

To the same effect, in a Hymn in honour of Beauty, divine Spenser, *platonizing*, sings:-

> '– – Every spirit as it is more pure,
> And hath in it the more of heavenly light,
> So it the fairer body doth procure
> To habit in, and it more fairly dight
> With cheerful grace and amiable sight.
> For of the soul the body form doth take:
> For soul is form, and doth the body make.'

But Spenser, it is clear, never saw Mrs Conrady.

These poets, we find, are no safe guards in philosophy; for here, in his very next stanza but one, is a saving clause, which throws us all out again, and leaves us as much to seek as ever:-

> 'Yet oft it falls, that many a gentle mind
> Dwells in deformed tabernacle drown'd,
> Either by chance, against the course of kind,
> Or through unaptness in the substance found,
> Which it assumed of some stubborn ground,
> That will not yield into her form's direction,
> But is perform'd with some foul imperfection.'

From which it would follow, that Spenser had seen somebody like Mrs Conrady.

And so he goes on, and on, and on, on poor Mrs Conrady's astonishing, unparalleled, 'symmetrical' ugliness while the reader smiles and is ashamed of smiling, but begins positively to wish to behold this spectacle, which is surely one of the wonders of the world: 'The first time you are indulged with a sight of her face, is an era in your existence ever after. You are glad to have seen it – like Stonehenge.' Charles's writing – whether humorous or serious – was at its most successful when it was about the length of a long letter or a short essay. This form gave him the time to unfold and develop his thoughts without losing the overall picture; newspaper paragraphs were always to be unsatisfying both to him and his editors.

The role played by Charles's drinking in the demise of his youthful journalistic career cannot, however, be ignored. Being clever and witty he often downplayed the subject, such as when Rickman had advised in a letter that Mary should take 'certain mixed Liquors'. Charles feigned having misunderstood this advice, thinking it meant for him, and complained he almost died in his enthusiastic attempt to carry out Rickman's instructions. 'I still keep my attachment to Brandy & Tobacco,' he wrote to his friend, adding, 'I certainly get more of a Christian than ever, for no man *repents* more than I do.'[55] His artful charm has, on the whole, successfully disarmed many critics from seriously considering Charles as a problem drinker. However, while many readers may ruefully recognize the equivalent of the rousing 'detestable rap of an old hag of a domestic' announcing the inevitable – always premature – manoeuvring of the hungover cranium from horizontal to vertical, few could synthesize the transformation from the night before to the morning after so readily as Charles had in *John Woodvil*:

> A weight of wine lies heavy on my head,
> The unconcocted follies of last night.
> Now all those jovial fancies, and bright hopes,
> Children of wine, go off like dreams.
> This sick vertigo here
> Preacheth of intemperance, no sermon better.

Crushing hangovers were not the only effect of Charles's drinking. Socially, he could become a handful. August 1801 provides an example of what was to become increasingly characteristic behaviour of Charles. A trip to Richmond on the river with friends began with Charles in high spirits and ended with him drunk and threatening to upset the boat and everyone in it by his 'bodily movements that were quite unsuited to so unsteady a conveyance in the watery element', as one po-faced witness reported.[56] His extremely alarmed companions restrained him with great difficulty, but were unable similarly to restrain his tongue, which he used to descant with what some considered unbecoming levity on the subject of religion. Admittedly, this occurred at a time of great stress for Charles (between the *Albion* and the *Chronicle* engagements) and he steadfastly maintained 'that a very little liquor will cause a considerable alteration in me'; however, subsequent evidence confirms that Charles was quite capable of drinking rather more than 'very little', although in a man of his slight build this may have produced more exaggerated effects than in other men. (He had only a few months earlier considered giving up alcohol for his health's sake.[57]) Either way, he got drunk and unmanageable and wrote a letter of apology to the one of his companions, Walter Wilson, who was most offended by his conversation, in which Charles explained that he was in no sense 'an inveterate enemy to all religion'.

I have had a time of seriousness, and I have known the importance and reality of a religious belief. Latterly, I acknowledge, much of my seriousness has gone off, whether from new company or some other new associations; but I still retain at bottom a conviction of the truth, and a certainty of the usefulness of religion.[58]

Neither Charles nor Mary were now regular churchgoers and when in need of solace during periods of Mary's illness Charles was more inclined to turn to the bottle than to God than he had been formerly. Towards the end of his period on the *Post* he wrote to a friend, 'The Lungs of Stentor could not sustain the Life I have led.'[59] A lifestyle combining heavy drinking and two jobs was not destined to be a happy one. A sacrifice would have to be made.

'I think I shall never engage to do task work any more,' Charles told Rickman in February 1802, 'for I am SICK.'[60] For both the Lambs the boundary between mental and physical distress was often blurred to the point of being indistinguishable. Moreover, the depression of one sibling often spread to the other, destabilizing the household. Charles simply could not afford to make himself ill. He therefore withdrew from newspaper writing, not without regret but with good reason. However, it is friction that creates pearls, and this abortive foray into journalism had at least produced the significant piece 'The Londoner'.

Many of the sentiments expressed in 'The Londoner' had appeared in letters from Charles to Manning and Wordsworth a year and more previous to its composition. Some close friend, if not more than one, knowing of Charles and Mary's financial difficulties, must have seen the potential in Charles's personal letters to appeal to a wider audience and suggested he write in the same, idiosyncratic, vein for publication. (This was, after all, a period in which entertaining letters were often read aloud, or copied to other correspondents, and had quite a different status to private correspondence today – possibly nearer to particularly amusing e-mails, which are now repeatedly forwarded, often in the process losing any sign of their origination.)

Charles had written to Manning in November 1800, in relation to his attitude towards his poet friends – as he saw it, smitten with rural scenes in a way which he could respect but not share:

For my part, with reverence to my friends northward, I must confess that I am not romance-bit about *Nature*. The earth, and sea, and sky (when all is said) is but as a house to dwell in . . . Just as important to me (in a sense) is all the furniture of my world. Eye-pampering but satisfys no heart. Streets, streets, streets, markets, theatres, churches, Covent Gardens, Shops sparkling with pretty faces of industrious milliners, neat sempstresses, Ladies cheapening, Gentlemen behind counters lying, Authors in the street with spectacles . . . Lamps lit at night, Pastry cook and Silver smith shops, Beautiful Quakers of Pentonville, noise of coaches, drousy cry of mechanic watchmen at night, with Bucks reeling home drunk if you happen to wake at midnight, cries of fire & stop thief, Inns of court (with their learned air and halls and Butteries just like Cambridge colleges), old Book stalls, Jeremy Taylors, Burtons on melancholy, and Religio Medici's on every stall −. These are thy Pleasures O London with-the-many-sins − O City abounding in whores − for these may Keswick and her Giant Brood go hang.[61]

This competitiveness, or at least defensiveness, against the 'Mountaineers' (led by Coleridge and Wordsworth) is again detected in a letter written the following January, to William Wordsworth:

Separate from the pleasure of your company, I dont mu[ch] care if I never see a mountain in my life. − I have passed all my days in London, until I have formed as many and intense local attachments, as any of you MOUNTAINEERS can have done with dead nature . . . I have no passion (or have had none since I was in love, and then it was the spurious engendering of poetry & books) to groves and vallies . . . I do not envy you. I should pity you, did I not know, that the Mind will make friends of any thing . . . So FADING upon me from disuse, have been the Beauties of Nature, as they have been confinedly called; so ever fresh & green and warm are all the inventions of men and assemblies of men in this great city −.[62]

And then again to Manning in February:

LONDON, whose dirtiest drab-frequented alley, and her lowest bowing Tradesman, I would not exchange for Skiddaw, Helvellyin, James, Walter, and the Parson in the bargain −. O! her Lamps of a night! Her rich goldsmiths, print shops, toy shops, mercers, hard-waremen, pastry cooks! − St. Paul's ch. yard, the Strand! Exeter Change! − Charing Cross, with the man *upon* a black horse! − These are thy Gods O London − . . . All the streets and pavements are pure gold, I warrant you. − At least I know an Alchymy that turns her mud into that metal − a mind that loves to be at home in Crowds −[63]

Charles's vehemence on this subject is telling: this is not merely London pride, but a critical reaction to a central tenet of the Romantic project. Wordsworth's Preface to the collection of his and Coleridge's poetry entitled *Lyrical Ballads* is widely regarded as 'probably the most important single document in English criticism'[64] and Charles's views are clearly a response to some of the ideas in what is arguably the Romantic manifesto.

There is much in the Preface with which Charles would have agreed. Wordsworth's much-quoted statement that 'all good poetry is the spontaneous overflow of powerful feelings', for example, is vindicated in Charles's own best work. However, Charles clearly found provoking Wordsworth's explanation of the subject-matter of the poems:

Low and rustic life was generally chosen, because in that condition the essential passions of the heart find a better soil in which they can attain their maturity, are under less restraint, and speak a plainer and more emphatic language; because in that condition of life our elementary feelings co-exist in state of greater simplicity, and consequently may be more accurately contemplated and more forcibly communicated; because the manners of rural life germinate from those elementary feelings, and from the necessary character of rural occupations are more easily comprehended, and are more durable; and lastly, because in that condition the passions of men are incorporated with the beautiful and permanent forms of nature.[65]

Wordsworth goes on to assert that 'the increasing accumulation of men in cities' and 'the uniformity of their occupations' conspire 'to blunt the discriminating powers of the mind and, unfitting it for all voluntary exertion, to reduce it to a state of almost savage torpor'. Ultimately, for Wordsworth (and, implicitly, Coleridge) 'Poetry is the image of man and nature.'[66]

It is quite possible to envisage that Charles – and Mary, who had the same passionate involvement with London – felt that what was becoming the Romantic movement, which he had had a not insignificant hand in co-creating, was, in exiling itself to countryside interests, monopolizing its values to its own exclusive rurally focused ends. A Londoner born and bred, Charles could participate in every emotion his Mountaineer friends evoked, but perceiving, as he did, every colour of human passion and emotion occurring all around him, he could not sanctify and elevate rural scenes simply because they were full of sheep and not people. His devaluation of the rural aesthetic by the use of the term 'eye-pampering' is crucially significant: the worth of human experience for the Lambs ultimately lived in people, and the sounds and shapes *they* made. 'Fresh & green and warm' humanity blasts 'dead nature' out of the water every time for Charles; it is the portrait, not the landscape, that feeds his soul; the mortal rather than the eternal. For both Charles and Mary, poetry was the image of *human* nature. (Coleridge had recognized this in the closing lines of 'This Lime-Tree Bower My Prison', when he addressed 'my gentle-hearted Charles, to whom/No sound is dissonant which tells of Life.')

When compared with the letters cited above, an extract

from 'The Londoner', published in the *Morning Post* for 1 February 1802, demonstrates how Charles translated his own thoughts and feelings into a formal address to an anonymous reader:

I was born, as you have heard, in a crowd. This has begot in me an entire affection for that way of life, amounting to an almost insurmountable aversion from solitude and rural scenes. This aversion was never interrupted or suspended, except for a few years in the younger part of my life, during a period in which I had set my affections upon a charming young woman. Every man while the passion is upon him, is for a time at least addicted to groves and meadows and purling streams. During this short period of my existence I contracted just familiarity enough with rural objects to understand tolerably well ever after the *poets*, when they declaim in such passionate terms in favor of a country life.

For my own part, now the fit is past, I have no hesitation in declaring, that a mob of happy faces crowding up at the pit door of Drury-lane Theatre, just at the hour of six, gives me ten thousand sincerer pleasures, than I could ever receive from all the flocks of silly sheep that ever whitened the plains of Arcadia or Epsom Downs.

Charles's indifference to the countryside is transformed into the essayist's 'aversion'; poets are gently damned along with the groves and meadows which enrapture them; and while the reader is encouraged to appreciate the writer's point of view, he is not expected to identify with it. We are to look on, amused at the character of the writer himself.

Manning liked the piece 'very much', adding, 'there is a deal of happy fancy in it'. He had reservations, however, about how broad the appeal of such idiosyncratic and apparently slight material might be, stating that 'it is not strong enough to be seen by the generality of readers. Yet if you would write a volume of Essays in the same stile you might be sure of its succeeding.'[67] Manning's advice was prophetic, but it was to be many years before such a volume appeared, and Charles's connection with the *Morning Post* was terminated shortly after the first tantalizing glimpse of 'Elia'. Charles was, for the time being, to abandon the voice he had found in 'The Londoner'. Although he believed that the '*personal*' was 'where my forte lies', this was not a view shared by those in a position to put it to the test of the reading public. He had closed one newspaper down, been sacked from a second and resigned from a third, all in the space of nine months. It was time to try something else.

7. The Critic and the Playwright

I am determined to take what snatches of pleasure we can, between the acts of our distressful drama.

(Charles Lamb to Samuel Taylor Coleridge [28 July 1800])

Charles's first experience of seeing his work performed on stage occurred when he wrote the Epilogue to Godwin's play *Antonio*. Charles and Mary set off in high spirits on the evening of 13 December 1800 to watch the first night from a box (a rare treat).

As the audience took their places, Lamb recalled, Godwin was cheerful and confident, Marshall silent and frightened. The first act passed without a sign from the audience – exactly as he intended, Godwin assured his companions, the dramatic tension was building up. During the second act, however, when Marshall tried to start a round of clapping, nobody followed. Kemble had warned Godwin not to invite too many friends to applaud on the first night for fear that the audience might suspect, but this risk had been exaggerated. The audience at one point expected a display of sword play and when they received instead a philosophical debate on the absurdity of duelling, coughing gradually drowned the actors' words. After that there was uproar and the performance was only completed with difficulty. *Antonio* was remembered as having been coughed off stage at its first and only night.[1]

The newspapers damned the Epilogue along with the play. Over the next few days, at Godwin's request, Charles suggested a number of cuts before Godwin had the play printed. Despite the failure of *Antonio*, Godwin was now hard at work on another play, about which he regularly consulted Charles. (As was the case with poetry, Charles was a much more able critic than creator and provided Godwin with some useful and pertinent advice.) Godwin was now courting, much to Charles and Mary's amusement. As Charles wrote to his friend John Rickman (a convivial neighbour from Southampton Buildings):

The Lady is a Widow with green spectacles & one child, and the Professor [their nickname for Godwin] is grown quite juvenile. He bows when he is spoke to, and smiles without occasion, and wriggles as fantastically as Malvolio, and has more affectation than a canary bird pluming his feathers when he thinks somebody looks at him. He lays down his spectacles, as if in scorn, & takes 'em up again from necessity, and winks that she may'nt see he gets sleepy about eleven oClock. You never saw such a philosophic coxcomb, nor any one play the Romeo so unnaturally.[2]

Charles asterisked the word 'Widow' and noted below: 'a very disgusting woman'.

Charles's opinion of Godwin's fiancée did not improve when she became his wife. He wrote to Manning two months after the wedding (which had taken place in December 1801): 'The Professor's Rib has come out to be a damn'd disagreeable woman, so much as to drive me & some more old CRONIES from his House. If a man will keep SNAKES in his House, he must not wonder if People are shy of coming to see him BECAUSE OF THE SNAKES.'[3] (As it happened, Charles's analogy held particular power for him, because he had been to see an exhibition of deadly snakes in a private house, including 'A LIVE RATTLE SNAKE 10 FEET IN LENGTH, and of the thickness of a big LEG' and had been scared witless when '*this monster*' flew at his hand on the cage. Jumping backwards in alarm he had bumped into another cage, and turned to see that another snake had managed to get its head through a gap in the wire 'not an inch from my back'. Charles was extremely shaken by the event, and suffered nightmares about snakes afterwards.[4]) By September 1802 Charles was describing Godwin's 'pitiful artificial Wife' bluntly as 'that Bitch', and complaining that she continued to alienate Godwin's friends, in particular James Marshall, an 'old steady, unalterable, friend of the Professor' who had found a place in Charles's heart by being 'the man who went to sleep when the Ancient Mariner was reading'.[5]

It is necessary to put Charles's aversion to his friend's wife into context. In 'A Bachelor's Complaint of the Behaviour of Married People' he was to describe the affronts the single man could expect to endure when his friends, as Etherage has it, 'committed matrimony':[6]

. . . if the husband be a man with whom you have lived on a friendly footing before marriage . . . look about you – your tenure is precarious . . . that the good man should have dared to enter into a solemn league of friendship in which they [the wife] were not consulted, though it happened before they knew him, – before they that are now man and wife ever met, – this is intolerable to them. Every long friendship, every old authentic intimacy, must be brought into their office to be new stamped with their currency, as a sovereign Prince calls in the good old money that was coined in some reign before he was born or thought of, to be new marked and minted with the stamp of his authority, before he will let it pass current in the world . . .

Innumerable are the ways which they take to insult and worm you out of their husband's confidence. Laughing at all you say with a kind of wonder, as if you were a queer kind of fellow that said good things, *but an oddity*, is one of the ways; – they have a particular kind of stare for the purpose; – till at last the husband, who used to defer to your judgment . . . begins to suspect whether you are not altogether a humorist, – a fellow well enough to have consorted with in his bachelor days, but not quite so proper to be introduced to ladies.

What Charles calls 'the staring way' is the first of a number of strategies he identifies used by new wives to mortify and alienate their husbands' old cronies in the essay, but while the tone is light, some genuine feeling is unmistakable. However, Charles's antipathy towards the new Mrs Godwin was not merely the resentment of the usurped; she was widely disliked for her moodiness, glibness and insincerity.[7]

Whether Charles and Mary knew it or not, the fact was that Godwin had married Mary Jane Clairmont because she was pregnant by him. Charles was mistaken in believing she was a widow with one child; she had two, both by different fathers, neither of whom was ever her husband. Ten years younger than Godwin, her relationship with him was initially kept a secret; James Marshall, the friend Charles mentioned as later ejected from Godwin's fireside by the second Mrs Godwin, was one of only a handful of close friends who met her in the early days of the relationship; he was also the only witness present at their wedding.

Whatever Mary Jane's faults, she had much to contend with. Her predecessor and namesake Mary Wollstonecraft watched over her from a picture-frame which dominated the parlour and no one, including Godwin, could resist comparing the two women. She had two step-children, as well as her own two (plus one thanks to Godwin) and money worries to manage. She was also a translator and writer and, like Mary Lamb, was never to see her name on the title page of any of her works. However, she was to have an important role in the Lambs' literary lives: the difficult woman whom Charles and Mary privately termed 'Bad Baby' was to be responsible for bringing the reading public their most successful and enduring work.

The extent to which friends of Charles, like Godwin, invited his advice and comments on their work is sometimes surprising. (Coleridge, for example, left the editing and organization of one of his manuscripts for publication entirely in Charles's hands.) Although his remarks uniformly mingle praise with criticism, the candour with which he habitually addressed them evidently occasionally stung. An interesting example of this originated in a piece of criticism to Wordsworth. Having thanked him for sending the second volume of *Lyrical Ballads*, Charles offered a suggestion regarding the poem 'The Old Cumberland Beggar, A Description':

An intelligent reader finds a sort of insult in being told, I will teach you how to think upon this subject. The fault, if I am right, is in a ten thousandth worse degree to be found in STERNE and many many novelists & modern poets, who continually put a sign post up to shew you WHERE YOU ARE TO FEEL. They set out with assuming their readers to be stupid. Very different from Robinson Crusoe, the Vicar of Wakefie[l]d, Roderick Random, and other beautiful bare narratives. – There is implied an unwritten compact between Author and reader; I will tell you a story, and I suppose you will understand it.[8]

In the same letter Charles tactlessly remarks that the standard of the poems in the second volume is not up to the standard of those in the first: 'I do not FEEL any one poem in it so forcibly as the Ancient Marinere, the Mad mother, and the Lines at Tintern Abbey in the FIRST.' Charles also utterly disagreed with Wordsworth's criticisms of Coleridge's 'The Ancient Mariner': 'I was never so affected by any human Tale. After first reading it, I was totally possessed with it for many days.' Finally, Charles expressed regret that Wordsworth's lengthy and didactic preface had not been published separately from the poems. Having been used to indulging in such critical freedoms, Charles was surprised to receive 'a long letter of four sweating pages' from Wordsworth, followed by 'four long pages, equally sweaty, and more tedious' from Coleridge. Wordsworth wrote unblushingly of his own genius and regretted Charles's 'range of SENSIBILITY' was so limited; Coleridge agreed that Charles's inability to appreciate Wordsworth's writing was a fault in him, not the work. 'What am I to do with such people?' an exasperated Charles wrote to Manning.

Writing to *you* I [must] may say, that the 2d vol. has no such pieces as the 3 I enumerated. − It is full of original thinking and an observing mind, but it does not often make you laugh or cry. − It too artfully aims at simplicity of expression. And you sometimes doubt if simplicity be not a cover for Poverty.[9]

It is a measure of the two men's closeness that Charles expressed such a sacrilegious doubt to Manning (who himself found the book 'utterly absurd from one end to the other'[10]). Nevertheless, the good opinion of Coleridge and Wordsworth was important to Charles and schoolboy-like he confessed to Manning: 'my ARSE *tickles red* from the northern castigation'.[11]

Ironically, since moving into town where they had sought anonymity, the Lambs' circle of acquaintances had rapidly expanded and they were either entertaining at home, or out themselves most evenings, quite apart from the many occasions when friends would drop in to see them casually. By the end of February 1801 Charles was complaining to Manning that their lodgings resembled 'a minister's levee' and he was beginning to long for space and time to himself. What was it about Charles and Mary Lamb that made them so popular? Neither of them was in any sense a glamorous figure. According to his friend P. G. Patmore, Charles could easily have been mistaken as 'a half-starved country curate, who has wandered up to the metropolis on a week's leave of absence'. He always dressed in black, though this was in fact a courtesy term for the colour of his suit, as 'he always contrived that it should exist in a condition of rusty brown'.[12] Other witnesses testify that his clothes 'indicated much wear', while an actor's wife archly observed that 'no man certainly was ever less beholden to his tailor'.[13] All accounts agree that his head seemed too big for his body, and his body, although slight, was yet too big for his legs, which were 'almost immaterial' – an impression not flattered by his black breeches and stockings.[14] The 'poor little spindles' ended in 'impossible feet, encased in large shoes, which placed flatly on the ground advanced slowly in the manner of a web-footed creature'. This distinctive walk was elsewhere described as 'a gait advancing with a motion from side to side, between involuntary consciousness and attempted ease'. Later in life Charles walked with 'a broken, uncertain step, as if he almost forgot to put one leg before the other'.[15] Many descriptions allude to a 'Jewish' character to Charles's features,

even to the sallow and uniform complexion, and the black and crisp hair standing off loosely from the head, as if every single hair were independent of the rest. The nose, too, was large and slightly hooked, and the chin rounded and elevated to correspond. There was altogether a *Rabbinical* look about Lamb's head which was at once striking and impressive.[16]

It is telling that there is no description of Charles's face which does not link it inextricably with his personality. Patmore recalled: 'Above all, there was a pervading sweetness and gentleness which went straight to the heart of every one who looked on it'; Mary Cowden Clarke agreed 'he had a smile of singular sweetness and beauty', while Thomas Allsop declared of his smile: 'There is nothing like it on earth . . . this *sunshine of the face.*'[17]

Like Charles, Mary dressed with Quaker-like simplicity, almost invariably in a plain black gown. There are far fewer descriptions of her, but Mary Cowden Clarke knew her well:

Miss Lamb bore a strong personal resemblance to her brother; being in stature under middle height, possessing well-cut features, and a countenance of singular sweetness, with intelligence. Her brown eyes were soft, yet penetrating; her nose and mouth very shapely; while the general expression was mildness itself. She had a speaking voice, gentle and persuasive; and her smile was her brother's own – winning in the extreme.[18]

B. W. Procter was also struck by Mary's placid expression and intelligent eyes, adding:

She was very mild in her manner to strangers; and to her brother gentle and tender, always. She had often an upward look of peculiar meaning, when directed towards him; as though to give him assurance that all was then well with her. His affection for her was somewhat less on the surface; but always present. There was great gratitude intermingled with it.[19]

Their generosity and kindness were proverbial and Charles's wit a byword, but there was also clearly an undefinable quality about them which made people seek their company.

Finding a balance between their need for peaceful domesticity and their natural gregariousness was an art Charles and Mary were never to master. Only three months before Charles was wanting to move, he had enthused to Manning about a neighbour:

This Rickman lives in our Buildings immediately opposite our house – the finest fellow to DROP in a nights about nine or ten oClock, cold bread & cheese time, just in the WISHING time of the night, when you *wish* for somebody to come in, without a distinct idea of a probable anybody.[20]

This Winnie-the-Pooh-ish appetite for something or someone pleasant to appear is highly characteristic. As Charles was to write: 'Not many sounds in life, and I include all urban and all rural sounds, exceed in interest a *knock at the door.* It "gives a very echo to the throne where Hope is seated."' However, 'its issues seldom answer to this oracle within. It is so seldom that just the person we want to see comes.'[21] There were many times when yet another knock at the door was the very last thing the endlessly hospitable Lambs needed at the end of a long day, especially as many of their friends were demanding guests. They decided to leave Chancery Lane for a more secluded spot and on 25 March 1801 moved to 16 Mitre Court Buildings. They were clearly delighted not only at being back in their beloved Temple where they had lived as children but at the set of 'delectable' rooms from which, Charles assured Manning, they had a fine prospect of the Thames and the Surrey Hills – if they stood on tiptoe. 'My bed faces the river so as by perking up upon my haunches, and supporting my carcase with my elbows, without much wrying my neck, I can see the white sails glide by the bottom of the King's Bench walks as I lie in my bed.'[22] The physical contortions required to enjoy the views notwithstanding, the Lambs were to be happy in their fourth-floor apartment, where they were to remain for the next eight years. Money remained in short supply: they had had to sell their spare bed in order to cover removal costs and were to keep no maid. However, they had bought – for a time at least – peace and quiet; here, Charles promised himself, 'I shall have all the privacy of a house without the encumbrance, and shall be able to lock my friends out as often as I desire to hold free converse with my immortal mind.' (Charles was actually no more capable of turning away visitors than he was of resisting a little self-mockery.)

An example of the Lambs' characteristic kindness and hospitality – which led to their being constantly at the mercy of friends in need – survives from their early period back in the Temple. One morning in the autumn of 1801 Charles and Mary were interrupted at breakfast by a knock at the door. Mary opened it to find George Dyer, unshaven and rain-sodden, holding out a piece of paper explaining that he had been ill with a fever. Unable to speak except by signs, laying his hand on his heart he communicated that 'his complaint lay where no medicines could reach it'. Mary managed to get him to eat and drink (they correctly suspected 'a vacuum' in this department) and he was comfortably settled in Charles's bed, so he believed, to die. Here he remained for three days, issuing instructions to his executor and bookseller for the posthumous publication of his unfinished works and bidding his relations farewell, while a doctor solemnly prescribed 'little white powders' (a placebo), which Dyer took believing that the doctor, knowing his case to be terminal, aimed to hasten his end as painlessly as possible. To his own astonishment, Dyer made a full recovery and Charles and Mary hoped to prevent future relapses by getting him to agree to eat at least one meal with them a day. On another occasion a couple of months later, Mary was alone in the house doing the laundry when Dyer dropped in with his latest friend, the elderly Earl of Buchan ('a pretty pickle to receive an Earl in! Lord have mercy upon us a LORD in my Garratt!'). Charles returned home to find he had missed the honour, but was to dine with Dyer and the Earl the following Sunday. Charles wrote to Rickman of Dyer's great pride in his new friend, 'always taking care to hedge in at the end, that he don't value Lords, & that the Earl has nothing of the Lord about him'. (It is small wonder that Charles thought Dyer would make a fine fictional character for a novel.) Perhaps what amused Charles in Dyer's character were elements of his own nature – or more general human failings – writ large; as he admitted to Rickman: 'O human nature! human Nature! For my part I have told every Body, how I had an EARL come to SEE ME – –.'[23]

It was clear that Dyer needed looking after and, according to Southey, Charles and Mary attempted a little match-making on his behalf:

Mary Lamb and her brother have succeeded in talking [George Dyer] into love with Miss Benjay or Bungey or Bungay; but they have got him into a quagmire and cannot get him out again, for they have failed in the attempt to talk Miss Bungay or Bungey or Benjey into love with him. This is a cruel business, for he has taken the injection, and it may probably soon break out into sonnets and elegies.[24]

Elizabeth Benger was the writer who had intimidated the Lambs over macaroons. Perhaps they hoped that a woman of her efficient principles was just what the disorganized Dyer needed, but it proved a vain endeavour; doubtless the unkempt academic constituted few women's idea of a desirable partner.

Although it had been rejected for production on the stage, Charles remained convinced of the merits of *John Woodvil* and the winter of 1801/2 saw its appearance in print – at his own expense. He had again revised the text, cutting out 'all the Ahs! & Ohs! and sundry weak parts, which I thought so fine three or four years ago.'[25] Dorothy Wordsworth, having read part of an early version of the play, had declared: 'The language is often very beautiful, but too imitative in particular phrases, words, etc. The characters except Margaret's unintelligible, and except Margaret's do not show themselves in action . . .'[26] Hazlitt was to go further, asserting that 'the character of his heroine Margaret is perhaps the finest and most genuine female character out of Shakespeare'. Rickman agreed that 'Lamb is particularly happy in his heroine,' adding that 'altogether I have not seen a play with so much humour, moral feeling and correct sentiment, since the world was young'.[27] Southey also approved of Margaret, but considered the play 'an exquisite picture in a clumsy frame'.[28] Ever candid, he informed a friend: 'Lamb . . . is printing his play, which will please you by the exquisite beauty of its poetry, and provoke you by the exquisite silliness of its story.'[29] Setting aside the many merits of the play's language and sentiments, it is clear that Charles had intended the play as a vehicle for poetry, but this was achieved at the expense of the mainstays of theatrical writing: characterization and plot. A reading of the play today reveals its many beauties – it must be approached as *homage* to, rather than imitation of, its genre – but also its utter unsuitability for stage representation. If Charles had hoped to resolve this problem by publishing the play – i.e. presenting it in a form in which it could be read, rather than watched – he was to be disappointed: the reviews were merciless, and he and Mary were left £25 poorer.[30]

On 10 August 1802, Charles and Mary set off northwards for a month's break, during which they would visit the homes of the Coleridges, the Lloyds (now at Ambleside) and the Wordsworths. The latter were not at Dove Cottage, having gone to France to resolve matters between William's former mistress and illegitimate child before his marriage to Mary Hutchinson, so their friends Thomas Clarkson, the anti-slavery campaigner, and his wife were the Lambs' hosts. During their stay with the Coleridges at Keswick Charles and Mary formed one of a sequence of special friendships with children which were to punctuate their lives. Already very fond of Hartley, their extended visit coincided with little Derwent arriving at the charming age when he was first attempting speech. The Lambs were captivated by 'Pi-pos', as he became known, due to his mispronunciation of Flying Opossum in a picture book. Charles described him on his return to London as 'the only child (but one) I had ever an inclination to STEAL from its parents. That one was a Beggar's brat, that I might have had cheap.' The robust pulling back from sentimentality evident here is, however, irresistibly undermined in his next remark: 'I hope his little Rash is gone.'[31]

Although they missed the Wordsworths during their trip, William and Dorothy were in London, having recently returned from France, when the Lambs went home and Charles was able to be their guide to one of his sights of London, Bartholomew Fair. Interestingly both Charles and Wordsworth appear to have relaxed their rather entrenched views of the country and the town respectively at about the same moment. It was while crossing the Thames on the roof of a stagecoach *en route* to France early in the morning that Wordsworth was struck by the beauty of the city, suggesting the germ of his poem 'Composed upon Westminster Bridge'. While Wordsworth opined that 'Earth has not anything to show more fair' than London at dawn, Charles was being bowled over by the landscape of the lakes and peaks. On his return to London he wrote to Coleridge: 'I feel that I shall remember your mountains to the last day I live. They haunt me perpetually. I am like a man who has been falling in Love unknown to himself, which he finds out when he leaves the Lady.'[32] The reversal of locations – each writer in the other's familiar element – combined with a more receptive maturity appears to have dispelled (or at least softened) their intellectual prejudices. Writing a couple of weeks later to Manning, having enumerated the glories of the lakes and mountains, Charles admitted: 'In fine I have satisfied myself, that there is such a thing as that, which tourists call *romantic*, which I very much suspected before.' The day they climbed Skiddaw, in particular, 'was a day that will stand out, like a mountain, I am sure, in my life'.[33]

On his return to London Charles realized that the experience had affected him deeply. 'I had been dreaming I was a very great man,' he reflected, but coming back to London and work he felt 'very *little*'. The break from London had also altered his perspective on another aspect of his life. He sounded Manning out on the subject.

My habits are changing, I think; i.e. from drunk to sober: whether I shall be happier or no, remains to be proved. I shall certainly be more happy in a morning, but whether I shall not sacrifice the fat & the marrow & the kidneys, i.e. the Night, the glor[iou]s, care-drowning, night, that heals all our wrongs, pours wine into our mortifications, changes the scene from indifferent & flat to bright & brilliant –. O Manning, if I should have formed a diabolical resolution, by the time you come to England, of not admitting any spiritous liquors into my house, will you be my guest on such shame worthy terms? Is life, with such limitations, worth trying. – The truth is that my liquors bring a nest of friendly harpies about my house, who consume me.[34]

Interestingly, Charles had expressed the same impressions and anxieties in *John Woodvil*, suggesting that these were not new revelations. John had talked about 'friendly harpies'

> . . . of that sort,
> Which haunt my house, snorting the liquors,
> And when their wisdoms are afloat with wine,
> Spend vows as fast as vapours, which go off
> Even with the fumes, their fathers.

Setting aside this evidence of the Lambs' famous (and often self-injurious) hospitality, Charles's characterization of 'Night' is strenuously self-revelatory. Apart from his rare 'holy' *days* when he might over-indulge and threaten to capsize, night – in company, at least – generally meant a drink (or three); hence night is glorious, care-drowning, healing of wrongs and mortifications, transformatory. Charles had written in *John Woodvil*, and was to write in his *Confessions of a Drunkard*, of the sense of needing to drink merely to arrive at the level that his peers found naturally. The born poet (which by now he was satisfied he was not) 'hath an internal wine, richer than lipparà or canaries, yet uncrushed from any grapes of earth, unpressed in mortal wine-presses . . . Its cellars are in the brain, whence your true poet deriveth intoxication at will.' This 'natural high' eluded Charles, or perhaps he was too shy or nervous to give it a chance; in any event he got into the habit of artificially inducing the sense of confidence, well-being and carefreeness that he assumed came easily to others. His addiction to tobacco, once he discovered it was a lubricant for conversation – never easy for a stammerer – was similarly inspired, and similarly impossible to refrain from.

Mary badgered Charles about his drinking, as she did about his smoking. Coleridge, a fellow indulger in both substances, was perhaps the least capable judge of such matters, which is probably why it was to him that Charles half-heartedly appealed for advice.

What do you think of smoking? I want your sober, *average, noon opinion* of it. – I generally am eating my dinner about the time I should determine it. Morning is a Girl, & c'ant smoke – she's no evidence one way or other. – & Night is so evidently *bought over*, that *he* ca'nt be a very upright Judge. – May be the truth is that *one* pipe is wholesome, *two* pipes toothsome, *three* pipes noisom, four *pipes* fulsom, *five* pipes quarrelsome, and thats the *sum* on't. But that is deciding rather upon rhime than reason.[35]

Charles was certainly prone to over-indulge in both when Mary was 'from home' and his spirits were low.

Following their return to London from Keswick the Lambs were busy carrying out errands for the Coleridges and Wordsworths, in particular sending fabrics, snuff, books and other items more easily procured in the city, including thick-soled shoes for Wordsworth custom-made to his own peculiar design which, according to a po-faced Charles, were 'very much admired at in London'.[36] Mary was disappointed on a hunt for children's books for Pi-pos, finding old favourites difficult to procure, their places supplanted by edifying manuals and instructive stories, designed more to educate than to fire the imagination. It was quite possibly this experience that led her to begin meditating on a new kind of literature designed especially for children.

The 600-mile round trip to visit their friends had exhausted Mary (now thirty-eight) and while there she had flagged somewhat on the long walks. Fatigue was often a catalyst to her illness and her health collapsed in late autumn. The nature and length of her malaise are not known, but she was still not herself at the beginning of December 1802. She was possibly still vulnerable when, in late March 1803, she happened to meet a Mr Babb at Rickman's home. Mr Babb turned out to be an old friend and admirer of Elizabeth Lamb and was evidently ignorant of the events surrounding her death. Initially the meeting seemed to produce no ill effects on Mary, but the following day she 'smiled in an ominous way'. Over the following weekend she became agitated and upset and told Charles 'that she was getting bad, with great agony'. Hoping the attack would prove to be a mild one, and would pass over without recourse to the madhouse, Charles comforted her but did not act. Coleridge was fortunately staying at Mitre Court at the time and on the Tuesday morning Mary, in a very disturbed state, grabbed hold of him, talking irrationally and wildly about George Dyer. Coleridge was sufficiently familiar with Mary's illness to recognize that her symptoms had advanced and, having sent words to Charles at the East India House, hailed a Hackney carriage and himself took Mary to the madhouse at Hoxton. Coleridge wrote to his wife, 'She was quite calm, and said it was the best to do so. But she wept bitterly two or three times, yet all in a calm way.'[37] This sorrowful resignation characterized Mary's going into confinement generally – at least, when her symptoms were caught in time. B. W. Procter, who met the Lambs at about this period, recalled meeting them on one such journey to Hoxton:

Whenever the approach of one of her fits of insanity was announced, by some irritability or change in manner, Lamb would take her, under his arm, to Hoxton Asylum. It was very affecting to encounter the younger brother and his sister walking together (weeping together) on this painful errand; Mary herself, although very sad, very conscious of the necessity for temporary separation from her only friend. They used to carry a strait jacket with them.[38]

Of the sorry episode occasioned by the unlucky appearance of Mr Babb, Coleridge's account to his wife ended: 'Charles is cut to the heart.' Shortly afterwards Charles knocked on Rickman's door, came in without a word, sat down and burst into tears. Rickman gradually got the whole story from him and managed to cheer him up a little. Charles stayed the night at Rickman's and Coleridge proposed staying with Charles for a few days afterwards. The support Charles's friends gave 'poor Lamb' at these times of distress was crucial.

This attack may have caught Charles at a particularly low ebb, for he had recently learnt of the death of Hester Savory, the young woman he had loved from afar at Pentonville. Hester had got married in July 1802 and died a bride of only seven months. To Charles the blow was apparently softened by the fact that Hester had always seemed to have something of heaven about her; the verse he wrote on the occasion of her death ending:

> My sprightly neighbour, gone before
> To that unknown and silent shore,
> Shall we not meet, as heretofore,
>   Some summer morning.
>
> When from thy cheerful eyes a ray
> Hath struck a bliss upon the day,
> A bliss that would not go away;
>   A sweet forewarning?

★

Following her return home, Mary continued 'very weak and dejected' until the first week of July. Writing to Dorothy Wordsworth congratulating her on becoming an aunt (William and Mary's first child, John, had been born on 18 June 1803), Mary admitted that the depression and fatigue following her last bout of illness had led her to doubt that she would ever feel completely well again: 'I strive against low spirits all I can, but it is a very hard thing to get the better of.'[39]

It is clear that Mary missed her close female friends, and her habit of storing up happy memories and moments to be brought out, like a child's box of treasures, when she needed consoling, is very evident in her letters. The judge John Stoddart and his sister Sarah had met the Lambs in July 1802 when the former were visiting London. Sarah became a particular friend of Mary's, although they saw each other rarely. In December 1802, when Mary was still feeling the effects of her recent illness, she vividly recalled elements of the visit in a letter to Sarah:

My poor head is just now full of the memory of our walks together – driving along the Strand so fast (lest the scotch broth should be spoiled in our absence) we were ashamed of shewing of red faces at your friend's in westminster, or bustling down Fleet-Market-in-all-its-glory of a saturday night, admiring the stale peas and co'lly flowers and cheap'ning small bits of mutton and veal for our Sunday's dinner's, returning home in all haste, to be scolded for not laying the cloth in time for supper (albeit it being nine o'clock) and then chidden for laughing in an unseemly manner. I have never half liked being at your brothers rooms since you left them: – they [Charles and John] sit and preach about learned matters, while I turn over an old book, and when I am weary look in the window in the corner where you and your work-bag used to be, and wish for you to rout them up and make us all alive.[40]

While Mary treasured Sarah's liveliness and her ability to shake everyone up (John Stoddart appears to have been something of a sobersides), the tranquillity of the Wordsworths' cottage was also a solacing memory and recuperating in the midst of the bustle of London she could imagine herself with Dorothy Wordsworth: 'how pleasant your little house and orchard must be now, I almost wish I had never seen it, I am always wishing to be with you, I could sit upon that little bench in idleness [all] day long'.[41]

Thinking the seaside would be good for Mary's health, the Lambs took their holiday that summer with the Burney family in the Isle of Wight. James Burney (brother of the novelist Fanny Burney) was a retired naval captain who had accompanied Captain Cook on his second and third voyages, on the latter commanding the *Discovery* on its voyage home following Cook's death; he now devoted his time to writing. He and his wife Sarah were both great card-players. (Members of the Burney family were to put in appearances in no less than three of the Elia essays.*) They appear to have had a very jolly time of it, spending their time, according to James Burney, doing 'every thing that is idle, such as reading books from a circulating library, sauntering, hunting little crabs among the rocks, reading Church Yard poetry which is as bad at Cowes as any Church Yard in the Kingdom can produce'. The only one who wasn't idle, ironically, was Mary: 'All the cares she takes into her keeping.' Burney also reported to Rickman that during a boat trip 'friend Lamb (to give a specimen of his Seamanship) very ingeniously and unconsciously cast loose the fastenings of the mast, so that Mast, sprit, sails, and all the

* Sarah is the model for Mrs Battle in 'Mrs. Battle's Opinions on Whist'; the marriage of their daughter Sarah is the model for 'The Wedding'; Martin Charles Burney, their son, is recalled in 'Detached Thoughts on Reading'.

rest tumbled overboard with a crash . . .'[42] Charles admitted that this report was 'partly true', adding the mitigating circumstance that 'it was never properly nailed down, or the accident could not have happened'.

Charles got his revenge on James Burney's tale-telling (he wrote his letter on the reverse of Burney's, so each was able to read the other's) by informing Rickman of the Burneys' son's misadventures (Martin was fifteen):

A volume might be made up of Martins Blunders which parental tenderness omits. Such as his letting the packet boat's boat go without him from the quay at Southampton, while he stood hiatusing, smit with the love of a Naiad; his tumbling back over a stone twice the height of himself, and daubing himself; his getting up to bathe at six o Clock, and forgetting it, and in consequence staying in his room in a process of annihilation &c. &c. Then the time expended in *Martin being scolded* would serve as great a sinner as Judas to repent in.

Having got the wind in his sails, Charles went on,

Capt Burney does nothing but teach his children bad habits. He surfeits them with cherries and black currents till they can eat no supper . . . There's a little girl he's brought with him that has cost I don't know what in codlings. – No ordinary orchard would be a jointure for her . . . To add to our difficulties Martin has brought down a Terence, which he renders out loud into canine Latin at Breakfast & other meals, till the eyes of the infatuated Parent let slip water for joy, and the ears of everybody beside shed their wax for being tired. More I could add but it is unsafe.[43]

Being rude to his friends was one of Charles's way of showing them affection. Mary Cowden Clarke (*née* Novello) recalled: 'His style of playful bluntness when speaking to his intimates was strangely pleasant – nay, welcome: it gave you the impression of his liking you well enough to be rough and unceremonious with you: it showed you that he felt at home with you.'[44] Mary's sister Clara recalled as a child being made by her father to sing for Charles, who delighted her by putting his hands over his ears, exclaiming 'Clara, don't make that d – – – – d noise!'[45] On another occasion, when the Novellos and Cowden Clarkes were visiting the Lambs, a neighbour arrived to go for a prearranged walk with Charles. Charles loudly explained for the benefit of his guests, 'You see I have some troublesome people just come down from town, and I must stay and entertain them; so we'll take our walk together tomorrow.'[46]

Mary was a favourite target for this off-handedness in company; he would slap her on the back and refer to her as 'my old woman', or turn to visitors explaining 'I call my sister "Moll" before the servants; "Mary" in presence of friends; and "Maria" when I am alone with her.'[47] One of the jokes Charles entertained himself with was the assertion that Mary had no sense of humour. He wrote to Wordsworth of querying a phrase in the great poet's 'The Force of Prayer'; he had asked Mary 'as if putting a riddle "What is good for a bootless bean"?' (the word in Wordsworth's poem is actually 'bene'), to which Mary immediately responded 'a shooless pea'. 'It was the first joke she ever made,' Charles languidly observed.[48]

Also for Mary's benefit, it amused him to pretend to despair of women who rose above their station. Discussing another woman writer, he said to Patmore: 'If she belonged to me, I would lock her up and feed her on bread and water till she left off writing poetry. A female poet, or female author of any kind, ranks below an actress, I think.'[49] If the Elia essay 'Modern Gallantry' does not give ample proof of his high regard for the female sex (including, specifically, actresses), his championing of the first professional female playwright, Aphra Behn, and serious defence of women writers in general, settles the matter. While he liked to be rude to his male friends about women writers, he was very friendly with many of those he met.[50] (When Wordsworth included three poems by his sister in his *Poems* of 1815 without acknowledging her authorship, it was Charles who chastised him for the omission.[51]) Mary appears to have complied in this double-act, where he behaved badly and she affected not to notice, one of the best examples being found in an account of a stranger's encounter with them quite late in their lives. Just as the Lambs had arranged for 'fans' of Coleridge and Wordsworth to meet the poets, in late middle age they found themselves the objects of a similar brand of curiosity. A friend arranged for N. P. Willis, a young American writer and a great 'Elian', to meet them, inviting them all to breakfast to his chambers in the Temple.

After the usual formalities, Willis pulled up a large armchair to the breakfast table for 'Miss Lamb'. 'Don't take it, Mary,' Charles warned, pulling the chair away from her with a very serious expression. 'It looks as if you were going to have a tooth drawn.' The conversation turned to other matters, at which point Charles took advantage of Mary's increasing deafness. 'Poor Mary!' he exclaimed. 'She hears all of an epigram but the point.'

'What are you saying of me, Charles?' inquired Mary.

'Mr Willis,' he replied, 'admires your "Confessions of a Drunkard" very much.' Not satisfied with this, he continued, 'And i was saying it was no merit of yours that you understood the subject.'

Mary still refused to rise to the provocation. Mr Willis then mentioned that he had bought a copy of the Elia Essays before leaving America.

'What did you give for it?' asked Charles.

'About seven and sixpence,' replied Willis.

'Permit me to pay you that,' Charles said and began counting the money out on the table. 'I never wrote anything that would sell. I am the publisher's ruin. My last poem won't sell a copy. Have you seen it, Mr Willis?'

Mr Willis had not.

'It's only eighteen pence, and I'll give you sixpence towards it.'

Charles had obviously hoped for a favourite sort of potted fish to be provided, but found they were having veal pie instead. After abusing the veal pie he asked whether his host was *positive* that there was no potted fish – not even a little scrap in the bottom of the dish? His host was not sure.

'Send and see,' said Charles, 'and if the pot has not been cleaned, bring me the cover. I think the sight of it would do me good.'

The lid of the pot was duly sent for. Charles tenderly considered the picture of the fish on it before kissing it, throwing out a reproachful glance at his host.[52]

While Henry Crabb Robinson knew Charles well enough to feel confident that 'C. Lamb says rude things, but always in so playful a style that you are sure he means nothing by what he says,'[53] we can be by no means certain that everybody took his good-humoured sallies so well. One lady may well have regretted lecturing him on his 'irregularities'. After she had been giving him some improving advice for some time, she began to feel that Charles's attention was straying. At last, she said: 'But, really, Mr Lamb, I'm afraid that all I'm saying has very little effect on you. I'm afraid, from your manner of attending to it, that it will not do you much good.' Charles assured her that her efforts were not wasted, as while her advice had indeed gone in one ear and out the other, it had done incalculable good to the gentleman standing on the other side of him.[54]

8. Toothache and Gumboil

Our sympathies are rather understood than expressed.

('Mackery End, in Hertfordshire')

'I am very uneasy about poor Coleridge, his last letters are very melancholy ones,' Mary wrote to Dorothy Wordsworth in July 1803.[1] Coleridge and his family had moved to Greta Hall three years before. Having achieved a comfortable home with sublime and inspiring views and proximity to Wordsworth, he hoped to embark on a period of great literary activity. Instead, an inability to write descended, weighing him down as much as the albatross had his mariner. Increased use of alcohol and opium somewhat relieved Coleridge's various ailments but caused nightmares so terrifying that he began to be afraid to go to sleep. He continued to dream and speak of various ambitious schemes, but actually did little to realize them. His interest in Sara Hutchinson (sister of Mary, who had married Wordsworth) grew proportionately with his dissatisfaction with his marriage. Regeneration, both of his spirits and his marriage, proved all too brief and by the winter of 1802 all the old demons had returned, along with a physical and intellectual restlessness.

November 1803 saw the first evidence of Charles encountering a serious bout of writer's block, although of a distinctly different character to Coleridge's. Charles's problem was rather a typical inability to organize his material systematically.

Charles had once remarked to Godwin that he was 'the worst hand in the world at a plot'[2] and indeed the failure of his stage plays lay not in their language but in their structure. It was this same way of thinking – to fix on particulars rather than to embrace the bigger picture – which characterized his poetry and later his essays, but which was also evident in his non-literary thinking: his politics focused on individual issues rather than an over-arching philosophy; his religious feeling was instinctive and personal rather than conformist, even his humour – typically the one-off pun – spoke of a sudden incisiveness often unrelated to (and increasingly socially inap-propriate to) the broader context. While, as an informal critic of his friends' poetry, he could hit on exactly what was wrong or right with a particular expression, he would have been extremely hard pressed to express his own philosophy of poetry. He had experienced such serious difficulties writing theatre reviews in the tight time-scale permitted by news-papers that he had been obliged to abandon them; he now faced his first major challenge as a literary critic in earnest. How would the self-confessed dilettante cope with a serious literary critical challenge?

Godwin had recently published his *Life of Geoffrey Chaucer* and asked Charles to write a review of it. Charles set about the task cheerfully enough, but soon found himself 'strangely hindered'. He attributed the difficulties he experienced first to the interruption of a visitor, then to poor health, but soon admitted defeat. Godwin, however, was not to be put off and suggested that the real reason Charles was deliberating over the review was that he did not like the book. It was true that Charles had some reservations about Godwin's approach – particularly his recourse to guessing at Chaucer's thoughts and motivations when evidence was scarce – but these were vastly outweighed by the merits he found in the work. The 'deadly blight' which led to the misunderstanding, and frayed tempers on both sides, was traced back to 'that Bitch' Mary Jane Godwin. She had attempted at an earlier date to draw Charles's opinion of the book from him, which he had refused to do until he had discussed it with her husband himself. Her persistence and a leading question (whether 'there was not too much fancy in the work') elicited Charles's admission of his general criticism but his stout refusal to go into details until he had seen Godwin. Bad Baby evidently, as Charles tellingly put it, immediately '*dropt*' this information to her husband and quite possibly presented it in a worse light than Charles intended. Charles was furious that what he was already finding a near impossible task was now clouded by the author's hurt feelings at a yet unwritten review. An attempt to clear such muddied water did, however, produce Charles's most perfect criticism of his own failings as a formal writer. As he wrote to Godwin:

You by long habits of composition, & a greater command gained over your own powers, cannot conceive of the desultory & uncertain way in which I (an author by fits) sometimes cannot put the thoughts of a common letter into sane prose. Any work which I take upon myself as an engagement, will act upon me to torment – e.g. when I have undertaken, as 3 or 4 times I have, a school boy copy of verses for Merch. Taylor's boys at a guinea a copy, I have fretted over them, in perfect inability to do them, & have made my sister wretched with my wretchedness for a week together. The same, till by habit I have acquired a mechanical command, I have felt in making paragraphs. – As to reviewing in particular, my HEAD is so whimsical a head, that I cannot after reading another man's book, let it have been never so pleasing, give any account of it, in any methodical way. I cannot follow his train. – Something like this you must have perceiv'd of me in conversation. Ten thousand times I have confessed to you, talking of my talents, my utter inability to remember in any comprehensive way what I read. – I can vehemently applaud, or perversely stickle at *parts*: but I cannot grasp at a whole. This infirmity (which is nothing to brag of) may be seen in my two little compositions, the tale & my play [*Rosamund Gray* and *John Woodvil*]. In both which no reader, however partial, can find *any story*.[3]

While this is perhaps a *little* harsh, the fact remained that when the subject and form of his solo writing was prescribed, or where a deadline was imposed, the intellectual discipline required to fulfil the task utterly eluded Charles. A natural digresser, he quickly became lost among the formal paths; self-doubt sprang up before him further impeding his way. Ironically, it was embracing this digressive habit – as a faculty rather than a failing – that was to lead to his period of greatest success as a writer; but the full discovery of Elia's wandering narrative (which yet fulfilled its own unique pattern) still lay in the future. (When he had transcribed 'The Londoner' in a letter to Manning, in order to explain that its whimsical meandering style was deliberate, Charles had tagged a familiar quotation from *Tristram Shandy* on to the end: 'What is all this about?, said Mrs Shandy –. A story of a Cock & a Bull, said Yorick', adding: '& so it is.'[4]) Pricked into a renewed attempt at the review, as a 'peace offering' to Godwin, Charles nevertheless finally had to admit defeat and bowed out, vexed at Godwin's continuing importunities. (As it happened, the reviews which did appear concurred with Charles's view that Godwin's biography contained too much 'imagination'.)

Coleridge set off on a characteristically evasionary trip to Sicily via Malta in April 1804, visiting Charles and Mary immediately before his departure. Charles and Mary's friends John and Sarah Stoddart were already in Malta and both hoped to keep tabs on Coleridge's progress through these intermediaries, as he himself could be prone to long epistolary silences. Mary continued to be extremely concerned about Coleridge's miserable and restless state and begged Sarah and her new sister-in-law to take particular care of him, 'to be to him kind affectionate nurses and . . . behave to him as you would to me, or to Charles if we came sick and unhappy to you'.[5]

Since Charles had ended his connection with the *Morning Post* money had been tight in the Lamb household. Financially constrained from moving very far afield from London, Charles and Mary spent their month of summer holiday of 1804 in Richmond, where they wandered the banks of the Thames and attempted to trace beauties which compared with Ullswater and Windermere, partially succeeding. Though Mary described themselves as 'poorer but happier', the former inevitably somewhat inhibited the latter, to the extent that Mary and Charles curtailed their letter-writing to a minimum in order to avoid the cost of return correspondence, and were uncomfortable when expensive unsolicited mail arrived. Similarly Charles had the embarrassment of having to ask Wordsworth for the money in advance when buying books for him in London. A proposed visit to the Wordsworths which would also encompass Sara Coleridge and the Clarksons was also, for lack of funds, repeatedly postponed.

On the morning of 7 February 1805 Charles arrived at the East India House to find a large crowd gathered outside. As he eased his way past them into his office he learned that they were friends and relations of those who had been aboard the *Earl of Abergavenny*, an East India vessel, which had sunk off Weymouth late on the night of the 5th. Members of the crowd were interrogating survivors of the wreck who were at intervals arriving at the Company's headquarters in order to give their account of the disaster. Rumour and misinformation abounded; one fact emerged with horrible certainty: well over half the souls on board had been drowned, including the captain. Charles knew him personally, but worse, knew that the news would devastate some of his closest friends: the captain of the *Earl of Abergavenny* was William and Dorothy Wordsworth's much-loved brother John.

Like Charles, John Wordsworth had joined the Company young, having served in its navy since the age of sixteen. Although separated from Dorothy and William in childhood, he later became very close to them and had come to see his role as that of provider and enabler, to subsidize financially a life that would free his brother to pursue a career in poetry. 'We were not Brother and Sister with him in blood only but had the same pleasures the same loves in almost everything,' William told Thomas Clarkson.[6] The three siblings had planned to live together following John's retirement. By 1805, when he was aged thirty-three, John had been captain of the *Earl of Abergavenny* for four years and had a reputation as a firm, honest and fair captain and a widely respected and admired individual. The *Earl of Abergavenny* had set out from Portsmouth on 2 February with a cargo which included luxury goods and about £70,000 in silver dollars, the latter to be used to purchase (unofficially) opium in Bengal and (officially) tea in China. The vessel also carried passengers, soldiers and sailors amounting to 400 souls. Three days into the voyage, probably due to the pilot being unfamiliar with the coast, the ship became grounded in Weymouth Bay, filled with water and sank with the loss of 260 lives.

William and Dorothy's grief was indeed terrible. William wrote to a friend: 'Our loss is one which never can be made up; had it come earlier in life or later it would have been easier to bear; we are young enough to have had hope of pleasure and happiness in each others company for many years, and too old to outgrow the sorrow.'[7] The same words might indeed have been used had Mary or Charles lost each other at the same age: the loss of a sibling was a sorrow with which they could empathize better than the loss of a child (which they did, very tenderly, on occasion); and when Mary wept beside Charles as he struggled to write some words of consolation to Dorothy and William, it was less for the dead captain that they grieved, but more for the bereaved brother and sister. Charles, who had been extremely low-spirited since the Godwin review period, became so depressed that he had to take time off work and the whole episode probably contributed to Mary's next breakdown, which occurred in June.

To wish to do something to help at such a time is natural; to be able to fulfil that wish is rarer. However, Charles's position at the East India House meant that he was able to render the Wordsworths real service which their letters demonstrate helped them to recover from their loss. To add to their initial distress, as soon as accounts of the shipwreck had appeared in the newspapers, aspersions had been cast over John Wordsworth's management of the situation. Various versions of the news asserted that the captain had not sent for help as early as he should, that he had not attempted to evacuate the crew and passengers, that he had been drunk, that he had been overwhelmed by the catastrophe and incapable of attempting to save even his own life. With access to eye-witnesses, Charles was able to reassure Dorothy and William that all these doubts were utterly unfounded: 'It is perfectly understood at the E.I. House, that no blame whatever belongs to the Captn. or Officers.'[8] He took great pains to solicit and copy to the Wordsworths first-hand accounts from the survivors, often tracking down crew members before they re-embarked on long voyages which would take them half way round the world and months away; 'for this,' Dorothy wrote to a friend, 'we must love him as long as we have breath. I think of him and his sister every day of my life, and many times in the day with thankfulness and blessings.'[9]

In late May the dreaded early symptoms of Mary's recurring illness began to manifest themselves. The management of this period – when Mary was not mad enough to be confined, but not well enough to lead a normal life – was extremely difficult for both of them. 'Being by ourselves is bad, & going out is bad,' Charles wrote to Dorothy Wordsworth. 'I get so irritable & wretched with FEAR, that I constantly hasten on the disorder. You cannot conceive the misery of such a foresight.'[10] Added to the guilt he felt at his reaction to the first signs of the approaching attack was the feeling that he was to blame to some extent for the anxiety he caused Mary. While he thought late nights had contributed, on this occasion, to Mary's illness, Charles confessed to Dorothy: 'I know I have been wasting & teazing her life for five years past incessantly with my cursed drinking & ways of going on.' By the end of July, however, Mary was improving, and she was back at Mitre Court Buildings before the end of the summer. In September she wrote to Sarah Stoddart (who had recently returned from Malta, her love-life still unresolved) that 'I begin almost to feel myself once more a living creature, and to hope for happier times.'[11]

Happier times remained elusive; although together at home once more, both Charles and Mary were depressed, a situation not helped by their precarious financial situation. Each other's company was possibly the worst thing for them both at this time – independently miserable, they also added to each other's gloom, as Mary described to Sarah Stoddart:

. . . indeed it has been sad & heavy times with us lately, when I am pretty well his low spirits, throws me back again & when he begins

to get a little chearful then I do the same kind office for him –. . .
You would laugh, or you would cry, perhaps both, to see us sit
together looking at each other with long and rueful faces, & saying
how do you do? & how do you do? & then we fall a crying & say
we will be better on the morrow – he says we are like tooth ach &
his friend gum bile, which though a kind of ease, is but an uneasy
kind of ease, a comfort of rather an uncomfortable sort.[12]

The idea of what we would now call an abscess actually
relieving toothache gives some idea of the independently
acquired, yet mutually exacerbated, pain which Mary and
Charles brought to their relationship at such times. While they
could be each other's greatest comfort, the intimate nature of
their relationship meant they could also be each other's most
exquisite torment.

One feature of Mary's state of mind following confinement
(or 'banishment', as she interestingly called it) after this particular bout of illness was a perpetual sense of uncertainty about the
fitness of her own actions. This insecurity is clearly expressed in
two consecutive letters, much of the subject matter of which is,
significantly, madness. Following her own return home Mary
had received a letter from Sarah Stoddart, who had recently
returned to England because her mother had 'gone out of her
mind'. Mary evaded replying to the letter because she would
have to address the subject of Mrs Stoddart's madness, which
too forcibly brought her own illness to mind – a topic which
both she and Charles strenuously avoided. The letter she
eventually did bring herself to write to Sarah about her mother
contains the first of only two examples of Mary discussing
mental illness and is illuminating about her own experience:

And do not I conjure you let her unhappy malady afflict you too
deeply – I speak from experience & from the opportunity I have

had of much observation in such cases that insane people in the fancy's they take into their heads do not feel as one in a sane state of mind does under the real evil of poverty the perception of having done wrong or any such thing that runs in their heads.

Think as little as you can, & let your whole care be to be certain that she is treated with *tenderness*. I lay a stress upon this, because it is a thing of which people in her state are uncommonly susceptible, & which hardly any one is at all aware of, a hired nurse *never*, even though in all other respects they are a good kind of people. I do not think your own presence necessary unless she *takes to you very much* except for the purpose of seeing with your own eyes that she is very kindly treated.[13]

Although Mary says that she speaks from experience, she distances herself from the patient by casting herself in the role of observer. Her emphasis on kind and caring treatment and equally emphatic statement that professional carers are unaware of its importance strongly suggests that Mary herself had experienced care that was less than tender.

As soon as she had sent the letter, in the feverish state of mind that such ruminations brought on, she regretted it, imagining that her 'impertinent interference' might imply that she felt Sarah did not know how to look after her mother. Not waiting for Sarah's reply, Mary wrote again immediately:

God knows nothing of this kind was ever in my thoughts, but I have entered very deeply into your affliction with regard to your Mother, & while I was writing, the many poor souls in the kind of desponding way she is in whom I have seen, came afresh into my mind, & all the mismanagement with which I have seen them treated was strong in my mind, & I wrote under a forcible impulse which I could not at that time resist, but I have fretted so much about it since, that I think it is the last time I will ever let my pen run away with me.

She added, by way of explanation:

. . . I do not think any one perceives me altered, but I have lost all self confidence in my own actions, & one cause of my low spirits is that I never feel satisfied with any thing I do – a perception of not being in a sane state perpetually haunts me. I am ashamed to confess this weakness to you, which as I am so sensible of I ought to strive to conquer.[14]

Mary delayed sending the letter, hoping for a reply to her first letting her off the hook, and eventually sent it with directions to Sarah to reply to her at her nurse's address. Her fear was that if Charles read Sarah's reply (as was likely) and saw that 'I had first written foolishly & then fretted about the event of my folly, he would both ways be angry with me'. She then felt guilty about conducting a 'secret correspondence' with Sarah – she had herself warned Sarah against keeping secrets from her brother John – and vowed in future always to show her letters to Charles before she sent them, 'which will be a proper check upon my wayward pen'.

The mess poor Mary worked herself into is even more strikingly pathetic in her attempts to hide her (imagined) mistake from her younger brother. (Even when writing about Toothache and Gumboil she had added, in her typically breathless way, 'Do not say any thing when you write of our low spirits it will vex Charles.') The depths to which her lack of self-confidence had plummeted are most clearly apparent when the letters referred to here are compared with the tone of a letter written to Sarah only eighteen months before.

Charles had caused some discomfort between the Lambs and the Stoddarts by remarking on the cost of receiving Mrs Stoddart's letters (presumably she had written to the Lambs at home rather than at the office), and Mary had written to Sarah: 'By entreaties & prayers I might have prevailed on my brother to say nothing about it. But I make a point of conscience never to interfere, or cross my brother in the humour he happens to be in.' A fittingly deferential attitude for a dependent spinster sister, it seems, but Mary goes on:

It always seems to me to be a vexatious kind of Tyranny that women have no business to exercise over men, which merely because *they* [women] *having a better judgement* they have the power to do. Let *men* alone, and at last we find they come round to the right way, which *we* by a kind of intuition perceive at once. But better, far better, that *we* should let them often do wrong, than that they should have the torment of [a] Monitor always at their elbows.[15]

Here Mary's submission to Charles is a strategy underpinned by a confidence in her own moral superiority; eighteen months later that confidence has all but evaporated into a sweating sense of guilt and fear of her own unfitness to make sound judgements.

By Christmas both Charles and Mary were in better spirits, Mary declaring on Christmas Day that she was glad to see the back of such a miserable year and looked forward to happier times. The year 1806 began auspiciously with Sarah Stoddart staying with the Lambs for all of January and most of February. 'She is one of the few people who is not in the way when she is with you,' Charles wrote to Hazlitt. In the spring Wordsworth paid them a solo visit. Once more the Lambs were in great demand both as visitors and hosts and Charles was complaining, 'I never have an hour for my head to work quietly in its own workings; which as you know is as necessary to the human system as SLEEP.'[16] The problem was to prove a perennial one. Years later Charles wrote: 'It is not of guests that we complain, but of endless, purposeless visitants; droppers in, as they are called. We sometimes wonder from what sky they fall.'[17] Typically, rather than discouraging the droppers-in, Charles rented a room where he worked every evening between 5p.m. and 8p.m. Here he wrote *Mr H—*, a stage farce, which Mary duly delivered to the manager of Drury Lane Theatre. Mary observed that he seemed more disposed to set to writing seriously than she had known him for a very long time and he proposed another two plays and a novel. While this arrangement left Mary alone to occupy the idle visitors, she also gained some extra spare time by it and she too was casting about for some writing employment, but could not make up her mind what form it should take.

Following a few days' break from his writing regime, Charles abandoned his writing-room, finding it too lonely, and convinced Mary that he would be able to work at home just as well. Mary, from long experience of Charles's procrastination, had rather dreaded this outcome, but resolved not to express her reservations. Since a period of coolness following the abandoned Chaucer review, the Lambs and Godwins had been reconciled and saw each other often. The Godwins had begun to establish a children's book publishing business, with Mary Jane as the official proprietor (it being considered that William's reputation as a radical might harm the business's chances of success). Charles had obliged them with a short verse work, *The King and Queen of Hearts*, and Mary Jane now engaged Mary to write a collection of summaries of Shakespeare's plays, which would give children enough of the plot and characterization to understand the plays when they later saw or read the authentic versions and to give an idea of their beauties. It was a brilliant idea – it is not known which of them thought of it, nor who suggested that Charles should lend a hand with the tragedies – and also solved a major problem for the Lambs, for Mary was to be paid sixty guineas.

Charles and Mary's imperative for writing for the Godwins' Juvenile Library was undoubtedly financial; however, the exercise enabled them to apply practically their controversial views of contemporary children's literature. The prevalent philosophy saw children's books as an extension of education: fiction, as much as non-fiction, should constitute a lesson. Popular children's writers such as Sarah Trimmer and Anna Letitia Barbauld (both caustically criticized by Charles) derived their rationale from the ideas of John Locke and Jean-Jacques Rousseau, who emphasized the importance of moral instruction. While such instruction should be presented in an entertaining form, Locke and Rousseau rejected fantasy and romance and mistrusted the folk- and fairy-tale. Consequently the majority of fiction available to children concerned likely events occurring in the lives of ordinary children where strong authority figures clearly directed both the protagonist and the reader to the appropriate response or course of action. Charles and Mary, in common with Coleridge and Wordsworth, strongly regretted this trend. As Coleridge expressed his view:

I infinitely prefer the little book of 'The Seven Champions of Christendom,' 'Jack the Giant Killer,' etc., etc. – for at least they make the child forget himself – to your moral tales where a good little boy comes in and says, 'Mama, I met a poor beggar man and gave him the sixpence you gave me yesterday. Did I do right?' – 'O, yes, my dear; to be sure you did.' This is not virtue, but vanity; such books and such lessons do not teach goodness, but – if I might venture such a word – goodyness.[18]

(It is interesting to recall here Charles's accounts of his own boy and beggar experience: having given away his aunt's plum-cake to a beggar, once his pride in his own charity had evaporated, the complex emotions Charles the child felt represented a realization of having been 'goody' rather than 'good'.) Coleridge continued:

The poet is one who carries the simplicity of childhood into the powers of manhood; who with a soul unsubdued by habit, unshackled by custom, contemplates all things with the freshness and wonder of a child; and connecting with it the inquisitive powers of riper years, adds, as far as he can find knowledge, admiration; and where knowledge no longer permits admiration, gladly sinks back into the childlike feeling of devout wonder.[19]

Charles and Mary shared the strong concern that without examples of the fantastic and the fanciful before him or her, the poetic impulse might be extinguished in the child.

Whereas Charles and Mary had clearly appreciated and benefited from being suffered 'to browse at will' on the fine pasture of 'good old English reading, without much selection or prohibition',[20] the likes of Barbauld and Trimmer believed children's reading material should be carefully chosen, closely supervised and – where necessary – censored. R. L. and Maria Edgeworth's advice to parents in Essays on Practical Education said it all: 'Few books can safely be given to children without the previous use of the pen, the pencil and the scissars.'[21] Particularly pernicious to children's moral development were fairy-tales, which were unnecessarily frightening and gave unrealistic impressions of the world. However, one of the main criticisms levelled at fairy-tales – that they, in Trimmer's words, operated 'too powerfully upon the feelings of the mind'[22] – was exactly what underpinned the value of them for the Lambs and their poet friends. What Trimmer, Barbauld *et al.* feared in the child was exactly what the Romantics celebrated and encouraged.

Charles's first piece of work for the Godwins, a new version of the nursery rhyme *The King and Queen of Hearts*, was a tale of crime and punishment which appears at first glance to conform to the instructive model favoured at the time. However, Charles added a new dimension to the story: Pambo the Knave's theft of the tarts is witnessed by a spying page, Mungo, who reports his crime to the King and Queen. Pambo then takes his revenge on Mungo. The illustrations, by William Mulready, depict a dissipate King and Queen who have evidently partaken of a bottle clearly marked GIN. Charles's rhyme ends subversively:

> Their Majesties so well have fed,
> The tarts have got up in their head,
> 'Or may be 'twas the wine!' hush, gipsey!
> Great Kings & Queens indeed get tipsey!
> Now, Pambo, is the time for you:
> Beat little Tell-Tale black & blue.

Whereas other children's literature portrayed infallible adult authority figures, Charles offered his diminutive readers a pair of inebriated royals; where others encouraged 'goodyness', in Charles's rhyme it was the goody-goody who came a cropper. (If there were a moral to be deduced from the rhyme, it would emerge as a warning against spying and telling tales, rather than against theft.) Charles clearly took the opportunity presented by his commission to adapt *The King and Queen of Hearts* to have a swipe at 'improving' literature for children. It was a wise commercial, if unadventurous, decision that the

Godwins did not solicit anything subsequently from him in the same vein.

The cultural respectability and iconic status of Shakespeare was an asset of incalculable value to the Lambs in the prosecution of their next work for children. Here were stories where good did not inevitably triumph over evil, where there was often no 'right' course of action, where virtues could bring their own attendant problems. As well as affording children a more sophisticated range of moral possibilities, Shakespeare's stories of course also offered them adventure, romance and magical transformations. While Charles and Mary believed, as Charles stated in their jointly-written Preface, that the plays were 'strengtheners of virtue', they were also 'enrichers of fancy': Shakespeare fed both the soul and the imagination.

This is not to say that the Lambs made no concessions to their youthful audience (or rather, its book-buying parents). The plays to be adapted were carefully selected and edited, and although much of the original language was retained, readers were spared some of Shakespeare's more graphic descriptions of sex and violence. However, just as the Lambs toned down some aspects of the stories to accommodate their audience, some of the more disturbing aspects were retained particularly to appeal to children. For example, recalling his own interest in the horrible and the frightening as a child, Charles pretty faithfully related the description of the witches' brew in *Macbeth*:

Their horrid ingredients were toads, bats, and serpents, the eye of a newt, the tongue of a dog, the leg of a lizard, and the wing of the night owl, the scale of a dragon, the tooth of a wolf, the maw of a ravenous salt-sea shark, the mummy of a witch, the root of the poisonous hemlock (this to have effect must be digged in the dark), the gall of a goat, the liver of a Jew, with slips of the yew tree that roots itself in graves, and the finger of a dead child: all these were set on to boil in a great kettle, or cauldron, which, as fast as it grew too hot, was cooled with a baboon's blood: to these they poured in the blood of a sow that had eaten her young, and they threw into the flame the grease that had sweaten from a murderer's gibbet.

Doubtless this morbidly thrilling passage was a great favourite with some young readers.

Charles and Mary's skills were clearly equally well adapted to this undertaking, both of them producing impressively efficient and economic reconstructions of the stories without losing many of the glories of their originals. Their work not only speaks of a deep and abiding love and respect for their model, but of a genuine commitment to render their treasures apparent to children and a belief that they would be able to appreciate them. Although we know which plays were adapted by whom (Mary doing approximately two-thirds of the work; Charles's contribution covering exclusively tragedies), it has rightly been observed that 'it must be said of the collaboration between Charles and Mary that their talents were so evenly matched and that they shared so many ideas that, at least in this work, it is impossible to disentangle their achievement and give credit to one and not the other'.[23]

When *Tales from Shakespeare* was published in the winter of 1806/7 it was an immediate success. The *Critical Review* declared that – apart possibly from Defoe's *Robinson Crusoe* – the *Tales* 'claim the first place, and stand unique, without rival or competitor'. While Mary could have had no idea how warm a critical reception her work would receive when she embarked on it, it seems no accident that she undertook the project soon after resolving on a new attitude. Expressing her doubts to Sarah Stoddart about Charles's ability to withstand the distractions of Mitre Court while writing, and her tendency to despondency on such occasions, she explained her determination to think and act positively, to alter 'my fretful temper to a calm & quiet one':

. . . I know my dismal faces have been almost as great a draw back upon Charles comfort, as his feverish teazing ways have been upon mine. Our love for each other has been the torment of our lives hitherto. I am most seriously intending to bend the whole force of my mind to counteract this, and I think I see some prospect of success.[24]

Why was it Mary, a relatively inexperienced writer, and not Charles, who was commissioned to write the *Tales*? Charles had by this time written a novella, two plays and a good deal of poetry as well as his journalistic œuvres, while all Mary had was a few poems to her name. While it could be suggested that it took a woman to perceive a woman's talent in this patriarchal age, there was probably a more practical factor at work. Charles had frequently protested at his inability to complete 'task work' and with the aborted review of her husband's book in mind Mary Jane Godwin may simply have felt the project was safer and more certain to be successfully completed with Mary Lamb at the helm. If Charles collaborated, that was certainly a bonus, and Mary Jane would have known that his sister would have been the very last person Charles would have felt able to let down. It has been established that he struggled, largely unsuccessfully, when faced with a formal engagement to write on a given theme, and that the torment that ensued made not only him, but Mary, 'wretched'. However, it has been largely unappreciated that his most enduring work of this type was only written – indeed *could* only have been written – when he worked closely with

Mary. Nonetheless he made very heavy weather of his comparatively modest contribution. Mary described their way of working to Sarah Stoddart thus:

. . . you would like to see us as we often sit writing on one table (but not on one cushion sitting) like Hermia & Helena in the Midsummer's Nights Dream. or rather like an old literary Darby and Joan. I taking snuff & he groaning all the while & saying he can make nothing of it, which he always says till he has finished and then he finds out he has made something of it.[25]

Somewhat amusingly, Charles represented the situation rather differently:

Mary is just stuck fast in All's Well that Ends Well. She complains of having to set forth so many female characters in boy's clothes. She begins to think Shakspear must have wanted Imagination. – I to encourage her, for she often faints in the prosecution of her great work, flatter her with telling her how well such a play & such a play is done. But she is stuck fast & I have been obliged to promise to assist her.[26]

Charles actually assisted Mary only by reading the finished tale and declaring it one of the best; however, this kind of assistance is not to be underestimated. Mary was considerably buoyed up by the experience of writing the *Tales* – which Charles, incidentally, genuinely thought she did 'capitally', although she referred to them with characteristic modesty as 'poor little baby-stories' – and anticipated making £50 a year out of writing, having 'no doubt but I shall alway[s] be able to hit upon some such kind of job to keep going on'.

Although Charles had not written poetry for some time, Mary wrote a number of poems during this period, one of which, 'Dialogue between a Mother and Child', which concerned a child's resistance to his widowed mother's remarriage, was warmly praised by Wordsworth. Charles and Mary's interest in the visual arts (they frequently attended exhibitions and auctions) is also reflected in Mary's choice of subject matter: a number of the poems she is known to have written in 1804 and 1805 were inspired by pictures; Charles also often rhapsodized on paintings he had recently seen in letters to Manning and a young artist he had met at Godwin's in March 1803, William Hazlitt. In the autumn of 1804 Hazlitt had painted Charles's portrait and a strong friendship developed which, unlike most of Hazlitt's other friendships, was an enduring one. According to Mary, Charles liked Hazlitt better than anyone except Manning, and following Manning's departure for China, Hazlitt supplied his place in Charles's life.

The absence of Manning in Charles's life and of Sarah Stoddart in Mary's incidentally inspired an idea which was to furnish Charles with material for one of his most successful Elia essays. The problematic nature of writing to people when the letter would take some time to reach them and the likelihood that the news it contained would be well out of date by the time it got there was one on which both Charles and Mary mused. Mary had had the first sense of the disparity between the moment that words were written and the moment that they were read when Sarah Stoddart had gone out to Malta: 'I sit writing here,' Mary wrote, 'and thinking almost you will see it tomorrow, and what a long, long, time it will be before you receive this – '[27] In another letter she wrote of an injury Sarah had sustained: 'I would condole with you upon the misfortune has befallen your poor leg, but such is the blessed distance we are at from each other, that I hope before you receiv[e] this you have forgot it ever happened.'[28] (It has been noted that the substance of both these statements appears in the Elia essay 'Distant Correspondents'; once again the germ of Charles's writing springs from an idea of Mary's.) Charles himself did not feel the frustrating irreconciliation of the writer's 'now' and the reader's 'now' – 'this confusion of tenses, this grand solecism of *two presents*' – until Manning went to China.

As bachelor and spinster Charles and Mary looked on with mixed feelings as their friends courted and married. Charles had already discovered that marriage had changed the character of his relationship with many of his friends and it is no accident that of his three current favourite companions (Manning, Hazlitt and – although mostly out of reach at this time – Coleridge) two were also bachelors and the third behaved as though he were, travelling without his wife and often not even writing to her for weeks on end. Not having children was certainly a regret for both Charles and Mary for which they compensated by investing time and interest in friends' children. They in turn were beloved. Hazlitt's niece, for example, 'a nice little girl of the Pypos kind', would accost strangers in the street with the important news that 'Mr Lamb is coming to see me.'[29]

Charles often affected a healthy contempt for children, complaining, as Elia, of smug parents ('I cannot for my life tell what cause for pride there can possibly be in having [children] . . . they are so common'[30]) and of children themselves ('Boys are capital fellows in their own way, among their mates; but they are unwholesome companions for grown people'[31]). On one occasion, finding himself in the midst of a large and noisy family, he proposed the health of the 'm-m-much ca–calumniated good King Herod'. Mary was also capable of affecting diffidence on the subject, describing children as a 'plaything for an hour'. While neither really subscribed to these views, their affection for children was by no means indiscriminate; Charles wrote: 'I think it unreasonable to be called upon to *love* them, where I see no occasion . . . to love all the pretty dears, because children are so engaging.' If children were to be loved, it must be for their own individual sakes and not because they happened to be sons and daughters of friends: 'a child's nature is too serious a thing to admit of its being regarded as a mere appendage to another being'.[32] Once, when visiting the Novello family, it was suggested to Charles that a jar of preserved ginger he had brought for the children would be wasted on them and should be offered instead to the grown-ups present. Charles would not hear of it, declaring children to be 'excellent judges of good things' and indeed the children never forgot the gift, nor the manner in which Charles appeared to 'find' it up a chimney.[33] Charles and Mary were not only very fond of certain children, but respected them, at least in part because they both naturally entered into children's way of thinking.

Even a cursory glance at Mary's stories in *Mrs Leicester's School* demonstrates how closely she was able to identify with a child's point of view – another aspect of her knack of seeing directly into other people's characters – but it is Charles's essay 'Dream-Children' which shows what a keen empathizing eye *he* trained on them. In the essay Elia dreams he is a widower telling his small children stories of his own childhood. His description of the slight preconscious gestures listening children make serves to make the depiction of the children highly realistic, yet this is an even more subtle manipulation of the reader than it first seems, for at the end of the essay Elia awakes from his sleep, to the reality that he is a childless bachelor, and Alice and John 'are nothing, less than nothing, and dreams'.

The extent to which both Charles and Mary empathized with children proceeded directly from their ability not only to recall vividly their own childhoods but, for Charles in particular, to remember the children they had been. For Charles such reflections were infused with strong emotion. While he did not entertain the highest opinion of himself as an adult, he cherished the memory of 'that "other me," there, in the back-ground' with a combination of pity and pride:

I can cry over its patient small-pox at five, and rougher mendicaments. I can lay its poor fevered head upon the sick pillow at Christ's, and wake with it in surprise at the gentle posture of maternal tenderness hanging over it, that unknown had watched its sleep. I know how it shrank from any the least colour of falsehood. – God help thee, Elia, how art thou changed! Thou art sophisticated. – I know how honest, how courageous (for a weakling) it was – how religious, how imaginative, how hopeful! From what have I not fallen . . .[34]

Why, Charles wondered, should he be preoccupied with these admiring thoughts of himself as a boy? Was it because he was unmarried and childless that 'I have not learned to project myself enough out of myself; and having no offspring of my own to dally with, I turn back upon memory, and adopt my own early idea, as my heir and favourite'? Or did Charles and Mary treasure their childhoods – which after all were not uniformly happy ones – because it was the one safe place in their lives? The day of horrors had neatly severed the past from the present: everything changed from that moment, leaving the seeming certainties of childhood behind. By striving to retain an idea of himself as a child, Charles could enjoy an idea of himself when the future seemed to hold limitless possibilities, when murder and madness had not yet closed so many doors to him.

A number of contemporaries remarked on Charles's childlike qualities; suggesting that 'that "other me," there, in the back-ground' – the boy Charles – was substantially preserved in him as an adult. Charles himself also recognized this. In the Preface to the *Last Essays of Elia*, writing in another persona, as though he were writing his own obituary, Charles observed:

His manners lagged behind his years. He was too much of the boy-man. The *toga virilis* never sate gracefully on his shoulders. The impressions of infancy had burnt into him, and he resented the impertinence of manhood. These were weaknesses; but such as they were, they are a key to explicate some of his writings.

While Charles had clearly thought a good deal on the subject of marriage and children, nothing is known about any hopes of becoming a wife and mother Mary may have entertained. Her correspondence with Sarah Stoddart gives only a tantalizing glimpse of her feelings. Sarah evidently openly shared with Mary her adventures with various admirers and while Mary claimed not to judge her friend, it is clear that she disapproved of some of Sarah's shenanigans, occasionally taxing her for a lack of modesty – not, she explained, modesty in the true sense, but a general freeness in demeanour which Mary felt allowed men to think less of Sarah. On the one hand, when Sarah was in Malta, Mary expressed the hope that she would come home and make a good 'English wife' and when Sarah did come home Mary took great interest in her romantic projects; on the other, she fantasized about Sarah coming to live with her and Charles – Sarah had certainly proved herself highly compatible with them during her long stay in 1806. A good example of Mary's idiosyncratic views on marriage appears in a letter to Sarah written in the summer of 1806:

What is Mr Turner? & what is likely to come of him? and how do you like him? and what do you intend to do about it? – I almost wish you to remain single till your Mother dies, & then come & live with us and we would either get you a husband or teach you how to live comfortably without, I think I should like to have you always to the end of our lives living with us, and I do not know any reason why that should not be except for the great fancy you seem to have for marrying, which after all is but a hazardous kind of an affair, but however do as you like, every man knows best what pleases himself best

Barely pausing to draw breath Mary continues:

I have known many single men I should have liked in my life (if it had suited them) for a husband: but very few husbands have I ever wished was mine which is rather against the state in general that one never is disposed to envy wives their good husbands, So much for marrying – but however get married if you can.[35]

Mary was forty-two when she wrote these words; it would be intriguing to know which men she might have fancied marrying. Of course marriage was infinitely more perilous – both emotionally and physically – for women than for men at the time, due to the hazards attending childbirth, and when Sarah did finally become a wife Mary wrote commiserating with her on a miscarriage: 'I am very sorry to hear of your mischance. Mrs Rickman has just buried her youngest child. I am glad I am an old maid, for you see there is nothing but misfortunes in the marriage state.'[36]*

* These words proved ominous: in the course of her first seven years of marriage Sarah experienced three miscarriages and three live births; only one of the babies survived infancy. She and Hazlitt later divorced.

Mary's advice on marriage matters was evidently widely sought; when Sarah seemed on the point of settling upon a husband, not only she but her brother John asked Mary to 'look at & examine into the merits of the said Mr D——' and if he passed muster to assist in drawing up the marriage settlement. John Stoddart was particularly concerned that his sister should not keep any money independently from her husband, which drew another interesting remark from Mary:

We will talk over these things when you [Sarah] come to town, and as to settlements, which are matters of which I never having had a penny in my own disposal I never in my life thought of, and if I had been blessed with a good fortune, & that marvellous blessing to boot a husband I verily believe I should have crammed it all uncounted into his pocket.[37]

Although there are very few extant letters to men from Mary it is clear from the correspondence of both her and her brother that she valued several close male friends. While Coleridge, whom she had known since his boyhood, was probably closest to her heart, her affection for Manning is also apparent. When Manning proposed going to China she expected to 'miss him very much . . . we love him dearly'.[38] Charles's first letter to Manning following his departure for China also gives an insight into his relationship with the Lambs: 'I will nurse the remembrance of your steadiness & quiet which used to infuse something like itself into our nervous minds.'[39] For this reason Mary used to refer to Manning as 'our ventilator'.

On 17 August 1806, Coleridge returned to England after more than two years of wandering, sick in mind and body and heavily addicted to laudanum. 'Shirtless & almost penniless', he pitched up at the Lambs', where he remained, dreading and procrastinating returning to his family at Keswick, until the end of the month. (Charles and Mary were often Coleridge's first port of call when he was in distress. When he all but collapsed in the street in 1807, his immediate instinct was to take a cab to the Lambs' home, where Mary dosed him with brandy and broth.) Charles and Mary were of course delighted to have their old friend back again, safe if not sound, as his long silences while abroad had caused much anxiety about his well-being, and his wife and children had been more or less abandoned, necessitating the rallying round of friends. However, Mary confessed to Dorothy Wordsworth that she was fatigued by Coleridge's conversation 'and the anxious care even to misery which I have felt since he has been here that something could be done to make such an admirable creature happy'.[40] They and others of his friends had dutifully kept open the lines of communication with Sara Coleridge and were now beside themselves with frustration that Coleridge still evaded resolving the marriage, one way or another. A month after he landed in England he had still not even written a line to his wife, while Mary was in the delicate position of corresponding with Wordsworth and Southey on how a separation might be arranged, and also with Sara Coleridge who clearly expected a joyful reunion with her husband. As concern, advice and exasperation whirled around him, Coleridge himself assiduously continued to do nothing. Eventually Mary took the bull by the horns in a letter which indicates the older-sisterly authority she had over Coleridge. She began with the upper hand, having evidently caught Coleridge and Charles smoking a 'Segar' (Charles had recently given up the habit – again), but assured Coleridge that 'your two odd faces amused me much more than the mighty transgression vexed me' and acquitted Coleridge of blame, assuring him that Charles would have taken up tobacco sooner or later without his friend's assistance.

She also reminded Coleridge that 'A few chearful evenings spent with you serves to bear up our spirits many a long & weary year', before beginning her assault:

You must positively must write to Mrs Coleridge this day, and you must write here that I may know you write or you must come and dictate a letter for me to write to her. I know all that you would say in defence of not writing & I allow in full force every thing that [you] can say or think, but yet a letter from me or you *shall go today*.[41]

Mary's 'musts' worked. Coleridge wrote to Sara and there-after kept her regularly updated on his movements – which marked the beginning of an – at last – forward-moving shift in his dealings with his family. He returned to Keswick in the middle of October, but was never to live permanently with his wife again.

June 1806 had brought the triumphant news that Charles's farce, *Mr H—*, had been accepted by the proprietors of Drury Lane Theatre. By the beginning of December it was in rehearsal and Mary was busy on her next project for the Godwins' Juvenile Library, *Mrs Leicester's School*. The pair had also established their famous Wednesday evenings (shifted to Thursdays later in life). As Charles told Manning: 'like other great men, I have a public day'. Pipes were smoked, cold meats consumed and cribbage played, punctuated by *bon mots* and wide-ranging debates.

Charles had high hopes for *Mr H—*, by which he hoped to make £300; if it failed, however, he would get nothing. His own description of the plot is as good as any:

The story is, a coxcomb appearing at Bath vastly rich – all the Ladies dying for him – all bursting to know who he is – but he goes by no

237

other name than Mr. H — a curiosity like that of the dames of Strasburg about the man with the great nose — . . . after much vehement admiration, when his true name comes out, HOGSFLESH, all the women shun him, [av]oid him & not one can be found to change their name for him — that's the idea . . .[42]

On 10 December, Charles and Mary, in the company of Hazlitt and another new friend, Henry Crabb Robinson, took their seats at Drury Lane to see the first performance. Earlier in the day Hazlitt had been pleased to hear 'the streets filled with the buzz of persons asking one another if they would go to see *Mr. H—*, and answering that they would certainly'. The house was packed and included many supporters (the fact that Charles and his brother both worked in large offices, he freely acknowledged, had helped in this respect). The Prologue — which Charles had only written at the last minute, at the Manager's request — went down a storm. A stunned Charles reported to Wordsworth, 'It was received with such shouts as I never witnessed to a Prologue. It was attempted to be ENCORED.' Even Charles, Hazlitt noted, laughed uproariously at his own wit.[43] The audience listened to the play attentively, but at its denouement, when Mr H's full name was disclosed, as Crabb Robinson recalled, 'the squeamishness of the vulgar taste in the pit showed itself by hisses'.[44] Dismayed, and then afraid of being recognized as the author, Charles again enthusiastically joined in, 'and was probably the loudest hisser in the house'.* The remainder of the play was rendered inaudible by barracking from the audience. Mary was at least as upset by the failure of *Mr H—* as Charles and while they both resolved to bear it stoutly, to receive both a

* The author's name did not appear on the play-bills.

critical and a financial disappointment in one blow went hard with them.*

The general opinion of those who commiserated with the Lambs over the damning of *Mr H—* was that a judicious editor could have turned it into a success. Mary acknowledged that its weakness lay in Charles's 'ignorance of stage effect' – which, in truth, had been the flaw at the root of *John Woodvil*. 'And I am much mistaken if he has not gained much useful knowledge, more than he could have learned from a constant attendance on the representation of other peoples pieces, by seeing his own fail, he seems perfectly aware why, & from what cause it failed.' Charles decided to have one more attempt at playwriting, to which he would bring to bear all the lessons he had learnt, and if that too failed, abandon the form forever.

Professionally undaunted by this setback, Charles and Mary spent Christmas as a working (writing) holiday at home, but planned a long visit with the Clarksons in the summer. The imminent publication of *Tales from Shakespeare* was something to look forward to, but in the event brought its own share of disappointments. Mary Jane Godwin had chosen the illustrations for the books (each tale was originally published in separate volumes) and proved herself a very bad baby indeed, having carelessly included representations of a number of scenes which Charles and Mary had cut in their necessarily shortened versions. These pictures therefore bore no relation to the text and would serve only to puzzle the intended audience, young readers. William Godwin had proved no better a midwife to their project, having not only pushed Charles into agreeing to put his name to the book – there was

---

* A successful run of the play was performed in Philadelphia in 1812 and *Mr H—* was published there the following year, Charles benefiting neither financially nor by being credited as the author.

no question of a woman with Mary's history being publicly attached to a book for children – but also having published an advertisement for the book in Charles's name, which, to Charles's great annoyance, emphasized their '*simplicity*'. No record survives of Mary's reaction, but she was not to live to see her name attached to her greatest and most enduring work; Mary's 'poor little baby-stories' were destined to become classics and are alone among the Lambs' work in being easily accessible even today.

One can only imagine what effect the publication of the *Tales* had on Charles and Mary, it being primarily *her* work, published in *his* name. However, Mary must have drawn some comfort from both Charles's free acknowledgement of Mary as the primary author, and the exceedingly warm critical reception that her adaptations achieved. (Interestingly, by this time 'As You Like It' had been demoted by Charles to the one 'we like least'.) However, when Charles sent a copy of *Poetry for Children* to Manning in 1810, explaining 'the best you may suppose mine; the next best are my coadjutor's; you may amuse yourself in guessing them out; but I must tell you mine are but one-third in quantity of the whole', he rather tantalizingly added, 'So much for a very delicate subject.'[45]

The long-wished-for visit to the Clarksons, now living at Bury St Edmunds, was finally accomplished in June 1807 and began well enough, for the Lambs were extremely fond of the Clarksons. However, at some point during their stay Mary began to exhibit signs of illness, one of which was demonstrated by her giving Charles's new coat away to the Clarksons' servant (Charles subsequently had to ask for it back, charitably offering the man compensation). Her symptoms accelerated before it was possible to accomplish the premature return journey to London; they left in great haste, leaving Charles's books and papers, and he was obliged to friends of the Clark-sons *en route* at Chelmsford who supplied a straitjacket to confine Mary's flailing arms (the Lambs had presumably on this occasion been sufficiently confident to leave her own at home). On the long journey back to London Mary talked incessantly 'in the most wretched desponding way conceiv-able', exhausting Charles, and it must have been some relief to deposit her, 'sadly tired and miserably depressed', at Hox-ton.[46] He spent the rest of the holiday at the British Museum, collecting materials for what would be his *Specimens of English Dramatic Poets*. The experience almost convinced them both that journeys so far from home were too hazardous to be attempted again.

Extreme talkativeness was evidently a common symptom of her attacks and just as she could witter on despondently as Charles describes, when 'high', according to Thomas Noon Talfourd, 'her ramblings often sparkled with brilliant description and shattered beauty'.

Though her conversation in sanity was never marked by smartness or repartee; seldom rising beyond that of a sensible quiet gentlewoman appreciating and enjoying the talents of her friends, it was otherwise in her madness . . . She would fancy herself in the days of Queen Anne or George the First; and describe the brocaded dames and courtly manners, as though she had been bred among them, in the best style of the old comedy. It was all broken and disjointed, so that the hearer could remember little of her discourse; but the fragments were like the jewelled speeches of Congreve, only shaken from their setting. There was sometimes even a vein of crazy logic running through them, associating things essentially most dissimilar, but connecting them by a verbal association in strange order. As a mere physical instance of deranged intellect, her condition was,

I believe, extraordinary; it was as if the finest elements of mind had been shaken into fantastic combinations like those of a kaleidoscope . . .[47]

Mary was still in 'banishment' in July, and Charles had not been allowed access to her since her confinement the previous month – 'NOR do they let me see her till she is getting pretty well.'[48] However, she appears to have been sufficiently recovered to return home before the end of the summer. During her absence an extraordinary liaison had taken root: her best friend, Sarah Stoddart, veteran of many an intrigue of the heart, had become seriously romantically entangled with Charles's current best friend, William Hazlitt. While Mary admitted to Sarah that 'You know I make a pretence not to interfere, but like all old maids I feel a mighty solicitude about the event of love stories'[49] and that her brother shared her vicarious satisfaction in the match ('for next to the pleasure of being married, is the pleasure of making, or helping marriages forward'[50]) she did not wholeheartedly endorse the proposed marriage – perhaps anticipating that Sarah or her suitor, as on a number of other occasions, would falter before the matter was brought to the altar. However seriously Sarah was taking the affair, Mary had her reservations. 'If I were sure you would not be quite starved to death, nor beaten to a mummy I confess I should like to see Hazlitt and you come together,' she said, mischievously admitting, 'if (as Charles observes) it were only for the joke sake.'[51]

The 'joke', against all expectations, was accomplished on 1 May 1808, when Mary officiated as bridesmaid at the wedding of Sarah Stoddart and William Hazlitt. Charles giggled helplessly throughout the ceremony, later confessing to Southey that 'any thing awful makes me laugh'.[52]

9. Friends and Confessions

I am a poor nameless egoist, who have no vanity to consult by
these Confessions. I know not whether I shall be laughed at, or
heard seriously. Such as they are, I commend them to the reader's
attention, if he finds his own case any way touched. I have told
him what I am come to. Let him stop in time.

('Confessions of a Drunkard')

Charles's collection of extracts and commentaries upon them,
*Specimens of English Dramatic Poets who Lived about the Time of
Shakespeare*, was published in the summer of 1808. To date,
Charles's critical acumen had been appreciated only by his
writer friends, all of whom, at some time or another, had
consulted him about their own work. *Specimens* was to establish him in the world's eye as a literary critic of the highest
order, leading a modern authority to assert that 'Lamb's judici-
ously brief comments are among the classics of English
criticism.'[1] Characteristically idiosyncratic and vested with
Charles's personal preferences (Ludwig Tieck said 'They are
written out of my heart'[2]), the collection retrieved a host of
Renaissance playwrights from near oblivion, their achievements at that time having been all but entirely obscured by
the attention paid to the exceptional genius of the bard himself.
Specimens was a labour of love for which Charles had, on and
off, been collecting materials throughout his adult life and he

was justly proud of the work. However, this kind of writing – however admirable – was not going to cover as many bills as a *Tales from Shakespeare*. Charles and Mary needed to capitalize on the foothold they had established in the market for children's literature.

Despite the problems the Lambs had encountered with the Godwins over *Tales from Shakespeare*, both now embarked on new projects for their publishing house. Mary's collection of children's stories, *Mrs Leicester's School* (1807) – to which Charles again contributed about a third of the material – demonstrated Mary's ability to translate her instinctive empathy with children into literature which would appeal to them. Mary Cowden Clarke, a child when she first knew the Lambs, recalled that Mary 'had a most tender sympathy for the young . . . She entered into their juvenile ideas with a tact and skill quite surprising. She threw herself so entirely into their way of thinking, and contrived to take an estimate of things so completely from *their* point of view.'[3] Using a device which allowed each of the stories to be told from the point of view of one of Mrs Leicester's pupils allowed Mary to exploit this constitutional empathy to her literary advantage.

Mrs Leicester's School attracted many adult admirers. The classicist Walter Savage Landor was particularly moved by a story which dealt with the remarriage of a widower, as seen through the eyes of his daughter. He wrote to Henry Crabb Robinson: 'Never have I read anything in prose so many times over, within so short a space of time, as The Father's Wedding-day . . . The story is admirable throughout, – incomparable, inimitable.'[4] To a female friend Landor confessed that as he read the story, 'I pressed my temples with both hands, and tears ran down to my elbows.'[5]

Charles had also been commissioned by the Godwins to work on a new title, along similar lines to the *Tales*: this was

The Adventures of Ulysses, a reworking for children of George Chapman's translation of Homer's classic. Although Charles and William Godwin saw a good deal of each other socially, their working relationship could be prickly – perhaps a legacy from the days of the abandoned Chaucer review, underscored by the form in which the *Tales* had been published.

Godwin had already insisted on a number of changes to the text of *Ulysses* and, now that it was ready for the printer, wanted more. Two of the letters which they exchanged during this period give a perfectly clear impression of the stresses obtaining between them at this time. While Godwin the idealist had expounded the view a decade before that children should be allowed 'to wander in the wilds of literature' and be trusted in some cases to select their own reading matter, Godwin the children's publisher and father of an expanding family had turned conservative.[6] As in so many cases where creativity and market forces collide, it is possible to see, and sympathize with, both points of view. First, from Godwin to Charles, written on 10 March 1808:

Dear Lamb

I address you with all humility, because I know you to be tenax propositi [tenacious in your proposals]. Hear me I intreat you with patience.

It is strange with what different feelings an author & a bookseller looks at the sam[e] manuscript. I know this by experience: I was an author – I am a bookseller. The author thinks what will conduce to his honour: the bookseller what will cause his commodities to sell.

You or some other wise man I have heard to say, It is children that read children's books (when they are read); but it is parents that choose them. The critical thought of the tradesman puts itself therefore into the place of the parent, &

enquires what will please the parent, & what the parent will condemn.

We live in squeamish days. Amidst the beauties of your manuscript, of which no man can think more highly than I do, what will the squeamish say to such expressions as these? 'devoured their limbs, yet warm & trembling, lapping the blood.' p.10, or to the giant's vomit, p.14, or to the minute & shocking description of the extinguishing the giant's eye, in the page following. You I dare say have no formed plan of excluding the female sex from among your readers, & I, as a bookseller, must consider that, if you have, you exclude one half of the human species.

Nothing is more easy than to modify these things, if you please; & nothing, I think, is more indispensible.

Give me, as soon as possible, your thoughts on the matter.

I should also like a preface. Half our customers know not Homer, or know him only as you & I know the lost authors of antiquity. What can be more proper, than to mention one or two of these obvious recommendations of his works, which must lead every human creature to desire a nearer acquaintance?

Believe me ever
faithfully yours
W Godwin.

I inclose the pages, 9–15.

Charles responded immediately:

Dear Godwin,
The Giant's vomit was perfectly nauseous, and I am glad that you pointed it out. I have removed the objection. – To the other passages I can find no other objection but what you may

bring to numberless passages besides, such as SCYLLA snatching up the six men &c – that is to say, they are lively images of *shocking* things. If you want a book which is not occasionally to *shock*, you should not have thought of a Tale which was so full of Anthropophagi & monsters. I cannot alter those things without enervating the Book, I will not alter them if the penalty should be that you & all the London Booksellers should refuse it. – But speaking as author to author, I must say, that I think *the* TERRIBLE in those two passages seems to me so much to preponderate over *the nauseous* as to make them rather FINE than *disgusting*. Who is to read them I do'nt know – who is it reads Tales of Terror & Mysteries of Udolpho? Such things SELL. – I only say that I will not consent to alter such passages which I know to be some of the best in the Book. As an author I say to you, an Author, Touch not my Work. As to a bookselle[r] I say, Take the work such as it is, or refuse it. You are as *free* to refuse it as when we first talk'd of it. As to a friend, *I say*, don't plague yourself or me with nonsensical objections. I assure you I will not alter one more word.

(Charles didn't sign the letter.) He did *not* alter one more word: the devouring of the still warm and trembling limbs stayed, as did the putting out of the Cyclops's eye; Charles did in fact pen a preface, but not of the type Godwin requested. Following such a blasting from Charles, Godwin was careful how he broached the subject of the preface, beginning his next letter: 'I tremble to speak my mind respecting whatever flows from your pen or your tongue, when I have to express any thing but satisfaction . . .' *but* he felt Charles's preface was 'too naked'; Godwin listed the merits of Homer to which Charles should draw attention. Charles's response was brief and to the point:

Dr. G—

I have read your letter and am fully of the opinion that such a drawling biography as you have chalk'd out is not my forte to write. I totally disagree with you; and prefer my own preface (as I am always likely to do) to any preface a man tells me I am qualified to write. You must take that, or none. I am SICK absolutely sick of that spirit of objection which you constantly shew, as if it were only to TEAZE ONE, or to warn one against having any more dealings with you in the way of trade. My preface is just such a one as I approve, & there is enough of it, but I had quite as lieve have *no preface* if you prefer it. I shall remember Ulysses as long as I live to write. –

Yours in the way of friendship
Still Ever
CL

Finally recognizing a man at the end of his tether, Godwin immediately backed off. As it turned out, Godwin may have been right about *Ulysses*. A review in the *Anti-Jacobin* declared the book 'almost too low for criticism', identifying the gross indecency of the language as a major negative factor.[7] The book was neither a critical nor a commercial success. It could not have escaped Charles's notice that when he collaborated with Mary his work sold like hot cakes, but so far all his solo enterprises had been dismal failures. *Ulysses* was only reprinted twice in Charles's lifetime, whereas his next joint venture with Mary was to be reprinted four times in six years.

Charles's vehemence over *Ulysses* is a stout reminder of the extremely strong views which he had always held on literature for children. To represent Homer (or indeed Chapman) in a way that was accessible to children was what he had set out to do; to water down or substantially sanitize the stories was to undermine an important aspect of the very nature of their appeal. The problem, of course, was not a new one; Mary and Charles had had to perform a delicate balancing act with their adaptations of Shakespeare's plays in order to render them acceptable to parents without losing their essential integrity. They had also addressed the problem alluded to by Godwin, of the young female reader. In her part of the preface to the *Tales* Mary stated her express intention of directing the books primarily towards girls, reasoning that boys were usually allowed access to their fathers' libraries at a younger age than girls and were consequently often already familiar with Shakespeare. There was clearly, if subtly expressed, a feminist agenda at work in Mary's thinking. From her point of view *Tales from Shakespeare* was as much an attempt to compensate for girls' educational and cultural disadvantages as anything else.

Coleridge remained a source of anxiety to the Lambs. He had told Southey he could not live much longer and Charles reported to Manning that Coleridge received visitors while he was on his close-stool – at once a symptom and symbol of his physical and moral degeneration.[8] Dorothy Wordsworth, who was used to Coleridge's reports of his own imminent death, remarked, 'we gather consolation from past experience, he has often appeared to be dying and has all at once recovered health and spirits'.[9] However, her brother William was sufficiently concerned to come to London to visit his sick friend. (The Wordsworths had tried – and failed – to help Coleridge by having him live with them.) Wordsworth was at this time growing in stature as a writer and Charles referred to him as 'Wordsworth the great poet', hinting at his friend's unabashed high opinion of his own powers. Even Coleridge baulked at Wordsworth's assertion that 'he does not see much difficulty in writing like Shakespeare, if he had a mind to try it'. Charles added wryly: 'It is clear then nothing is wanting but the mind.'[10]

Of course the Lambs could tolerate more than a few flaws

in their friends and were pleased to welcome warmly 'the great poet' to their home. Wordsworth had promised to read them some of his new epic 'The White Doe' and was prevailed upon to do so one evening when the now engaged William Hazlitt and Sarah Stoddart were also present. Wordsworth actively disliked Hazlitt, who had caused a scandal at Keswick some five years earlier by unbecoming conduct with a young woman from the village. In addition to this inauspicious circumstance, Wordsworth was disappointed that Charles and Mary did not give the poem the rapturous reception the poet felt he had a right to expect for what he considered a masterpiece. In a long letter to Coleridge Wordsworth expressed the view that Charles should be ashamed of his inability to meet the poem imaginatively, and concluded: 'of one thing be assured, that Lamb has not a reasoning mind, therefore cannot have a comprehensive mind, and, least of all, has he an imaginative one'.[11]

Coleridge and the Lambs also drifted apart for a period at this time. Although Coleridge was in London, he saw little of his old friends and some of the tension similar to that obtaining between the Lambs and 'Wordsworth the great poet' is detectable in this cooling; as Mary explained to Mrs Clarkson: 'we could not submit to sit as hearers at his lectures and not be permitted to see our old friend when *school-hours* were over'.[12] Mary's nose was clearly put out of joint by the fact that she and Charles were obliged to share Coleridge with a growing coterie of admirers who hung on his every word. If anyone could good-naturedly puncture Coleridge's magical bubble of spell-binding talk, it was his oldest friend. Having studied, originally, for a career in the church, Coleridge once paused his flow of speech and turned to Charles to ask him if he had ever heard him preach? 'N-n-never heard you do anything else!' replied Charles, to much laughter.[13]

If Charles could do no more than gently tease Coleridge, Mary, who had known Coleridge since he was a boy when she was already a young woman, had been used to the freedom of reprimanding him on occasion ('I know he thinks I am apt to speak unkindly of him: I am not good tempered, and I have two or three times given him proofs that I am not'). However, Mary reminded herself, Coleridge was Coleridge: according to her own philosophy, she should love him for the good that was in him and look for no change.

Do not imagine that I am now *complaining* to you of Coleridge, perhaps we are both in fault. We expect *too much*, and he gives *too little*. We ought many years ago to have understood each other better. Nor is it quite all over with us yet, for he will some day or other come in with the same old face, and receive (after a few spiteful words from me) the same warm welcome as ever.[14]

Indeed, on the very day Mary wrote this letter, she and Charles received an upbeat letter from Coleridge announcing his next project: a weekly paper called *The Friend*. The same post brought a notice for a turkey which the Clarksons had sent, 'which I am more sanguine in expecting the accomplishment of than I am of Coleridge's prophecy', Charles could not help adding.[15]

Charles had 'a horror' of removals and tended to leave the arrangements to Mary, who merely found them 'great labour, and pain, and grief'. His comments on the subject to Manning again suggest something of the voice of Elia:

What a dislocation of comfort is comprized in that word MOVING! – Such a heap of little nasty things, after you think all is got into the cart, old drudging boxes, worn out brushes, gallipots, vials, things that it is impossible the most necessitous person can ever want, but which the Women, who preside on these occasions, will not leave behind if it was to save your soul, they'd keep the cart ten minutes to stow in dirty pipes and broken matches, to shew their economy. Then you can find nothing you want for many days after you get into your new lodgings. You must comb your hair with your fingers, wash your hands without soap, go about in dirty gaiters . . .[16]

Worse, the Lambs were to move twice in 1809: first, in March, temporarily back to Southampton Buildings where they were to stay in Hazlitt's bachelor lodgings until their new chambers were ready, then, in May, into what they hoped would be their permanent home. However, there were three great consolations in the move: the rent was only £30; the new rooms were much more conveniently arranged and spacious and had been freshly decorated; but better yet, they were situated only a few doors from Charles and Mary's childhood home. From their new lodgings Charles could look out one way into Inner Temple Lane, and out through the back into Hare Court (where the trees touched the windows, so that 'it's like living in a garden') and see the very pump he had drunk from as a six-year-old. He declared his intention of remaining at this address until he died.

Money worries having eased slightly as a result of their children's books (Charles's salary at the East India Company also rose incrementally each year), they bought new furniture and curtains and took on a maid. However, only a few days after their arrival at Inner Temple Lane Mary fell ill. Exhausted by the move, she then found she could not get to sleep in the new house: as in so many cases of her illness, fatigue led to a breakdown. 'What sad large pieces it cuts out of life, out of her life who is getting rather old and we may not have many years to live together,' Charles wrote miserably to Coleridge. (Actually, Mary was forty-five and only just over half-way through her life.) Left alone in a strange house with an unfamiliar maid, Charles was downcast: 'I am weaker & bear it worse than I ever did.'[17] It was at about this time that Robert Lloyd marked Charles and Mary's co-dependence in a letter to his wife: 'If we may use the expression, their Union of affection is what we conceive of marriage in Heaven. They are the World *one* to the *other*.'[18]

Poetry for Children, another joint venture for the Godwins, was published that summer and the pressure both of them had been under shows in the writing. The book had been undertaken entirely for economic reasons; as Robert Lloyd noted: 'It is *task* work to them, they are writing for money, and a Book of Poetry for Children being likely to sell has induced them to compose one.'[19] Again Mary supplied approximately two-thirds of the work, Charles the remainder.* The poems are a mixture of moral tales on the usual prescribed themes (humility, responsibility, envy, tolerance, filial duty, vanity, charity, pride, etc.), but also of tragic and happy events and natural phenomena. When the mood took them, versifying was relatively easy for both Charles and Mary, but the constraints of the brief in this case and the pressures of moving did not conspire to produce their best work. While both had a facility at prose for readers of any age, their poetry directed at adult readers is much more successful than the poems they wrote for children.

Mary was ill for six weeks and was very weak when she returned home. However, a long-anticipated 'dear quiet lazy

---

* Unlike the *Tales* and *Mrs Leicester's School*, of eighty-four poems only a handful can certainly be ascribed either to Charles or to Mary and one is by their brother John; E. V. Lucas's guess (in his edition of the *Works*) is probably the most educated: he ascribes fifty-eight to Mary and twenty-five to Charles.

delicious month' spent with the Hazlitts at Winterslow in Wiltshire, fine weather and long walks effected her complete recuperation (her improved looks on her return to London 'almost made Mrs Godwin die with envy') and a revival of Charles's spirits. Incidentally, the fact that Charles was already known to his friends as a problem drinker is evident in Hazlitt writing to Leigh Hunt after this visit that Charles 'neither smoke nor drank any thing but tea and small beer, while he was here'.[20] They got home to find Jane (the maid) had broken the glass of two of their treasured framed Hogarth prints 'whereat I [Mary] made a great noise'. She was clearly back on form.

Charles returned to work to the good news of a colleague's resignation, whereby he was promoted and his salary increased by £20 a year. His buoyant state of mind brought out his mischievous side, as he exploited Mary Jane Godwin's extreme curiosity about the Hazlitts' household. Charles entertained himself by telling her that the Hazlitts had discovered a well in their garden and – water being so scarce in that part of the world – it would bring them an income of £200 per year. Bad Baby rushed round to Inner Temple Lane the next morning to ask Mary whether it was true. Mary wrote with some relish to Sarah Hazlitt, 'She longs to come to Winterslow as much as the spiteful elder sister did to go to the well for a gift to spit diamonds.'[21] Mary Jane Godwin was not insensitive to some of her husband's friends' dislike of her, complaining to Henry Crabb Robinson of 'the persecution she has to bear from the Lambs, Mrs. Holcroft etc.' However, she got short shrift from 'Crabby', who 'would hear nothing on that subject'.[22]

January 1810 found Mary in 'excellent health' and both of them well settled in their new home. 'May I never MOVE again, but may my next Lodging be my COFFIN,' Charles grimly resolved.[23] In early February Charles complained that his brother John 'teazes me to death' by supposing that he could use his literary connections to get a book John had written widely reviewed. Charles not only resented the pressure, but the assumption that he held any sway with the critics ('I!! who have been set up as a mark for them to throw at'). John, of whose progress Charles and Mary's correspondence is otherwise almost uniformly silent, was at this time, according to his brother, 'a plump good looking man of seven & forty'. The 'book' he had written was a political pamphlet, *A Letter to the Right Hon. William Windham, on His Opposition to Lord Erskine's Bill, for the Prevention of Cruelty to Animals.*

John's argument devolved upon the premise that when God gave man dominion over animals He expected man to discharge that responsibility with the same compassion with which God exercised His dominion over man: God never authorized man to torture, maltreat and otherwise abuse his fellow creatures. John goes on to give lurid examples of unnecessary brutality, such as the practice of boiling lobsters to death slowly and the preparation of eels, which involved sticking a fork in the eel's eye to hold it securely while it was skinned, then coiling it on a skewer – all while it was still alive – and finally broiling it. He calls for legal penalties to be introduced for wanton cruelty to animals, comparing the attitude of men to beasts with that of white people to black people, before black people were introduced into 'our section of the circle of justice'.

While John's argument at first seems entirely reasonable in its criticisms, it soon begins to become slightly more idiosyncratic. Again citing biblical precedent, he argues that in the description of the Creation in Genesis, God provided 'every green herb for meat' but gave no permission for one creature to eat another. Neither was strict vegetarianism enough: the fourth commandment ordered cattle to be given a rest on

Sundays. As the 104th Psalm has it: 'a man hath no pre-eminence above a beast, for all is vanity: all go to one place: all are of the dust, and all turn to dust again'. Admissible though all this may be, it is in his description of the suffering of live fish bait that John makes an allusion which suggests a slightly obsessive preoccupation with the subject:

On Sunday goes forth the angler to his innocent recreation (as men humorously call it) and impales the poor earthworm, which in its torture writhes about with strength prodigious in so small and soft an animal, and almost baffles the determined angler in his attempts to put it on the hook; while a copious slimy sweat, as of blood, exudes from every pore; all this, which is no unlike representation of crucifixion, declares its agony in vain.[24]

Is this a hint at why Charles feared, on one occasion, for his brother's mind? (Years later John was to refer again to his preoccupation with images of crucifixion: 'When a child,' he wrote, 'I have had my feelings so affected by [Christ's] suffer-ings, that I never can give up his dying for me upon the dreadful cross.'[25]) If he expressed himself in his pamphlet somewhat eccentrically, John clearly felt very strongly on the subject, having devoted much time and energy to the work, the reason being found in his rhetorical question: 'For what can the mind of a wise man rest upon, when his body decays, but the faithful performance of his duty?'[26]

Given the dearth of information about John, it is tempting to try to read something of his personality into this pamphlet – the style suggests a certain pomposity, for example – but all that can properly be deduced from it is how far the concept of 'duty' expressed here differs from John's attitude to his obligations as a brother and as a son. While his Christian compassion for the eel and the humble earthworm may be admirable, the hard fact remains that when faced with the real and immediate needs of his family, he had washed his hands of them. This double standard, where what John said and what John did were vastly at variance, was identified by Charles in the portrait of his brother he left in the Elia essay 'My Relations'. John, Charles observed, was 'made up of contradictory principles'. 'The genuine child of impulse, the frigid philosopher of prudence . . . With always some fire-new project in his brain J.E.* is the systematic opponent of innovation, and crier down of every thing that has not stood the test of age and experiment.' Charles goes on to give numerous further examples of the gulf between John's practice and his preaching, concluding that 'Whereas mankind in general are observed to wrap their speculative conclusions to the bent of their individual humours, *his* theories are sure to be in diametrical opposition to his constitution.' It must be admitted that *A Letter to the Right Hon. William Windham* tells us nothing so much as that John's moral and theological reasoning on the subject of compassion towards 'our humble earth-born fellow-mortals'[27] bore not the slightest resemblance to his actual general conduct towards his fellow man.

In July Charles and Mary returned to the Hazlitts' home at Winterslow for a holiday, but it was not to be compared with the golden month they had spent there the previous year. The failure of the bank at Salisbury had depressed the area, from large manufacturers to private individuals, and the town was 'full of weeping and wailing'. Some people had literally lost everything. The Lambs found the experience disturbing, Charles observing that 'It is the next thing to seeing a city undone with the plague within its walls.' They returned home via Oxford (both the university cities were great favourites of

---

* Elia's subterfuge masks John Lamb as James Elia.

Charles's), vowing no more night travelling as sleep deprivation gave Charles headaches and had more serious effects on Mary. Nevertheless, for all their careful preparations, although Mary appeared well on the journey back to London, she was taken ill soon afterwards and 'banished'. Charles resolved, not for the first time nor the last, that they would undertake no more long journeys. 'I have lost all wish for sights,' he sighed to Hazlitt.

Although Mary was well enough to come home after about six weeks, she was extremely weak and depressed for some time. A visit from Dorothy Wordsworth in October 1810 would generally have enlivened Mary, but on the night she arrived 'that damn'd infernal bitch Mrs Godwin' also visited and kept them up so late that Mary had lain wide awake all night. Loss of sleep was again the catalyst and Mary fell into a decline. The offer of a friend, Dr George Leman Tuthill, to treat Mary at home fortunately prevented her becoming worse and having to return to Hoxton, but she continued in a 'feeble and tottering condition'.[28] However, he prescribed a strict regime: Mary was to do no work, go out or receive visitors as little as possible, and to have no late nights. Although she claimed idleness made her feel 'so helpless & so useless',[29] in any case Mary's rest was interrupted by a string of domestic problems. Their maid, Jane, had been replaced by Betty who left soon after Dorothy Wordsworth's visit. Betty's replacement, a country girl, had stayed with the Lambs for only a few days before her sister came and took her home, having conceived the view that the Temple was a den of iniquity where a respectable girl would surely be ruined. Mary then secured the services of another girl who, she told Dorothy Wordsworth, 'is seven & twenty with a very plain person,' adding wryly, 'therefore I hope she will be in little danger here'.[30] According to Charles the new maid was 'a big stupid country wench' who immediately fell ill, took to her bed and looked likely to die on them.[31]

If Charles could do nothing to ameliorate their servant problems, he could at least address the number of visitors they received, which he was well aware was doing his sister no good. He screwed himself up to turn them away, writing uncomfortably to Hazlitt:

I have made up my mind that she shall never have anyone in the house again with her, and that no one shall sleep with her not even for a night, for it is a very serious thing to be always living with a kind of fever upon her, & therefore I am sure you will take it in good part if I say that if Mrs. Hazlit comes to town at any time, however glad we shall be to see her in the daytime, I cannot ask her to spend a night under our roof. Some decision we must come to, for the harassing fever that we have both been in, owing to Miss Wordsw*t*— coming, is not to be borne, & I had rather be dead than so alive.[32]

He added that although Tuthill's regime had made Mary much calmer, she was still 'too much harrassed by Company, who cannot or will not see how late hours & society teaze her'. If it was a difficult task to ask Mary's best friend to be considerate in her visits, it was a much harder task to deter those who could not or would not see that their visits were unhelpful. Mary Jane Godwin was one of the worst offenders in this respect and Charles wrote to her husband explaining the situation. That the Godwins were likely to take offence at Charles's letter is plain, as he several times begs them not to do so before ending:

If you were to see the agitation my sister is in between the fear of offending you & Mrs. G. – and the difficulty of maintaining a system which she feels we must do to live without wretchedness, you would excuse this seeming strange request: which I send with a trembling anxiety as to its reception with you, whom I would never offend.[33]

He also had the awkward task of asking Dorothy Wordsworth not to request Mary to do her London errands. While staying with them she had clearly been unaware of the pressures on Mary, only noting the 'boundless' kindness and hospitality which made the Lambs' home the most comfortable place she had ever stayed in London;[34] now that Charles wrote in embarrassment she felt guilty at her lack of sensitivity. She wrote to Henry Crabb Robinson:

I feel as if I *ought* to have perceived that everything out of the common course of her own daily life caused excitement and agitation equally injurious to her – Charles speaks of the necessity of absolute quiet and at the same time being obliged sometimes to have company that they would be better without. Surely in such a case as theirs it would be right to select whom they will admit, admit those only when they are likely to be bettered by society; and to exclude *all* others! They [have not] one true Friend who would not take it more kindly of them to be so treated.[35]

The affection and concern the Lambs attracted from their friends finds a typical voice in Dorothy's: 'Pray, as you most likely see *Charles* at least from time to time, tell me how they are going on. There is nobody in the world out of our own house for whom I am more deeply interested.' However, letters from their circle prove that the Lambs were by no means left in the solitude they sought and by the middle of November had much company in the evenings.

Charles must also have been conscious that he could do

more to prevent Mary being 'teazed' by his own conduct. He now frequently got very drunk when he went out and on at least one occasion had to be carried up the stairs to their lodgings by the coachman who had brought him home. ('I got home tolerably well, as I hear, the other evening. It may be a warning to any one in future to ask me to a dinner party. I always disgrace myself.'[36]) In March 1810 Mary had written wearily to Sarah Hazlitt:

Charles was drunk last night, and drunk the night before, which night before was at Godwins . . . We finished there at twelve Oclock, Charles and Liston [the comic actor] brimfull of Gin & water & snuff, A[f]ter which Henry Robinson spent a long evening by our fireside at home and there was much gin & water drunk, albeit only one of the party partook of it . . . Charles could not speak plain for tipsyness . . . Last night was to be a night of temperance, but it was not.[37]

An important part of Dr Tuthill's regime for Mary was that she was to drink nothing but water. It is testament to Charles's commitment to her recovery that he now manfully kept her company in this deprivation (he also gave up smoking – again), but further proof of the fact that his drinking had become excessive that a friend noted, 'We shall all rejoice, indeed, if this experiment succeeds.'[38] A painful exercise for Charles was made doubly difficult by Coleridge's frequent presence (it appears he was exempt from the strictures on visitors, probably because of Mary's particular fondness for him). Coleridge was about to embark on a course of treatment to wean him off both alcohol and drugs, but in the meantime was making the most of his drinking days. As Charles told Dorothy Words-worth: 'He is going to turn sober, but his Clock has not struck yet, meantime he pours down goblet after goblet, the 2d to see where the 1st is gone, the 3d to see no harm happens to the second, a fourth to say there's another coming, and a 5th to say he's not sure he's the last.'[39] Despite Charles's ability to make light of the subject, Crabb Robinson noted that his change of habits, 'though it on the whole improves his health, yet when he is low-spirited leaves him without a remedy or relief'.[40]

Charles and Mary continued to see a good deal of Coleridge while he remained in town and were peripherally involved in his falling out with Wordsworth. The cause of this was, briefly, that hearing of Basil Montagu's generous plan to have Coleridge live in his house while he underwent treatment, Wordsworth – knowing what it was to have Coleridge in one's home, and knowing the experience would certainly lead to Montagu's alienation from Coleridge – warned Montagu against the scheme. Montagu, who shortly learned this for himself and resolved to keep Coleridge in separate lodgings nearby, however made the error of repeating Wordsworth's reservations to Coleridge, who was at first furious and then terribly hurt. Mary continued to be about the only person with licence to boss Coleridge about (for example, writing to a friend, 'he offered to write to you, but as I found it was to be done *Tommorrow*, and as I am pretty well acquainted with his to-morrows, I thought good to let you know his determination *to-day*'[41]), and had been corresponding with Dorothy Wordsworth in an attempt to reconcile the two. Coleridge appears never to have resented Mary playing the elder sister and continued to turn to her in his distress. Having avoided his other friends, he went to see her and immediately burst into tears, sobbing 'Wordsworth – Wordsworth has given me up. *He* has no hope of me – I have been an absolute Nuisance in his family.'[42]

The whole affair deeply saddened Mary, clouding as it did

her relationship with the Wordsworths but chiefly Dorothy, and because Coleridge's constant presence with them in London exposed their loyalties to misinterpretation. Her equilibrium was quite possibly disturbed by the ongoing feud, and it only took a close bereavement to open the chasm beneath her feet. Coleridge was with Mary when she was informed abruptly of the death of her friend George Burnett. Charles and Mary had known Burnett for at least eight years. Richard Holmes has described his life as 'a curious version of Coleridge's life as a real failure'.[43] He had met Coleridge and Southey at Oxford, become a Pantisocrat and proposed marriage to Martha Fricker (sister of Coleridge and Southey's brides). She rejected him and he shifted between various posts thereafter, including medicine, writing and education. He became hopelessly addicted to opium and died in great poverty in a workhouse. The shock of the news and the distressing circumstances surrounding Burnett's demise, Coleridge related, 'overset my dear, most dear, and most excellent friend and heart's sister, Mary Lamb — and her illness has almost overset me'.[44] It was off to the asylum again for Mary, where she remained for about two months.

Although Charles could easily have blamed Coleridge for Mary's breakdown, and while he was well aware of his friend's many failings, Charles never forgot the man Coleridge had been and, indeed, the man who remained intact though handicapped through his own capacity for self-destruction. One evening while at the Lambs', Crabb Robinson happened to use the expression 'poor Coleridge': 'Lamb corrected me, not angrily, but as if really pained. "He is," he said, "a fine fellow, in spite of all his faults and weaknesses. Call him Coleridge; I hate *poor*, as applied to such a man. I can't bear to hear such a man pitied." '[45] Similarly, Charles continued to maintain Coleridge's unparalleled genius as a writer. Crabb Robinson

reported that Charles, astonished at hearing Leigh Hunt referring to Coleridge as a bad writer, 'in his droll and extravagant
way, abused every one who denied the transcendent merits of
Coleridge's writings'.[46] Without fail, and without failing to
pay Wordsworth his due, Charles always insisted Coleridge
to be the superior writer. Wordsworth, he felt, was 'too apt
to force his own individual feelings on the reader, instead of,
like Shakespeare, entering fully into the feelings of others'.[47]

However, Charles was by no means uncritical of his old
schoolfriend. On 18 November 1811 Charles joined many of
Coleridge's friends when they rallied to support the beginning
of a series of lectures he was giving at the London Philosophical
Society, off Fleet Street. According to Crabb Robinson, 'In
this he surpassed himself in the art of talking in a very interesting way, without speaking at all on the subject announced.'
Having advertised the lectures as discussing the influence of
Shakespeare and Milton on later poetry, Coleridge began
with a defence of corporal punishment in schools and took a
rambling circuit through the courts of Elizabeth I, James I and
Charles I, via the difference between wit and fancy, poetic
diction and European languages. 'This is not much amiss,'
Charles whispered to Crabb Robinson. 'He promised a lecture
on the Nurse in "Romeo and Juliet", and in its place he has
given us one in the *manner* of the Nurse.'[48]

An unpleasant event of 1811 – which incidentally demonstrates that the East India clerks were by no means the sober
scribes one might imagine – occurred in July when a colleague
threw a pen full of ink at Charles, nearly blinding him. A
happier occasion in September was the birth of a healthy son
to the Hazlitts. Benjamin Haydon, the first guest to arrive at
the child's christening, appeared at the appointed hour to find
nothing ready, the house untidy and Sarah in her dressing-
gown. Hazlitt, having left it to the last minute, had been

unable to find a priest and – worst of all, to Haydon's mind – there was no sign of any food. ('On my life there is nothing so heartless as going out to dinner and finding no dinner ready.')

Other guests began to arrive, including the Lambs, and a plate of cold potatoes and a hunk of beef 'with a bone like a battering ram' eventually appeared on the table. Watching the baby (who needed changing) grizzling and trying to stick his fingers in the gravy, Haydon could not reconcile himself to 'such violation of all the decencies of life'. The occasion demonstrated the Lambs' tendency to take people uncritically as they found them. Charles, Haydon noted, seemed entirely undisturbed and perfectly unconcerned at the state of the Hazlitts' household.[49] (It was possibly at another christening that Charles made Keats smile by grabbing hold of the baby's long gown saying, 'Where, God bless me, where does it leave off?'[50] On yet another occasion a doting mother asked Charles how he liked babies. 'Boiled,' he replied.[51])

Both Mary and Charles continued to take careful precautions in order to keep Mary's illness at bay, for example, avoiding situations which might tire her. Hence, when the Fenwick family (including their dog) descended on them for a week in October, Charles was left to hold the fort, Mary having decamped to the Burneys' at Richmond, where she intended to do nothing more strenuous than read novels and play cards. However, there were inevitably factors which they could not control. On 26 February 1812 Crabb Robinson arrived at the Lambs' to be immediately collared by Mary, who showed him a review of Charles's *Specimens* in the *Quarterly Review*. In the article William Gifford tore apart Charles's critique of John Ford's plays, branding his fulsome praise as 'the blasphemies of a poor maniac' and describing Charles as an 'unfortunate creature [for whom] every feeling mind will find an apology for his calamitous situation'. While Crabb Robinson, who was well aware of Mary's condition, could well have understood Mary's distress at the veiled reference to herself (Charles's 'calamitous situation'), he would not have fully appreciated the reference to Charles himself as a 'poor maniac', as he was not to learn until after Charles's death that Charles had himself at one time been committed to a madhouse.[52] The distress and guilt occasioned by this public humiliation of Charles and broadcasting of their history may well have been the cause of the bout of illness which arrested Mary shortly afterwards.

Charles had been feeling sadly out of step with prevailing trends in literature for some time. The children's fiction market seemed to have become even narrower and writing for adults seemed no less prescriptive. 'The sense of humour is utterly extinct,' Charles told Crabb Robinson. When Crabb Robinson was asked, by an admirer of Charles's work, why he did not write more, Crabb Robinson unhesitatingly asserted as one reason 'the bad character given him by the reviewers'. It was true that Charles was utterly sick of the critical hammerings he had taken over the years, to the extent that when he introduced Thomas Noon Talfourd to Wordsworth he said: 'Mr Wordsworth, I introduce you to Mr Talfourd, *my only admirer.*'[53]

While Mary was still in confinement following the revelations implied in the *Quarterly Review*, Charles appears to have thrown caution to the wind and penned 'The Triumph of the Whale' for Leigh Hunt's *Examiner*. Though he was not generally a politically motivated animal, Charles may now have considered that if even literary criticism could attract the kind of blistering personal attack Gifford had published, why should Charles not say exactly what he liked? It was not as though he could be hurt worse than he had been. Furthermore, the voice of reason, who in the normal course of events might well have checked Charles's pen, was raving in a madhouse. 'The Triumph of the Whale' was sufficiently seditious to be attributed by some to Lord Byron. Charles characterized the Prince of Wales in the poem as a fat floundering fish, surrounded by crooked dolphins, fawning eels and a host of courtiers and hangers-on, depicted as 'Monsters of the Deep'. But right at the bottom of the hierarchy,

> Last and lowest in his train,
> Ink-fish (libellers of the main)
> Their black liquor shed in spite:
> (Such on earth the things *that write*.)

'The Triumph of the Whale' appeared in the *Examiner* on 15 March 1812. The following week an article appeared in the same publication, asserting that the Prince of Wales was 'A violator of his vow, a libertine over head and heels in disgrace, a despiser of domesticities, a company of gamblers and demi-reps'. While no more treacherous, substantially, than Charles's verse, the paper was prosecuted and Leigh and John Hunt imprisoned in Surrey Gaol. 'Everything is a libel, as the law is now declared,' Leigh Hunt had announced to his friends, 'and our security lies only in their shame.'[54]

While the Hunts took their punishment stoically, Charles felt an enormous debt of loyalty to them and during 1813 and 1814 he and Mary were Leigh Hunt's most steadfast visitors. Hunt was later to write: 'But what return can I make to the L.'s, who came to comfort me in all weathers, hail or sunshine, in daylight or in darkness, even in the dreadful frost and snow of the beginning of 1814? I am always afraid of talking about them, lest my tropical temperament* should seem to render me too florid.'[55] He also wrote a poem 'To C.L.' in appreciation of these visits when he needed them most, and the welcome sound of the knock at the door, 'Then the lantern, the laugh, and the "Well, how d'ye do!" '[56]

In May 1813 Hunt recorded Charles and Mary dining with him in jail, noting in his diary that Charles 'was very *temperate* and pleasant; – poor fellow! He has every excuse for being otherwise, and therefore twenty times the usual credit for self-restraint.'[57] The casual reference to Charles being sober – one of several dropped *en passant* by the Lambs' circle – implies that the circumstance was noteworthy. The fact that Hunt links Charles's drinking with his 'calamitous situation' is also important and has a strong bearing on an extraordinarily powerful essay which Charles produced at this time.

'Confessions of a Drunkard', which was published in 1813 in *The Philanthropist*,[58] is Charles's most controversial piece of writing as far as his autobiographical work is concerned. Widely believed to be a gross exaggeration of the facts – if not outright fiction – it nevertheless represents a major inconvenience to those who have argued that Charles's drinking was not a problem. The difficulty seems to lie in the fact that those who have most appreciated Charles Lamb's writing, particularly as 'Elia', have been warmly attracted to Charles the man – to the personality that his writings appear to reveal. Swinburne was to observe that 'No good criticism of Lamb, strictly speaking, can ever be written; because nobody can do justice to his work who does not love it too well to feel himself capable of giving judgment on it.' The over-identification of the reader with Charles the writer is yet more pernicious than Swinburne suggests: lovers of Charles's writing believe they

* Leigh Hunt mistakenly gives 'experiment' for 'temperament'.

love, or would have loved, *him*. In the period at which the popularity of Charles Lamb's writing was at its height, the ideas of the 'good' writer and the 'bad' man were almost irreconcilable. For his admirers to acknowledge that their icon was an alcoholic would have done at least as much damage to his name as a writer as Coleridge's reputation for radicalism or Godwin's for atheism did to theirs. Responses of Elians, as some of his adherents have styled themselves, divide into two camps: those whose sense of loyalty blinds them to the incontrovertible evidence of his frequent excessive and problematic drinking, and those who, while downplaying it, have cast themselves in the role of apologist.

Charles's first biographer, Thomas Noon Talfourd, referred only to his subject's 'frailties' and only barely acknowledged the 'relaxing' effect of 'the glass' on Charles until the final few pages of his book: describing the stresses and strains Mary's condition exerted on her brother he asks:

Will any one, acquainted with these secret passages of Lamb's history, wonder that, with a strong physical inclination for the stimulus and support of strong drinks – which man is framed moderately to rejoice in – he should snatch some wild pleasure 'between the acts' (as he called them) 'of his distressful drama,' and that, still more, during the loneliness of the solitude created by his sister's absences, he should obtain the solace of an hour's feverish dream?[59]

Talfourd, while skilfully not giving any sense of the extent of Charles's drinking, makes it plain that any criticism or exaggeration of his over-indulgence is plain churlishness.

It is small wonder that readers of Charles's work merge the identity of the writer with the authorial voice of Elia, when some of those who knew him personally found the line difficult to draw. Talfourd wrote of 'that quaint sweetness . . . that peculiar union of kindness and whim, which distinguished him from all other poets and humorists' – clearly referring to his writing – a description which overlaps with his description of the *man*'s 'guileless simplicity of character and gentleness of nature'. Man and writer are indivisible in Talfourd's observation that 'The sweetness of his character, breathed through his writings, was felt even by strangers.'[60]

Talfourd's argument is apparently so reasonable that it almost escapes notice that it is irreconcilable with Charles's authorship of 'Confessions of a Drunkard' – an essay, incidentally, to which Talfourd conveniently never alludes. However well presented Talfourd's argument is (and it is), he cannot have it both ways: if man and writer are indivisible, and the man's drinking represents no more than the occasional glitch ('an hour's feverish dream'), it would be impossible for this same man to have written 'Confessions of a Drunkard'.

Charles himself was clearly aware of this; when one critic asserted that he had reason to know that the 'fearful picture of the consequences of intemperance' delineated in 'Confessions' was a 'true tale', Charles responded by explaining that what the – officially anonymous – author of the 'Confessions' described were no more than 'imagined experiences'. Well aware that he had done his job only too well – readers were struck by the powerful and graphic nature of the account, which seemed to attest to its authenticity – Charles was reduced to claiming that this was 'mock fervor, and counterfeit earnestness'.[61] The question which nobody appears to have asked is why anyone should wish to *imagine* what it was like to be an alcoholic, let alone write quite so effectively and feelingly on the subject.

Before asking why Charles should have chosen to write 'Confessions of a Drunkard', it is as well to consider what he wrote. The piece opens with a light enough tone, more characteristic of the later essays by Elia, introducing the alcoholic as someone known to the author. He goes on to describe the withdrawal symptoms he has observed in his acquaintance when he has tried to kick the habit as like 'going through fire' or being flayed alive; when this person has tried to abstain even for one evening, 'I have known him to scream out, to cry aloud, for the anguish and pain of the strife within him.' The piece becomes progressively darker; subsequently the narrator admits that *he* is the subject he describes and the descent into guilt and self-disgust begins in earnest.

Hitherto, Charles's attitude to drinking, as expressed in his familiar letters, had been characterized as the ruefulness of the regularly hung-over, rather than the unmistakable self-pity and self-disgust of the drunk. As the narrator he reveals more and more the depths of his suffering, guilt and self-loathing; he writes, he tells us (and by this time we can quite believe it), with tears trickling down his cheeks. He describes in great detail a painting which he has seen in which a man is being ministered to by three female figures (Sensuality, Evil Habit and Repugnance), commenting: 'When I saw this, I admired the wonderful skill of the painter. But when I went away, I wept, because I thought of my own condition.' Amongst the symptoms he describes is the sense of feeling unequal to his business; although he was never particularly adapted to his work he had coped cheerfully enough (this is a convincing picture of the poet resignedly but efficiently listing quantities of calico in the ledger at his desk in East India House), but his work now 'wearies, frightens, perplexes' him. In common with other symptoms he describes, this may speak more of depression than of alcoholism specifically: 'The slightest commission given me by a friend, or any small duty which I have to perform for myself, as giving orders to a tradesman, &c. haunts me as a labour impossible to be got through.' He lacks concentration, and is overwhelmed by feelings of shame and the acute awareness of his own deterioration: 'I perpetually catch myself in tears, for any cause, or none.' Again, this may indicate a state of mind which the narrator may seek to assuage by drinking, rather than one necessarily brought on by addiction to it. Similarly, although enjoying reasonable health in the past, he now feels ill all the time; even getting out of bed is a trial: 'Life itself, my waking life, has much of the confusion, the trouble, and obscure perplexity, of an ill dream. In the day time I stumble upon dark mountains.'

The narrator (if we yet resist identifying him completely with Charles) casts himself as one of those who 'feel the want of some artificial aid to raise their spirits in society to what is no more than the ordinary pitch of all around them without it'; in order to give himself a role in such society, he sets himself up as a wit: 'I, who of all men am least fitted for such an occupation which I experience at all times of finding words to express my meaning, or natural nervous impediment in my speech!' If Charles wished expressly to distance himself from the drunkard of the 'Confessions' why on earth did he give so many proofs of his authorship?

Although some of what has been written about the 'Confessions' (and interestingly it is one of his works which has received least attention, just as Mary's essay 'On Needlework', in which she reveals an aspect of her character almost invisible from the extraneous evidence, has been largely ignored) seeks to distance Charles Lamb from the authorial voice, Gerald Monsman in his examination of the autobiographical aspect of Charles's writing may hit near the mark when he suggests that in the persona of the drunkard of this essay, 'he gives voice to his own doubts, fears, sorrows, and guilts by exteriorizing or objectifying his inner states, a mode of dramatic detachment that creates a double who can cry out upon the world with the full force of his corrosive misery'.[62] Monsman goes on to claim that in Charles's early prose personae (in which he includes the drunkard of 'Confessions'), though they are in his view 'very distant from Lamb's own circumstances', the 'major' point of similarity and identification is 'that of their guilt. In this they are very close indeed to Lamb's true sense of himself.'[63]

Though the circumstances of the drunkard of the 'Confessions' are *not* 'very different from Lamb's own circumstances' when he was at the height of his drinking, Monsman's point is sound: the 'Confessions' provided an outlet for his general feelings of anxiety, inadequacy and shame focused on the one tangible aspect of alcohol abuse. He could not write about the miseries of enforced celibacy, or the effective imprisonment of being responsible for someone perpetually on the brink of madness, nor could he discuss alcoholism as a symptom of his depression without addressing these issues. However, he *could* substitute alcoholism as a cause, rather than a symptom, of his state of mind, and on that premise open the floodgates of his feelings. What emerges from the essay is indeed 'the full force of his corrosive misery', even though it merges the boundaries of psychological problems and those associated with, or intensified by, drinking. This, then, may explain not only why he wrote the 'Confessions', but why he appears to have been surprised at it being believed a true account: the significant subterfuge of 'Confessions' lies not in the concealment of the identity of its narrator, but in the suppression of its true subject.

Shortly after a visit from their friend Barbara Betham in the summer of 1814, a peculiar discovery was made by Charles and Mary which had all the qualities of a strangely satisfying dream. It began with an odd sound emanating from a room on the other side of their party wall. Charles's bedroom was in the attic and, as was often the case in the days when people leased sets of rooms in large houses, a locked door in this room (for which the Lambs had no key) barred the way between the Lambs' apartments and those which they adjoined. The noise, which was identified as the miaowing of a cat, emanated from the other side of the locked door.

Forcing the door open, Charles and Mary rescued the cat, which had got stuck behind some panelling. Further investigation revealed the existence of 'four untenanted, unowned rooms'. At first Mary and the maid used the extra space for hanging up washing to dry in; emboldened by the experiment, one of the rooms being much bigger than Charles's bedroom, he moved his bed in. Then Mary hit upon an idea which was to solve the problem of Charles being constantly interrupted in his writing by visitors calling, and she moved a firegrate, a table and chair into another room, and presented him with a study. Here, Mary persuaded him, he might write at his ease, 'as he could not hear the door knock, or hear himself denied to be at home, which was sure to make him call out and convict the poor maid in a fib. Here I said he might be almost really not at home.' Leaving him highly pleased with his new premises, Mary congratulated herself on their good fortune and her clever idea. However, Charles reappeared a few hours later with a 'sadly dismal face'. The bare white-washed walls were anathema to inspiration, he complained: he could not work in 'that dull unfurnished prison'.

Determined not to give up, while Charles was at work the next day Mary moved in rugs and some old prints and for the following week both spent all their spare time decimating their library by cutting out every picture they could find and pasting them on to the walls of the stolen garret. (Occasionally Charles would consult Mary 'to ask my leave to strip a fresh poor author, which he might not do you know without my permission as I am elder sister', she was pleased to report to Barbara Betham.) In the end, 'the print room' became their favourite sitting-room. They also kept the cat.[64] (Shortly afterwards Henry Crabb Robinson called on the Lambs and found Charles 'as delighted as a child' with his new apartment. 'It was pleasant to observe his innocent delight. Schiller says all great men have a childlikeness in their nature.'[65])

The Lambs continued to see a good deal of Crabb Robinson, whose diary entries afford many glimpses into the Lambs' everyday lives. He records, for example, walking to Enfield with Charles, Crabb Robinson reciting Wordsworth's 'Daffodils' – a poem of which he was very fond – while Charles hummed tunes, interspersed with chats about poetry. 'Lamb cared more for the walk than the scenery, for the enjoyment of which he seems to have no great susceptibility. His great delight, even in preference to a country walk, is a stroll in London.'[66] Charles's old prejudice was one shared by Mary. Wordsworth sent them his great poem 'The Excursion' in August of this year, in which he emphasized Nature's role in teaching 'the lesson deep of love', his protagonist drinking in the rural spectacle and, in that transcendental moment when 'thought was not', communing with the living God. Wordsworth's evocative and inspirational descriptions of the rural world about him were acknowledged teasingly by Charles as 'a deal of noble matter about mountain scenery', whereas Mary wondered aloud, her tongue firmly in her cheek, whether town dwellers *had* souls, let alone whether they could be saved, and affected great anxiety about 'that invisible part of us' in herself.[67] Despite their inability to resist alluding to the old argument with Wordsworth, the Lambs recognized the greatness of his work and Charles devoted three weeks of his holiday that year to writing a review of

'The Excursion' for William Gifford's *Quarterly Review* (the organ, incidentally, which had affected to pity him as a poor maniac), although he had niggling reservations about what Gifford might do to his article before it appeared in print – forebodings which were to prove all too justified.

Unfortunately Charles was unable to make much use of his borrowed garret that autumn, the absence of some of his colleagues and poor speculations leading to an increased and stressful workload. He was having to return to the office in the evenings to keep up with the paperwork. He wrote to Wordsworth: 'The nature of my work too, puzzling & hurrying, has so shaken my spirits, that my sleep is nothing but a succession of dreams of business I cannot do, of assistants that give me no assistance, of terrible responsibilities.'[68] Charles felt 'fagged & disjointed' and it was probably as much for his health as for Mary's that their regular parties were reduced to one a month.[69] Mary was also busily occupied at this time, having been commissioned to write an essay ('On Needlework') for the new *British Lady's Magazine*. Always conscientious in her work, Mary had even been teaching herself Latin in order to acquire the conventional style of such writing which appeared to come so easily to her male peers who had had the benefits – unlike her – of a classical education. When Crabb Robinson called on her in early December when she had finished the piece, she was completely exhausted by her endeavours and told him that she found writing 'a most painful occupation, which only necessity could make her attempt'. He was not the first to be astonished by this idea, finding the apparently effortless 'grace and talent' manifested in works such as *Mrs Leicester's School* and *Tales from Shakespeare* impossible to reconcile with the fatiguing struggle Mary had endured to complete them.[70]

The pressures of the East India House as well as the onerous task of 'The Excursion' review meant that by the end of the year Charles was in no better state than Mary; he told Wordsworth, 'I write with great difficulty & can scarce command my own resolution to sit at writing an hour together.'[71] He also faced a new commitment, agreeing in early December to write regularly for John Scott's *The Champion*. Unfortunately, less than a fortnight later he was obliged to break off the arrangement: Charles had either not the leisure or the heart to write. Discussing 'The Excursion' only a day or two later he might have been thinking of himself when he remarked that 'there are deeper sufferings in the mind of man than in any imagined hell'.[72] The next evening Crabb Robinson recorded in his diary: 'Late in the evening Lamb called, to sit with me while he smoked his pipe. I had called on him late last night and he seemed absurdly grateful for the visit. He wanted society, being alone. I abstained from inquiring after his sister, and trust he will appreciate the motive.'[73]

Silence, once again, told Mary's story.

10. Crimes and Horrors

An angel's wing is waving o'er thy head,
While they, the brother and sister, walk;
Nor dare, as heedless of its fanning, talk
Of woes which are not buried with the dead.

(Opening of a poem about Charles and Mary, by
Valentine Le Grice, 1849)

During the period 1811 to 1814 Charles had completed a number of short works. He had written the Prologue to Coleridge's tragedy *Remorse* (1813) and the Epilogue to James Kenney's comedy *Debtor and Creditor* (1814). He had written essays for a variety of titles and the style which was to characterize 'Elia' had begun to emerge. Most significant of these was 'A Bachelor's Complaint of the Behaviour of Married People', in which the narrator casts a jaundiced and querulous eye over the change in his bachelor friends once they become married men. It has been suggested that the Complaint, although explicitly critical of the influence of wives (and it is principally women whom the narrator blames), belies Charles's latent envy of the married state. Geoffrey Tillotson also observes that in the essay, 'Lamb's method is to make the Bachelor speak of other people, and speak interestingly of them, and yet to interest us most in what we gather about himself.'[1] However, this threatens to fudge the distinction between Charles's identity and the emerging identity of Elia.

While Charles may well have envied some of his married friends (though certainly not all of them), he was a sufficiently sophisticated writer to stand at a distance from his narrator, whom he distinguishes by hinting at certain character traits – some his own, some borrowed or observed. Thus while many of the essays do tell us about Charles (especially when they are cross-referenced with his letters), his art is to make it appear that *Elia*, his creation, is preconsciously revealing *him*self.

Charles was not yet writing under the name Elia, however (although the Complaint was subsequently reprinted as an Elia essay), and had not yet commenced the regular series which was to immortalize that name. His review of Wordsworth's long autobiographical poem 'The Excursion' represented an altogether different challenge and was to form his most avowedly literary contribution to the Romantic discourse. It was the first review of its kind Charles had undertaken and was composed in trying circumstances; however, Mary considered it the best prose he had ever produced. Although he had feared that Gifford might 'put words in its mouth', in the event Gifford – either through maliciousness or incompetence – succeeded in mutilating the article almost beyond recognition. Charles wrote immediately to Wordsworth:

I never felt more vexd in my life than when I read it. I cannot give you an idea of what he has done to it out of spite at me because he once sufferd me to be called a lunatic in his THING. The *language* he has altered throughout. Whatever inadequateness it had to its subject, it was in point of composition the prettiest piece of prose I ever writ, & so my sister (to whom alone I read the MS) said. That charm if it had any is all gone: more than a third of the substance is cut away & that not all from one place, but *passim*, so as to make utter nonsense. Every warm expression is changed for a nasty cold one.[2]

Worse, the original had been lost or withheld by Gifford so Charles was unable even to show Wordsworth the product of three weeks' hard work and prove his sincere high regard for the poem. Fortunately Wordsworth did not for a moment doubt the truth of Charles's account and was as aggrieved on Charles's behalf as Charles was on his. Despite Southey's efforts to retrieve the original manuscript, it was never found. Doubtless it is one of the lost treasures of this period of literary history.

Mary returned home about the beginning of February 1815 to further domestic problems. A letter from Charles to an unidentified 'Mrs H' gives an idea both of the Lambs' compassion towards their string of maidservants and of Charles's typical habit of subverting any idea that he might have a heart on such matters:

Dear Mrs. H.,

Sally who brings this with herself back has given every possible satisfaction in doing her work, etc., but the fact is the poor girl is oppressed with a ladylike melancholy, and cannot bear to be so much alone, as she necessarily must be in our kitchen, which to say the truth is damn'd solitary, where she can see nothing and converse with nothing and not even look out of [the] window. The consequence is she has been caught shedding tears all day long, and her own comfort has made it indispensable to send her home. Your cheerful noisy children-crowded house has made her feel the change so much the more.

Our late servant always complained of the *want of children*, which she had been used to in her last place. One man's meat is another man's poison, as they say. However, we are eternally obliged to you, as much as if Sally could have staid. We have got an old woman coming, who is too stupid to know when she is alone and when she is not.

Yours truly,

C. Lamb, for self and sister[3]

Nevertheless, Mary returned home to find one significant improvement. From the date of her last 'banishment' Charles had renounced gin, and was still on the wagon in April of the following year. However, he was extremely low-spirited, continuing to find the pressures of work demoralizing. He had forgone a number of his days off in order to keep up with his work and continued to work late often, a twelve-hour day (with two hours for dinner) being unexceptional. 'I have had my day,' he sighed to Wordsworth. 'I had formerly little to do. So of the little that is left of life I may reckon two thirds as dead, for TIME that a man may call his own is his LIFE, and hard work & thinking about it taints even the leisure hours, stains Sunday with workday contemplations . . .'[4] But work was having a more disturbing effect on Charles than causing him to resent the time it took up; he was not only 'tired with thoughts of it' but 'frightened with fears of it'; more seriously for him as a writer, employing his pen all day at work, he was less and less willing to pick it up at home and when he did found it impossible to marshal his thoughts.

A refreshing break from the daily grind of the East India House and Mary's round of domestic chores was afforded by a trip into the countryside in mid-May 1815, taking in St Albans Cathedral and Verulam House (built by Sir Francis Bacon); but the place which most delighted the Lambs was Mackery End, their aunt's farm, at which Mary especially had spent so many happy childhood holidays. Although the house had been rebuilt, the orchard and garden were still recognizable, and

Charles and Mary were warmly and hospitably received by their relations. A strong wave of nostalgia washed over Mary, who had much clearer memories of the old farm than Charles, who had been little more than a toddler when he had last visited:

Charles says he never saw me look so happy in his life, and he was not much less so for in the evening he said it was the pleasantest day he ever had in his life, When I saw him smoking his pipe with the farmer I wished to realize a dream I have twice had lately that he was with me and he himself a little child also, for I seemed to feel as much loss of him as his cousin Sophy a little girl of his own age who is dead and who he well remembers playing with.[5]

The subconscious desire – manifest in Mary's dreams – to turn back the clock, while in some senses typical of both her and her brother, may well speak more specifically of her concern for him, his drinking, his depression and the toll his work was taking on him and her inability – unlike when he was a child and she was his world – to do anything to ameliorate his trials. Mary never ceased to feel responsible for Charles; as he was to write, just as 'in the days of weakling infancy I was her charge' so 'I have been her care in foolish manhood since'.[6] Perhaps this awareness of Charles's own frailties somehow preserved her health, as for the first time in a long time following a fairly extended journey Mary retained her equilibrium.

She survived a trip to Cambridge with Charles in August in similarly robust health and loved tramping around the colleges and the old haunts of Coleridge, Manning and Lloyd as much as Charles ever had, nearly crying on the way home at the thought that it was all over. However, in the middle of September the darkness once again descended. Mary was sent away, leaving Charles depressed and distraught. 'I cannot attend to any thing but the most simple things,' he wrote to Mary Matilda Betham, whom he had offered to help with her 'Lay of Marie'; 'I am very much unhinged indeed.'[7] What had particularly shaken Charles was the speed of the recurrence of Mary's illness – barely six months had elapsed since she had returned home from her last 'banishment'. Charles had previously applied for a reduction in his hours of work, and now asked to take early retirement on a reduced pension. The East India Company turned a characteristically deaf ear to his pleas, causing Charles to wish fervently that God would curse '& fire it to *the ground*'. 'No one can tell how ill I am because it does not come out to the exterior of my face but lies in my scull deep & invisible. I wish I was leprous & black jaundiced skin-over and that all was as well within as my cursed LOOKS.' Charles was also feeling increasingly resentful about the small amount of his time that he could call his own: 'Why the devil am I never to have a chance of scribbling my own free thoughts verse or prose again?' he railed at Betham. 'Why must I write of Tea & Drugs & Piece goods & bales of Indigo –.'[8] To add to his miseries, Charles suspected that the problems he was bringing home from work might be partially responsible for Mary's relapse . . .

. . . but one always imputes it to the cause next at hand; more probably it comes from some cause we have no controul ove[r or con]jecture of. – It cuts sad great slices out of the time the lit[tle] time we shall have to live together. I dont know but the recurrence of these illnesses might help me to sustain her death better than if we had had no partial separations.[9]

The kind of twilight world Charles inhabited during Mary's absences induced a feeling of incompleteness which inevitably inspired thoughts of ultimate closure: while Charles had on at least one occasion almost wished Mary would die, freeing them both of the blight to their lives, the idea of her death was to Charles – who had never known a world without Mary – actually unimaginable. Yet it was also inconceivable to him that he should predecease her; after all, who would look after Mary? Certainly not their brother John.

'You must go first, Mary,' he was once heard to say to her.

'Yes, Charles,' she replied. 'I must go first.'[10]

Confused by the ambivalence of his feelings contemplating Mary's death, 'I will imagine us immortal,' Charles resolved, 'or forget that we are otherwise.'[11]

At the end of March 1816, returning to London for the first time in almost two and a half years, Coleridge made a beeline for the Lambs and remained with them for nearly three weeks before moving into the family home of Dr James Gillman of Highgate, where he was to undergo a detoxification programme to cure him of his drug addiction; or, as Charles uncharitably put it, where 'he PLAYS AT LEAVING OFF LAUD—M'. Charles and Mary still retained their deep affection for their old friend, though knew better than to expect him to see through anything he started. It was at this time that Charles gave the famous description of him: 'I think his essentials not touched,' he assured Wordsworth, 'he is very bad, but then he wonderfully picks up another day, and his face when he repeats his verses hath its ancient glory, an Arch angel a little damaged –.'[12] Coleridge had not moved far; he was only four miles away, and Charles was not being entirely ironic when he told Wordsworth that 'the neighbourhood of such a man is as exciting as the presence of 50 ordinary Persons. Tis enough to be within the whiff and wind of HIS genius, for us not to possess our souls in quiet. IF I lived with him or,' he hastily added, 'the *Author of the Excursion*, I should in a very little time lose my own identity, & be dragged along in the current of other peoples thoughts, hampered in a net.' While we have seen that when Charles was particularly vulnerable as a very young man, in the Salutation and Cat days when his feelings about Ann Simmons were at their most raw and painful, Coleridge's presence had had an unsettling effect similar to that Charles describes here, it is interesting that the mature Charles still keenly felt the intellectual power Coleridge emanated as an almost spiritual or visionary quality, as irresistible as a Siren's song: 'what amuses others ROBS ME OF MYSELF', he confessed.[13] Gillman, however, evidently considered Charles an unhelpful influence in his attempts to encourage his patient into healthier habits. Charles and other friends were – in the early days at least – made to feel unwelcome at Highgate and Charles later complained about the 'apron strings' which bound Coleridge to Gillman.

Charles and Mary's brother John puts in a brief and rare appearance in both Talfourd's and Haydon's accounts of this year (1816), not for any great service to literature or humanity but because he gave Hazlitt a black eye. (Mary and Charles appear to have loyally avoided criticizing their brother, but Crabb Robinson found him 'grossly rude and vulgar'.[14]) The conjunction of these two men of equally forthright opinions must have resembled the proverbial unstoppable ball meeting the immovable post. Apparently John and Hazlitt had both been at one of Charles and Mary's card parties when John flatly asserted that Holbein's colouring was as fine as Vandyke's. This was as good as a red rag to a bull and Hazlitt fairly exploded, leapt to his feet and swore that if John did not hold his tongue he would expose him in the newspapers.

'And if you do,' John retorted, 'I'll pound you in a mortar!'

Hazlitt maintained he would and John punched him in the face. A scuffle ensued, the card table went over, the company rose in confusion and succeeded in parting the combatants.

'By God, Sir, you need not trouble yourself,' Hazlitt spluttered as he was restrained. 'I do not mind a *blow*, Sir! Nothing affects me but an *abstract idea*!'[15]

Coleridge, whom Hazlitt had ferociously attacked in print earlier in the year, was 'not displeased' to hear of the incident. Even Crabb Robinson broke off with Hazlitt at this time as a result of Hazlitt's relentless abuse of Wordsworth. At this Mary checked Crabb Robinson, with the words: 'We cannot afford to cast off our friends because they are not always what we wish.' Aware of the general justness of the rebuke, but unrepentant in the case of Hazlitt, Crabb Robinson nevertheless uncomfortably recalled Charles's remark that 'Hazlitt does bad actions without being a bad man.'[16] This distinction between character and action was a central theme in both Mary and Charles's thinking. In the royal controversy raging at the time Mary once said, 'They talk about the Queen's innocence. I should not think the better of her, if I were sure she was what is called innocent.' Crabb Robinson reflected, 'There was a profound truth in this. She, doubtless, means that she thought more of the mind and character than of a mere act, objectively considered.'[17]

The only other memorable anecdote relating to John Lamb happened to be related to royalty. Given the task, on some occasion, of conducting Princess Charlotte round an art exhibition, he pointed out what he considered to be the *pièce de résistance*: a painting of Elizabeth I. The princess took one look at the portrait and exclaimed, 'Christ! What a fright!'[18]*

Charles's work pattern at the East India House had settled down by the spring of 1816 to a six-hour day, and while he

* Benjamin Haydon, who probably heard the story at (at least) second hand, says, I think erroneously, the painting belonged to John.

still resented it taking up the 'golden' part of the day, 'it does not kill my peace as before'.[19] In October 1816 Charles was obliged to inform all the friends who received mail free of charge via him at the East India House that the company had ended this kind custom. During that summer Charles and Mary spent a month at Calne, but on their return to London Charles 'drooped sadly', fought a losing battle to quit smoking, and Mary persuaded him to try another change of scene. They found a cottage at Dalston, planning to stay a week, but ended up remaining ten weeks, discovering the benefits of quiet and leisure and early hours – clearly feeling London was injurious to their well-being. They calculated they had walked 350 miles during their holidays. Mary began to consider 'that if ever Charles is superannuated on a small pension, which is the great object of his ambition, and we felt our income straitened I do think I could live in the country entirely'.[20] However, rather than regenerating Charles, when he returned to London he found the contrast too great, describing himself 'somewhat effeminate from country hours' and late nights tormenting.

By November 1817 Charles and Mary had moved house once again. The rooms in the Temple now needed renovating and redecorating and had become 'inconvenient'. They exchanged the peace and quiet of the Temple for the hustle and bustle of Covent Garden, moving to 20 Russell Street. The move from the Temple was 'an ugly wrench', Charles acknowledged, 'but like a tooth, now 'tis out and I am easy'.[21] Here, above a brazier's shop, they were in the centre of all the commotion surrounding the market behind them as well as the comings and goings at Drury Lane Theatre opposite their front door and the Bow Street courts just a few steps away, where Mary was able to indulge her pleasure in watching street life from her window.

The regular gatherings at the Lambs' were relaxed events.

Their rooms were tidy and comfortable, if their furniture was on the shabby side. All visitors were struck by the scruffy condition of their library – unbound books, books with broken spines and stained covers, and books still carrying their prices from the second-hand stall – which testified to both the Lambs' love of reading and a life of economy. As a fire blazed in the grate Mary would encourage guests to help themselves from the spread set out on a side table: cold meat, hot roast potatoes and Fleet Street's best beer. Whist and conversation were the order of the evening, which often extended far into the night. The mixture of writers, artists, musicians and actors with friends of the Lambs from all manner of other walks of life found the only pertinent social division at Russell Street depended on whether or not one was a serious card player. 'It was humanity's triumph,' Leigh Hunt declared.[22]

Coleridge and Wordsworth met at the Lambs' on several occasions in 1817, one occasion at Christmas in their new rooms in Covent Garden proving rather uncomfortable. The company divided into three groups: the women gathered around Mary while the men divided into two groups: round Wordsworth at one end of the room, and round Coleridge at the other. Crabb Robinson moved between the groups, observing that at one point Coleridge was quoting Wordsworth's poetry at the same time that Wordsworth was quoting . . . Wordsworth's poetry.

On 28 December 1817 Charles attended a dinner given by Benjamin Haydon, an artist with whom he had been friendly since at least 1813, who was now at the peak of his reputation. Haydon had earlier engineered a meeting between his friend Keats and Wordsworth, at the younger poet's request, and hoped to facilitate their better acquaintance. Also present were John Landseer (the artist) and Thomas Monkhouse (a merchant and patron of the arts, who was also a cousin of

Mary Wordsworth and Sara Hutchinson). The table was laid in Haydon's studio, dominated by the vast canvas on which he was then working, 'Christ's Triumphal Entry into Jerusalem'. If Haydon's unfinished painting lent an august air to the proceedings, it also had a surreal aspect, for two of the diners – Keats and Wordsworth – were also numbered among the figures surrounding Christ. As well as including his contemporaries in the tableau, Haydon had incorporated historically significant characters, notably Voltaire and Newton.

As old men, Wordsworth and Haydon were to recall what became known as 'the immortal dinner'. Wordsworth was everything his host could have wished, 'in fine and powerful cue', and the evening began with 'a glorious set to on Homer, Shakespeare, Milton, & Virgil. Lamb got excessively merry and witty, and his fun in the intervals of Wordsworth's deep and solemn intonations of oratory was the fun & wit of the fool in the intervals of Lear's passion. Lamb soon gets tipsey, and tipsey he got very shortly, to our infinite amusement.'[23] Haydon left three slightly different accounts of the meeting, and Keats one, which collated give the following impression:[24]

Charles votes their host absent, descants on the excellence of his port and proposes a vote of thanks in which all concur. They all drink a toast to Monkhouse's port.

Charles then votes Monkhouse present and apprises him of the honour done him while he was away (Monkhouse has not moved). They drink another toast.

Charles examines the head of Voltaire in Haydon's painting before turning on the guest of honour.

CHARLES (*to Wordsworth*): Now, you old lake poet, you rascally old poet, w-w-why do you call Voltaire dull?

The others defend Wordsworth, affirming there is a state of mind in which Voltaire would be dull.

CHARLES (*raising his glass*): Here's to Voltaire – the Messiah of the French nation, and a very proper one too.

ALL (*raising their glasses*): Voltaire!

They drink.

Charles turns his attention to Newton in the painting.

CHARLES: Now here is a fellow who believes nothing unless it is as clear as the three sides of a triangle. (*Raising his glass*) To Newton's health!

KEATS (*raising his glass*): And confusion to mathematics!

WORDSWORTH: Confusion to mathematics? How's that, Sir?

KEATS: Because he destroyed all the poetry of the rainbow –

CHARLES: – by reducing it to a prism.

ALL (*raising their glasses*): To Newton's health and confusion to mathematics!

They drink.

Later. They have left the table. Charles dozes by the fire. Late-night droppers-in begin to arrive. The first is the explorer Joseph Ritchie, who is about to pioneer a new route to Timbuctoo. Keats makes him promise to take a copy of his poem 'Endymion' ('A thing of beauty is a joy for ever . . .') with him and throw it into the middle of the Sahara desert. A discussion ensues on the attendant perils of Ritchie's proposed journey.

CHARLES (*suddenly awake, in confusion*): – and pray, who is the gentleman we are going to lose?

Ritchie joins in the general laughter.

The next visitor is of a different cast to the other guests. John Kingston is a civil servant, Deputy Comptroller of the Stamp Office, and a Wordsworth fan. Having learnt that the great poet is to dine with Haydon, he has that morning introduced himself to the artist and begged an introduction to Wordsworth, with whom, he says, he has frequently corresponded. Haydon thinks it a liberty; 'but still, as he had the appearance of a gentleman, I told him he might come'. Kingston duly arrives and is introduced to Wordsworth. In order to subsidize his writing, Wordsworth has taken up the post of Distributor of Stamps for his region of the Lake District, a fact Kingston is well aware of. However, in introducing the two men, Haydon neglects to mention Kingston's title, which makes him Wordsworth's senior.

Enter the Comptroller, frilled, dressed and official, with a due awe of the powers above him and a due contempt for those beneath him. Charles appears to doze by the fire. Formalities over, Kingston searches for a way to start a literary conversation.

KINGSTON (*eventually, to Wordsworth*): Don't you think, Sir, Milton was a great genius?

Keats looks at Haydon; Wordsworth looks at Kingston; all wonder at the crassness of the question.

CHARLES (*as if from nowhere*): Pray, Sir, did you say Milton w-w-was a great genius?

KINGSTON (*with milk and water insipidity*): No, Sir, I asked Mr Wordsworth if he were not.

CHARLES: Did you say so, Sir?

KINGSTON: Yes, Sir.

CHARLES: Why then, Sir, I say, you are – (*he hiccups*) – you are a silly fellow.

WORDSWORTH: Charles! My dear Charles!

But Charles is already asleep. Kingston does not know what to make of it. A long pause.

KINGSTON: Don't you think Newton a great genius?

Keats hides his face in a book; Ritchie keeps a straight face with difficulty; Wordsworth looks confused. Charles picks up a candle and approaches Kingston as though enormously impressed.

CHARLES (*holding the candle close to Kingston's face*): Sir, w-w-will you allow me to look at your phrenological development?

Kingston continues to attempt to make an impression. Landseer (who is deaf) strains to understand what is going on.

CHARLES (*retiring to the fire*): Diddle diddle dumpling my son John, w-w-went to bed with his trousers on . . .

Kingston smiles uncomfortably and commences saying some fine things.

CHARLES: . . . one shoe off and the other shoe on . . .

Kingston says some more fine things.

CHARLES: . . . diddle diddle dumpling my son John.

Kingston hits on another way to make an impression.

KINGSTON (*to Wordsworth, in a spasmodic and half-chuckling anticipation of assured victory*): I have the honour of some correspondence with you, Mr Wordsworth.

WORDSWORTH: With me, Sir? Not that I remember.

KINGSTON: Don't you, Sir? (*He pauses for effect*) I am a Comptroller of Stamps.

A long pause. Wordsworth squirms. Haydon observes this and feels pain at the slavery of office, reflecting with some unhappiness on the despotic power relations which obtain in administrative hierarchies. Charles considers the gloves are now off.

CHARLES (*singing*): Hey diddle diddle, the cat and the fiddle, the cow jumped over the moon . . .

WORDSWORTH: My dear Charles . . .

Charles unsteadily approaches Kingston with his candle again.

CHARLES: Do let me have another look at the gentleman's organs.

Keats and Haydon each take one of Charles's arms and haul him into the next room. Muffled guffaws emanate from behind the closed door. They return – without Charles. All attempt to mollify the offended Comptroller while . . .

CHARLES (*off-stage, rattling the door*): Who is that fellow? Allow me to see his organs once more!

Shortly after this it took the combined efforts of Monkhouse, Wordsworth and Haydon to pour Charles into his coat while he continued to demand to be allowed one last examination of the Comptroller's skull. But if the most amusing part of the evening was at its end, just as memorable for Haydon had been the serious talk earlier. Before he went to bed that night he wrote in his diary:

There was something interesting in seeing Wordsworth sitting, & Keats & Lamb, & my Picture of Christ's entry towering up behind them, occasionally brightened by the gleams of flame that sparkled from the fire, & hearing the voice of Wordsworth repeating Milton with an intonation like the funeral bell of St. Paul's & the music of Handel mingled, & then Lamb's wit came sparkling in between, & Keats's rich fancy of Satyrs & Fauns & doves & white clouds, wound up the stream of conversation. I never passed a more delightful day, & I am convinced that nothing in Boswell is equal to what came out from these Poets. Indeed there were no such Poets in his time. It was an evening worthy of the Elizabethan age, and will long flash upon 'that inward eye which is the bliss of Solitude.'

The periods Mary spent in exile in the Hoxton madhouses have tended to be represented as little more than blank spaces in her life and little attention has been paid to what her experiences might have been. Since the 'day of horrors', at the onset of each of her recurring bouts of insanity Mary had been taken to one of the madhouses. After 1817 it appears that she was instead boarded out with one of the female keepers. This change in strategy has tended to be attributed to the increased comfort and convenience of such an arrangement, and to the slight improvement in the family's finances which made it possible. However, it seems highly probable that her removal from the private madhouse is linked to a sequence of scandals, revelations and official reports concerning the management of private madhouses at this time.

A Statement of the Cruelties, Abuses and Frauds, which are practised in Mad-Houses, by J. W. Rogers, which appeared in 1815, constitutes a catalogue of crimes against the inmates of these institutions which Rogers, in his capacity as visiting physician, had witnessed with his own eyes. Rogers described a regime of brutality and inhumanity which, he said, amounted to 'a combination of evils, moral and physical, sufficient to overpower the soundest intellect'. It was not unusual, he said, for patients to be left chained to their beds indefinitely; unable to turn, they developed sores which, due to the general filth, became infected: 'In this state some constitutions will hold out long, and endure the greatest torture, before death relieves them.' Patients who refused food were often brutally force-fed, leading to horrible injuries: in one case Rogers knew of 'the upper part of the mouth was forced through with the handle of a spoon' – less fortunate patients suffocated. Lunatics who talked too much were gagged, or had their whole heads bandaged, he said, 'with such indifference to the consequences, that respiration is rendered extremely difficult and painful, and it becomes a species of torture consistent with the general barbarity of the place'. One of the most disturbing sights Rogers witnessed was that of patients being beaten while chained hand and foot, secured in chairs. One man was blinded in one eye by such a beating. Almost worse than the physical cruelty towards patients was the evident indifference of the keepers to their charges. 'Dirty' patients were whipped out of bed in nothing but their shirts to be mopped down at an outside pump even when snow was on the ground. Rogers saw three wretched women occupying a bunk designed for one, naked and covered only with a piece of old carpet. He found another in a similarly pathetic state; no one had noticed she was dead.[25] *A Description of the Crimes and Horrors in the*

Interior of Warburton's Private Mad-House was anonymously published (although its writer has been identified as John Mitford) in about 1822 and painted a depressingly similar picture.

Why are these two publications significant to our story? It is apparent from minutes of the evidence submitted to the Select Committee appointed to look into the abuses in madhouses in 1815 that Rogers had been a visiting surgeon at Warburton's madhouse; parallels between the evidence he gave to the committee and his published account (which did not mention the institution by name) strongly suggest that many of the incidents of abuse he related had occurred at Warburton's. Further parallels between these incidents and those described in Mitford's *A Description of the Crimes and Horrors in the Interior of Warburton's Private Mad-House* confirm the fact that both writers were describing Warburton's madhouse. William Warburton was master of Whitmore House, Hoxton, and just as Sir Jonathan Miles's madhouse, Hoxton House, was now known familiarly as Miles's madhouse, so Whitmore House was now known as Warburton's madhouse. Whitmore – or Warburton's – was the very madhouse in which Mary Lamb was regularly confined.

Is it possible that Mary Lamb, as a private patient whose care was paid for by her family rather than by her parish, and who was after all something approaching middle-class, might have been in a different bracket, a different part of the building, receiving a different standard of treatment? The evidence is not encouraging. Rogers saw 'gentlemen', including 'a gallant officer, who had highly distinguished himself', beaten while manacled hand and foot to a chair; he saw 'the wife of a respectable tradesman' treated with 'excessive cruelty by her keeper' (being beaten against the bedstead, and fed spoonfuls of salt), while a 'young married lady' (significantly not merely a 'woman') 'died in great misery' having been so violently force-fed that her teeth were falling out and 'her gums were putrid'.[26] Mitford took advantage of publishing anonymously to name names, should anyone be in any doubt as to the indiscriminate brutality of the keepers at Warburton's. William Congreve Alcock, once MP for the county of Wexford, in Ireland, was regularly knocked down by his keeper and often had 'his mouth stuffed with human ordure, in order', so his keeper said, 'to make him know good victuals when they were placed before him.' Mitford also happened to walk in in time to witness Miss Rolleston, daughter of Stephen Rolleston, Chief Clerk in the Secretary of State's Office, being 'beaten with a broom-stick on the breast'. He goes on: 'I have seen the person of that child, for so I must call one bereft of reason, prostituted on the steps leading to the lodge, by more than one keeper. I have heard it mentioned to Warburton, and his answer has been, "it is no matter; she don't know what is done to her." . . . Mary Wilson, her keeperess, would often say, "Go to your den, you bitch, or I'll beat your brains out."' On another occasion Mitford writes, 'Poor Miss Rolleston one morning was found in the room of Mr. Daniels, a gentleman called to the bar, but unfortunately deranged. The keeperess, who had not sanctioned this visit, dragged her out by the hair of her head, beat her head repeatedly against the wall, and then tying her legs, flogged her as children are flogged at school, in the presence of half-a-dozen monsters in the shape of men, whose remarks at the time are too indelicate – too shocking for repetition.' The author concludes: 'A greater sink of villainy never was erected than Warburton's Mad-house. A more helpless being exists not within its walls than Miss Rolleston.'[27] There are, unfortunately, many more hideous examples.

Mitford also describes a case disturbingly similar to Mary Lamb's. He writes: 'Mrs Wakefield, the authoress of many good books for little children, is frequently an inmate of Whitmore House,' he tells us. 'When she recovers, and the paroxysm goes off, she returns to society, but when she is ill they (the keepers) rob her of all she possesses. I remember – can I ever forget it? – when they stripped her in the cellar of all her apparel, which was new, and sent her up naked, all but her shift, into the parlour, pretending she had thrown them down the necessary; a new dress was ordered, and the keep-eresses divided her garments amongst them.'[28] (The insane being well known to be 'great destroyers of apparel', this scam was widely employed in corrupt madhouses.) The fact that Mrs Wakefield, like Mary, was an occasional patient at Warburton's begs the question why she did not complain to her friends and family of her treatment there. Two possible explanations are admissible: that she was in such a state that she was unaware of the abuses, or could not later remember them, or that she did not think she would be believed, and would possibly be thought mad again – she would have been only too aware of the consequences of her complaint if she found herself at Warburton's again. If Mary was similarly abused, either of the same factors might explain her silence on the subject. There is also the more distressing possibility that Mary felt she had no right to complain of the treatment she received, that she bore in silence what she perceived in some sense to be a just punishment for her terrible crime.

It is an inescapable fact that these abuses were occurring within the same walls that confined Mary, at the time that she was confined there and to people like her. While we cannot conclude from this that she personally was abused, we can be far from certain that she was not. Even taking the most optimistic view, that she escaped the ill-treatment which seemed universally practised at Warburton's madhouse, she could not have failed to hear the blows, the curses and the screams, nor, unless she was kept perpetually in solitary confinement, to witness the consequences of the abuse of those women or her own class whose 'whole appearance demonstrated extreme ill treatment', or those who, as a result of being routinely punched in the face, 'exhibited an appearance truly horrible'.[29] It seems impossible that Mary could have been unaware of what went on at Warburton's unless she was completely insensible throughout her sojourns, which we know she was not. Whether Charles knew is a different, and more delicate, matter. What is certain is that Warburton's keepers were adept at presenting an entirely misleading 'front' to visitors. Mitford, who was himself incarcerated there, knew that while the conditions in which pauper patients were kept excited very little interest, patients paying at the higher rate would be cleaned up and brought into the front parlour to receive visitors, who assumed this was where they generally spent their day.

It is clear from his letters that Charles placed great faith in the women who had immediate responsibility for Mary. Presumably he was under the impression that these were of a different breed from those encountered by Rogers while he was a visiting surgeon at the same madhouse at the same time, in whom he was 'sorry to be obliged to say' he observed 'even a greater degree of ferocity, if possible . . . than in the men'.[30] Mitford's account of the methods by which visitors were deceived by the female keepers is worth quoting at length. Like Miss Rolleston, one harmless lunatic known as Crazy Jane was routinely raped by the male keepers, only to be beaten afterwards by her female keeper who declared 'she could not keep her from the men'. This was, Mitford wrote:

. . . a burning lie to my certain knowledge; depraved in themselves, they knew not what virtue meant, and the sacred stream of pity never flowed in their corrupt veins. Mr. Chawner, the clergyman, once emphatically denounced those women to the housekeeper as 'the sweepings of Hell,' if so, it is a pity that place should ever be swept; at all events, they are the scum of the earth, and were the kennels of St. Giles's to be raked for infamy, none would be found to equal them; yet they dressed well, and could assume a look of cheerful humility, and shew tenderness to their patients when occasion called for them thus to do penance to the real sentiments of their base hearts. I have seen them receive presents from the afflicted friends for their kindness, when those, from whom they received this reward, were worse used by them than any others.

One afternoon, Miss Rolleston ran up stairs before the house-keeper in a rude romping way, as might be expected from her situation. The old lady, to teach her respect, as she said, ordered her to be straight-waistcoated; it was hardly done before her parents came, when the old sycophant herself brought her down stairs into the parlour neatly dressed, and received from her mother, as a reward for her humanity, a silk dress, and when they were gone, she laughed at their folly, and ordered the punishment of the waistcoat again to be inflicted on the poor girl, unconscious of giving any offence.

There was a lady confined by her husband, labouring under melancholy madness, or rather a powerful nervous complaint; he called every Sunday to see her, and she always entreated him with tears, to have her removed, but gave no reason why she wished it, and the keeperesses took care they should never be left alone together, from fear that she might tell 'the secrets of her prison-house.'[31]

This lady was sufficiently in control of her senses to know better than to be seen to tell her secrets. Another female patient whose letter of complaint was intercepted was, 'as a general admonition for her presumption . . . well flogged with a rope, and tied to her bed-post for a week, not permitting her to retire for the purposes of nature, and the stench in the room was abominable'. Patients deemed likely to blow the whistle on their gaolers were heavily drugged when visitors were expected and Mitford confidently asserted that even 'the medical visitors of Hoxton mad-house knew nothing of its general management'.[32]

While there were obvious methods of discouraging inmates from telling their stories to their families and friends, published revelations were also easily cried down. The journalist John Mitford's observations could be discredited on the grounds that he was himself mad, having been confined in the madhouse he described. Rogers, who had been a visiting surgeon at Warburton's, was a more 'reliable' witness, but accusations of lying and theft (both unsubstantiated) by the superintendent of one of Warburton's madhouses ensured his ruin and also served as a warning to other professional witnesses. However, the close consonance of the accounts of Mitford, Rogers and witnesses to the Select Committees repeatedly confirm the authenticity of their reports.[33]

Armed with these testimonies which are external to, and independent of, the Lambs' story, remarks in their correspondence which otherwise seemed insignificant (appearing to say nothing of her experiences) now regain their full importance. For example, during Mary's first confinement following the murder, Charles told Coleridge that he and Mary wrote to each other almost every day because 'we can scarce see each other but in company with some of the people of the house'.[34] He later mentioned to Manning – *en passant* – that he had been to visit Mary but had been refused access to her.[35] We know that Mary posed no danger to Charles on the first occasion at least – she had allowed him to take the murder weapon out of her hand immediately following the murderous attack on her parents – yet her contact with him when he visited the madhouse was clearly closely supervised and subsequently controlled. It would appear, then, that Charles did not see Mary while she was confined, except on the permission of her keepers and then only in their presence.

While Charles trusted the women who had charge of his sister, he hints that their capacity for patience and kindness was not infinite. He wrote:

They love her, and she loves them, and makes herself very useful to them. Benevolence sets out on her journey with a good heart, and puts a good face on it, but is apt to limp and grow feeble, unless she calls in the aid of self-interest by way of crutch. In Mary's case, as far as respects those she is with, 'tis well that these principles are so likely to cooperate.[36]

In other words, though he believed Mary's keepers had good intentions he was well aware of their all-too-human failings and of the absolute necessity of Mary ameliorating her vulnerability by making herself both agreeable and useful to them.

While regular visitors to the Hoxton madhouses – including Charles Lamb – could not be expected to suspect the crimes which were perpetrated within its walls, it does seem peculiar that Charles continued to return Mary to Warburton's after 1815–16, when a Select Committee of the House of Commons reported itself horrified by the regime and conditions in the Hoxton madhouses, stating 'a case cannot be found where the necessity for a remedy is more urgent'.[37] Presumably, Charles had some reason for giving the institution the benefit of the doubt for a further two years before changing the regular arrangements for Mary's care. The loss or suppression of any correspondence on the subject of Mary's periods in

Warburton's madhouse makes it impossible to do more than speculate on how closely her experiences corresponded to those reported in accounts of the same institution at the same time. However, such evidence does suggest that Mary's bouts of confinement represented something more subtle and more disturbing than mere blank spaces in her life.

11. C.L. and Co.

Farewell the most distant thoughts of marriage; the finger-circling
ring, the purity-figuring glove, the envy-pining bridesmaids, the
wishing parson, and the simpering clerk. Farewell, the ambiguous
blush-raising joke, the titter-provoking pun, the morning-stirring
drum. – No son of mine shall exist, to bear my ill-fated name.
No nurse come chuckling, to tell me it is a boy. No midwife,
leering at me from under the lids of professional gravity. I
dreamed of caudle.

(*Mr H—*)

The Lambs' indefatigable hospitality continued to eat away at
the time they could call their own and by February of 1818
Charles was again complaining of too much society. In
addition to the constant traffic in and out of their home Charles
was seen as something of a man of letters at the East India
House, and was often interrupted in his work by colleagues
and visitors who had what Charles called 'the form of reading
men' but actually read only in order to fund their conversation.
They sought his opinions on a range of literary matters but
also ferreted him out in his vicarious fame as a friend of
Coleridge and Wordsworth. No peace at work and no peace
at home led Charles to complain to Mary Wordsworth, 'I am
never C.L. but always C.L. and Co.'[1] Charles's status was
exalted to that of literary celebrity in his own right in 1818,
when his *Works* were published and he found more earnest

young men making their way to his desk at East India House. However, it is misleading to suppose that the East India Company was in any sense a relaxed organization, overlooking the vagaries or peculiarities of some of its staff. The misadventure of one of Charles's colleagues, Tommy Bye (also a sonneteer, whose poems Charles likened to those of Petrarch, 'or what we may suppose Petrarch would have written if Petrarch had been born a fool'[2]), is a stark reminder of how unforgiving the company could be.

Tommy had served thirty-six years at East India House and Charles had known him 'man and mad-man' twenty-seven of these. A friend of Charles's, although they were not close, Tommy was fond of a drink and on this particular morning came into work spectacularly drunk, having stopped off on the way to the office to top up the previous night's intake. His appearance was not improved by the fact that he had washed himself with a bit of new calico which had transferred its bright blue dye to his face. When this was pointed out to him (he hadn't noticed) he refused to wash it off, claiming 'it was characteristic, for he was going to a sale of indigo, and set up a laugh which I did not think the lungs of mortal man were competent to'. Tommy was rewarded for his misbehaviour by having his salary savagely cut from £600 to £100 per annum.[3]

Charles's letters of this period give absolutely no inkling of a surprising fact: he had fallen in love. Were one to scour the correspondence for clues to where he might have fixed his affections, the most likely candidate would seem to be the writer Mary Matilda Betham, a woman he wrote to in the warmest terms and whose work he also respected and admired. (In June 1816 he wrote saying how much he and Mary were looking forward to seeing her in London: 'Let *us* be among the very first persons you come to see. Believe me that you can have no friends who respect & love you more than ourselves.'⁴) But the woman Charles had fallen in love with is mentioned only in passing as one of their circle.

Charles had admired Fanny Kelly's work as an actress for many years and had been moved to write a sonnet to her which had recently appeared in the *Chronicle*. The sonnet applauded Kelly for the integrity and dignity with which she approached her craft (Charles disliked *obvious* stage performances, which pleased the crowd but failed to touch the heart), but also spoke of the peculiar intelligence she brought to her stage work, which made her actions and responses seem to proceed from the authentic thought of the character she was playing. The sonnet ends:

> Your tears have passion in them, and a grace
> Of genuine freshness, which our hearts avow;
> Your smiles are winds whose ways we cannot trace,
> That vanish and return we know not how –
> And please the better from a pensive face,
> And thoughtful eye, and a reflecting brow.

He once asked Kelly whether actors evoked emotions on stage by remembering a feeling they had experienced in the past, or by actively expressing the emotion at the moment of performance. She emphatically endorsed the latter method, recalling that as a girl she had acted opposite Sarah Siddons in a scene where Siddons had had to weep over her; Kelly never forgot the sensation of Siddons's hot tears on her collar which 'perfectly scalded' her back.⁵

Charles admired Kelly not only for her professional skills, but because her life had been full of trials which she had nevertheless risen above through hard work and selflessness, always retaining her good humour. Her father, who had been an apothecary, brought the family to its knees by his drinking and then walked out on them. From the age of eight Fanny supported her mother and three siblings as a child actress. In adult life she would tell a touching anecdote of how one day the theatre manager inadvertently gave her a whole guinea, instead of half a guinea, for her wages. Charles went on to record the incident in his Elia essay 'Barbara S—', in which he portrayed the child's competing instincts as she weighed the much-needed clothes the extra money could provide for her little sisters against the sense of wrongdoing by not telling the manager of his mistake. His instinct for participating in a child's feelings and being capable of evoking them in the reader make this moral fable on the quality of honesty especially palatable. Little Fanny of course returned the money, but was somewhat mortified 'to see the coolness with which the old man pocketed the difference, which had caused her such mortal throes'.

By the time Kelly met the Lambs she was a well-respected actress but life was still hard. Not only did she have to keep herself on wages far lower than her male counterparts earned, but maintaining a good reputation in an age when actresses were considered by many to be little better than prostitutes was a constant struggle. Matters were not helped by the unwanted interest of numerous admirers, including the strenuous attentions of the Earl of Essex, who could not comprehend why Kelly should not accede to his proposal to become his kept mistress. (So assiduous was the Earl in his campaign that Kelly was only able to shake him off by threatening to lay the matter open to his wife.) However, a far more dangerous threat was posed not only to her reputation but to her life by an obsessive fan called George Barnett (not to be confused with Mary Lamb's friend George Burnett).

Barnett, who was widely considered to be extremely eccen-

tric, but who was actually seriously unbalanced, was obsessively opposed to women wearing men's clothes. This was not
as odd in itself as it perhaps first seems: since the introduction
of women to the English stage following the Restoration of
Charles II, 'breeches roles' for women had been popular with
audiences as much for the view of actresses' bodies they
afforded as for the confusions they introduced to plots of plays.
They also afforded women – both on stage and in the audience
– the rare opportunity to mock masculine behaviour and were
on occasions more subversive than is often appreciated. This
'immodest' apparel confirmed the actress in her already tar-
nished status while also representing a threat to those who felt
the status quo was under siege by the growing independence
of women. The cross-dressed actress, therefore, symbolized
for many the usurpation of male dominance as well as –
usefully – labelling her as a loose woman. These attitudes had
largely receded by the early eighteenth century, but they were
clearly the anxieties exercising George Barnett. He wrote
Kelly a series of letters of complaint, one of which contained
a verse ending:

> Mistaken Girl! Ambition would you sway,
> To assume a part in each voluptuous Play;
> Your Sex's softness endeavouring to abuse,
> And for defence advance not one excuse.[6]

Another was more threatening:

I love the sex, and once esteemed you as an ornament to it, till you
raised my indignation by your impertinence and scandalous abuses.
You are very partial to a disguised Male Dress, but let me not
experience any more of your folly, for if you do I'll secure you as
an Imposter, and punish you for your temerity![7]

Kelly ignored Barnett's broadsides, which clearly incensed him. On 15 February 1816 he wrote his maddest letter yet.

Years ago I was your Admirer, but always met with disappointment. Coquetry indulged you, though often obtained at the expense of others. Without vanity to myself, I think my good intentions towards you have been more trifled with than any of my contemporaries. My claim to your person is therefore greater, which determines me to demand your hand, or, in other words, to make you my wife.

Anticipating that Kelly might not willingly comply with his demand, the clearly confused Barnett went on to challenge her to a duel; a pistol, he supposed, would be her preferred weapon.

Two days later, Charles and Mary were in the audience at Drury Lane as Kelly's guests to see her in *Modern Antiques*. The play was well under way when they became aware of a disturbance in the auditorium. They turned to see Barnett on his feet aiming a duelling pistol at Kelly on stage. He fired and she dropped to the floor. After a short struggle Barnett was overpowered and arrested, while Kelly was carried into the wings. Fortunately, Barnett had missed his target; the bullet had ricocheted off the scenery and bounced harmlessly back into Mary Lamb's lap. As she and Charles were recovering from the shock, Kelly, who had fainted, came back on stage to a tremendous ovation. It was one of the Lambs' more memorable evenings at the theatre.

After their removal to Covent Garden the following year, Kelly became a more frequent visitor at the Lambs', often dropping in on her way home – she lived only a few doors away – from the theatre. Mary also gave her Latin lessons. She had numerous personal virtues – Crabb Robinson, who had introduced her to the Lambs' circle, described her as 'an unaffected, sensible, clear-headed, warm-hearted woman'[8] and it is easy to understand why Charles should have been attracted to her. However, there is no clue of his interest in the letters prior to the significant correspondence of 20 July 1819. The only noticeable reference in the letters is a mention of Kelly's 'divine plain face' in a letter to Mrs Wordsworth of 18 February 1818 (Charles was not given to describing women's features), but then again as a well-known actress this mention can pass as unexceptional. He had, however, complimented her in print. If she was flattered by his sonnet, she would not have failed to pick up the hint in his review of Richard Brome's *The Jovial Crew* on 4 July 1819. He wrote of Kelly in the role of Rachel: '"What a lass that were," said a stranger who sate beside us, "to go a-gypsying through the world with . . . !"'

It is not known whether Charles discussed his feelings for Fanny with anyone other than his sister and, from the tone of his letter to her, it seems unlikely that he saw fit to mention it even to Fanny before diving in at the deep end. His letter to her, of 20 July 1819, is worth quoting in full:

Dear Miss Kelly, – We had the pleasure, *pain* I might better call it, of seeing you last night in the new Play. It was a most consummate piece of Acting, but what a task for you to undergo! At a time when your heart is sore from real sorrow! It has given rise to a train of thinking, which I cannot suppress.

Would to God you were released from this way of life; that you could bring your mind to consent to take your lot with us, and throw off for ever the whole burden of your Profession. I neither expect or wish you to take notice of this which I am writing, in your present over occupied & hurried state. – But to think of it at your leisure. I have quite income enough, if that were all, to justify for me making such a proposal, with what I may call even a handsome provision for my survivor. What you possess of your own would naturally be appropriated to those, for whose sakes chiefly you have made so many hard sacrifices. I am not so foolish as not to know that I am a most unworthy match for such a one as you, but you have for years been a principal object in my mind. In many a sweet assumed character I have learned to love you, but simply as F.M.Kelly I love you better than all. Can you quit these shadows of existence, & come & be a reality to us? Can you leave off harassing yourself to please a thankless multitude, who know nothing of you, & begin at last to live to yourself & your friends?

As plainly & frankly as I have seen you give or refuse assent in some feigned scene, so frankly do me the justice to answer me. It is impossible I should feel injured or aggrieved by your telling me at once, that the proposal does not suit you. It is impossible that I should ever think of molesting you with idle importunity and persecution after your mind [was] once firmly spoken – but happier, far happier, could I have leave to hope a time might come, when our friends might be your friends; our interests yours; our book-knowledge, if in that inconsiderable particular we have any advantage, might impart something to you, which you would every day have it in your power ten thousand fold to repay by the added cheerfulness and joy which you could not fail to bring as a dowry into whatever family should have the honour and happiness of receiving *you*, the most welcome accession that could be made to it.

In haste, but with entire respect & deepest affection, I subscribe myself

C. Lamb

The terms of the proposal are extraordinary on a number of counts, the most noticeable of which is that Charles refers to 'we' and 'us' seven times, implicitly emphasizing that Mary would continue to be a significant party in the matrimonial household. Charles appears, above all, to be offering Kelly the opportunity to retire and reserve her own money for her own use (this would not happen automatically at this time without it being explicitly stated) – the proposal forming more of a charitable offer at a difficult time (we do not know under what personal sorrow Kelly was labouring). The notion that Kelly had been 'a principal object' in his mind for years comes, as mentioned above, as a complete surprise but his frank 'I love you' is clearly entirely sincere. While Charles might have thought better of suggesting that Kelly could benefit from the Lambs' 'book-knowledge', the terms in which he anticipates her refusal and the guarantees he makes saving her any future embarrassment could not be more delicately expressed. Miss Kelly penned her response immediately. It ran:

An early & deeply rooted attachment has fixed my heart on one from whom no worldly prospect can well induce me to withdraw it but while I thus *frankly* & decidedly decline your proposal, believe me, I am not insensible to the high honour which the preference of such a mind as yours confers upon me – let me, however, hope that all thought on this subject will end with this letter, & that you will henceforth encourage no other sentiment towards me than esteem in my private character and a continuance of that approbation of my humble talents which you have already expressed so much & so often to my advantage and gratification.
    Believe me I feel proud to acknowledge myself
              Your obliged friend
                F.M.Kelly

It is not known whether the attachment Kelly described actually existed, or whether it was a kind invention on her part, but she never married. One of her biographers, L. E. Holman, has suggested that her dedication to her profession (she was now twenty-nine and at the height of her career) precluded any thoughts of retirement. Significantly, she told a colleague that the match was impossible on account of '*their* constitutional malady*' – i.e. both Charles's and Mary's mental instability. While Charles undoubtedly had qualities which a potential bride might find attractive, suffering from bouts of crushing depression and having a sister subject to violent attacks of insanity were not among them.

Charles could not have been entirely surprised by Kelly's polite refusal; he was possibly even slightly relieved. In any case, he took it squarely on the chin and sat down to pen the third letter of the day's correspondence:

Dear Miss Kelly, – *Your injunctions shall be obeyed to a tittle.* I feel myself in a lackadaisacal no–how–ish kind of a humour. I believe it is the rain, or something. I had thought to have written seriously, but I fancy I succeed best in epistles of mere fun; puns & *that* nonsense. You will be good friends with us, will you not? Let what has past 'break no bones' between us. You will not refuse us them next time we send for them?

Yours very truly,

C.L.

Do you observe the delicacy of not signing my full name?

N.B. Do not paste that last letter of mine into your Book.

(The reference to breaking bones is a pun on the ivory tokens which allowed friends of the cast and theatre management free entry to performances.)

Kelly wrote to her sister Lydia about the affair and described seeing Charles a week after the proposal.

I was indeed sorry to refuse him, for he shows the most tender and loyal affections. But even at the peril of my decision causing him great despondency, which I rather feared, I could have no other course than to say the truth that I could not accept his offer. I could not give my assent to a proposal which would bring me into that atmosphere of sad mental uncertainty which surrounds his domestic life. Marriage might well bring us both added causes for misery and regrets in later years. But he seems to guard his feelings well, we did not speak of the matter . . .[9]

(Kelly's penultimate statement seems to refer to the possibility of the marriage producing children who might inherit the Lambs' 'constitutional malady'.) There is no evidence that the matter was ever mentioned again and Charles and Fanny continued lifelong friends. However, a decade later 'the great attention he paid to every word she uttered' was observable even by strangers.[10]

In November 1819 the Lambs played hosts to William Wordsworth, nine-year-old son of the poet, taking him sight-seeing in London. William entertained the Lambs with his sage remarks on what he saw, observing when taken over Waterloo Bridge (only completed two years before) that 'if we had no mountains, we had a fine river at least', and 'he supposed they must take at least a pound a week Toll'. At the Exeter Change he was disappointed to learn the new lion cubs had died, as had his favourite, the Orang Outan, and the tiger was looking decidedly peaky. He was much cheered, however, by the golden eagle.[11]

The year 1820 saw a bold attempt to reconcile the problems

of too much company in town and too little in the country. The previous year they had experimented by taking a cottage in Dalston, from which Charles walked to work every day. While Mary had delighted in the garden, full of fruit trees and flowers, she confessed that 'flowers are flowers still; and I must confess I would rather live in Russell Street all my life, and never set my foot but on the London pavement, than be doomed always to enjoy the silent pleasures I now do'. Perhaps only the Lambs could have considered as a possible solution the idea of spending alternate weeks in town and country, dividing their time between 'quiet rest and dear London weariness'.[12] They appear to have kept this routine up until mid-July 1820 when they spent a month in their increasingly beloved Cambridge. There they met up with Crabb Robinson, there on circuit, who spent a day with them walking through the colleges. 'All Lamb's enjoyments are so pure and hearty,' he wrote in his diary, 'that it is an enjoyment to see him enjoy.'[13] It was probably during this visit that they met and became interested in Emma Isola, grand-daughter of William Wordsworth's tutor, Agostino Isola, and daughter of Charles Isola, lately Esquire Bedell of Cambridge University. Charles Isola's wife having died, Emma lived with her aunt, Miss Humphries, in Trumpington Street. Miss Humphries appears to have been a difficult person and it may have been a recognition of this, combined with sympathy for the motherless twelve-year-old, that led Charles and Mary to offer to take Emma off Miss Humphries's hands the following Christmas. In the event the visit was postponed due to Mary falling ill. However, Mary made a comparatively quick recovery (after less than four weeks), possibly because she was cared for at Dalston rather than being removed to a madhouse.* Except for about a

---

* Henry Crabb Robinson certainly thought this was the case.

week in mid-November when they welcomed the Wordsworths back from Europe, the Lambs did not return to Russell
Street until shortly after Christmas. In January 1821 Emma
arrived for her promised visit, enlivening the childless household by playing with the Lambs' dog, Pompey, while Charles
taught her *not* to turn down the pages of his books. Mary took
Emma to the theatre and Charles took her back to Exeter
Change – the animals there evidently proving a great favourite
with children in general and Charles in particular. Emma was
a very lively child and the Lambs flattered themselves that they
returned her to her aunt in Cambridge with 'her gait, gesture,
and general manners . . . considerably improved'.[14]

In March 1821 the Lambs recommenced shuttling between
Russell Street and Dalston and in late May left London for a
month's holiday in Margate. The holiday was enlivened by
the beaching of a huge whale, which stimulated great local
interest. Charles was telling a friend who had dropped in to
see them about the giant, which had been taken away on a
reinforced cart 'on which it lay a huge mass of colossal height'.
Charles then looked past his guest, then back at him 'with one
of his sudden droll penetrating glances' and informed him:
'The *eye* has just gone past our window.'[15]

Charles and Mary's brother John Lamb became extremely
ill towards the end of September 1821, occasioning a breakdown of Mary's equilibrium. Charles remained with her at
Dalston and on 26 October broke the news of John's death to
her. Experience had taught Charles that keeping bad news
from Mary until she was better generally provoked a relapse,
and that it was better to inform her while she was ill, repeating
it over time until it gradually sank in. She recovered around
the middle of November and they returned to Russell Street.
Mary was still weak, pale and thin and both she and Charles,
Crabb Robinson observed, seemed 'softened by affliction,

and to wish for society'.[16] Charles and Mary continued in somewhat low spirits through the winter and into the following spring, when Charles wrote to Wordsworth of 'a certain deadness to every thing' which he dated from his brother's death. William and Dorothy of course particularly empathized with Charles and Mary at this time, although Dorothy with her usual acumen recognized that the problematic nature of their relationship with John inevitably mingled their grief with regret. Responding to Crabb Robinson's account of Charles and Mary she wrote back to him:

It concerns us very much to hear such an indifferent account of Lamb and his sister; the death of their brother, no doubt, has afflicted them much more than the death of any brother, with whom there had, in near neighbourhood, been so little personal or family communication, would afflict any other minds.[17]

Charles and Mary had reached the age when one starts to lose one's friends in greater proportion, which Charles was feeling keenly:

One sees a picture, reads an anecdote, starts a casual fancy, and thinks to tell of it to this person in preference to every other – the person is gone whom it would have peculiarly suited. It won't do for *another*. Every departure destroys a class of sympathies. There's Capt. Burney gone! – what fun has whist now? What matters it what you lead, if you can no longer fancy him looking over you? . . . Common natures do not suffice me. Good people, as they are called, won't serve. I want individuals. I am made up of queer points and I want so many answering needles.[18]

Charles was wishing to retire more than ever – 'O for a few years between the grave and the desk!' – but had been informed in no uncertain terms that nothing but an incapacitating illness would set him free from the East India House. The idea of a few years of good health and the leisure to enjoy it was becoming the only thing sustaining Charles, and he dreaded the thought of having to wait 'till years have sucked me dry'. He told Wordsworth, 'I sit like Philomel all day (but not singing) with my breast against this thorn of a Desk, with the only hope that some Pulmonary affliction may relieve me.'[19] However, if Charles did not have time he at least now had money. Since August 1820 he had been writing regular essays for the *London Magazine* under the pen-name Elia.

In the Elia essays Charles had found the voice which was to make his name famous and which was to have a lasting influence on the essay as a literary genre. The character of Elia, while not identical with Charles's own personality, draws extensively on his own thoughts and experiences. Elia offers no objective view of the subject he discusses but rather casts the reader in the role of fellow-traveller on a journey which has a poignancy or special significance for the narrator. Some of these journeys are tangible, as when he takes us to revisit the scenes of his childhood, while others are expeditions through Elia's mind, exposing his preferences and prejudices. Simultaneously funny and sad, the peculiar tone of the essays which renders them so appealing is almost indefinable, so dependent is its success on the individual reader's receptivity to and empathy for Elia's idiosyncrasies. E. V. Lucas probably comes closest with his simple observation that Elia is treasured by readers because he 'describes with so much sympathy most of the normal feelings of mankind'.[20] Blending fact and fiction had always appealed to Charles. Just as he amused himself by representing Mary as a hopeless alcoholic, he wrote several 'hoax' letters to friends and delighted in misleading obfuscations as well as the impertinence of the arrant lie.

Wordsworth was to observe that 'Lamb's veracity was unquestionable in all matters of a serious kind; he never uttered an untruth either for profit or through vanity, and certainly never to injure others. Yet he loved a quizzing lie, a fiction that amused him like a good joke, or an exercise of wit.'[21] Whereas some men were approvingly described as 'matter-of-fact', Charles affected to pride himself on being a 'matter-of-lie' man. He liked to consider his tendency to the mischievous fib as a byword, characterizing anything which could be accomplished with the minimum of effort as 'as easy as lying is to me'.[22] He had written in ironical vein to a friend in 1817: 'the same steady adherence to principle, and correct regard for truth, which always marked my conduct, marks it still. If I am singular in anything it is in too great a squeamishness to anything that remotely looks like a falsehood. I am call'd Old Honesty; sometimes Upright Telltruth, Esq., and I own it tickles my vanity a little.'[23] Charles had even stolen the name Elia from a clerk at the South Sea House – conveniently, it formed an anagram of 'a lie' and, pronounced correctly, constitutes a homophone for 'a liar'.

However, Elia rarely offered pure fiction; his essays represented, rather, the truth fictionalized, and sometimes pure autobiography. Charles enjoyed his friends' attempts to separate truth and untruth in the essays, as when Bernard Barton asked him whether Joseph Paice (Charles's first employer and the subject of the essay 'Modern Gallantry') was a real person. Charles replied soberly: 'A careful observer of life, Bernard, has no need to invent. Nature romances it for him.'[24] The Elia essays were to bring Charles fame and fortune, both in modest but significant degree. If he could not afford to quit the East India House, he could at least now afford a few 'extras'.

In June 1822 Charles and Mary were forty-seven and fifty-eight respectively and neither had ever been abroad. They decided to visit France. Twenty years earlier Charles had mocked his own gauche fascination for things foreign, writing to Manning who was in France: 'Have you seen a man Guillotined yet? Is it as good as Hanging? Are the Women *all* painted, & the men *all* monkeys?' But he did have a serious interest in travel: to be in a new place was tantamount to becoming a new person. 'It appears to me, as if I should die with joy at the first Landing in a foreign Country. It is the nearest Pleasure, which a grown man can substitute for that unknown one, which he can never know, the pleasure of the first entrance into Life from the Womb.' Their appetite whetted by Manning, who had told them that 'Paris to a stranger is a desert full of Knaves and Whores – like London', and also that the architecture was superior to that in London, they set off on 18 July 1822.[25]

Henry Crabb Robinson went to say goodbye to the Lambs the day before they left and noted that Charles was in high spirits but that Mary was rather nervous. 'Her courage in going is great,' he added, knowing that long journeys had in the past often proved a catalyst to Mary's attacks.[26] As a precaution, Mary's nurse, Sarah James, accompanied them. At Amiens their worst fears were realized; Mary's attack came on suddenly, while they were in a coach, and Charles was at his wits' end to know what to do. Fortunately he ran into some acquaintances who were able to help him get Mary into secure accommodation. In what unfamiliar surroundings Mary was confined is not known, but Charles's determination to enjoy the holiday was undaunted. He went on to Versailles and stayed with James and Louisa Kenney (friends of Mary Shelley), where he spent much time sampling French wine and playing with the Kenneys' little girl, Sophy, whom he called his 'dear wife'. He later wrote assuring her that some of the happiest days of his life were those spent with her among the pears and apricots of Versailles. Charles went on to Paris with Kenney's friend John Howard Payne. (Payne was an actor-turned-playwright who, interestingly, had made his début in the part of Young Norval in *Douglas*, the character Charles had imagined himself during the fit of insanity which sent him to the madhouse at Hoxton in 1795.) In Paris, as in London, Charles considered the streets and shops the best sights of the city. He particularly impressed himself by eating frogs' legs, recommending them to John Clare as 'the nicest little rabbity things you ever tasted'.[27] 'Imagine a Lilliputian rabbit!' he exclaimed to Barron Field.[28]

Satisfied that Mary was in good hands, Charles returned to England in the middle of August in order to return to work, while Mary recuperated with the Kenneys. She was well enough to see the sights of Paris with Louisa Kenney, Crabb Robinson and Payne, where she loved 'the dear long dreary Boulevards' before she too returned home early in September. In a very delicate gesture Crabb Robinson lent Mary his waistcoat for her return journey (it seems extraordinary that they should have set out without a straitjacket, but perhaps it had been lost). Fortunately it was not needed, but to Mary's embarrassment it was confiscated at the Custom House, its officers clearly unconvinced that a waistcoat labelled Henry Robinson could form a legitimate item of her wardrobe.

After returning from France Charles began to drink heavily in the evenings again. In September 1822 he wrote to Bernard Barton: 'I am, like you, a prisoner to the desk. I have been chained to that gally thirty years, a long shot. I have almost grown to the wood . . . I am very tired of clerking it, but have no remedy.'[29] Things were no better by Christmas, when the customs of the season dictated that the Lambs' free time was engaged by frequent visitors and visiting. 'All work and no play dulls me,' he complained to Barton. 'Company is not play, but many times hard work. To play, is for a man to do what he pleases, or to do nothing – to go about soothing his particular fancies.' Charles had always maintained, and continued so to do, that he was only envious of the rich because of the leisure their money bought. 'Books are good, and Pictures are good, and Money to buy them therefore good, but to buy *TIME!* In other words, LIFE – '[30]

Charles's frequent recourse to lamenting his lot as an office-worker, however, belies the fact that he was keenly aware of the necessity of a regular income. He had seen too many of his friends who lived entirely by their writing struggling – and failing – to make ends meet. While he and Mary had survived on a very modest income – particularly in the early years – it had been regular and dependable and on more than one occasion when friends with literary aspirations had considered giving up their day jobs Charles had counselled forcefully against it. Bernard Barton, a bank clerk, had considered giving up his job in 1812, when Byron had warned him that deserving success did not ensure it: 'Do not renounce writing, but never trust entirely to authorship. If you have a profession, retain it.' The bank, Byron counselled, represented 'a last and sure resource'.[31] Now, in 1823, Barton was again champing at the bit and it was Charles who remonstrated with him:

Throw yourself on the world without any rational plan of support, beyond what the chance employ of Booksellers would afford you!!!

Throw yourself rather, my dear Sir, from the steep Tarpeian rock, slap-dash headlong upon iron spikes. If you had but five consolatory minutes between the desk and the bed, make much of them, and live a century in them, rather than turn slave to the Booksellers . . . I have known many authors for bread, some repining, others envying the blessed security of a Counting House, all agreeing they had rather have been Taylors, Weavers, what not? rather than the things they were. I have known some starved, some to go mad, one dear friend literally dying in a workhouse.[32]

The spectre of poor George Burnett's pathetic end as a pauper dependent on the parish continued to constitute a cautionary example to Charles in his moments of desk-bound gloom. When seriously contemplating life as a freelance writer, Charles could become a positive champion of the wage economy.

Keep to your Bank, and the Bank will keep you. Trust not to the Public, you may hang, starve, drown yourself, for anything that worthy *Personage* cares. I bless every star that Providence, not seeing good to make me independent, has seen it next good to settle me upon the stable foundation of Leadenhall. Sit down, good B.B., in the Banking Office; what, is there not from six to Eleven P.M. 6 days in the week, and is there not all Sunday? Fie, what a superfluity of man's time, – if you could think so! . . . Henceforth I retract all my fond complaints of mercantile employment, look upon them as Lovers' quarrels. I was but half in earnest. Welcome, dead timber of a desk, that makes me live.[33]

As always, Charles's advice sprang directly from his current mood.

Charles often drew on humour at work merely to entertain himself, alleviating the drudgery of his office and more particularly dissipating his resentment of its rules and authority figures. For example, all the clerks were required to sign an attendance book on arrival at work and one morning, although he arrived on time, Charles neglected to do so. Several hours later he theatrically slapped himself on the forehead, as if suddenly remembering something, and exclaimed: 'Lamb! Lamb! I have it!' before rushing across the room to write the same in the book, much to his fellow clerks' amusement. On another occasion an unpopular head of department came to check what Charles was working on.

'Pray, Mr Lamb, what are you about?' he asked.

'Forty, next birthday,' Charles replied.

The head of department was not amused. 'I don't like your answer,' he said.

'Nor I your question,' said Charles.

Another superior complained one morning of his tardiness: 'Really, Mr Lamb, you come very late!'

'Yes,' Charles admitted. 'But consider how early I go!'[34]

If Charles was somewhat shy of the attention his work brought him, he was nonetheless sensible of the cultural significance of the circle in which he moved and the momentous nature of some of the gatherings he attended. Due to the appearance of the Elia essays, which gained something of a cult following, the Lambs' home more than ever constituted one of the hubs around which many avant-garde writers and artists of the day gathered and 'gossipped about writing' as Crabb Robinson put it. More serious discussions also took place. With the benefit of hindsight some of the more significant cultural events of the period seem to have been received in a refreshingly off-hand fashion; for example, Robinson was at a large gathering at the Lambs' one evening when Southey arrived, who had himself just left William Blake. Blake, Robinson noted, had shown Southey 'a perfectly mad poem, called "Jerusalem"'.[35] (Charles, with his usual perspicacity, was one of Blake's earliest admirers.) He was also conscious of his place in that firmament, although never appeared to take it seriously. He wrote, for example, to Bernard Barton on 5 April 1823: 'I wishd for you yesterday. I dined in Parnassus, with

Wordsworth, Coleridge, Rogers, and Tom Moore – half the Poetry of England constellated and clustered in Gloster Place!'[36]

'Parnassus' was Thomas Monkhouse's house. Monkhouse too was conscious of the Olympian status of the invited company, whom he described in a letter as *'five of the most distinguished Poets of the Age* . . . Wordsworth – Coleridge – Lamb – Moore & Rogers'. Interestingly Crabb Robinson listed the poets present in exactly the same order in his diary, commenting, 'Five poets of very unequal worth and most disproportionate popularity, whom the public probably would arrange in the very inverse order, except that it would place Moore above Rogers.' Their host, Monkhouse, was described by one of his guests as 'a Maecenas of the school, contributing nothing but good dinners and silence'. He had attended 'the immortal dinner' at Haydon's and Wordsworth generally stayed with him when he came to London.

A comparison of three accounts of the evening serves to demonstrate what a very imperfect science biography is. Had only Charles's account survived, for example, there would be no way of guessing that Mary was also present, which suggests the strong possibility that she was present on a number of other occasions when Charles reports that 'I' did something which in fact 'we' did. (The habit of failing to mention female company is pretty much universal in contemporary accounts; only Monkhouse mentions that his wife Jane was present, while only Crabb Robinson includes the names of Miss Hutchinson and Mrs Gillman.) Thomas Moore's account of the evening described Charles as 'the hero at present of the *London Magazine*', but Charles had mixed feelings about the fame brought by the Elia essays. On the one hand, he was persecuted by 'fans' of the kind that had pursued Coleridge, and in January 1823 he records anticipating a meeting with 'a literary lady' who wanted to see 'Elia'. 'Now, of all God's creatures, I detest letters-affecting, authors-hunting ladies,' he complained.[37] On the other, he confessed that 'I like a bit of flattery tickling my vanity as well as anyone.'[38]

Charles's fame now went before him on social occasions; Mary, however, arrived with a different kind of 'baggage'. Whereas Moore described Charles as 'the hero at present of the *London Magazine*', he identified Mary, not as the author of *Tales from Shakespeare* or *Mrs Leicester's School*, but as 'the poor woman who went mad in a diligence on the way to Paris'.[39] Moore, who it seems had not met the Lambs before, described Charles as 'a clever fellow, certainly, but full of villainous and abortive puns, which he miscarries of every minute. Some excellent things, however,' Moore allowed, 'have come from him,' suggesting that Charles's reputation as a writer somewhat inhibited criticism of his social behaviour. Crabb Robinson – described by Moore as 'one of the *minora sidera* of the constellation of the Lakes' – in turn noted that Moore 'seemed very conscious of his inferiority' and while he was attentive to Coleridge 'seemed to relish Lamb, whom he sat next'. Significantly, Crabb Robinson reports that Charles was on good form, 'kept himself within bounds and was only cheerful at last' and Monkhouse described him as 'most witty – but perfectly steady' – both gentlemanly codified references to the fact that Charles did not get blind drunk on this occasion. Nevertheless, as Charles confessed to Barton, his 'cheerfulness' resulted in a hangover the next morning.[40]

There is general agreement that Coleridge was on his most excellent eloquent form, as Charles reported to Barton: 'Coleridge was in his finest vein of talk, had all the talk, and let 'em talk as evilly as they do of the envy of Poets, I am sure not one there but was content to be nothing but a listener. The Muses were dumb, while Apollo lectured on his and their fine art.'

Charles's sensation of losing his sense of self when continuing for any extended period of time in the company of Wordsworth and especially Coleridge – that of feeling his own identity swamped and suffocated by the brilliance and originality of their thought – was nevertheless undiminished. By the time Wordsworth left London, Charles felt he had been 'over-watched and over-poeted'. 'I was obliged for health sake to wish him gone; but now he is gone I feel a great loss,' he admitted. The use of the word 'over-watched' is interesting, especially as Charles resolved to spend some time in Dalston 'to recruit, and have serious thoughts – of altering my condition, that is, of taking to sobriety'.[41] Had Wordsworth been lecturing him about his drinking? He was certainly drinking as much now as he ever had. Having finally found a popular voice in Elia he had begun to find the demands of that persona straitening, describing himself as trapped in 'the body of this death'.

12. Bridget and Elia

And everywhere that Mary went,
Her lamb was sure to go.

(Traditional nursery rhyme)

Much of 1823 saw Charles and Mary looking on while many of their friends were embroiled in or disentangling themselves from marital affairs of one kind or another. Coleridge continued to live apart from his estranged wife, at the Gillmans'. Charles expressed the view that, hopelessly ill-suited to marriage, Coleridge 'ought not to have a wife or children; he should have a sort of diocesan care of the world – no parish duty.'[1] Sarah and William Hazlitt's marriage – the idea of which Mary and Charles had considered such a great joke – turned out not nearly so funny. Having settled on a divorce in the Scottish courts, Sarah now seemed to Mary to look forward to the trip with inappropriate high spirits. Mary Shelley reported to Leigh Hunt Mary's difficulty as she 'in vain endeavoured to make [Sarah] look on her journey to Scotland in any other light than a jaunt'.[2] Undaunted by these disconcerting examples of the wedded state, the Lambs' friend Thomas Alsager (at that time financial editor of *The Times*) married scandalously 'beneath him'. Alsager, it appears, delayed introducing his bride to his circle for some time, but when she did finally appear, a lady making polite conversation asked whether she were acquainted with a certain Mrs

Mitchel. 'I can't say I does, ma'am,' replied Mrs Alsager, 'but the same doctor as lays me, lays her.' Mrs Alsager was very beautiful and she and her husband proved to have a happier marriage than either the Coleridges or the Hazlitts. Or, as she herself put it: 'Oh, Alsager and me, we lives like doves.'[3]

In June 1823 Charles and Mary, accompanied by Sarah James, visited Tunbridge Wells and Hastings, spending their holidays agreeably walking, sight-seeing, eating turbot and drinking smuggled Dutch gin. In their spare time Sarah James, who had picked up a smattering of French during their continental trip and was eager to learn more, was taught the language by Mary. (It is an example of Mary's willpower and dedication that in middle age she taught herself Latin, French and Italian and tutored a number of their friends' children in a range of academic subjects.) On their return to London the Lambs found it difficult to settle back into their old routines. The contrast between Charles's sedentary habits at the East India House and the vigorous walking he had enjoyed by the sea was one thing, but even home didn't feel like home after the break. In Covent Garden their landlady seemed always to be quarrelling with their maid and Dalston provided more stress than rest, the landlord's family

always beating one another, brothers beating sisters (one a most beautiful girl lamed for life), father beating sons and daughters, and son again beating his father, knocking him fairly down, a scene I never before witnessed, but was called out of bed by the unnatural blows, the parricidal colour of which, tho' my morals could not but condemn, yet my reason did heartily approve, and in the issue the house was quieter for a day or so than I had ever known.[4]

Disturbed by the constant arguments and fights at both addresses and feeling the need for a change of lifestyle, Charles and Mary decided to give up their rooms in Covent Garden and Dalston and made their most radical move yet, to Islington, then little more than a village on the outskirts of London. Mary Shelley, visiting shortly after the move, wrote to Leigh Hunt: 'I cannot say much for the beauty or rurality of the spot but they are pleased.'[5] From here Charles could walk to work while enjoying the benefits of a more secluded home life. He described their new domicile to Bernard Barton thus:

I have a Cottage, in Colebrook row, Islington. A cottage, for it is detach'd; a white house, with 6 good rooms; the New River (rather elderly by this time) runs (if a moderate walking pace can be so termed) close to the foot of the house; and behind is a spacious garden, with vines (I assure you), pears, strawberries, parsnips, leeks, carrots, cabbages, to delight the heart of old Alcinous. You enter without passage into a cheerful dining room, all studded over and rough with old Books, and above is a lightsome Drawing room, 3 windows, full of choice prints. I feel like a great Lord, never having had a house before.[6]

Unused, also, to having a garden, Charles managed to upset an elderly neighbour the first day they were there by lopping some branches off a tree which had served the purpose of screening her window from passers-by. Despite Charles's conciliatory 'fine words', the old lady was furious and 'talk'd of the Law'. Yet even this premature *faux pas* could not dampen his spirits; although, Elia-like, Charles gave a deliberately subversive impression of his aptitude for rural life, reflecting on his new-found interest in horticulture with some satisfaction: 'I do now sit under my own vine, and contemplate the growth of vegetable nature. I can now understand in what sense they speak of FATHER ADAM. I recognise the paternity, while I watch my tulips' – this was in September.[7]

Mary had not been involved in the removal. Having become ill – Charles suspected – at the mere prospect of it, she lingered at Dalston with Sarah James until the dust had settled. She was well enough to join Charles at Islington in September 1823 only a few days after the move, but was not right for some time. One day soon after she had come home George Dyer called in to see her *en route* to a lunch engagement with Anna Letitia Barbauld (one of the 'bald' women, whom Charles and Mary had once strenuously attempted to link romantically with Dyer). Dyer's eccentricities and absent-mindedness were now compounded by failing eyesight and as he left the house, having forgotten to put on his spectacles, instead of turning to go along the path which ran parallel to the New River, he strode purposefully straight ahead and vanished from sight. (As he later explained to Procter, 'I soon found that I was in the water, Sir.'[8]) Fortunately, as it was the middle of the day, passers-by retrieved him from the river and sent for a doctor. A dirty one-eyed sot was summoned from the nearest pub ('where it seems he lurks,' Charles told Sarah Hazlitt, 'for the sake of picking up water practice'), the limit of whose expertise lay in administering copious amounts of brandy. Not for the first time, Mary put Dyer – now drunk – to bed and Charles came home to find him raving. 'He sung, laughed, whimpered, screamed, babbled of guardian angels, would get up and go home; but we kept him there by force . . .' Dyer went home the next morning none the worse for wear and the Lambs dined out on the tale for some time, Charles making it the subject of one of his most amusing Elia essays, 'Amicus Redivius'.

An important event of 1823 was the publication in book form of all the Elia essays to date. Their reception was mixed and sales were slow, a situation which was not helped by a casual reference of Southey's in the January issue of the *Quar-*

terly Review. He described *Elia* as 'a book which wants only a sounder religious feeling, to be as delightful as it is original'. Southey's remark stung Charles, on three counts. First, it was likely to prejudice the book-buying public against *Elia*; second, there was an element of the pot calling the kettle black ('If all his UNGUARDED expressions on the subject were to be collected –' Charles reflected . . . [9]); third, this seemed further evidence of the *Quarterly*'s entrenched antipathy to Charles (having exposed his and Mary's history of mental illness, exploited the candour of 'Confessions of a Drunkard', and maliciously made mincemeat of his review of Wordsworth's 'Excursion' – the *Quarterly* now cast doubts on Charles's spiritual integrity).

Charles responded with his 'Letter to Southey', published in the *London Magazine*. By defending Leigh Hunt and Hazlitt, whom Southey had criticized, at a time when, according to Crabb Robinson, 'there are not two characters more generally detested in the country', Charles characteristically allowed his loyalty to his friends to expose himself to further brickbats.[10] Southey was genuinely shocked at how much his comments had hurt Charles and following an exchange of apologetic letters on both sides, the two were reconciled. Charles's libellous poem 'The Triumph of the Whale' had been written when Mary (whom Charles called 'my second conscience') was in confinement and Charles explained that 'my guardian angel was away' when he composed his rebuke to Southey.[11] Mary's presence, it seems, generally prevented Charles's more dangerous forays into print.

Charles and Mary were both to become 'guardian angels' following the death of Emma Isola's father in 1823. Emma was now an orphan, alone in the world apart from her siblings (for whom various provisions had been made) and her rather severe aunt. Having a tender concern for all their friends' children, the Lambs now took a particular interest in Emma to the extent that they assumed responsibility for her education (paying for her to attend a school in Dulwich run by a Mrs Richardson) and having her to stay with them in her holidays. Although Miss Humphries was never to relinquish entirely her guardianship of her niece, from this time on Emma effectively became part of Charles and Mary's household and an important part of their lives.

Charles was now forty-eight and Mary fifty-nine. Charles continued to hope he would be allowed to retire early and made preparations for making his will soon after they settled into their new home. They looked forward to a future of peace and tranquillity at Islington. Contentment, however, proved elusive. Winters often had a depressing effect on Charles's spirits but he continued to feel miserable well into their first summer at the cottage. He had always needed to feel in the mood to write even a letter, but now he complained of an absolute inability to put pen to paper. A new friend he made at about this time, Peter George Patmore, observed that 'it was a task of almost insuperable difficulty and trouble to him to write'.[12] Charles himself told Barton: 'I cannot write without a genial impulse, and I have none.'[13] For nearly a year he wrote nothing for the *London Magazine*, but his depression became more generally incapacitating. 'To have to do anything – to order me a new coat, for instance, tho' my old buttons are shelled like beans – is an effort.'[14]

Although they had planned to visit Reigate with the Allsops and Ramsgate to see the Monkhouses, Charles and Mary made no long journeys during their first year in Islington. These decisions may well have preserved Mary's health as she escaped her 'sad yearly visitation', suffering only one mild attack in March 1824. Visits from Manning and Emma Isola enlivened them for a time, but Charles continued to feel low and miserable, increasingly ascribing his depressed spirits to the nature of his work at the East India House.

During his years at Leadenhall Charles had seen his working conditions become progressively more restrictive. The clerks had lost many of the holidays they had traditionally enjoyed – Charles got only Christmas Day off, for example, at that season – and any absence from the office which exceeded half an hour had to be recorded in a book. Perhaps the only aspect of his employment which might seem surprisingly liberal today is that Charles frequently welcomed visitors on personal business at the Accountants' Office: fans of Elia and hopeful young writers arrived clutching letters of introduction and friends popped in to catch up on the news.

On 10 February 1825 Charles celebrated his fiftieth birthday. At around this time he was astonished to pick up a hint that, should he apply to retire on the grounds of ill-health, the application might at last be kindly considered. He consulted Dr Tuthill (who had been treating Mary) and Dr Gillman (who had been treating Coleridge), both of whom made medical statements in support of his retirement, and waited in an apprehensive fever. He eventually heard he was to be liberated on 29 March 1825. Transported with elation, he wrote briefly and to the point to Robinson: 'I have left the d – – – – d India house for ever! Give me great joy.'

When he had had time to recover from the initial shock of finally achieving freedom, he wrote in a more considered tone to Wordsworth:

I came home for ever on Tuesday in last week. The incomprehensibleness of my condition overwhelm'd me. It was like passing from life into Eternity. Every year to be as long as three, i.e. to have three times as much real time, time that is my own, in it! I wandered about thinking I was happy, but feeling I was not. But that tumultuousness is passing off, and I begin to understand the nature of the gift. Holydays, even the annual month, were always uneasy joys: their conscious fugitiveness – the craving after making the most of them. Now, when all is holyday, there are no holidays. I can sit at home in rain or shine without a restless impulse for walkings. I am daily steadying, and shall soon find it as natural to me to be my own master, as it has been irksome to have had a master.[15]

When Robinson called on Charles to congratulate him he said he had never before seen Charles 'so calmly cheerful'. Charles told him, and no doubt he meant it, that 'he would not do another seven years at the East India House for a hundred thousand pounds'.[16]

Charles felt that Tuthill and Gillman, who had testified that his health was not up to the pressures and anxieties of his office, had – as an act of kindness – rather exaggerated his case, but when Mary read over their certificates she 'shook her head and said it was all true'. Mary was immensely relieved at Charles's emancipation, and following the day of his release, woke up every morning 'with an obscure feeling that some good has happened to us'.[17] This pleasurable sensation was enhanced by concrete securities: Charles was to receive a pension of £450 (his salary had been £730), which he reckoned to augment by 'scribbling occasionally'.[18]

Charles enlarged on his feelings of elation and the calm which followed in his Elia essay 'The Superannuated Man', and the relish with which he regarded his yearned-for leisure:

I have indeed lived nominally fifty years, but deduct out of them the hours which I have lived to other people, and not to myself, and you will find me still a young fellow . . . My ten next years, if I stretch so far, will be as long as any preceding thirty. A man can never have too much Time to himself, nor too little to do.

While attractive in the anticipation, time itself was to become a burden to Charles.

Mary was finding it increasingly difficult to keep up with Charles on his marathon walks. (This is not to suggest that she was unfit: she could comfortably accomplish a regular twelve-mile walk well into her sixties, but Charles usually walked about twenty miles.) He had, however, acquired a new companion in the shape of a dog called Dash. Dash had belonged to Thomas Hood and was later to belong to at least two other friends of the Lambs, one of whom described him as 'a large and very handsome dog, of a rather curious and sagacious breed'. Dash made his presence in the household strongly felt, creating an insufferable fuss if anyone went out without him. According to Patmore, Charles made himself 'a perfect slave' to this dog, who paid not the slightest attention to instructions and ran away the minute he was off the lead. A regular walk in Regent's Park always ended with a vexed Charles enduring a half-hour wait for Dash to reappear – 'and they used to take this walk oftener than any other, precisely because Dash liked it and Lamb did not'. Eventually Mary took Patmore – who had been so foolhardy as to express admiration for Dash – aside and begged him to take the dog, 'if only out of charity', she said, 'for if we keep him much longer, he'll be the death of Charles'. Unsurprisingly, in Patmore's charge Dash subsided into a model of canine obedience.[19]

Just as the Lambs were slaves to their dog, so they submitted to the authority of a particularly strident maid they had at this time. Beckey had been the Hazlitts' maid before coming to the Lambs and it was perhaps this experience of living with literary types which strengthened her constitutional resistance to anything 'odd'. Hence she made it her role in life to instruct the Lambs in the ways of the world and keep their behaviour within the bounds of what was – to her mind – respectable.

Very fond of her master and mistress, she was continually having to remind them of what was, and was not, 'good for them', always being prepared to offer them 'a bit of her mind' when they threatened to veer off the paths of convention. While visitors to the Lambs' household were often shocked at the liberties Beckey took with her employers (Crabb Robinson thought her 'a plague and a tyrant to them'), the Lambs themselves not only did not resent her impertinence but, Patmore observed, seemed 'highly gratified and amused by, the ineffable airs of superiority, amounting to nothing less than a sort of personal patronage, which she assumed'.[20]

Although they were out of the city, the city continued to come to them. A typical gathering at Colebrooke Cottage included Bryan Waller Procter, Henry Francis Cary, Edwin Herbert, Thomas De Quincey and John Clare, in his green coat and yellow waistcoat, looking like 'a very cowslip'. Thomas Hood (the original owner of Dash) had become a near neighbour of the Lambs when they moved to Islington, although Charles had known him since 1821 when Hood was a young editorial assistant on the *London Magazine*. Despite their age difference (when the Lambs moved to Colebrooke Cottage, Hood, at twenty-four, was half Charles's age), the Hoods and the Lambs became close friends and continued so after the Hoods moved to an area known as Adelphi. Hood particularly enjoyed the 'extempore assemblies' at the cottage, at one of which he met the now legendary Coleridge. Coleridge's conversation had evidently lost none of its enthralling appeal, as Hood recalled:

With his fine, flowing voice, it was glorious music, of the 'never-ending, still-beginning' kind; and you did not wish it to end. It was rare flying, as in the Nassau Balloon; you knew not whither, nor did you care. Like his own bright-eyed marinere; he had a spell in his voice that would not let you go. To attempt to describe my own feeling afterward, I had been carried, spiralling, up to heaven by a whirlwind intertwisted with sunbeams, giddy and dazed, but not displeased, and had then been rained down again with a shower of mundane stocks and stones that battered out of me all recollection of what I had heard, and what I had seen![21]

To describe the Lambs' friends as a 'circle' is actually misleading, as many of their friends had little or nothing to do with the literary set and Charles's reasons, in particular, for choosing some of his companions, continued to appear obscure if not perverse. As Patmore observed:

. . . he was a gentle, amiable, and tender-hearted misanthrope. He hated and despised men with his mind and judgment, in proportion as (and precisely because) he loved and yearned towards them in his heart; and individually, he loved those best whom everybody else hated, and for the very reasons for which others hated them.[22]

Although Patmore shared Charles and Mary's rare ability to appreciate their friend Hazlitt's finer qualities while tolerating his extremely volatile personality (Hazlitt had successfully alienated so many of his acquaintances that Charles and Patmore were the only people who attended his funeral, saving only his own son), he was not so enamoured of others of their circle and cast a disapproving eye over the Lambs' circumstances at Islington. Their home had, in his view,

. . . degenerated, for the most part, into the trysting place of a little anomalous coterie of strenuous idlers and 'Curious Impertinents,' who, without the smallest power of appreciating the qualities of mind and character which nominally brought them together, came there to pass the time under a species of excitement a little different from their ordinary modes of social intercourse – alternating 'an evening at the Lambs' with a half-price to the play, or a visit to the wild beasts at Exeter 'Change.[23]

While the Lambs were always hospitable, Charles providing the entertainment while Mary 'used to bustle and potter about like a gentle housewife, to make everybody comfortable',[24] even at Islington they were too accessible to idle visitors.

On 27 May 1825, having attended the funeral of his late brother's widow, Charles succumbed to what he described as a 'nervous fever'. If writing was ever therapeutic for him, it was now. Unable to come up with an idea for his regular essay, he capitalized on what he identified as the sick man's 'incapacity of reflecting upon any topic foreign to itself' and wrote 'The Convalescent', in which he enlarged on the king-like status of the invalid: 'How sickness enlarges the dimensions of a man's self to himself! He is his own exclusive object!' The patient's introspection, Elia observes, insulates him from the world's misfortunes: 'He has put on the strong armour of sickness, he is wrapped in the callous hide of suffering; he keeps his sympathy, like some curious vintage, under trusty lock and key, for his own use only.' 'The Convalescent' is observational black comedy of a particularly piquant kind.

The Lambs began to consider moving even further out of town, to Enfield, in order to avoid the constant stream of visitors at Islington ('never any poor devil was so befriended as I am,' moaned Charles).[25] Reluctant to make such a radical move rashly, they experimented by staying with the Allsops, friends they had met through Coleridge, who were boarding with a Mrs Leishman. Charles felt calmer by the time they returned to Islington at the beginning of September, but was immediately laid low again with 'a most violent nervous fever' which now rendered him incapable of sleep. The doctor applied leeches to his temples, but Charles's ailment was deeper: he was having a nervous breakdown. Not having work to worry about, he now transferred the focus of his anxieties to money, or the lack of it, wondering how they were going to manage on the pension from the East India Company if he could not supplement their income by writing. As always, anxiety threatened to prevent him from writing, which in turn prevented him resolving the cause of his anxiety. Living with Charles while he was in this state would have taken its toll on the strongest constitution and given the nature and long duration of his illness it is a wonder that Mary's own health did not collapse sooner than it did. Miss James, now an old lady, came to the rescue, nursing Mary at home. She and Charles lived apart under the same roof and Charles shunned all visitors. Although both had begun to recover by the beginning of December, it proved – for Charles at least – a temporary reprieve.

'Summer has set in with its usual severity,' Coleridge wryly observed to Charles at the beginning of May 1826. The unusually cold and windy weather depressed Charles. 'A cold Summer is all I know of disagreeable in cold. I do not mind the utmost rigour of real Winter, but these smiling hypocrites of Mays wither me to death.' The miserable weather exacerbated Charles's uncomfortable condition: he was experiencing a continual sensation of bells ringing in his head. It is not clear whether this was a physical phenomenon, such as tinnitus, or a symptom of his mental state, but he described his head as 'a ringing Chaos', rendering writing difficult and reading impossible.[26]

Retirement had been the golden objective sustaining Charles through his later years at the East India House and he had never anticipated any difficulty in adjusting to his change of circumstance. However, it had been plain enough to Crabb Robinson as early as June 1825 that Charles was constitutionally unsuited to leisure. 'I do not doubt, I do not fear, that he will be unable to sustain the "weight of chance desires",' he confided to Dorothy Wordsworth. 'Could he – but I fear he cannot – occupy himself in some great work requiring continued and persevering attention and labour, the benefit would equally be his and the world's.'[27] Perhaps he suggested this to Charles, as when he recovered from his illness Charles determined on a change of routine and established for himself a programme of study at the British Museum. The primary factor which resulted in the subsequent great improvement in his spirits he ascribed, perhaps unaware of the irony, to his keeping office hours.

In January 1827 Charles made a sad pilgrimage to visit Randal Norris on his deathbed. (Norris had been the librarian at the Temple who had gravely cautioned Charles about the unreliability of Chaucer's spelling.) Charles wrote to Henry Crabb Robinson:

In him I have a loss the world cannot make up. He was my friend and my father's friend all the life I can remember. I seem to have made foolish friendships ever since. Those are friendships which outlive a second generation. Old as I am waxing, in his eyes I was still the child he first knew me. To the last he called me Charley. I have none to call me Charley now.[28]

With Norris's death Charles and Mary's last link with the Temple was severed. With his typical solicitude, Charles made it his business to secure a pension for Norris's widow and to find a position for his son.

Charles and Mary spent the summer of 1827 again at Enfield

at Mrs Leishman's, where they were once again 'weighing the advantages of dulness over the over-excitement of too much company'. Dullness was alleviated by the presence of Emma Isola who, having spent all her holidays with the Lambs, now lived with them full-time for a year while Charles and Mary took upon themselves the task of educating her to a standard where she could get a position as a governess. Although a bright and perceptive girl, Emma was according to Mary 'sadly deficient' in arithmetic and found Latin impossible, causing Charles to castigate her as 'a lazy, block-headly supine'.[29] (Mary wrote her an encouraging poem on the subject: 'To Emma, Learning Latin, and Desponding'.[30]) Charles was reduced to making Emma sit with her back to the window to help her concentrate (he complained of her yawning and gaping), but she seemed to have eyes in the back of her head and as visitors approached the house would suddenly 'jump up and shriek out "there are the Hoods!"'[31] Though Emma did not now 'run wild about our house' as she had as a child, she brought a welcome liveliness to the couple's home; in return they did everything they could for her.

Emma had an understandable distraction from her studies in the shape of Edward Moxon, a young man in publishing in whom Charles had taken an interest and whose career he would attempt to advance (Moxon later became Wordsworth's publisher). Moxon had almost certainly met Emma through the Lambs and while they appear to have been sufficiently relaxed as chaperones, they were always aware of the superior authority of her aunt, Miss Humphries, who was 'so queer a one' that she would not permit Emma to go unaccompanied with Moxon to meet the Hoods at Vauxhall. Worried that Miss Humphries 'would withdraw [Emma] from us altogether in a fright', the Lambs deferred to her wishes.[32]

Having tried Enfield for a stretch of four months and having found the peace and quiet beneficial, at the end of September 1827 Charles and Mary with Emma in tow moved there – as they hoped – permanently. Although the decision to retreat to Enfield has often been ascribed to the benefits for Mary's health, it was Charles who claimed he had had '*no* health' at Islington and good health at Enfield, which was sufficient reason for decamping. The house they chose was of recent construction and comfortable, having every convenience of the period; moreover the rent was £10 less a year than that in Islington. Their landlords, Mr and Mrs Westwood, lived only next door and the sight of the odd family who came to inspect the house impressed itself sufficiently on their son that many years later he recalled a slight middle-aged man, a bundle-like old lady and a girl with a dog (this would be Dash, before his exile to Patmore's) with a 'to let' sign in its mouth. Charles's constitutional dislike of moving house was undiminished in this, almost his last, experience of it. He told Thomas Hood that it had been difficult leaving Colebrooke Cottage ('You may find some of our flesh sticking to the door posts'):

To change habitations is to die to them, and in my time I have died seven deaths. But I dont know whether every such change does not bring with it a rejuvenescence. Tis an enterprise, and shoves back the sense of death's approximating, which tho' not terrible to me, is at all times particularly distasteful.[33]

Despite Charles's optimism, Enfield did not bring the hoped for 'rejuvenescence'; the move out of town began inauspiciously and was to prove a fatal misjudgement. Although once again Mary had no hand in the removal to their new house in Enfield – the capable Beckey managing it single-handed – she was taken ill the night before they moved in. As Mary now always remained at home during her periods of derangement, cared for, on this occasion, by a local nurse, it was impossible for Charles to receive visitors. 'I see her, but it does her no good,' he told Bernard Barton.[34] December came with no sign of any improvement in Mary and Charles's spirits sank lower and lower. 'It is perfectly exhausting,' he told Barton. 'Enfield and every thing is very gloomy.'[35]

As the period of Mary's illness lengthened, making it the longest yet, Charles began to face the awful possibility that Mary might never recover her senses. Continuity of care was always important in Mary's progress; the Enfield nurse had to leave in mid-November and Miss James was summoned, the change causing Mary to get worse. In the middle of December Miss James too had to leave and another nurse was procured. As Christmas approached, however, the clouds began to lift and though visits and visitors were out of the question, Charles, Mary and Emma spent the time quietly together under Beckey's management. Although Mary improved, Charles continued feeling low and fatigued.

Walking continued to be a favourite pastime of Charles, Mary and Emma, Charles encouraging friends to visit 'the delightful vicinages of Enfield' and writing proprietorially of 'our pleasant farms and villages'.[36] Yet Enfield High Street was not the Strand and the slow pace of provincial Middlesex life had nothing to compare with the eternal activity, vibrancy and noise of motley London. The Lambs had known Enfield would be dull – it was precisely why they had settled there – but the tedium of living there full-time outdid even Charles's gloomiest expectations. The bright glimmer of his wit nevertheless sparkled mischievously through his description of Enfield in all its banality in a letter to Mary Shelley:

If you ever run away, which is problematical, don't run to a country village, which has been a market town, but is such no longer. Enfield, where we are, is seated most indifferently upon the borders of Middlesex, Essex, and Hertfordshire, partaking of the quiet dullness of the first, and the total want of interest pervading the latter two Counties. You stray into the Church yard, hoping to find a Cathedral. You think, I will go and look at the Print shops, and there is only one, where they sell Valentines. The chief Bookseller deals in prose versions of Melodramas, with plates of Ghosts and Murders, and other Subterranean passages. The tarts in the only Pastry-cook-looking shop are baked stale. The Macaroons are perennial, kept torpid in glass cases, excepting when Mrs **** gives a card party. There is no jewellers, but there's a place where brass knobs are sold. You cast your dreary eyes about, up Baker Street, and it gets worse. There was something like a tape and thread shop at that end, but here – is two apples stuck between a farthing's-worth of ginger bread, and the children too poor to break stock.

The week days would be intolerable, but for the superior invention which they show here in making Sundays worse. Clowns stand about what was the Market Place, and spit minutely to relieve ennui. Clowns, to whom Enfield trades-people are gentle people. Inland Clowns, Clods, and things below cows. They assemble to infect the air with dulness from Waltham marshes. They clear off o' the Monday mornings, like other fogs. It is ice, but nobody slides, nobody tumbles down, nobody dies as I can see, or nobody cares if they do; the Doctors seem to have no Patients, there is no Accidents nor Offences, a good thief would be something in this well-governed hamlet. We have for indoors amusement a Library without books, and the middle of the week hopes of a Sunday newspaper to link us by filmy associations to a world we are dead to. Regent Street was, and it is by difficult induction we infer that Charing Cross still is. There may be Plays. But nobody here seems to have heard of such contingencies.[37]

It was later observed of Charles that 'he had a habit of venting his melancholy in a sort of mirth'.[38] However, this strategy could not alter the fact that he was essentially miserable away from the cut-and-thrust of city life, not to mention the 'old familiar faces'.

Soon after the move to Enfield Patmore visited them, accompanying Charles on one of his long walks. Patmore made the error of commenting on how much more pleasant such walks were here than Charles's old rambling places in Islington and Dalston, and immediately realized he had touched a nerve. Charles declared,

with a vehemence of expression extremely unusual with him, and almost with tears in his eyes, that the most squalid garret in the most confined and noisome purlieu of London would be a paradise to him, compared with the fairest dwelling placed in the loveliest scenery of 'the country'. 'I *hate* the country!' he exclaimed.

Patmore was shocked, not only at the strength of Charles's feelings, which seemed to come 'from the bottom of his soul', but at the recognition that 'it was working ungentle and sinister results there, that he was himself almost alarmed at'.[39] Charles was right to be alarmed. Whatever the pitfalls of living in London were, he was completely unfit for life in the country. The extremity of the alteration would prove fatal.

Although it is difficult to derive a sense of continuity from the sporadic nature of the surviving correspondence, it is clear that while Charles suffered periods of deep depression in Middlesex, the Enfield ennui was on many occasions enlivened by visits from their old friends, whose company, though less frequently enjoyed, was more welcome than ever. Fanny Kelly, Crabb Robinson and Moxon were with them for Easter 1828 and Mary Victoria Novello, the daughter of their friend the musician, had married Charles Cowden Clarke in July 1828 and both visited the Lambs shortly afterwards. Charles had written a song lyric in honour of the occasion of their wedding which he had intended to send to the bride's father, but Mary had prevented him on the grounds that it was too light in tone for the occasion. Charles, who found weddings and funerals equally hilarious, could not imagine *anything* being too light for a wedding, but submitted to his sister 'to whose judgment,' he explained, 'I am apt to defer too much in these kind of things.'[40] The notion that one sibling had all the control in their relationship was one which both Charles and Mary amused their friends with, Mary referring to Charles as 'his honor, who decides all things here'.[41]

A friend of the Lambs once observed that the next best thing to reading a book by Charles was listening to a conversation between him and his sister.[42] Mary Balmanno met the Lambs at a supper party at the Hoods' and was impressed at Mary's 'saint-like good-humour and patience [which] were as remarkable as his strange and whimsical modes of trying them. But the brother and sister perfectly understood each other.'[43] Balmanno observed of Mary that:

Her behaviour to her brother was like that of an admiring disciple; her eyes seldom absent from his face. Even when apparently engrossed in conversation with others, she would, by supplying some word for which he was at a loss, even when talking in a distant part of the room, show how closely her mind waited upon his.[44]

Balmanno invited the Lambs to visit her the following evening. On arrival Charles affected to forget that they had previously met.

'Allow me, madam,' he said, 'to introduce to you my sister Mary. She's a very good woman, but she drinks.'

'Charles, Charles!' Mary blushed deeply.

'Why,' Charles reproved his sister, 'you know it's a fact. Look at the redness of your face. Did I not see you in your cups at nine o'clock this morning?'

'For shame, Charles,' Mary said. 'What will our friends think?'[45]

What *did* their friends think? When Jane Hood once asked Charles whether Mary minded his constant teasing, Charles admitted that he did on one occasion think he had gone too far and resolved not to tease her at all for several days. According to Charles, 'Mary did nothing but keep bursting into tears every time she looked at me, and when I asked her what she was crying for, when I was doing all I could to please her, she blubbered out: "You're changed, Charles, you're changed; what have I done, that you should treat me in this cruel manner?"' Charles explained that he had only been trying to be kind, but Mary was having none of it.

'Joke again, Charles,' she begged, '– I don't know you in this manner. I am sure I should die, if you behaved as you have done for the last few days.'

'So you see I joke for her own good,' Charles solemnly explained to Jane Hood. 'It saved her life then, anyhow.'[46]

By the summer of 1828 the Lambs had finally succeeded in their plan of finding Emma Isola a place as a governess, thus setting her on a path of respectable independence. She had gone to the family of a clergyman, Mr Williams, at Fornham in Suffolk, but continued to return to the Lambs' home during her holidays. That Edward Moxon's interest in her was undiminished is indicated by him having sent her a Valentine that year, of which she was, according to Charles, 'very proud'. Charles described Emma as 'a girl of gold', to his friend Procter, and as 'somewhat of a pensive cast', following her stay at Christmas 1828. His 'silent brown girl' had evidently calmed down considerably from the wild child of a few years earlier.[47]

Both Charles and Mary looked forward to Emma's next visit in the summer, but in the event Mary did not see her. She was so ill that Charles was obliged to send her away from home. Despite the fact that Emma came, accompanied by an old schoolfriend, the house without Mary felt to Charles at times 'a frightful solitude'.[48] At the end of her stay, Charles accompanied Emma as far as Charing Cross. As he stood in the teeming rain, watching the Cornwallis coach disappear from view, the full weight of his solitude descended on him. 'Never did the waters of heaven pour down on a forlorner head,' he later wrote. He thought to console himself by staying a few days in London with a friend, which he did . . .

But Town, with all my native hankering after it, is not what it was. The streets, the shops are left, but all old friends are gone. And in London I was frightfully convinced of this as I past houses and places – empty caskets now. I have ceased to care almost about any body. The bodies I cared for are in graves, or dispersed. My old Clubs, that lived so long and flourish'd so steadily, are crumbled away.[49]

On his return home he visited Mary, who was in Fulham. Although she looked physically healthy, she was 'sadly rambling, and scarce showing any pleasure in seeing me, or curiosity when I should come again'. Charles acutely felt the sense in which the chunks of their life together that were cut out by Mary's illness were growing larger and larger, now depriving them of three months of every year. He slunk back to Enfield to 'hide like a sick cat in my corner'. But Enfield held no comforts – even the redoubtable Beckey had decamped to be married. Charles tried to communicate the almost inexplicable character of the loss of this odd specimen of humanity to Barton:

And to make me more alone, our illtemperd maid is gone, who with all her airs, was yet a home piece of furniture, a record of better days; the young thing that has succeeded her is good and attentive, but she is nothing – and I have no one here to talk over old matters with. Scolding and quarreling have something of familiarity and a community of interest – they imply acquaintance – they are of resentment, which is of the family of dearness. I can neither scold nor quarrel at this insignificant implement of household services; she is less than a cat, and just better than a deal Dresser.[50]

Charles's relief, when Mary did finally come home after twelve weeks' absence, soon evaporated as she gave way to crushing depression, lapsing into 'the saddest low spirits that ever poor creature had'.[51] Charles was almost in despair, her case seeming utterly hopeless.

While Mary had been away Charles had found only one source of relief from the introspection which inevitably attended his solitude: 'What I can do, and do overdo, is to walk, but deadly long are the days – these summer all-day days, with but a half hour's candlelight and no firelight.' The Leadenhall clerk who had spoken so feelingly of having to work by candlelight all day, the London winters rendering the Accountant's Office so dark; the writer who had painfully lamented the remorseless demands of the East India Company which ate away great slices of his life; both now united in confessing to having become 'a sanguinary murderer of time'.[52] Longed-for leisure seemed revealed as a sinister phantom, a siren which sang its summoning song only in order to dash him to pieces on its rocks.

Yet even in his darkest moments, though emotionally he could not see past the day before him, intellectually Charles knew that there would be better times, that 'weariness is not eternal'. He reassured his friend Barton, 'Something will shine out to take the load off, that flags me, which is at present intolerable.'[53] This 'something' sprang from necessity itself. The lease being up on their Enfield house, the Lambs hesitated at the prospect of taking another, both being in moods not conducive to making sound long-term decisions. Since removals had become irresistibly associated with the onset of Mary's bouts of insanity, they were apprehensive about moving at all. They settled on the shortest move possible: to next door, where they would 'cast off the cares of house-keeping', give up the responsibilities of a garden and become boarders with their present landlords, the Westwoods. It was a decisive step – selling their furniture, for one thing, spoke of no going back. Within less than a week, Charles claimed, Mary already looked two and a half years younger. Suddenly and almost inadvertently it seemed they had fallen into the best solution possible.

The Westwoods, the Lambs had found, were good, solid country people. Thomas Westwood, a hunchback, had been at various times a travelling salesman for a wholesaler's and a haberdasher and was now an insurance agent and landlord. Through carefulness and diligence he and his wife were now widely respected members of the Enfield community. Aimiable and pleasant as he was, Mr Westwood's faculties were now somewhat failing. Accompanying Mary back from her visit to the Gillmans at the end of 1829, they were passing the house of one of his friends when Westwood remarked, 'I cannot think what is gone of Mr. Mellish's rooks. I fancy they have taken flight somewhere; but I have missed them two or three years past.' Mary could not help noticing that even as he spoke 'the rookery was darkening the air above with undiminished population, and deafening all ears but his with their cawings'.[54] This characteristic lack of self-awareness and the fact that Mr Westwood had but *one* anecdote were exactly the sort of idiosyncrasies guaranteed to endear him to Charles and Mary. Living with the Westwoods, who took all responsibility from the Lambs ('We are fed we know not how, quietists, confiding ravens'), suited their constitutions admirably and the first winter they passed under their roof found them in better health than they had ever enjoyed since coming to Enfield.

But it was at a cost. The Londoner in Charles rose up like a chained dog, by turns straining at the leash and subsiding into resigned boredom. He wrote to Wordsworth in January 1830 that he had gained physical well-being at the intolerable price of dullness. 'O let no native Londoner imagine that health, and rest, and innocent occupation, interchange of converse sweet and recreative study, can make the country any thing better than altogether odious and detestable.'[55] He dreaded the approach of the long bright days of summer, preferring candlelit winter evenings when he could imagine he was in Holborn or St Giles or anywhere but Enfield. The only way to eat up such days was with 'purposeless exercise'.

Even when Mary was at home, Charles was not free of his restlessness; his time-murdering walks became longer; latterly he contrived to use up the whole of the morning in walking, rain or shine, going nowhere in particular, but seeking by exercising his body to shake off the torpor that had settled on his mind. Mary must have recognized that when he remained at home he would brood obsessively on 'dangerous and intractable questions, on which his strong common sense told him there was no satisfaction to be gained, but from which his searching spirit could not detach itself'.[56] Having suffered from overwork, he now found leisure worse. 'The mind preys on itself, the most unwholesome food,' he confessed to Barton.[57] But his walks also offered a further source of relief – inevitably there was an alehouse at the end of them. He habitually walked visitors part of the way home when they left him. As they left the house, Mary's mantra was always the same: 'Now, Charles, you're not going to take any ale?', as was Charles's irritable reply 'No, no.'[58]

Patmore, who only knew Charles and Mary following Charles's retirement from the East India Company, had a very interesting view of Charles's relationship with drink, which is also singular in that it involves gentle criticism of Mary's attitude. Mary, Patmore observed, had a proper and laudable concern for her brother's *physical* health, and it was on these grounds that she objected to his drinking, indeed frequently nagging him on the subject. But what Mary failed to take into account, Patmore argued, was the use 'of those artificial stimuli which were to a certain extent indispensable to the healthy tone of his *mental* condition'.[59] No conversation was as good as Charles's, and Charles's was never better than when he had had a few drinks; alcohol being the key which 'not only unlocked the poor casket in which the rich thoughts of Charles Lamb were shut up, but set in motion that machinery in the absence of which they would have lain like gems in the mountain, or gold in the mine'. Charles was only truly in his element and at his most articulate when the inhibiting faculties had been relaxed by alcohol. Hence Patmore could say of Mary that 'to keep him from the chance of being ill, she often kept him from the certainty of being well and happy'. It is clear from his account that Patmore never saw Charles dead drunk, and he consequently defends him from the charge of alcohol abuse, but he does not shrink from using the word 'addicted' in relation to Charles and drink.[60]

It cannot be ignored that when he was a clerk at the East India House Charles ascribed his fits of anxiety and gloom to his work, but that when he retired they became, if anything, worse. Similarly, he attributed his ills to the excitement of the city when he was in London and to the dullness of the country when rusticated. The shortness of the days in winter sank his spirits and the length of the days in the summer seemed unendurable. He was depressed when Mary was ill, and also depressed when she was well. He blamed drinking and smoking for making him miserable, but when he gave them up regretted their capacity for making him happy. In short, he was always looking outside himself for the cause of his pain and, having fixed on something, looked to its opposite as his cure. Patmore may come closest to identifying Charles's nameless grief when he describes 'a *constitutional* sadness about Lamb's mind'.[61] Patmore's opinion is significant in that at the time of writing his memoirs he was yet unaware of the tragedy which had shaped the lives of the Lambs and so naturally looked to Charles, rather than Mary, for the source of Charles's malaise. He did, however, know of Charles's early bout of mental illness and confinement in the Hoxton madhouse. As a result Patmore ascribed Charles's inability to find peace either in company or in solitude to his having been permanently unbalanced by this early bout of mental illness. He noted the irreconcilability of Charles's desire for solitude and need for company, ascribing the latter to an intellectual difference between him and his peers:

Unlike his friends, Coleridge and Wordsworth, Lamb was not a man whose mind was sufficient to itself, and could dwell for ever, if need were, in the world of its own thoughts, or that which the thoughts of others had created for it. He delighted to *visit* those worlds, and found there, it may be, his purest and loftiest pleasures.

But the *home* of his spirit was the face of the common earth, and in the absence of human faces and sympathies, it longed and yearned for them with a hunger that nothing else could satisfy.[62]

Patmore had the opportunity to observe Charles at home in Islington and later in Enfield and noticed that he seemed incapable of relaxing for more than half an hour at a time, to be persecuted by a restlessness which would not let him sit still or even settle on one topic of conversation for long. Though he wished for visitors he had lost the art of enjoying them to the extent that, Patmore observed, 'every knock at the door sent a pang to his heart; and this without any distinction of persons: whoever it might be, he equally welcomed and wished them away'.[63]

On 26 February 1830 news arrived from Fornham which swept away all other unhappy preoccupations. Mrs Williams wrote to say that Emma was desperately ill with a 'brain fever' (almost certainly meningitis). She was far too sick to be brought home and Charles and Mary waited 'gasping for news'; Mrs Williams had warned them to expect the worst. Charles meditated going to Suffolk, but hesitated at leaving Mary to bear the awful suspense alone. On 1 March another letter arrived which provoked Mary to 'an agony of tears' – but of relief. Emma, though still dangerously ill, was improving. It was another month before she was considered fit enough to undertake the journey to Enfield and Charles travelled to Fornham to escort her home by stage coach. Emma was very weak but had strength enough to laugh uproariously when a fellow passenger attempted to engage Charles in a serious conversation on whether it would turn out to be a good season for turnips.

It is a measure of Charles's usual behaviour that following

his arrival at Fornham, the moment he was alone with Emma she took him into a corner and begged him not to drink, especially after dinner, promising he should have as much as he liked when they got home 'and I won't say a word about it'.[64] Emma had clearly experienced acute embarrassment on his account on previous occasions and was extremely anxious not to repeat the exercise with the Williamses. Dining with the local doctor and his wife at Enfield at about this time had ended typically with Mary making a hungover Charles write a letter of apology to his host and hostess for having to be carried home. Charles acceded but was characteristically unrepentant, claiming that far from disgracing their party, as Mary insisted, he had rather honoured it, 'for every one that was not drunk (and one or two of the ladies, I am sure, were not) must have been set off greatly in the contrast to me. I was the scapegoat. The soberer they seemed.'[65] On another occasion his note of apology to a hostess was followed by a solemn assurance that she need not fear inviting him again, for he never got drunk in the same house twice. While Charles continued to make light of his drinking, Mary and Emma both clearly dreaded the appearance of the bottle on any social occasion.

Emma's sister joined them at Enfield at Easter and by the end of April Emma was well enough to return to the Williamses. Mary and Charles appear to have gone to London for a period in the summer and stayed at Southampton Buildings. Mary succumbed to her 'annual visitation', leaving Charles feeling 'when not at foot, very desolate'; nothing and nobody stimulated his interest: 'I am in an interregnum of thought and feeling,' he told Barton.[66] Deciding in November that London was not conducive to Mary's recovery, Charles took her back to Enfield. This attack seemed the worst yet; Charles told Moxon: 'Her state of mind is deplorable beyond any example.

I almost fear whether she has strength at her time of life ever to get out of it.'[67] Mary's condition meant that she became abnormally excited by the smallest event. Although she was confined to her room, the slightest hint of activity in the world outside upset her. For example, learning that Southey had called at the house (though she had not seen nor heard him) agitated her and Charles could neither receive nor write letters in her presence. As Christmas 1830 approached, with the prospect of Emma coming home for the holidays, she began to mend. However, Charles felt trapped at Enfield, the desire to see friends like the Wordsworths while they were in town the following spring pulling him one way but the fear of leaving and upsetting Mary keeping him back. It was difficult for them to receive overnight visitors at the Westwoods' and Charles ached for company. Many of his letters from this time onwards are characterized by almost pathetic invitations to their friends to take a day trip out to Enfield, however spur-of-the-moment, assuring them that he and Mary are *always* at home.

Due to Charles's increased fame as a result of the success of the Elia essays, many more of his *bons mots* are recorded from later life than from his earlier years, giving the perhaps illusory impression that he became funnier as he got older. Posterity, however, as identified earlier, is often no friend to the humorist. Thomas Allsop prefaced his recollections of Charles with this *caveat*:

I am quite aware that I can convey no notion of what Charles Lamb *was*, hardly even of what he said, as for the greatest part of its value depended on the manner in which it was said. Even the best of his jokes – and *how good* they were you can never know – depended upon the circumstances, which to narrate would be to overlay and weary the attention.[68]

One of the circumstances which renders the modern reader's ability to appreciate Charles's wit even more difficult than it was for Allsop's first readers is simply that our ideas of what is funny are so different. (Plays on words, for example, hold fewer charms now than they did for his contemporaries and Charles was particularly addicted to homophones.) As if to prove the point Allsop includes a number of (to our ear) deplorable examples of Charles's puns, one of which suffices here: 'Martin Burney, whilst earnestly explaining the three kinds of acid, was stopped by Lamb's saying, – "The best of all kinds of acid, however, as you know, Martin, is uity – assid-uity." '[69] Some of his jokes appear not to have been considered funny even at the time. He told Haydon and Talfourd that he had been with his friend Hume and his wife and children when Hume had repeated the old saying 'One fool makes many.' 'Ay, Mr Hume,' Charles rejoindered, 'you have a fine family.' Charles considered this one of his best jokes ever, but as Crabb Robinson confessed in his diary, 'Neither Talfourd nor I could see the excellence of this.'[70]

That Charles's general manner was amusing, however, has better stood the test of time, and as Charles and Mary got older the odder and more quirky they seem to have become. It was, for example, from this later period that the meeting with Mr Willis occurred, when Charles amused himself by telling the American that Mary had written 'Confessions of a Drunkard' and reproachfully kissed the fish. A reverend gentleman, also a fan of Elia, similarly secured an introduction and visited the Lambs at home. He noted that Charles made free use of a bottle of rum in the cupboard, refraining only when upbraided by his sister. After a while, Charles asked, 'May I have a little drop now? Only a *leetle* drop?'

'No,' said Mary. 'Be a good boy.'

Eventually he got his own way. The Reverend Russell

found that Charles required encouragement to talk: 'He would throw out a playful remark, and then pause awhile. He spoke by fits and starts, and had a slight impediment in his utterance, which made him, so to say, grunt once or twice before he began a sentence.' He and the Reverend Russell agreed that Moore's poetry was akin to rich plum-cake – 'very nice, but too much of it made one sick'. While discussing literature (or anything else) he continually referred to Mary:

'Mary, don't you hate Byron?'

'Yes, Charles.'

'That's right,' he approved, playfully slapping her on the back.

To those who knew them, or thought they knew 'Elia', such oddities were merely quaintly characteristic. However, not everyone was won over by what others found irresistible. 'The fact is,' Patmore explained, 'that in ordinary society, if Lamb was not an ordinary man, he was only an odd and strange one.' When away from the challenging and provoking minds on which his intellectual stimulation depended, Charles reverted to the entertainer: the joker, the punster, the clown. Chameleon-like, Charles reinvented himself to match the company he was in.

The consequence was, that to those who did not know him, or, knowing, did not or could not appreciate him, Lamb often passed for something between an imbecile, a brute, and a buffoon; and the first impression he made on ordinary people was always unfavourable – sometimes to a violent and repulsive degree.[71]

Charles's childlike qualities either charmed or appalled people. On one occasion, retiring to the drawing-room after dinner at a friend's house, on seeing another guest bending over he failed to resist the sudden temptation to leapfrog the gentleman's back. At the age of fifty-three he managed to strain a tendon while skipping with a rope. While drink might have relaxed his inhibitions on these occasions, there was something in Charles which derived immense satisfaction from small acts of recklessness. But why? Perhaps these breaches of decorum fell into the same category as his general habit of jesting and fibbing; these little rebellions made him feel he was not merely Fortune's pawn. According to Desmond McCarthy, humour 'is after all only a way of coming to terms with a reality which one despairs of altering; it is a make-shift, a get-out'.[72] 'Wit' of all kinds was possibly a necessary diversion to Charles, a temporary solution to the intractable problem of life.

To one young Scotsman, determined to hate England and everything in it, Charles's appeal was utterly incomprehensible.

Charles Lamb I sincerely believe to be in some considerable degree insane. A more pitiful, ricketty, gasping, staggering, stammering Tomfool I do not know. He is witty by denying truisms and abjuring good manners. His speech wriggles hither and thither with an incessant painful fluctuation, not an opinion in it, or a fact, or a phrase that you can thank him for – more like a convulsion fit than a natural systole and diastole. Besides, he is now a confirmed, shameless drunkard; *asks* vehemently for gin and water in strangers' houses, tipples till he is utterly mad, and is only not thrown out of doors because he is too much despised for taking such trouble with him. Poor Lamb! Poor England, when such a despicable abortion is named genius![73]

This was Thomas Carlyle's impression of Charles in 1831. A subsequent account of Carlyle's calls Charles and Mary 'a very sorry pair of phenomena', defines Charles's talk as 'contemptibly small . . . more like "diluted insanity"' and gives his overall impression of Charles as an 'emblem of imbecility bodily and spiritually'.[74]

While attention should be paid to Carlyle's view, it should perhaps be remembered that Charles had always affected to hate Scots. Indeed, one account has him inviting Carlyle to dinner and serving him porridge. The only concrete evidence to hand which might possibly have influenced Carlyle's predisposition to Charles, lies in the Elia essay 'Imperfect Sympathies', which had been published three months prior to Carlyle's encounter with him. Elia opens his assault with characteristic candour: 'I have been trying all my life to like Scotchmen,' he says, 'and am obliged to desist from the experiment in despair.' The principal problem, Elia identifies, is that the standard Caledonian does not doubt, imagine, explore or consider; he has a stock of opinions of which he is certain.

Between the affirmative and the negative there is no border-land with him. You cannot hover with him upon the confines of truth, or wander in the maze of a probable argument. He always keeps the path. You cannot make excursions with him – for he sets you right. His taste never fluctuates. His morality never abates. He cannot compromise, or understand middle actions. There can but be a right and a wrong. His conversation is as a book. His affirmations have the sanctity of an oath. You must speak upon the square with him. He stops a metaphor like a suspected person in an enemy's country.

Elia illustrates his point by recalling an occasion when he showed a favourite print of a da Vinci, a portrait of a woman, to a Scotsman:

After he had examined it minutely, I ventured to ask him how he liked MY BEAUTY (a foolish name it goes by among my friends) – when he very gravely assured me, that 'he had considerable respect for my character and talents' (so he was pleased to say), 'but had not given himself much thought about the degree of my personal pretensions.'

This reminds him of another example of Caledonian literal-mindedness:

I was present not long ago since at a party of North Britons, where a son of Burns was expected; and happened to drop a silly expression (in my South British way), that I wished it were the father instead of the son – when four of them started up at once to inform me, that 'that was impossible, because he was dead.'

'An impracticable wish,' he concluded, 'was more than they could conceive.'

'Not an opinion in it, or a fact,' Carlyle had complained of Charles's conversation, unwittingly falling into the very stereotype he very probably resented. His painful characteriz-ation of Charles's drinking, however, cannot be so amusingly disposed of.

Emma was at Enfield again in the summer of 1832, but Mary was 'from home'. This time she had been sent to a small private madhouse in Edmonton. Charles despaired as her illness dragged on for five months. As always, Emma's presence cheered him. When Henry Crabb Robinson visited them at the end of July he took a walk with Charles, who was 'in excellent health and in tolerable spirits, and was . . . quite eloquent in praise of Miss Isola. He says she is the most sensible girl and the best female talker he knows.'[75]

At the end of April 1833 all the Westwoods and both the Lambs were ill with influenza. Although they were in good spirits, Mary was obliged to keep house for everyone and the fatigue took its toll. However, for once this cloud had a silver lining. Since the autumn of 1831 overcrowding and illness in the Westwood family had caused Charles and Mary to begin to feel uncomfortable at Enfield and they had at times been heartily fed up with their landlords. One of the first observations the formidable Beckey had made about the Lambs was that they never questioned domestic accounts. The butcher, the baker, or the candlestick maker could easily cheat them and the Lambs would pay up with a smile – a subject on which Beckey was often wont to give them 'a bit of her mind'. But the cupidity of the Westwoods galled Charles. Already paying handsomely for their own board and lodging, the Lambs were expected to pay for every last cup of tea their visitors consumed. On one occasion an extra sixpence appeared on the bill beside one of the 'extra' teas and on inquiring what it was for Charles was informed that 'the elderly gentleman' who had visited them had taken rather a large quantity of sugar in his tea. (The sweet-toothed old gentleman was Wordsworth.)

Although Charles would complain to his friends of his landlords' greed, it was the Westwoods' own short-sightedness in the affair that he most regretted; how could they not perceive that by cheating the Lambs they put almost their sole source of income at risk? Patmore believed that it was out of a sense of charity to the old couple that the Lambs remained there as long as they did, as Charles reasoned: 'What would become of the poor people if we left them?'[76] However, by the time of the flu outbreak Charles's patience with the Westwoods was exhausted; he had demoted them to 'most *hated* and *detestable* people'.[77] Mary's breakdown at the end of

April seemed to offer a way out. Charles took her to Edmonton, to the small private madhouse run by Mr and Mrs Walden that she had gone to the year previously. As Mary's periods of illness grew longer each year (the last bout of madness had lasted three months, followed by two more of deep depression), he reasoned, he would correspondingly see less and less of her. Rather than remove her from *his* company, why did he not move in with *her*, at the Waldens'? This extraordinary solution came to Charles suddenly and he acted on his decision immediately. Little more than a week after Mary became ill, both he and she were settled at the Waldens' as their sole inmates. Though he was cheered by the fact that he had escaped an increasingly difficult situation, with the added bonus that Edmonton was nearer to dear old London, Charles was not romantic about his new home. 'I have got out of hell, despair of heaven, and must sit down contented in a half-way purgatory,' he told Sarah Hazlitt, subsequently referring to their home at Edmonton as 'my half way house'.[78]

Charles had once spoken of 'the hypostatical union' between him and his sister. 'When Mary calls, it is understood that I call too, we being univocal.'[79] As a result of this legendary inseparability their last home together would be a madhouse.

13. Emma and the End

There is something inexpressibly shocking in first hearing of a dear friend's death through the medium of a public newspaper, at a time, perhaps, when you believe him to be in perfect health, and are on the point of paying him a too long delayed visit. Such was my case in respect to Charles Lamb. Still more painful was the case of a lady [Fanny Kelly], formerly a distinguished ornament of the English stage, to whom Lamb was attached by the double tie of admiration and friendship. Several days after Lamb's death, she was conversing of him with a mutual friend, who, taking for granted her knowledge of Lamb's death, abruptly referred to some circumstance connected with the event, which for the first time made her acquainted with it.

(Patmore, *My Friends and Acquaintance*, pp. 99–100)

Emma and Moxon had become formally engaged at the end of April 1833 and were to marry on 30 July. In anticipation of the happy event Moxon made Emma a present. 'For god's sake, give Emma no more watches,' wrote Charles.

One has turn'd her head. She is arrogant, and insulting. She said something very unpleasant to our old Clock in the passage, as if he did not keep time, and yet he had made her no appointment. She takes it out every instant to look at the moment-hand. She lugs us out into the fields, because there the bird-boys ask you 'Pray, Sir, can you tell us what's a Clock,' and she answers them punctually. She loses all her time looking 'what the time is.' I overheard her whispering, 'Just so many hours, minutes, &c. to Tuesday – I think St. George's goes too slow' – This little present of Time, why, 'tis Eternity to her –

He adds at the bottom of the letter: 'Never mind opposite nonsense. She does not love you for the watch, but the watch for you.'[1] While Charles must have been looking forward to Emma's marriage with mixed feelings, it is symptomatic of his kindness that he wrote Moxon the very kind of letter a young bridegroom-to-be might most like to receive.

Plans for the wedding continued apace without Mary, who remained insensible of the arrangements or their occasion. Emma went to meet her aunt in London (where they were both to stay with friends, the Misses Buffams) three days before the wedding and were joined by Charles two days later. Samuel Rogers, Moxon's patron, was to give Emma away, but at the last minute was unable to come. It therefore fell to Charles to do a father's honours. Bearing in mind the difficulty he always had maintaining a straight face on such occasions, it appears that he acquitted himself well, though Emma doubtless kept a steely eye on him at the wedding breakfast, which he took with the bride, her sister and her formidable aunt, while the groom kept table with his brother and sister. (If this spoke of a *froideur* between Miss Humphries and Moxon, it was shortly to break out into full-scale cold war.) Charles left the happy couple preparing for their honeymoon in France and returned home *'half as sober as a judge'*.[2]

Back in Edmonton nothing short of a miracle had occurred. On Emma's wedding day Mrs Walden had been sitting with her patient, who yet appeared dead to the world. Noting that by the hour Emma must now have been married, Mrs Walden took a glass of wine – Mary, from the depths of her insensibility, sensed 'a total change of countenance' – and asked Mary's leave to drink to Mr and Mrs Moxon's health. 'It restored me, from that moment: as if by an electrical stroke,' Mary reported, 'to the entire possession of my senses.' Moreover, her astonishing recovery left her feeling unusually serene. 'I never felt so calm and quiet after a similar illness as I do now. I feel as if all tears were wiped from my eyes, and all care from my heart.' Charles could barely believe the change in Mary on his return home. 'Never was such a calm, or such a recovery,' he wrote to Emma and Moxon.[3]

The suddenness and occasion of her recovery seem to indicate that some anxiety surrounded Emma and Moxon's marriage for Mary, which the news of its successful accomplishment resolved. Miss Humphries certainly appears to have been less than helpful and Mary may perhaps have feared that at the last moment she would produce some impediment. Charles's own explanation was itself a guess: 'I can impute [it] to nothing but the turn given to her mind by the certainty of the Marriage, which as a mystery so puzzled her.'[4] An alternative explanation touches somewhat deeper. In her 1948 biography, Katherine Anthony argued that 'the personal sadness of Lamb's later years came from his unhappy love for Emma Isola'. Anthony believed that this aspect of the story had remained untold 'because it tended to discount the romantic fraternal legend'.[5] Anthony, incidentally, was not alone in this view. The novelist Neil Bell had already (in 1945) stated that 'All the evidence (except to the wilfully blind) points to the love of these two people for one another.'[6] In these analyses, Emma, rather than having the role of a kind of niece to Charles and Mary, actively came between them, trespassing on their mutually exclusive intimacy.

The interpretation of the relationship between Charles, Mary and Emma thus puts a different weight on Emma's marriage. Anthony interprets Mary's sudden recovery thus:

Mary, having been jealous because her brother had shared his hitherto undivided attention with his ward, had been haunted by the fear that she might slay Emma in a fit of insanity, as she had slain her mother; and therefore . . . Mrs Walden's sudden announcement of Emma's marriage relieved Mary of that fear and effected her equally sudden recovery.[7]

In order to entertain this theory it is necessary to accept that Mary was indeed jealous of Emma. It is worth noting that even Ernest Carson Ross, who is the most energetic and thorough debunker of the notion that there was a 'special' relationship between Emma and Charles, does accept that Mary was 'subconsciously jealous of Emma'.[8]

If Mary was indeed jealous of Emma, did she have reason to be? In other words, did Charles love Emma in a substantially different way from the way he loved Mary? Ross, who has strenuously resisted the idea that Charles's feelings for Emma ever strayed beyond purely avuncular affection, nevertheless identifies the year she lived full-time with the Lambs, between the spring of 1827 (when she left school) and the spring of 1828 (when she left them to take up her post as a governess), as the period in which, *if* Charles entertained amorous thoughts towards Emma, he would have become most keenly aware of them. Ross consequently concentrates his examination of the evidence on this period. While this is reasonable given that this was certainly the period when Emma and Charles were in each other's company more than any other, it does ignore an earlier significant period.

Before Charles's retirement Emma spent much of her time

at the Lambs' alone with Mary, Charles's holidays not being nearly so generous as hers. Following his retirement in 1825, however, he was at home at least as much as Mary and it is known that Emma increasingly became his walking companion. Emma was now seventeen years old, had inherited her family's Italian colouring and was, in Robinson's estimation, 'beautiful'. Whatever Emma's charms were, Ross is again generous in allowing that 'we may be sure that Lamb exercised the charm of his personality on her, as he was wont to do on the youthful daughters of his acquaintances'.[9]

The joint circumstances of Emma having attained sexual maturity and her being suddenly so much in Charles's company are coincident with Charles's own dating of the beginning of their serious friendship. Writing to Emma's friend Miss Fryer following Emma's marriage to Moxon in 1833, he said: 'I want to talk to someone. I know in my reason this is a good match but I cannot but remember a companionship of 8 years in my almost solitude.' This again brings us back to 1825. Having established the significance of this year in their relationship it seems wilful to ignore – if not to connect – the fact of Charles experiencing his two nervous breakdowns (described as bouts of 'nervous fever') in the same year.

Moving on to 1827–8, the year Emma lived full-time with the Lambs, due to Mary's attack she and Charles were alone together much of the time. (Emma was now twenty, Charles fifty-three.) However, it is vain to search the correspondence for any evidence of the distinct character of his feelings. He acknowledged that although he knew she had to leave in order to work, 'it grieves me to give her up' and when the time came for her to go, he found the experience 'unhinging'. Crabb Robinson also records Charles reading him 'some feeling lines' he had written on Emma's coming-of-age.[10] Yet it would be a hard matter to prove that these emotions spoke of more than love of a paternal nature. On the other hand, it is extremely unlikely that if he were sexually attracted to Emma – given his position as Emma's guardian in all but legal name – he would have committed such feelings to paper, let alone communicated them to a friend in a letter. (It is as well to bear in mind that there would be no evidence amongst Charles's writings that he had any special regard for Fanny Kelly, but for the survival of two letters: one proposing marriage and one acknowledging rejection. He nowhere else mentions his feelings for her at all.) It is known that much correspondence was destroyed or lost, and well into the twentieth century letters and parts of letters were suppressed even by Charles's most exhaustive biographer, E. V. Lucas, in order to protect the feelings of living relations of those concerned. Many of these are now lost for all time. It is at least a pity, if not suspicious, that hardly any correspondence between Charles and Emma has survived.

Regardless of the difficulty of characterizing Charles and Emma's relationship, there remains the mystery of Mary's sudden and complete recovery. There are a number of possible explanations why Mary experienced such a strong feeling of relief on hearing of Emma and Moxon's marriage. Mary may have feared that Miss Humphries would prevent it. She may, subconsciously, have been wishing Emma away so that she would regain her position as Charles's principal significant 'other'. She may, if we accept Anthony's theory, have feared she would harm Emma in a moment of madness. She may even have felt her own feelings for Emma were 'unhealthy' – an area impossible to investigate, but not impossibly relevant. It is also possible that a mélange of doubts and anxieties encompassing some or all of these factors conspired to make the marriage seem an unrealizable solution. It is interesting to note Dorothy Wordsworth's feelings, expressed in a letter to an old schoolfriend, in anticipation of her brother's wedding. While she loved William's fiancée and was delighted at the prospect of becoming her sister-in-law, she confessed, 'happy as I am, I half dread that concentration of all tender feeling, past, present, and future which will come upon me on the wedding morning'.[11] Perhaps it was simply the relief of Emma's future being resolved that swept the clouds away for Mary that day.

Mary's recovery also led to a revival in Charles's spirits. 'I am calm, sober, happy,' he told Moxon. 'Tell E. I am *very good* also.'[12] By the end of November, both he and Mary appeared to be in good spirits, Charles bidding Moxon tell Emma that every day he loved her more and missed her less. In the new year, however, Mary slipped into her familiar 'fever' and was 'as bad as poor creature can be'. He again doubted her capacity to recover, telling Mary Betham, 'She has less and less strength to throw it off, and they leave a dreadful depression after them.'[13] This illness did not drag Charles down with it as it usually did and he reflected that he was happier with her — even when she was insane — than without her, as he explained to Emma's schoolfriend:

When she is not violent, her rambling chat is better to me than the sense and sanity of this world. Her heart is obscured, not buried; it breaks out occasionally; and one can discern a strong mind struggling with the billows that have gone over it. I could be nowhere happier than under the same roof with her. Her memory is unnaturally strong; and from ages past, if we may so call the earliest records of our poor life, she fetches thousands of names and things that never would have dawned on me again, and thousands from the ten years she lived before me. What took place from early girlhood to her coming of age principally lives again (every important thing and every trifle) in her brain with the vividness of real presence. For twelve hours incessantly she will pour out without intermission all her past life, forgetting nothing, pouring out name after name to the Waldens as if in a dream; sense and nonsense; truths and errors huddled together; a medley between inspiration and possession.[14]

In Miss Fryer he seemed to have found the repository for his feelings he had long suffered without: she counselled hope without judging; she offered solace but required nothing in return. Charles could unbosom himself to Emma's friend in a way he could not to either Emma or Mary. At a distance he could admit the positive aspects of a madness he had hitherto acknowledged only privately.

Coleridge had been threatening to die for much of his life. Eventually it proved one of the few intentions he saw through. The sense in which Charles and Mary now lived at a distance from the world they had once inhabited was demonstrated in the fact that Charles did not learn of his dearest, oldest friend's death until it was too late to attend the funeral. As it transpired, Charles was relieved to have been spared the experience; he felt he had no words to express himself to his fellow mourners. Neither could he write, as he was asked, a few lines on Coleridge for the *Athenaeum*. He assured the editor he was 'incapable'.

However, a little while later he put down the following:

When I heard of the death of Coleridge, it was without grief. It seemed to me he had long been in the confines of the next world, that he had a hunger for Eternity. I grieved that I could not grieve! But since I feel how great a part he was of me, his great and dear Spirit haunts me. I cannot think a thought, I cannot make a criticism of men and books, without an ineffectual turning and reference to him. He was the proof and touchstone of all my cogitations . . . Never saw I his likeness, nor probably can the world see it again.

Coleridge had been reading his recently published *Poetical Works* before he died. Next to 'This Lime-Tree Bower My Prison', which he had written during Charles's first visit to Nether Stowey and dedicated to him, he had pencilled: 'Ch. And Mary Lamb – dear to my heart, yea, as it were my Heart. – S.T.C. Aet. 63; 1834 – – – – – 1797 – 1834 = 37 years!' Coleridge had left a gold mourning ring and a lock of his hair 'to my oldest Friend, & ever-beloved Schoolfellow, Charles Lamb, and in the deep and almost life-long affection, of which this is the slender record, his equally beloved Sister Mary Lamb, will know herself to be included.'

When he felt they could bear it, Charles visited the Gillmans, who had given Coleridge a caring home for the last eighteen years of his life. Typically, asking to see Harriet, the woman who had nursed Coleridge, he was 'struck and affected by the feeling she manifested towards his friend' and made her a gift of five guineas. Nothing but Mary's death could have touched Charles so deeply as that of Coleridge; it was Words-worth's view that it hastened his own.

Early in the winter, several months after Coleridge's death, some old friends went to visit the Lambs. Mary was buried in madness and Charles was disturbed and still much preoccupied with the inconceivability of his 'touchstone' being gone.

He thought of little else (his sister was but another portion of himself) . . . He had a habit of venting his melancholy in a sort of mirth. He would, with nothing graver than a pun, 'cleanse his bosom of the perilous stuff that weighed' upon it. In a jest, or a few light phrases, he could lay open the last recesses of his heart. So in respect of the death of Coleridge. Some old friends saw him two or three weeks ago, and remarked the constant turning and reference of his mind. He interrupted himself and them almost every instant with some play of affected wonder, or astonishment, or humorous melancholy, on the words, *Coleridge is dead*. Nothing could divert him from that, for the thought of it never left him.[15]

'I had thought in a green old age,' Charles had written to Wordsworth, more than twelve years before, 'to have retired to Ponder's End – emblematic name how beautiful! in the Ware road, there to have made up my accounts with Heaven and the Company, toddling about between it and Cheshunt, anon stretching on some fine Izaac Walton morning to Hoddesdon and Amwell, careless as a Beggar, but walking, walking ever, till I fairly walkd myself off my legs, dying walking!'[16] He never made it to Ponder's End, but he did, indirectly, manage to die walking.

There was some talk that he was drunk – that would have been unsurprising; he had been carried home unconscious on at least one occasion since Coleridge's death – others hotly denied what they considered a slur on his name: the myth of St Charles was already taking root. Three days before Christmas, in the year of Coleridge's death, Charles tripped and fell over in Edmonton High Street and grazed his face. It didn't seem serious and he went home, possibly to sleep it off. Unknown to Charles, he had contracted erysipelas, also known as St Anthony's Fire, an acute streptococcal infectious disease of the skin. A week later he was dead.

'You must go first, Mary,' he had said and she had agreed. Given their age difference this circumstance seemed quite possible, but now Mary was left alone in the world. William Wordsworth had likened the couple to a single tree with a double trunk; as his sister Dorothy now observed, old, frail and mad, Mary was now 'a solitary twig'. Mary's friends feared that her brother's death would provoke a serious attack of her illness from which, this time, she would never recover. She was already unwell, her illness described as 'then in mild type', which indicates that she was not violent, but gives little clue to the extent of her ability to comprehend what had happened. When she was taken in to see her brother's body 'she observed on his beauty when asleep and apprehended nothing further'. This statement is probably more significant than it at first seems. As Thomas De Quincey observed:

. . . over Lamb, at this period of his life [about 1821] there passed regularly, a brief eclipse of sleep . . . It descended upon him as softly as a shadow . . . Motionless in his chair as a bust, breathing so gently as scarcely to seem certainly alive, he presented the image of repose midway between life and death, like the repose of sculpture; and to one who knew his history a repose affectingly contrasting with the calamities and storms of his life. I have heard more persons than I can now distinctly recall, observe of Lamb when sleeping – that his countenance in that state assumed an expression almost seraphic, from its intellectual beauty of outline, its childlike simplicity, and its benignity . . . The eyes it was that disturbed the unity of effect in Lamb's waking face. They gave a restlessness to the character of his intellect, shifting, like Northern Lights, through every mode of combination with fantastic playfulness, and sometimes by fiery gleams obliterating for the moment that pure light of benignity which was the predominant reading on his features.[17]

It may be that Mary understood perfectly well that Charles was not going to wake up, but that just as he found rare peace in sleep, death came, in one sense, as a relief or respite from the restlessness which had tormented his latter years. It may be the case that, as was the case when her other brother died, the reality sank in slowly, by degrees. Whatever was going on inside her head, externally she appeared 'resigned and composed'.[18] Talfourd and Ryle, an old colleague of the East India House, as Charles's executors, arranged the funeral, Mary having taken Ryle to Edmonton churchyard and pointed out the spot Charles had chosen, on one of their walks together, as his final resting place.

On 3 January 1835, a small group of mourners gathered in the churchyard to attend the funeral; Mary was among them. Her state of mind on that occasion can only be guessed at, but Crabb Robinson, who visited her a few days afterwards, noted: 'A stranger would have seen little remarkable about her. She was neither violent nor unhappy; nor was she entirely without sense. She was, however, out of her mind, as the expression is . . .'[19]

Although when Charles had suggested it would be better if Mary predeceased him, Mary had agreed, Southey's view on the matter is significant. Having known the couple for forty years – even before the 'day of horrors' – he had had ample opportunity to observe and reflect on their relationship and concluded, on Charles's death, that 'Forlorn as his poor sister will feel herself . . . it is better that she should be the survivor. Her happiness, such as it was, depended less upon him than his upon her.'[20]

When a great or good man dies, it is tempting to review his final days or words with a kind of awe, to look for something significant and enduring yet, at the same time, typical of the person. On the day of what turned out to be his fatal accident, Charles wrote his last letter. Of course, he had no idea it would be elevated to a status of such import; if he had, he might have taken a deal more trouble over it. It has more of the everyday than the eternal about it, but most of all, more of Charles Lamb than of anyone else.

> Dear Mrs. Dyer, – I am very uneasy about a *Book* which I either have lost or left at your house on Thursday. It was the book I went out to fetch from Miss Buffam's, while the tripe was frying. It is called Phillip's Theatrum Poetarum; but it is an English book. I think I left it in the parlour. It is Mr. Cary's book, and I would not lose it for the world. Pray, if you find it, book it at the Swan, Snow Hill, by an Edmonton stage immediately, directed to Mr. Lamb, Church-street, Edmonton, or write to say you cannot find it. I am quite anxious about it. If it is lost, I shall never like tripe again.
>
> With kindest love to Mr. Dyer and all,
> Yours truly,
>
> C. LAMB

On 12 January Henry Crabb Robinson steeled himself to visit Mary. That evening he wrote the following account in his diary.

It was a melancholy sight, but more so to the reflection than to the sense . . . On my going into the room where she was sitting with Mr. Waldron [*sic*], she exclaimed with great vivacity, 'Oh! Here's *Crabby*.' She gave me her hand with great cordiality, and said, 'Now this is very kind – not merely good-natured, but very, very kind to come and see me in my affliction.' And then she ran on about the unhappy, insane family of my old friend – – – – –. It would be useless to attempt recollecting all she said; but it is to be remarked that her mind seemed turned to subjects connected with insanity, as well as with her brother's death. She spoke of Charles repeatedly . . . She spoke of his birth, and said that he was a weakly, but very pretty child. I have no doubt that if ever she be sensible of her brother's loss, it will overset her again. She will live for ever in the memory of her friends as one of the most amiable and admirable of women.[21]

Just as the name of his old friend with the insane family was censored, this published version of his diary omitted a more significant detail: that Mary had told Crabb Robinson that Emma and Charles had been in love with each other.

Given Mary's state of mind Crabb Robinson interpreted the statement as 'utterly wild and groundless'. There is no way of knowing whether there was any truth in Mary's assertion. If it were true, this would be the first opportunity she had of expressing it and Crabb Robinson, as her closest male friend since Coleridge's death, would have been the person to whom she would have opened her heart. If it were not true, however, what did it mean? One way of approaching the subject is to begin with the premise that having all her life suppressed her own sexuality as an unmarriageable woman, Mary subconsciously expressed her strong emotional feelings for her brother by transferring them to Emma, who *could* feasibly respond to Charles in a sexual way. In other words, Emma became a conduit for Mary's suppressed feelings for her brother. Alternatively, she could have entertained genuine hopes that Charles and Emma might become a couple, so that Charles, having sacrificed the best years of his life to caring for his sister, could in later life enjoy the comforts of the married state. (Crabb Robinson claimed Mary did not think Moxon good enough for Emma.) If Mary subconsciously hoped for this, she could easily have begun to imagine that such an attachment really existed. A further explanation for her statement harks back to the idea that she was jealous of Emma intruding on her hitherto exclusive intimacy with Charles and feared Charles's feelings for Emma might be of a nature that would in turn exclude her. Whether her notion that Charles and Emma were in love was based in fact, wishful thinking, or fear, her expression of it cannot be ignored. In any event it spoke of an aspect of her relationship with her brother which clearly disturbed her.

Charles's qualities, both as a writer and as a man, were sufficiently esteemed by many of his friends that soon after his death plans were afoot to collect and publish a selection of his letters and a brief biography. Thomas Noon Talfourd, who had stood at his graveside on that winter morning, was delegated the task of gathering and organizing both the letters and the information on Charles's life supplied by his friends. His edition of *The Letters of Charles Lamb, with a Sketch of His Life* appeared in 1837 and was dedicated to Mary. Mary had already been critical of things that had been made public about her brother's life. William Wordsworth had drawn on his intimate knowledge of the couple, in an epitaph for Charles which contained references of which Mary strongly disapproved. 'She does not like any allusion to his being a clerk, or to family misfortunes,' her friend Henry Crabb Robinson observed, adding understandingly: 'This is very natural. Not even dear Mary can overcome the common feeling that would overcome lowness of station, or a reference to ignoble sufferings.'[22] Dear Mary, however, had little reason to fear what her friends might write about her brother, or what portions of his correspondence they would permit to be published. The whole of Talfourd's project, along with numerous other memoirs and letters published in the twelve and a half years between the deaths of Charles and Mary, carefully excluded all references to the factors which had most powerfully determined the course of her brother's life: Mary's insanity and her murder of their mother. It was not until after Mary's death in

1847 that Talfourd, with the assent of mutual friends of the Lambs, felt it appropriate to restore many passages in the letters which he had excised from his earlier edition, and to include in the account of Charles's life certain events not previously known even to some of the Lambs' closest friends. A number of other personal memoirs of the Lambs followed, all of which remained careful, however, to play down Charles's drinking and his own black moods. As a result of the vagaries of time and pride much evidence is now lost; at any time new letters could come to light which would fill in more of the gaps and answer many of the questions arising from a life that sat so uncomfortably between laughter and sorrow.

Mary had lived eleven years before Charles arrived in her life and was to outlive him by over twelve more. To universal astonishment, he had left her an estate amounting to between fifteen hundred and two thousand pounds. This plus an annuity from East India House left her perfectly comfortable. Old friends continued to visit her at Edmonton; she would often take a short walk with them, inevitably ending up beside her brother's grave. She appears to have enjoyed continuous good health at least until August 1837. Her periods of illness then lengthened, until she was 'out of her mind' for a greater portion of every year than she was well. Crabb Robinson visited her in August 1839, when she had already been ill for ten months. He wrote,

. . . these severe attacks have produced the inevitable result. Her mind is gone, or, at least, has become inert. She has still her excellent heart, – is kind and considerate, and her judgment is sound. Nothing but good feeling and good sense in all she says; but still no one would discover what she once was. She hears ill, and is slow in conception. She says she bears solitude better than she did.

In June 1841 B. W. Procter – the friend who had many years earlier been touched by meeting Charles and Mary, both in tears, on their way to the madhouse at Hoxton, carrying a straitjacket between them – called on Mary unannounced. He was horrified to find her alone in the house and in a state of neglect. Apparently Mrs Walden had developed 'a very evil temper' and Mary was 'in danger of being unduly and unnecessarily excited'. Procter promptly wrote to Talfourd:

She tells me that whilst the children were young, she was desirous of staying, to mediate between them and the mother (whose temper she says amounts to a disease) and partly (as far as I could collect) because she thought it might be serviceable to the people themselves. Miss Lamb was, yesterday, perfectly well ... In my opinion, her mere desire to leave the place – repeatedly and strongly expressed – is a sufficient reason for her leaving it. No one could talk more sensibly or better in any respect than she did yesterday. She enquired after all her friends and acquaintance – and I think if she were nearer London, the friends of her brother and herself would have *many* opportunities of rendering the last days of her life more happy than they are at present.[23]

It is clear in many respects that she was still the same old Mary.

After this short spell in hell Mary moved to St John's Wood, to live with her old nurse Sarah James's sister, Mrs Parsons, at 41 Alpha Road, the last of many removals. August 1842 found Mary again paying and receiving visits, in full possession of her faculties and her memory still strong. But by March 1843 Crabb Robinson acknowledged she was 'a mere wreck of herself' and very hard of hearing.

Her death, on 20 May 1847, aged eighty-three, came as a relief both to her and to her friends. Among those who saw her into her brother's grave were Talfourd, Ryal, Moxon, Martin Burney, Forster and Allsop. Charles's grave had deliberately been dug deep enough to receive his sister's remains when the time came. As their mutual friends stood around the burial plot, the mourners noticed that Charles's coffin had been partially exposed, forcefully bringing his memory to mind. Crabb Robinson wrote afterwards: 'There was no sadness assumed by the attendants, but we all talked with warm affection of dear Mary Lamb, and of her brother Charles, – all of the men of genius I ever knew, the one most intensely and universally to be loved.'[24] In fact, there was an exception to the 'no sadness'. Martin Burney, one of the children of their circle of friends in whom the Lambs had taken a particular and affectionate interest, now a man, wept inconsolably at the graveside of those who 'had been among the dearest objects of existence to him'.[25]

Although Charles and Mary died childless, their names lived on, and not only through their writings. Two friends named sons after Charles: Charles Lamb Talfourd, born in 1828, died aged only six; but Charles Lamb Kenney, born in 1821, lived to be sixty – older than his namesake. Although most of the buildings associated with the Lambs have vanished, Islington now has an Elia Mews and an Elia Street, while Lamb's Gardens can be found in Widford, scene of Charles's romance with Ann Simmons.

On Mary's death, the remainder of their estate passed to Emma Moxon; their only other legacy to the world was their work.

While *The Essays of Elia* remain works of great charm and originality – 'The Wedding', for example, is still able to melt the hardest heart – they are now neglected. *Tales from*

Shakespeare, however, remains in print, the stories retaining both their original utility and beauty. How long before they too disappear from bookshelves remains to be seen.

Charles Lamb's importance to the literature of his period, however, lies as much in the contributions he made to the work of other writers as it does in his own achievements. While his advice to Coleridge to 'cultivate simplicity' is legendary, many others drew inspiration from him. Wordsworth's most recent biographer, Juliet Barker, has drawn attention to Charles's responsibility for 'one of the liveliest passages in "The Prelude"', where Wordsworth paraphrases a letter Charles wrote him, to give one small example, and it is probably impossible to establish how significant to Wordsworth was Charles's encouragement to write 'The Recluse'.[26] Richard Holmes, the most recent biographer of Coleridge, finds that it was not – as is usually supposed – Wordsworth who was primarily responsible for the emergence of Coleridge's 'plain style', but Charles.[27] Coleridge would regularly send his work in progress to Charles, 'whose *taste and judgement* I see reason to think more correct and philosophical than my own, which yet I place pretty high'.[28] He also left all the business of proof corrections and the arrangement of the material in the third edition of his *Poems* to Charles.

Aside from their various contributions to the literature of their age, the work of Charles and Mary Lamb was destined to endure, although sometimes in the most unexpected ways.

The *Charles Lamb Society Bulletin* included in its issue for October 1941 a report from Mr C. McKay, Secretary of Native Affairs (Western Samoa). One of the more ambitious ways in which the London Missionary Society promulgated the values of Western civilization to the Samoans was in encouraging them to put on Shakespeare's plays. However, there were no translations of Shakespeare in Samoan, the only available versions being those printed in the Mission's vernacular journal, *O le Sulu Samoa*. Mr McKay thought the Society would be interested to know that these versions were freely adapted from the Lambs' *Tales from Shakespeare*. That Charles and Mary Lamb were responsible for bringing Shakespeare to Samoa seems a fitting achievement in an odd but well-intentioned life.

Bibliography

Aaron, Jane, *A Double Singleness: Gender and the Writings of Charles and Mary Lamb* (Clarendon, 1991).

Allen, G. A. T., *Christ's Hospital* (Blackie & Son, 1937).

Allsop, Thomas (ed.), *Letters, Conversations and Recollections of S. T. Coleridge*, 2 vols. (Moxon, 1836).

Anderson, G. A. (ed.), *The Letters of Thomas Manning to Charles Lamb* (Harper, New York, 1926).

Anon., *A Description of the Crimes and Horrors in the Interior of Warburton's Private Mad-House at Hoxton, commonly called Whitmore House* (Benbow, ?1822).

Barker, Juliet, *Wordsworth: A Life* (Viking, 2000).

Barnett, George L., *Charles Lamb: The Evolution of Elia* (Indiana University Press, 1964).

Bate, Jonathan (ed.), *Elia and the Last Essays of Elia* (Oxford University Press, 1987).

Beer, John (ed.), *Samuel Taylor Coleridge: Poems* (Dent, 1974).

Bennett, Betty T. (ed.), *The Letters of Mary Wollstonecraft Shelley*, 3 vols. (Johns Hopkins University Press, 1980–88).

Blainey, Ann, *Immortal Boy: A Portrait of Leigh Hunt* (Croom Helm, 1985).

Blunden, Edmund (ed.), *Charles Lamb: His Life Recorded by his Contemporaries* (Hogarth, 1934).

Brewer, Luther A. (ed.), *Some Lamb and Browning Letters to Leigh Hunt* (The Torch Press, 1924).

The Christ's Hospital Book (Hamish Hamilton, 1958).

Coombs, Tony, *'Tis a Mad World at Hogsdon: A short history of Hoxton and surrounding area* (Hoxton Hall, ?1975).

Coote, Stephen, *John Keats: A Life* (Hodder & Stoughton, 1995).

Courtney, Winifred Fisk, *Young Charles Lamb 1775–1802* (Macmillan, 1982).

Cowden Clarke, Charles and Mary, *Recollections of Writers* (Centaur, 1969; first published in book form 1878).

Curry, Kenneth (ed.), *New Letters of Robert Southey* (Columbia University Press, 1965).

De Quincey, Thomas, 'Recollections of Charles Lamb', in George Gordon (ed.), *Charles Lamb: Prose and Poetry, with essays by Hazlitt and De Quincey* (Clarendon, 1928).

De Selincourt, Ernest (ed.), *The Letters of William and Dorothy Wordsworth* (Clarendon, 1967–93), 8 vols. (*I: The early years, 1787–1805*, revised by Chester L. Shaver; *II: The middle years: pt. 1. 1806–1811*, revised by Mary Moorman; *III: The middle years: pt. 2. 1812–1820*, revised by Mary Moorman and Alan G. Hill; *IV: The later years: pt. 1. 1821–1828*, revised, arranged, and edited by Alan G. Hill; *V: The later years: pt. 2. 1829–1834*, revised, arranged, and edited by Alan G. Hill; *VI: The later years: pt. 3. 1835–1839*, revised, arranged, and edited by Alan G. Hill; *VII: The later years: pt. 4. 1840–1853*, revised, arranged, and edited by Alan G. Hill; *VIII: A supplement of new letters*).

Edgeworth, R. L. and Maria, *Essays on Practical Education* (R. Hunter, 1815).

Francis, Basil, *Fanny Kelly of Drury Lane* (Rockliff, 1950).

Frank, Robert, *Don't Call Me Gentle Charles: An Essay on Lamb's 'Essays of Elia'* (Oregon State University Press, 1976).

Garton, Charles, *Schola Lincolniensis* (The Old Christ's Hospital Lincolnians' Society, 1988).

Gates, Eleanor M. (ed.), *Leigh Hunt: A Life in Letters* (Falls River, 1998).

Gilchrist, Anne, *Mary Lamb* (W. H. Allen, 1883).

Godwin, William, *The Enquirer: Reflections on Education, Manners and Literature* (J. Moore, 1797).

Gordon, George (ed.), *Charles Lamb: Prose and Poetry, with essays by Hazlitt and de Quincey* (Clarendon, 1928).

Griggs, E. L. (ed.), *Collected Letters of Samuel Taylor Coleridge*, 6 vols. (Oxford University Press, 1956–71).

Hayter, Alethea, *The Wreck of the Abergavenny* (Macmillan, 2002).

Hazlitt, William, 'The Spirit of the Age', in George Gordon (ed.), *Charles Lamb: Prose and Poetry, with essays by Hazlitt and De Quincey* (Clarendon, 1928).

Hazlitt, William, 'On the Conversation of Authors', in George Gordon (ed.), *Charles Lamb: Prose and Poetry, with essays by Hazlitt and de Quincey* (Clarendon, 1928).

Hazlitt, W. C., *Mary and Charles Lamb: Poems, Letters and Remains* (Chatto & Windus, 1874).

Holman, L. E., *Lamb's 'Barbara S—': The Life of Frances Maria Kelly, Actress* (Methuen, 1935).

Holmes, Richard, *Coleridge: Early Visions* (Flamingo, 1999).

Holmes, Richard, *Coleridge: Darker Reflections* (Flamingo, 1999).

Howe, Will D., *Charles Lamb and His Friends* (Bobbs–Merrill, 1944).

Hunt, Leigh, *Lord Byron and some of his contemporaries* (Henry Coburn, 1828).

Ingrams, Allan (ed.), *Patterns of Madness in the Eighteenth Century: A Reader* (Liverpool University Press, 1998).

Jerrold, Walter (ed.), *Thomas Hood and Charles Lamb: The Story of a Friendship* (Ernest Benn, 1930).

Johnson, Edith Christina, *Lamb Always Elia* (Methuen, 1935).

King, H. G. L., 'The Lamb Tragedy and the Law', *CLS Bulletin 56*, October 1942.

Lamb, John, *A Letter to the Right Hon. William Windham, on His Opposition to Lord Erskine's Bill, for the Prevention of Cruelty to Animals* (Maxwell & Walter Wilson, 1810).

Lawson, Philip, *The East India Company: A History* (Longman, 1993).

Logan, J. V., Jordan, J. E. and Frye, Northrop (eds.), *Some British*

Romantics: a Collection of Essays (Ohio State University Press, 1966).

Lucas, E. V. (ed.), *Charles Lamb and the Lloyds* (Smith, Elder & Co., 1898).

Lucas, E. V. (ed.), *The Works of Charles and Mary Lamb*, 7 vols. (Methuen, 1903–5).

Lucas, E. V., *The Life of Charles Lamb*, 2 vols. (Methuen, 1905).

Marrs, Edwin W. Jr (ed.), *The Letters of Charles and Mary Anne Lamb*, 3 vols. (Cornell University Press, 1975–8).

McKenna, Wayne, *Charles Lamb and the Theatre* (Smythe, 1978).

Monsman, Gerald, *Confessions of a Prosaic Dreamer: Charles Lamb's art of autobiography* (Duke University Press, 1984).

Moorman, Mary (ed.), *Journals of Dorothy Wordsworth: The Alfoxden Journal 1798; The Grasmere Journals 1800–1803*, 2nd edn (Oxford University Press, 1980).

Morley, Edith J., *Correspondence of Henry Crabb Robinson with the Wordsworth Circle* (Clarendon, 1927).

Morley, F. V., *Lamb Before Elia* (Jonathan Cape, 1932).

Morris, Arthur D., *The Hoxton Madhouses* (Goodwin Bros., 1958).

Moxon, Edward, *Contemporary Notices of Charles Lamb* (private reprint, 1891).

Nabholtz, John R., *'My Reader My Fellow-Labourer': A Study of English Romantic Prose* (University of Missouri Press, 1986).

North, Ernest Dressel (ed.), *The Wit and Wisdom of Charles Lamb* (G. P. Putnam's Sons, 1893).

Norton, Charles Eliot (ed.), *Thomas Carlyle, Reminiscences* (J. M. Dent, 1972).

Novello, Clara, *Reminiscences* (Edward Arnold, 1910).

Parry-Jones, William Ll., *The Trade in Lunacy: A Study of Private Madhouses in England in the Eighteenth and Nineteenth Centuries* (Routledge & Kegan Paul, 1972).

Patmore, P. G., *My Friends and Acquaintance* (Saunders & Otley, 1854).

Penrose, P. D. (ed.), *The Autobiography and Memoirs of Benjamin Robert Haydon 1786–1846* (G. Bell, 1927).

Polowetzky, Michael, *Prominent Sisters: Mary Lamb, Dorothy Wordsworth and Sarah Disraeli* (Praeger, 1996).

Pope, Willard Bissell (ed.), *The Diary of Benjamin Robert Haydon*, 5 vols. (Harvard University Press, 1963).

Porter, Roy, *Mind-Forg'd Manacles: A history of madness in England from the Restoration to the Regency* (Athlone, 1987).

Randel, Fred V., *Charles Lamb's Essayistic Romanticism* (Kennikat, 1975).

Riehl, Joseph E., *Charles Lamb's Children's Literature* (Institut für Anglistik und Amerikanistik, Universität Salzburg, 1980).

Rogers, J. W., *A Statement of the Cruelties, Abuses and Frauds, which are practised in Mad-Houses* (E. Justins, 1815).

Rollins, Hyder E. (ed.), *The Letters of John Keats 1814–1821*, 2 vols. (Harvard University Press, 1958).

Roper, Derek (ed.), *Lyrical Ballads* (Northcote House, 1987).

Ross, Ernest Carson, *The Ordeal of Bridget Elia* (University of Oklahoma Press, 1940).

Ross, Ernest Carson, *Charles Lamb and Emma Isola: A survey of the evidence relevant to their personal relationship* (Charles Lamb Society, 1950).

Rysor, Thomas M. (ed.), *Coleridge's Shakespearean Criticism* (Dent, 1964).

Sadler, Thomas (ed.), *Diary, Reminiscences and Correspondence of Henry Crabb Robinson*, 3 vols. (Macmillan, 1869).

St Clair, William, *The Godwins and the Shelleys: the Biography of a Family* (Faber & Faber, 1990).

Talfourd, Thomas Noon, *Final Memorials of Charles Lamb* (Moxon, 1850).

Thompson, A. S., 'Lamb', in *The Cambridge History of English Literature*, vol. XII (Cambridge University Press, 1961).

Tillotson, Geoffrey, 'The Historical Importance of Certain *Essays of Elia*', in J. V. Logan, J. E. Jordan and Northrop Frye (eds.), *Some British Romantics: A Collection of Essays* (Ohio State University Press, 1966).

Wild, Antony, *The East India Company: Trade and Conquest from 1600* (HarperCollins, 1999).

A Note on the Text

Quotations from the *Essays of Elia* are from the edition most easily accessible by the reader: *Elia and the Last Essays of Elia*, ed. Jonathan Bate, 'The World's Classics' series (Oxford University Press, 1987). Other quotations from the Lambs' works are taken almost exclusively from E. V. Lucas's seven-volume edition of *The Works of Charles and Mary Lamb* (Methuen, 1903–5).

There exists no complete edition of the Lambs' letters. The work of updating Lucas's edition (included in his edition of the *Works*) was commenced by Edwin W. Marrs, whose first three volumes cover letters up to the autumn of 1817 and appeared in 1975–8, but remains yet unfinished. Therefore letters dated after this period are taken from Lucas's edition except where otherwise stated.

The problem with using two editions is that each editor uses different means of indicating the Lambs' emphasis of certain words. Marrs renders words written in large letters in bold face, and those underlined in bold face italics. We have rendered all emphasized words in small capitals and where it is known that the word was also underlined, in underlined small capitals. Lucas appears only rarely to differentiate between degrees of emphasis, rendering all such words in italics, which we have retained. (It is as well to be aware, also, that Lucas tidies up the Lambs' punctuation and spelling much more than Marrs, who usually preserves their many eccentricities.)

Where dates are given in square brackets, this indicates that no date appeared on the actual letter but the date has been established by editors of the letters.

Abbreviations Used in the Notes

CL	Charles Lamb
ML	Mary Lamb
Lucas	E. V. Lucas, *The Works of Charles and Mary Lamb* (Methuen, 1903–5); vols. I and II of the letters are equivalent to vols. VI and VII of the *Works*
Lucas, *Life*	E. V. Lucas, *The Life of Charles Lamb*, 2 vols. (Methuen, 1905)
Marrs	Edwin W. Marrs Jr (ed.), *The Letters of Charles and Mary Anne Lamb*, 3 vols. (Cornell University Press, 1975–8)

Notes

Introduction

1. *Critical Review*, May 1807.
2. A. S. Thompson, 'Lamb', in *The Cambridge History of English Literature*, XII (Cambridge University Press, 1961), p. 189.
3. Thomas De Quincey, 'Recollections of Charles Lamb', in George Gordon (ed.), *Charles Lamb: Prose and Poetry, with essays by Hazlitt and de Quincey* (Clarendon, 1928), p. 30; William Wordsworth, 'Written After the Death of Charles Lamb', in Edmund Blunden (ed.), *Charles Lamb: His Life Recorded by his Contemporaries* (Hogarth, 1934), p. 252; Edward Moxon, *Contemporary Notices of Charles Lamb* (1891).
4. CL to Dorothy Wordsworth, 14 June 1805, Marrs, II, p. 169. The letter, which is missing several words, has been reconstructed by the editor.
5. ibid, p. 170.
6. 'Written on Christmas Day, 1797'.
7. ML to Sarah Stoddart, [21 September 1803], Marrs, II, p. 124.
8. William Hazlitt, 'The Spirit of the Age', in Gordon (ed.), *Charles Lamb*, pp. 20–21.
9. Thomas Noon Talfourd, *Final Memorials of Charles Lamb* (Moxon, 1850), p. 351.
10. William Hazlitt, 'On the Conversation of Authors', in Gordon (ed.), *Charles Lamb*, p. 2; cited by Ann Blainey, *Immortal Boy: A Portrait of Leigh Hunt* (Croom Helm, 1985).
11. Hazlitt, 'On the Conversation of Authors', in Gordon (ed.), *Charles Lamb*, p. 3.

Chapter 1: Polly and Charley

1. Winifred Courtney, *Young Charles Lamb 1775–1802* (Macmillan, 1982), p. 11.
2. See the Elia essays 'The Old Benchers of the Inner Temple' and 'New Year's Eve' and also Charles's poem 'Gone or Going'.
3. CL to William Wordsworth, [13 October 1804], Marrs, II, p. 146.
4. 'Dream-Children'.
5. ML to Mrs Vincent Novello, [spring of 1820], Lucas, I, pp. 538–9.
6. CL to Samuel Taylor Coleridge, [17 October 1796], Marrs, I, p. 52.
7. CL to Samuel Taylor Coleridge, 14 November 1796, Marrs, I, p. 64, and CL to Samuel Taylor Coleridge, [3 October 1796], Marrs, I, p. 48.
8. Charles and Mary Cowden Clarke, *Recollections of Writers* (Centaur, 1969; first published in book form 1878), p. 185.
9. ML to Mrs Morgan and Charlotte Brent, [22 May 1815], Marrs, III, pp. 159–60.
10. ML to Sarah Stoddart, [early November 1805], Marrs, II, p. 184.
11. 'Poor Relations'.
12. CL to Miss Fryer, [no date], Lucas, II, p. 929.
13. 'My Relations'.
14. ML to Sarah Stoddart, [21 September 1803], Marrs, II, pp. 123–4.
15. 'My Relations'.
16. CL to Samuel Taylor Coleridge, 28 October 1796, Marrs, I, p. 57.
17. 'Mackery End, in Hertfordshire'.
18. 'All Fools' Day'.
19. 'Witches and Other Night Fears'.

20. CL to Samuel Taylor Coleridge, [23 October 1802], Marrs, II, pp. 81–2.

21. 'Witches and Other Night Fears'.

22. ibid.

23. 'The Old Benchers of the Inner Temple'.

24. ibid.

25. F. V. Morley, *Lamb Before Elia* (Jonathan Cape, 1932), p. 74.

26. CL to Henry Crabb Robinson, 20 January 1827, Lucas, II, pp. 720–21.

27. ML to Sara Hutchinson, [November? 1816], Marrs, III, p. 234, and CL to Dorothy Wordsworth, [21 November 1817], Lucas, I, p. 507.

28. CL to William Wordsworth, [30 January 1801], Marrs I, p. 267.

29. CL to Robert Lloyd, [7 February 1801], Marrs, I, p. 271.

30. Moxon, *Contemporary Notices*, pp. 8–9.

31. 'The Praise of Chimney-Sweeps' and 'A Complaint of the Decay of Beggars in the Metropolis'.

32. Charles's account of Mackery End is in his 'Elia' essay of the same name; Mary mentions it in a letter: ML to Mrs Morgan and Charlotte Brent, [22 May 1815], Marrs, III, pp. 159–60.

33. See CL to Samuel Taylor Coleridge, [3 October 1796], Marrs, I, p. 49.

34. 'Dream-Children'.

35. CL to Samuel Taylor Coleridge, [17 October 1796], Marrs, I, p. 52.

36. CL to Samuel Taylor Coleridge, [13–16 June 1796], Marrs, I, p. 30.

37. ibid., and CL to Robert Southey, 31 October 1799, Marrs, I, pp. 171–2.

38. 'Blakesmoor in H—shire'.

39. ibid.

40. 'My First Play'.

41. ibid.

Chapter 2: The Schoolboy and the Mantua-maker

1. 'Captain Starkey' (1825), in *Hone's Every-Day Book*.
2. 'Detached Thoughts on Books and Reading'.
3. Jane Aaron, *A Double Singleness: Gender and the Writings of Charles and Mary Lamb* (Clarendon, 1991).
4. Leigh Hunt, *Lord Byron and some of his contemporaries* (Henry Coburn, 1828), pp. 346–7.
5. ibid., p. 347.
6. T. S. Surr, in *The Christ's Hospital Book* (Hamish Hamilton, 1958), p. 72.
7. Samuel Taylor Coleridge, *The Courier*, 1811.
8. Hunt, *Lord Byron*, pp. 352–3.
9. Cited by G. A. T. Allen, *Christ's Hospital* (Blackie & Son, 1937), p. 31.
10. Samuel Taylor Coleridge in a letter to Thomas Poole, cited in *The Christ's Hospital Book*, p. 71.
11. 'Christ's Hospital Five and Thirty Years Ago'.
12. CL to Samuel Taylor Coleridge, [5–6 February 1797], Marrs, I, p. 96.
13. 'A Dissertation Upon Roast Pig'.
14. Samuel Taylor Coleridge in a letter to Thomas Poole, cited in *The Christ's Hospital Book*, p. 70.
15. Hunt, *Lord Byron*, p. 371.
16. 'Christ's Hospital Five and Thirty Years Ago'.
17. Samuel Taylor Coleridge, *Biographia Literaria*, cited in *The Christ's Hospital Book*, p. 70.
18. Hunt, *Lord Byron*, p. 346.
19. Edmund Blunden (ed.), *Charles Lamb: His Life Recorded by his Contemporaries* (Hogarth, 1934), p. 19.
20. Hunt, *Lord Byron*, p. 356.
21. Leigh Hunt, *Autobiography*, in *The Christ's Hospital Book*, p. 77;

Hunt, *Lord Byron*, p. 362, and W. P. Scargill, *Recollections of a Blue-coat Boy*, in *The Christ's Hospital Book*, p. 128.

22. 'Christ's Hospital Five and Thirty Years Ago'.
23. Allen, *Christ's Hospital*, p. 36.
24. Samuel Taylor Coleridge, *Table Talk*.
25. E. L. Griggs (ed.), *Collected Letters of Samuel Taylor Coleridge*, 6 vols. (Oxford, 1956–71), I, p. 347.
26. Samuel Taylor Coleridge to Thomas Poole, Griggs (ed.), *Collected Letters of Samuel Taylor Coleridge*, I, pp. 354–5.
27. Samuel Taylor Coleridge to Thomas Poole, Griggs (ed.), *Collected Letters of Samuel Taylor Coleridge*, I, pp. 348 and 347.
28. 'Oxford in the Vacation'.
29. CL to George Dyer, 22 February 1831, Lucas, II, p. 870.
30. 'The Old Margate Hoy'.
31. Samuel Taylor Coleridge to Robert Southey, Griggs (ed.), *Collected Letters of Samuel Taylor Coleridge*, I, p. 136.
32. 'Modern Gallantry'.
33. ibid.
34. ibid.
35. 'The South-Sea House'.
36. 'Old China'.
37. CL to Robert Lloyd, [22 July 1800], Marrs, I, p. 214.
38. ML to Sarah Stoddart, [21 September 1803], Marrs, II, p. 124.

Chapter 3: The Salutation and Cat

1. 'A Chapter on Ears'.
2. 'Dream-Children'.
3. Cited in Antony Wild, *The East India Company: Trade and Conquest from 1600* (HarperCollins, 1999), pp. 62–3.
4. Philip Lawson, *The East India Company: A History* (Longman, 1993), p. 126.

5. Winifred Courtney, *Young Charles Lamb 1775–1802* (Macmillan, 1982), p. 90.

6. 'Poor Relations'; Lucas, *Life*, I, p. 75.

7. Robert Southey to Edward Moxon, 2 February 1836; in Edmund Blunden (ed.), *Charles Lamb: His Life Recorded by his Contemporaries* (Hogarth, 1934), p. 23.

8. Samuel Taylor Coleridge to Robert Southey, December 1794, in Blunden (ed.), *Charles Lamb*, pp. 22–3.

9. 'To a Friend', in John Beer (ed.), *Samuel Taylor Coleridge: Poems* (Dent, 1974), p. 43.

10. *Popular Fallacies*: 'That home is home though it is never so homely.'

11. 'Christ's Hospital Five and Thirty Years Ago'.

12. ibid.

13. E. L. Griggs (ed.), *Collected Letters of Samuel Taylor Coleridge*, 6 vols. (Oxford, 1956–71), I, pp. 67–8.

14. William Hazlitt, 'On the Living Poets', *Misc. Works*, 3 vols. (Routledge, 1887), III, pp. 198–9.

15. William Wordsworth to John Payne Collier, [December 1817/January 1818], in Ernest de Selincourt (ed.), revised by Mary Moorman and Alan G. Hill, *The Letters of William and Dorothy Wordsworth: The Middle Years: Part II* (Clarendon, 1970), p. 664.

16. CL to Samuel Taylor Coleridge, [8–10 June 1796], Marrs, I, p. 18.

17. CL to Samuel Taylor Coleridge, [1 December 1796], Marrs, I, pp. 65–6; CL to Thomas Manning, 26 February 1808, Marrs, II, p. 274; CL to Samuel Taylor Coleridge, [28 January 1798], Marrs, I, p. 126; CL to Thomas Manning, [17 May 1800], Marrs, I, p. 204.

18. CL to Samuel Taylor Coleridge, [8–10 June 1796], Marrs, I, p. 18.

19. CL to Samuel Taylor Coleridge, 10 December 1796, Marrs, I, p. 78.

20. ibid.

21. Published anonymously by John Lamb, *A Letter to the Right Hon. William Windham, on His Opposition to Lord Erskine's Bill, for the Prevention of Cruelty to Animals* (Maxwell & Walter Wilson, 1810), p. 16.

22. F. V. Morley, *Lamb Before Elia* (Jonathan Cape, 1932), pp. 116–17.

23. *Charles Lamb Bulletin*, April 1974, 118.

24. CL to Samuel Taylor Coleridge, [27 September 1796], Marrs, I, p. 45.

25. Robert Southey to Edward Moxon, 2 February 1836, in Blunden (ed.), *Charles Lamb*, p. 25.

26. CL to Samuel Taylor Coleridge, [8–10 June 1796], Marrs, I, p. 19.

27. ibid., p. 22.

28. CL to Samuel Taylor Coleridge, [13–16 June 1796], Marrs, I, p. 32.

29. CL to Samuel Taylor Coleridge, [8–10 June 1796], Marrs, I, p. 17.

Chapter 4: Friend-confessor, Brother-confessor

1. See, for example, William Ll. Parry-Jones, *The Trade in Lunacy: A Study of Private Madhouses in England in the Eighteenth and Nineteenth Centuries* (Routledge & Kegan Paul, 1972), p. 12.

2. W. F. Bynum *et al.* (ed.), *The Anatomy of Madness: Essays in the History of Psychiatry* (Tavistock, 1985), II, p. 28.

3. Roy Porter, *Mind-Forg'd Manacles: A history of madness in England from the Restoration to the Regency* (Athlone, 1987), p. 23.

4. Allan Ingrams (ed.), *Patterns of Madness in the Eighteenth Century: A Reader* (Liverpool University Press, 1998), pp. 250–51.

5. J. W. Rogers, *A Statement of the Cruelties, Abuses and Frauds, which are practised in Mad-Houses* (E. Justins, 1815), p. 41.

6. Arthur D. Morris, *The Hoxton Madhouses* (Goodwin Bros., 1958), unpaginated.

7. Anon., *A Description of the Crimes and Horrors in the Interior of Warburton's Private Mad-House at Hoxton, commonly called Whitmore House* (Benbow, ?1822), p. 12.

8. Parry-Jones, *The Trade in Lunacy*, p. 83.

9. CL to Samuel Taylor Coleridge, [3 October 1796], Marrs, I, pp. 47–8.

10. ibid.

11. CL to Samuel Taylor Coleridge, 8 November 1796, Marrs, I, p. 60.

12. CL to Samuel Taylor Coleridge, [27 September 1796], Marrs, I, p. 44. Marrs gives 'that' for 'than'.

13. ibid., pp. 44–5. Marrs gives 'best' for 'rest'.

14. CL to Samuel Taylor Coleridge, [3 October 1796], Marrs, I, p. 47.

15. CL to Samuel Taylor Coleridge, [23 October 1802], Marrs, II, p. 81.

16. CL to Samuel Taylor Coleridge, [3 October 1796], Marrs, I, p. 47.

17. ibid., p. 49. Marrs gives 'he' for 'be'.

18. ibid., p. 50.

19. CL to Samuel Taylor Coleridge, [17 October 1796], Marrs, I, p. 52.

20. CL to Samuel Taylor Coleridge, 28 October 1796, Marrs, I, p. 56.

21. CL to Samuel Taylor Coleridge, 8 November 1796, Marrs, I, pp. 58–61.

22. ibid., pp. 60–61. My italics.

23. Richard Holmes, *Coleridge: Early Visions* (Flamingo, 1999), p. 115.

24. CL to Samuel Taylor Coleridge, 14 November 1796, Marrs, I, p. 62.

25. ibid., pp. 63–4.

26. CL to Samuel Taylor Coleridge, [1 December 1796], Marrs, I, p. 66.

27. CL to Samuel Taylor Coleridge, 10 December 1796, Marrs, I, p. 79.

28. CL to Samuel Taylor Coleridge, 9 January 1797, Marrs, I, p. 89.

29. CL to Samuel Taylor Coleridge, 10 December 1796, Marrs, I, p. 79.

30. CL to Samuel Taylor Coleridge, 9 January 1797, Marrs, I, p. 89.

31. CL to Samuel Taylor Coleridge, 8 November 1797, Marrs, I, p. 59.

32. CL to Samuel Taylor Coleridge, [1 December 1796], Marrs, I, pp. 66–7.

33. ibid., p. 66.

34. CL to Samuel Taylor Coleridge, [9 December 1796], Marrs, I, p. 73.

35. CL to Samuel Taylor Coleridge, 10 December 1796, Marrs, I, p. 77.

36. CL to Samuel Taylor Coleridge, 5 February 1797, Marrs, I, p. 96.

37. CL to Samuel Taylor Coleridge, 7 April 1797, Marrs, I, p. 106.

38. CL to Samuel Taylor Coleridge, 24 June 1797, Marrs, I, p. 113.

Chapter 5: Lloyd and Southey

1. Ernest de Selincourt, cited in Margaret Drabble (ed.), *The Oxford Companion to English Literature* (Oxford University Press, 1995), p. 1095.

2. Juliet Barker, *Wordsworth: A Life* (Viking, 2000), pp. 200–201.

3. Wordsworth, 'The Prelude', X, 918–20.

4. Cited by Barker, *Wordsworth*, p. 18.

5. E. V. Lucas (ed.), *Charles Lamb and the Lloyds* (Smith, Elder & Co., 1898), p. 17.

6. CL to Samuel Taylor Coleridge, [?20 September 1797], Marrs, I, p. 123.

7. 'Written on Christmas Day, 1797'.

8. CL to Samuel Taylor Coleridge, [28 January 1798], Marrs, I, p. 126.

9. ibid., p. 127.

10. 'A Quaker's Meeting'.

11. 'Grace Before Meat'.

12. 'A Quaker's Meeting'.

13. See, for example, F. V. Morley, *Lamb Before Elia* (Jonathan Cape, 1932), p. 194.

14. Samuel Taylor Coleridge to Joseph Cottle, E. L. Griggs (ed.), *Collected Letters of Samuel Taylor Coleridge*, 6 vols. (Oxford University Press, 1956–71), I, pp. 357–8; see also Samuel Taylor Coleridge, *Biographica Literaria*, ch i.

15. Griggs (ed.), *Collected Letters of Samuel Taylor Coleridge*, I, p. 403.

16. CL to Samuel Taylor Coleridge, [*c.* 23 May–6 June] 1798, Marrs, I, pp. 128–9.

17. *Analytical Review*, May 1798.

18. CL to Robert Lloyd, [13 or 23 August 1798], Marrs, I, p. 134.

19. CL to Robert Southey, [29 October 1798], Marrs, I, p. 139, and 21 January 1799, Marrs, I, p. 156.

20. CL to Robert Lloyd, [13 or 23 August 1798], Marrs, I, pp. 134–5.

21. CL to Robert Lloyd, 13 November 1798, Marrs, I, p. 144.

22. *Critical Review*, no. 24, October 1798.

23. CL to Robert Southey, 8 November 1798, Marrs, I, pp. 142–3.

24. W. C. Hazlitt, *Mary and Charles Lamb: Poems, Letters and Remains* (Chatto & Windus, 1874), p. 164.

25. CL to Robert Southey, [28 November 1798], Marrs, I, p. 152.

26. Winifred Courtney, *Young Charles Lamb 1775–1802* (Macmillan, 1982), p. 227.

27. CL to Robert Southey, [28 November 1798], Marrs, I, p. 152.

28. Lucas (ed.), *Charles Lamb and the Lloyds*, p. 99.

29. CL to Robert Southey, 21 January 1799, Marrs, I, p. 156.

30. CL to Robert Southey, [29 October 1798], Marrs, I, p. 139.

31. CL to Robert Southey, [23 January 1799], Marrs, I, p. 160.

32. 'Written on the Day of my Aunt's Funeral'.

33. CL to Robert Lloyd, [23 April 1799], Marrs, I, p. 169.

Chapter 6: Toad and Frog

1. Thomas De Quincey, *Literary Reminiscences* (1851), I, pp. 67–70.

2. See Edith Christina Johnson, *Lamb Always Elia* (Methuen, 1935), p. 39.

3. Cited by Lucas, *Life*, II, p. 57.

4. Preface to *The Last Essays of Elia*.

5. 'All Fools' Day'.

6. 'Oxford in the Vacation'.

7. Winifred Courtney, *Young Charles Lamb 1775–1802* (Macmillan, 1982), p. 204.

8. Kenneth Curry (ed.), *New Letters of Robert Southey* (Columbia University Press, 1965), p. 190.

9. 'Curious Fragments'.

10. CL to Robert Southey, 31 October 1799, Marrs, I, pp. 171–2.

11. CL to Thomas Manning, [mid-] December 1799, Marrs, I, p. 173.

12. 'Oxford in the Vacation'.

13. CL to Thomas Manning, 27 December 1800, Marrs, I, p. 263.

14. CL to Thomas Manning, [late September or early October 1801], Marrs, II, p. 25.

15. CL to Samuel Taylor Coleridge, [23 January 1800], Marrs, I, p. 180.

16. CL to Thomas Manning, [18 February 1800], Marrs, I, pp. 185–6.

17. ibid.

18. CL to Thomas Manning, [1 March 1800], Marrs, I, p. 187.

19. CL to Samuel Taylor Coleridge, [16 or 17 April] 1800, Marrs, I, p. 200.

20. CL to Thomas Manning, [17 March 1800], Marrs, I, p. 189.

21. Samuel Taylor Coleridge to William Godwin, E. L. Griggs (ed.), *Collected Letters of Samuel Taylor Coleridge*, 6 vols. (Oxford University Press, 1956–71), I, pp. 579–80.

22. ML to Sarah Stoddart, [21 September 1803], Marrs, II, pp. 123–4.

23. Lucas, *Life*, II, p. 966.

24. 'Mackery End, in Hertfordshire'.

25. CL to Samuel Taylor Coleridge, [3 October 1796], Marrs, I, p. 50.

26, CL to Samuel Taylor Coleridge, 6 August 1800, Marrs, I, p. 217.

27. CL to Thomas Manning, [17 March 1800], Marrs, I, pp. 189–90.

28. CL to Thomas Manning, [5 April 1800], Marrs, I, pp. 191–2.

29. The whole event is recounted in CL to Samuel Taylor Coleridge, [16 or 17 April] 1800, Marrs, I, pp. 198–201.

30. CL to Samuel Taylor Coleridge, [12 May 1800], Marrs, I, pp. 202–3.

31. CL to Thomas Manning, [17 May 1800], Marrs, I, pp. 203–4.

32. CL to Thomas Manning, [20 May 1800], Marrs, I, p. 207.

33. CL to Thomas Manning, [1 June 1800], Marrs, I, p. 208.

34. CL to Thomas Manning, [8 June 1800], Marrs, I, pp. 208–9.

35. Cited in Lucas, *Life*, I, p. 298.

36. Thomas Sadler (ed.), *Diary, Reminiscences and Correspondence of Henry Crabb Robinson*, 3 vols. (Macmillan, 1869), II, p. 247; III, p. 59; III, p. 60.

37. Cited in Courtney, *Young Charles Lamb*, p. 195.

38. CL to Thomas Manning, [3 November 1800], Marrs, I, p. 245.

39. 'Newspapers Thirty-Five Years Ago'.

40. Lucas, *Life*, I, p. 200.

41. CL to Thomas Manning, [31 August 1801], Marrs, II, p. 16.

42. *The Albion and Evening Advertiser*, 30 June 1801, p. 3; reprinted in Courtney, *Young Charles Lamb*, Appendix B, pp. 343–6.

43. CL to John Rickman, 16 September [1801], Marrs, II, p. 21.

44. Cited by George L. Barnett, *Charles Lamb: The Evolution of Elia* (Indiana University Press, 1964), p. 10.

45. Cited by Edmund Blunden (ed.), *Charles Lamb: His Life Recorded by his Contemporaries* (Hogarth, 1934), pp. 36–7.

46. Griggs (ed.), *Collected Letters of Samuel Taylor Coleridge*, I, p. 569.

47. 'Newspapers Thirty-Five Years Ago'.

48. CL to John Rickman, [mid-January 1802], Marrs, II, p. 45.

49. CL to Samuel Taylor Coleridge, [11 October 1802], Marrs, II, pp. 77–9.

50. Marrs, II, p. 53n.

51. CL to William Godwin, [10 November 1803], Marrs, II, p. 128.

52. ML to Dorothy Wordsworth, [13 October 1804], Marrs, II, p. 148, and ML to Sarah Stoddart, [30 May–2 June 1806], Marrs, II, p. 229.

53. *Popular Fallacies*: 'That the worst Puns are the Best.'

54. CL to John Rickman, [?14 February 1802], Marrs, II, p. 52.

55. CL to John Rickman, [early December 1801], Marrs, II, pp. 39–41.

56. Cited by Marrs, II, p. 12.

57. CL to Thomas Manning, April 1801, Marrs, II, p. 3.

58. CL to Walter Wilson, 14 August 1801, Marrs, II, p. 11.

59. CL to John Rickman, 9 January [1802], Marrs, II, pp. 42–4.

60. CL to John Rickman, [?14 February 1802], Marrs, II, p. 52.

61. CL to Thomas Manning, [29 November 1800], Marrs, I, p. 248.

62. CL to William Wordsworth, [30 January 1801], Marrs, I, pp. 267–8.

63. CL to Thomas Manning, [?27 February 1801], Marrs, I, p. 277.

64. Derek Roper's preface to his edition of Wordsworth's *Lyrical Ballads* (Northcote House, 1987), p. 9.

65. Wordsworth's preface, ibid., p. 21.

66. ibid., pp. 25 and 33.

67. G. A. Anderson (ed.), *The Letters of Thomas Manning to Charles Lamb* (Harper, New York, 1926), p. 74.

Chapter 7: The Critic and the Playwright

1. William St Clair, *The Godwins and the Shelleys: the Biography of a Family* (Faber & Faber, 1990), p. 232.

2. CL to John Rickman, 16 September [1801], Marrs, II, p. 22.

3. CL to Thomas Manning, 15 February 1802, Marrs, II, p. 55.

4. CL to Thomas Manning, [16 October 1800], Marrs, I, pp. 241–2.

5. CL to Thomas Manning, 24 September 1802, Marrs, II, p. 70.

6. Sir George Etherage, *She Would If She Could* (1668), V, i, 557–8.

7. See, for example, Robert Lloyd's opinion, cited by E. V. Lucas, in *Charles Lamb and the Lloyds* (Smith, Elder & Co., 1898), pp. 154–5.

8. CL to William Wordsworth, [30 January 1801], Marrs, I, pp. 265–6,

9. CL to Thomas Manning, [15 February 1801], Marrs, I, pp. 272–3.

10. Anderson (ed.), *The Letters of Thomas Manning to Charles Lamb* (Martin Secker, 1925), [25 February 1801], p. 52.

11. CL to Thomas Manning, [?27 February 1801], Marrs, I, p. 276.

12. P. G. Patmore, *My Friends and Acquaintance* (Saunders & Otley, 1854), pp. 11–12 and 18.

13. Lucas, *Life*, II, pp. 202 and 63–4.

14. ibid., II, p. 93.

15. ibid., II, pp. 7–8; I, p. 77; II, p. 265.

16. P. G. Patmore, *My Friends and Acquaintance*, p. 14.

17. ibid., p. 15; Charles and Mary Cowden Clarke, *Recollections of Writers* (Centaur, 1969; first published in book form 1878), p. 57; Thomas Allsop (ed.), *Letters, Conversations and Recollections of Samuel Taylor Coleridge*, 2 vols. (Moxon, 1836), p. 36.

18. Cowden Clarke, *Recollections*, p. 177.

19. Lucas, *Life*, II, p. 202.

20. CL to Thomas Manning, [3 November 1800], Marrs, I, p. 243.

21. 'Valentine's Day'.

22. CL to Thomas Manning, [?27 February 1801], Marrs, I, p. 277, and April 1801, Marrs, II, p. 3.

23. The whole incident of Dyer's 'illness' is told in a letter by CL to John Rickman, [late October or early November 1801], Marrs, II, pp. 28–32, and the encounter with the Earl in CL to John Rickman, 9 January [1802], Marrs, II, pp. 42–4.

24. 17 February 1802, Robert Southey writes to John Rickman, in Edmund Blunden (ed.), *Charles Lamb: His Life Recorded by his Contemporaries* (Hogarth, 1934), p. 36.

25. CL to John Rickman, 24 November 1801, Marrs, II, p. 37.

26. Mary Moorman (ed.), *Journals of Dorothy Wordsworth: The Alfoxden Journal 1798; The Grasmere Journals 1800–1803*, 2nd edn (Oxford University Press, 1980), p. 42.

27. Cited by Blunden (ed.), *Charles Lamb*, p. 35.

28. Robert Southey to John Rickman, 17 February 1802, cited by Blunden (ed.), *Charles Lamb*, p. 37.

29. Kenneth Curry (ed.), *New Letters of Robert Southey*, (Columbia University Press, 1965), p. 184

30. F. V. Morley, *Lamb Before Elia* (Jonathan Cape, 1932), p. 233.

31. CL to Samuel Taylor Coleridge, [8 September 1802], Marrs, II, pp. 65–7.

32. ibid.

33. CL to Thomas Manning, 24 September 1802, Marrs, II, pp. 68–71.

34. ibid.

35. CL to Samuel Taylor Coleridge, [13 April 1803], Marrs, II, pp. 108–9.

36. CL to Samuel Taylor Coleridge, 4 November 1802, Marrs, II, p. 84.

37. Samuel Taylor Coleridge to his wife, 4 April 1803, Blunden (ed.), *Charles Lamb*, p. 38.

38. Lucas, *Life*, I, p. 173.

39. ML to Dorothy Wordsworth, 9 July [1803], Marrs, II, pp. 117–19.

40. ML to Sarah Stoddart, 1 December [1802], Marrs, II, pp. 89–91.

41. ML to Dorothy Wordsworth, 9 July [1803], Marrs, II, pp. 117–19.

42. James Burney to John Rickman, 27 July 1803, Marrs, II, p. 121.

43. CL to John Rickman, 27 July 1803, Marrs, II, p. 122.

44. Cowden Clarke, *Recollections*, p. 54.

45. Clara Novello, *Reminiscences* (Edward Arnold, 1910), p. 33.

46. Cowden Clarke, *Recollections*, p. 173.

47. ibid., p. 184.

48. CL to William Wordsworth, [28 April 1815], Marrs, III, pp. 147–8.

49. Patmore, *My Friends and Acquaintance*, p. 84.

50. Allsop (ed.), *Letters of S. T. Coleridge*, p. 218.

51. CL to William Wordsworth, [16 April 1815], Marrs, III, p. 141.

52. Lucas, *Life*, II, pp. 263–5.

53. Thomas Sadler (ed.), *Diary, Reminiscences and Correspondence of Henry Crabb Robinson*, 3 vols. (Macmillan, 1869), 15 December 1811.

54. Patmore, *My Friends and Acquaintance*, p. 89.

Chapter 8: Toothache and Gumboil

1. ML to Dorothy Wordsworth, 9 July [1803], Marrs, II, p. 117.
2. CL to William Godwin, [16 September 1801], Marrs, II, p. 18.
3. CL to William Godwin, [10 November 1803], Marrs, II, pp. 127–9.
4. CL to Thomas Manning, 15 February 1802, Marrs, II, pp. 54–8.
5. ML to Sarah Stoddart, [?27 March 1804], Marrs, II, pp. 133–5.
6. William Wordsworth to Thomas Clarkson, 16 February [1805], Ernest de Selincourt (ed.), *The Letters of William and Dorothy Wordsworth*, 8 vols. (Clarendon, 1967–93), I, pp. 544–5.
7. ibid.
8. CL to William Wordsworth, 4 March [1805], Marrs, II, pp. 157–9.
9. Dorothy Wordsworth to Mrs Thomas Clarkson, [c. 16 April 1805], De Selincourt (ed.), *Letters of William and Dorothy Wordsworth*, I, pp. 584–5.
10. CL to Dorothy Wordsworth, 14 June 1805, Marrs, II, pp. 169–71.
11. ML to Sarah Stoddart, [18 September 1805], Marrs, II, pp. 173–5.
12. ML to Sarah Stoddart, [early November 1805], Marrs, II, pp. 182–5.
13. ibid.
14. ML to Sarah Stoddart, [9 and 14 November 1805], Marrs, II, pp. 185–7.
15. ML to Sarah Stoddart, [mid-June 1804], Marrs, II, pp. 141–4.
16. CL to William Hazlitt, 15 January 1806, Marrs, II, pp. 199–201. The same sentiment appears in *Popular Fallacies*: 'That home is home . . .' and also in Charles's play *The Wife's Trial*.
17. *Popular Fallacies*: 'That home is home though it is never so homely.'

18. Thomas M. Rysor (ed.), *Coleridge's Shakespearean Criticism* (Dent, 1964), II, p. 11.

19. ibid., II, p. 12.

20. 'Mackery End, in Hertfordshire'.

21. R. L. and Maria Edgeworth, *Essays on Practical Education* (R. Hunter, 1815), p. 412.

22. Cited by Joseph E. Riehl in *Charles Lamb's Children's Literature* (Institut für Anglistik und Amerikanistik, Universität Salzburg, 1980), p. 28.

23. ibid., pp. 83–4.

24. ML to Sarah Stoddart, 14 March [1806], Marrs, II, pp. 218–21.

25. ML to Sarah Stoddart, [30 May–2 June 1806], Marrs, II, pp. 227–30.

26. CL to William Wordsworth, 26 June 1806, Marrs, II, pp. 230–33.

27. ML to Sarah Stoddart, [?27 March 1804], Marrs, II, pp. 133–5.

28. ML to Sarah Stoddart, [mid-June 1804], Marrs, II, pp. 141–4.

29. ML to Mrs Coleridge, [13 October 1804], Marrs, II, pp. 148–9.

30. 'A Bachelor's Complaint on the Behaviour of Married People'.

31. 'The Old and the New School Master'.

32. 'A Bachelor's Complaint on the Behaviour of Married People'.

33. Charles and Mary Cowden Clarke, *Recollections of Writers* (Centaur, 1969; first published in book form in 1878), p. 163.

34. 'New Year's Eve'.

35. ML to Sarah Stoddart, [30 May–2 June 1806], Marrs, II, pp. 227–30.

36. ML to Sarah Stoddart Hazlitt, [30 March 1810], Marrs, III, pp. 49–52.

37. ML to Sarah Stoddart, [23 October 1806], Marrs, II, pp. 241–3.

38. ML to Mrs Clarkson, 13 March 1806, Marrs, II, pp. 215–18.

39. CL to Thomas Manning, 10 May 1806, Marrs, II, pp. 225–7.

40. ML to Dorothy Wordsworth, [29 August 1806], Marrs, II, pp. 238–9.

41. ML to Samuel Taylor Coleridge, [early to mid-September 1806], Marrs, II, pp. 240–41.

42. CL to Thomas Manning, 5 December 1806, Marrs, II, pp. 244–8.

43. William Hazlitt, *London Magazine*, in Edmund Blunden (ed.), *Charles Lamb: His Life Recorded by his Contemporaries* (Hogarth, 1934), pp. 40–41.

44. Thomas Sadler (ed.), *Diary, Reminiscences and Correspondence of Henry Crabb Robinson*, 3 vols. (Macmillan, 1869), I, p. 230.

45. CL to Thomas Manning, 2 January 1810, Marrs, III, p. 35.

46. CL to Mr and Mrs Thomas Clarkson, [June 1807], Marrs, II, pp. 257–8.

47. Thomas Noon Talfourd, *Final Memorials of Charles Lamb* (Moxon, 1850), pp. 351–2.

48. CL to Mrs Clarkson, [?20 July 1807], Marrs, II, p. 259.

49. ML to Sarah Stoddart, [28 November 1807], Marrs, II, pp. 261–2.

50. ML to Sarah Stoddart, [12 February 1808], Marrs, II, pp. 268–70.

51. ML to Sarah Stoddart, [28 November 1807], Marrs, II, pp. 261–2.

52. CL to Robert Southey, 9 August 1815, Marrs, III, p. 181. Also see 'The Wedding'.

Chapter 9: Friends and Confessions

1. A. H. Thompson, 'Lamb', in *The Cambridge History of English Literature* (Cambridge University Press, 1961), XII, p. 190.

2. Thomas Sadler (ed.), *Diary, Reminiscences and Correspondence of Henry Crabb Robinson*, 3 vols. (Macmillan, 1869), III, p. 487.

3. Charles and Mary Cowden Clarke, *Recollections of Writers* (Centaur, 1969; first published in book form 1878), p. 178.

4. Edmund Blunden (ed.), *Charles Lamb: His Life Recorded by his Contemporaries* (Hogarth, 1934), p. 55.

5. Lucas, *Life*, II, p. 284.

6. William Godwin, *The Enquirer: Reflections on Education, Manners and Literature* (London, 1797), p. 144.

7. Joseph E. Riehl, *Charles Lamb's Children's Literature* (Institut für Anglistik und Amerikanistik, Universität Salzburg, 1980), pp. 95–6.

8. CL to Thomas Manning, 26 February 1808, Marrs, II, pp. 271–5.

9. Dorothy Wordsworth to Jane Pollard Marshall, [23] and 24 February [1808], Ernest de Selincourt (ed.), *The Letters of William and Dorothy Wordsworth*, 8 vols. (Clarendon, 1967–93), II, i, pp. 198, 200.

10. CL to Thomas Manning, 26 February 1808, Marrs, II, pp. 271–5.

11. William Wordsworth to Samuel Taylor Coleridge, 19 April 1808, de Selincourt (ed.), *Letters of William and Dorothy Wordsworth*, II, i, pp. 217–23.

12. ML to Mrs Clarkson, [10 December 1808], Marrs, II, pp. 289–91.

13. Lucas, *Life*, II, p. 267.

14. ML to Mrs Clarkson, [10 December 1808], Marrs, II, pp. 289–91.

15. ML to Sarah Stoddart Hazlitt, with a postscript from CL, [9 and 10 December 1808], Marrs, II, pp. 286–8.

16. CL to Thomas Manning, 28 [29] March 1809, Marrs, III, pp. 3–5.

17. CL to Samuel Taylor Coleridge, [7 June 1809], Marrs, III, pp. 12–16.

18. E. V. Lucas, *Charles Lamb and the Lloyds* (Smith, Elder & Co., 1898), p. 159.

19. ibid., p. 161.

20. Eleanor M. Gates (ed.), *Leigh Hunt: A Life in Letters* (Falls River, 1998).

21. ML to Sarah Stoddart Hazlitt, [7 November 1809], Marrs, III, pp. 30–33.

22. Sadler (ed.), *Diary of Henry Crabb Robinson*, 15 December 1811.

23. CL to Robert Lloyd, [1 January 1810], Marrs, III, pp. 33–4.

24. John Lamb, *A Letter to the Right Hon. William Windham, on His Opposition to Lord Erskine's Bill, for the Prevention of Cruelty to Animals*, p.19.

25. Lucas, *Life*, II, p. 80.

26. ibid., p. 12.

27. John Lamb, *A Letter*, p. 7, citing Robert Burns.

28. Henry Crabb Robinson to Dorothy Wordsworth, 23 December 1810, Sadler (ed.), *Diary of Henry Crabb Robinson*, I, p. 316.

29. ML to Dorothy Wordsworth, 13 November 1810, Marrs, III, pp. 60–62.

30. ibid.

31. ML and CL to Dorothy Wordsworth, [23 November 1810], Marrs, III, p. 65.

32. CL to William Hazlitt, 28 November 1810, Marrs, III, pp. 68–9.

33. CL to William Godwin, [November or December 1810?], Marrs, III, p. 70.

34. Dorothy Wordsworth to Catherine Clarkson, 30 October [1810], de Selincourt (ed.), *Letters of William and Dorothy Wordsworth*, II, i, p. 439.

35. Dorothy Wordsworth to Henry Crabb Robinson, 6 November 1810, de Selincourt (ed.), *Letters of William and Dorothy Wordsworth*, II, i, pp. 443–4.

36. CL to Henry Crabb Robinson, [May 1809], Marrs, III, p. 10.

37. ML to Sarah Stoddart Hazlitt, [30 March 1810], Marrs, III, pp. 49–52.

38. Henry Crabb Robinson to Dorothy Wordsworth, 23 December 1810, Sadler (ed.), *Diary of Henry Crabb Robinson*, I, p. 316.

39. ML to Dorothy Wordsworth, 13 November 1810, Marrs, III, pp. 60–64 (postscript by Charles).

40. Henry Crabb Robinson to Dorothy Wordsworth, 23 December 1810, Sadler (ed.), *Diary of Henry Crabb Robinson*, I, p. 316.

41. ML to Mary Matilda Betham, [6 March 1811], Marrs, III, pp. 71–3.

42. Juliet Barker, *Wordsworth: A Life* (Viking, 2000), p. 417.

43. Richard Holmes, *Coleridge: Early Visions* (Flamingo, 1999), p. 366.

44. Samuel Taylor Coleridge to Henry Crabb Robinson, Sadler (ed.), *Diary of Henry Crabb Robinson*, I, p. 364.

45. Sadler (ed.), *Diary of Henry Crabb Robinson*, 3 August 1811, I, p. 340.

46. ibid., 17 January 1812, I, p. 370.

47. ibid., 8 January 1811, I, p. 319.

48. ibid., 5 December 1811, I, p. 348.

49. P. D. Penrose (ed.), *The Autobiography and Memoirs of Benjamin Robert Haydon 1786–1846* (G. Bell, 1927), pp. 138–9.

50. Hyder E. Rollins (ed.), *The Letters of John Keats 1814–1821*, 2 vols. (Harvard University Press, 1958), I, p. 215.

51. Cited in supplement to *CLS Bulletin*, no. 51, July 1941.

52. See the footnote in Sadler (ed.), *Diary of Henry Crabb Robinson*, I, p. 383.

53. Sadler (ed.), *Diary of Henry Crabb Robinson*, 20 April 1812, I, p. 379; 15 May 1811, I, p. 329; I, p. 409; 12 April 1812, I, p. 378.

54. ibid., 16 March 1812, I, pp. 375–6.

55. Blunden (ed.), *Charles Lamb*, p. 65.

56. ibid., pp. 64–5.

57. Gates (ed.), *Leigh Hunt*.

58. No. ix.

59. Thomas Noon Talfourd, *Final Memorials of Charles Lamb* (Moxon, 1850), p. 341.

60. ibid., p. x; p. 337.

61. Cited by Gerald Monsman, *Confessions of a Prosaic Dreamer: Charles Lamb's art of autobiography* (Duke University Press, 1984), pp. 33–4.

62. ibid., p. 17.

63. ibid., p. 32.

64. The discovery is fully described in ML to Barbara Betham, 2 November 1814, Marrs, III, pp. 116–18.

65. Sadler (ed.), *Diary of Henry Crabb Robinson*, 29 June 1814, I, p. 432.

66. ibid., 3 July 1814, I, pp. 432–3.

67. CL to William Wordsworth, 9 August 1814, Marrs, III, p. 96.

68. CL to William Wordsworth, [19 September 1814], Marrs, III, p. 111.

69. Sadler (ed.), *Diary of Henry Crabb Robinson*, 17 November 1814, I, p. 461.

70. ibid., 11 December 1814, I, pp. 463–4.

71. CL to William Wordsworth, [28 December 1814], Marrs, III, p. 125.

72. Sadler (ed.), *Diary of Henry Crabb Robinson*, 19 December 1814, I, p. 465.

73. ibid., 20 December 1814, I, pp. 465–6.

Chapter 10: Crimes and Horrors

1. 'The Historical Importance of Certain *Essays of Elia*', by Geoffrey Tillotson, pp. 89–116 in J. V. Logan, J. E. Jordan and Northrop Frye (eds.), *Some British Romantics: a Collection of Essays* (Ohio State University Press, 1966), pp. 112, 93, 95.

2. CL to William Wordsworth, [7 January 1815], Marrs, III, pp. 128–30.

3. CL to Mrs Joseph Hume?, [March 1815?], Marrs, III, p. 138.

4. CL to William Wordsworth, [16 April 1815], Marrs, III, p. 141.

5. ML and CL to Mrs Morgan and Charlotte Brent, [22 May 1815], Marrs, III, pp. 159–62.

6. 'Mackery End, in Hertfordshire'.

7. CL to Mary Matilda Betham, [?16 September 1815], Marrs, III, p. 197.

8. CL to Mary Matilda Betham, [early October? 1815], Marrs, III, p. 200.

9. CL to Sara Hutchinson, 19 October 1815, Marrs, III, p. 203.

10. Lucas, *Life*, II, p. 281.

11. CL to Sara Hutchinson, 19 October 1815, Marrs, III, p. 203.

12. CL to William Wordsworth, 26 April 1816, Marrs, III, p. 215.

13. ibid., pp. 215–16.

14. Lucas, *Life*, I, p. 362.

15. Willard Bissell Pope (ed.), *The Diary of Benjamin Robert Haydon*, 5 vols. (Harvard University Press, 1963), III, pp. 319–20.

16. Thomas Sadler (ed.), *Diary, Reminiscences and Correspondence of Henry Crabb Robinson*, 3 vols. (Macmillan, 1869), 22 December 1816, II, p. 40.

17. ibid., 27 May 1831, II, p. 505.

18. Pope (ed.), *Diary of Benjamin Robert Haydon*, III, p. 320.

19. CL to William Wordsworth, 26 April 1816, Marrs, III, p. 216.

20. ML to Sara Hutchinson, [November? 1816], Marrs, III, p. 234.

21. CL to Dorothy Wordsworth, [21 November 1817], Lucas, I, p. 507.

22. Lucas, *Life*, II, p. 115.

23. Pope (ed.), *Diary of Benjamin Robert Haydon*, II, p. 173.

24. ibid., pp. 173–6; P. D. Penrose (ed.), *The Autobiography and Memoirs of Benjamin Robert Haydon 1786–1846* (G. Bell, 1927), pp. 231–3 and (in a letter to William Wordsworth of 1842)

563–4; John Keats to George and Tom Keats, 5 January 1818, in Hyder E. Rollins (ed.), *The Letters of John Keats 1814–1821*, 2 vols. (Harvard University Press, 1958), II, pp. 197–8.

25. J. W. Rogers, *A Statement of the Cruelties, Abuses and Frauds, which are practised in Mad-Houses* (E. Justins, 1815), pp. 13–30.

26. ibid., pp. 31 and 39.

27. Anon., *A Description of the Crimes and Horrors of the Interior of Warburton's Private Mad-House at Hoxton, commonly called Whitmore House* (Benbow, ?1822), pp. 6–8.

28. ibid., pp. 14–15.

29. Rogers, *A Statement of the Cruelties*, p. 31.

30. ibid., p. 19.

31. Anon., *A Description of the Crimes*, p. 25.

32. ibid., pp. 8 and 19.

33. See William Ll. Parry-Jones, *The Trade in Lunacy: A Study of Private Madhouses in England in the Eighteenth and Nineteenth Centuries* (Routledge & Kegan Paul, 1972), pp. 240–41, p. 252.

34. CL to Samuel Taylor Coleridge, [17 October 1796], Marrs, I, p. 52.

35. CL to Thomas Manning, [1 June 1800], Marrs, I, p. 208.

36. CL to Samuel Taylor Coleridge, 28 October 1796, Marrs, I, p. 56.

37. Cited by Parry-Jones, *The Trade in Lunacy*, p. 16.

Chapter 11: C.L. and Co.

1. CL to Mary Wordsworth, 18 February 1818, Lucas, I, p. 511.

2. See Lucas, I, p. 518.

3. CL to Thomas Manning, 28 May 1819, Lucas, I, p. 522 and CL to William Wordsworth, [7 June 1819], Lucas, I, p. 524.

4. CL to Mary Matilda Betham, 1 June 1816, Marrs, III, p. 218.

5. This is related in 'Barbara S——' and is also mentioned in Thomas

Sadler (ed.), *Diary, Reminiscences and Correspondence of Henry Crabb Robinson*, 3 vols. (Macmillan, 1869), III, p. 19.

6. L. E. Holman, *Lamb's 'Barbara S—'* (Methuen, 1935), p. 38.

7. ibid., p. 37.

8. Sadler (ed.), *Diary of Henry Crabb Robinson*, 4 April 1828, II, p. 388.

9. Holman, *Lamb's 'Barbara S—'*, p. 69.

10. E.g. by Mrs Balmanno in Walter Jerrold (ed.), *Thomas Hood and Charles Lamb: The Story of a Friendship* (Ernest Benn, 1930), p. 12.

11. CL to Dorothy Wordsworth, [25 November 1819], Lucas, I, p. 534.

12. ML to Mrs Vincent Novello, [spring of 1820], Lucas, I, p. 539.

13. Sadler (ed.), *Diary of Henry Crabb Robinson*, II, p. 165.

14. CL to Miss Humphries, 27 January 1821, Lucas, II, p. 550.

15. Charles and Mary Cowden Clarke, *Recollections of Writers* (Centaur, 1969; first published in book form 1878).

16. Sadler (ed.), *Diary of Henry Crabb Robinson*, 18 November 1821, II, p. 218.

17. Dorothy Wordsworth to Henry Crabb Robinson, 3 March 1822, Sadler (ed.), *Diary of Henry Crabb Robinson*, II, p. 225.

18. CL to William Wordsworth, 20 March 1822, Lucas, II, p. 563.

19. ibid.

20. Lucas, *Life*, II, p. 44.

21. Sadler (ed.), *Diary of Henry Crabb Robinson*, 1 February 1836, III, pp. 89–90.

22. CL to Mrs William Ayrton, [(16) April 1833], Lucas, II, p. 907.

23. CL to John Chambers, [late May or early June 1817], Marrs, III, pp. 247–8.

24. CL to Bernard Barton, [25 February 1830], Lucas, II, p. 831.

25. CL to Thomas Manning, 15 February 1802, Marrs, II, pp. 54–5, and G. A. Anderson (ed.), *Letters of Thomas Manning to Charles Lamb* (Martin Secker, 1925), 2 February 1802, p. 62.

26. Sadler (ed.), *Diary of Henry Crabb Robinson*, 17 June 1832, II, p. 233.

27. CL to John Clare, 31 August 1822, Lucas, II, p. 570.

28. CL to Barron Field, 22 September 1822, Lucas, II, p. 573.

29. CL to Bernard Barton, 11 September 1822, Lucas, II, p. 572.

30. CL to Bernard Barton, [23 December 1822], Lucas, II, pp. 588–9.

31. See Lucas, II, p. 595n.

32. CL to Bernard Barton, 9 January 1823, Lucas, II, p. 594.

33. ibid., II, p. 595.

34. Ernest Dressel North (ed.), *The Wit and Wisdom of Charles Lamb* (G. P. Putnam's Sons, 1893), pp. 245–6, p. 230.

35. Sadler (ed.), *Diary of Henry Crabb Robinson*, I, p. 338.

36. Lucas, II, pp. 605–6.

37. CL to John Howard Payne, [January 1823], Lucas, II, p. 590.

38. CL to Bernard Barton, [11 October 1828], Lucas, II, p. 780.

39. Cited by Lucas, II, p. 606.

40. Accounts of the evening can be found in Sadler (ed.), *Diary of Henry Crabb Robinson*, II, pp. 246–9 and Edith J. Morley (ed.), *Correspondence of Henry Crabb Robinson with the Wordsworth Circle* (Clarendon, 1927), pp. 125–6; Lucas, *Life*, II, pp. 102–3.

41. CL to B. W. Procter, 13 April 1823, Lucas, II, p. 607.

Chapter 12: Bridget and Elia

1. Thomas Sadler (ed.), *Diary, Reminiscences and Correspondence of Henry Crabb Robinson*, 3 vols. (Macmillan, 1869), 8 January 1823, II, p. 240.

2. Mary Shelley to Leigh Hunt, 19 August 1823, in Betty T. Bennett (ed.), *The Letters of Mary Wollstonecraft Shelley*, 3 vols. (Johns Hopkins University Press), I, p. 375.

3. Mary Wollstonecraft Shelley to Marianne Hunt, 27 November

[1823], Bennett (ed.), *Letters of Mary Wollstonecraft Shelley*, I, p. 403.

4. CL to Bernard Barton, [17 August 1824], Lucas, II, p. 652.

5. Mary Wollstonecraft Shelley to Leigh Hunt, 26 October 1823, Bennett (ed.), *Letters of Mary Wollstonecraft Shelley*, I, p. 397.

6. CL to Bernard Barton, 2 September [1823], Lucas, II, p. 618.

7. ibid., p. 619.

8. Mary Wollstonecraft Shelley to M. Hunt, 27 November 1823, Bennett (ed.), *Letters of Mary Wollstonecraft Shelley*, I, p. 403.

9. CL to Bernard Barton, [10 July 1823], Lucas, II, p. 616.

10. Henry Crabb Robinson to Dorothy Wordsworth, 31 October 1823, in Lucas, *Life*, II, p. 111.

11. Lucas, *Life*, II, p. 164; CL to Robert Southey, 21 November 1823, Lucas, II, p. 627.

12. P. G. Patmore, *My Friends and Acquaintance* (Saunders & Otley, 1854), p. 56.

13. CL to Bernard Barton, 15 May 1824, Lucas, II, p. 643.

14. CL to Bernard Barton, [17 August 1824], Lucas, II, p. 653.

15. CL to William Wordsworth, 6 April 1825, Lucas, II, p. 674.

16. Sadler (ed.), *Diary of Henry Crabb Robinson*, 22 April 1825, II, p. 293.

17. CL to William Wordsworth, 6 April 1825, Lucas, II, p. 674.

18. CL to Sara Hutchinson, [18 April 1825], Lucas, II, p. 677.

19. Patmore, *My Friends and Acquaintance*, pp. 29–32.

20. Sadler (ed.), *Diary of Henry Crabb Robinson*, 9 May 1829, II, p. 416; Patmore, *My Friends and Acquaintance*, pp. 41–4.

21. Walter Jerrold (ed.), *Thomas Hood and Charles Lamb: The Story of a Friendship* (Ernest Benn, 1930), pp. 123–4.

22. Patmore, *My Friends and Acquaintance*, pp. 16–17.

23. ibid., pp. 20–21.

24. ibid., p. 21.

25. CL to Samuel Taylor Coleridge, [2 July 1825], Lucas, II, p. 684.

26. CL to Bernard Barton, [16 May 1826], Lucas, II, pp. 704–5.

27. Sadler (ed.), *Diary of Henry Crabb Robinson*, June 1825, II, p. 298.

28. CL to Henry Crabb Robinson, 20 January 1827, Lucas, II, p. 721.

29. ML to the Thomas Hoods, [?summer 1828], Lucas, II, p. 777; CL to Mary Wollstonecraft Shelley, 26 July 1827, Lucas, II, p. 739.

30. The poem was published in *Blackwood's Magazine* for June 1829 – see Lucas, II, p. 740.

31. CL to Thomas Hood, [?May 1829], Lucas, II, p. 809.

32. CL to Edward Moxon, 17 July 182[7], Lucas, II, p. 734.

33. CL to Thomas Hood, [18 September 1827], Lucas, II, p. 753.

34. CL to Bernard Barton, [late 1827], Lucas, II, p. 761.

35. CL to Bernard Barton, [4 December 1827], Lucas, II, p. 762.

36. CL to Bernard Barton, [11 October 1828], Lucas, II, p. 780.

37. Luther A. Brewer (ed.), *Some Lamb and Browning Letters to Leigh Hunt* (The Torch Press, 1924), pp. 16–17. It is interesting to compare this account with CL's letter to William Wordsworth, [22 January 1830], Lucas, II, p. 827.

38. John Forster in Edmund Blunden (ed.), *Charles Lamb: His Life Recorded by his Contemporaries* (Hogarth, 1934), p. 241.

39. Patmore, *My Friends and Acquaintance*, p. 49.

40. CL to Vincent Novello, [6 November 1828], Lucas, II, p. 782.

41. ML to the Thomas Hoods, [?summer 1828], Lucas, II, p. 777.

42. Edward Moxon, *Contemporary Notices of Charles Lamb* (private reprint, 1891), p. 17.

43. Jerrold (ed.), *Thomas Hood and Charles Lamb*, p. 11.

44. ibid., p. 12.

45. Ernest Dressel North (ed.), *The Wit and Wisdom of Charles Lamb* (G. P. Putnam's Sons, 1893), p. 232.

46. ibid., p. 235.

47. CL to B. W. Procter, [19 January 1829] and 22 January 1829, Lucas, II, pp. 794–6.

48. CL to Bernard Barton, [3 June 1829], Lucas, II, p. 811.

49. CL to Bernard Barton, 25 July 1829, Lucas, II, p. 813.

50. ibid., p. 814.

51. CL to Edward Moxon, [22 September 1829], Lucas, II, p. 815.

52. CL to Bernard Barton, 25 July 1829, Lucas, II, p. 814.

53. ibid.

54. CL to James Gillman, 30 November 1829, Lucas, II, pp. 821–3. I think this letter is mistakenly interpreted as addressed to Gillman, (a) because it appears to address the *reader* as Coleridge (see p. 823); (b) because Mary had just returned from a visit to the Gillmans', where Coleridge was residing, and (c) because the tone of the writing seems more consonant with Charles's other letters to Coleridge. The only clue to its addressee seems to be 'Dear G' which has possibly been mistaken and may have been intended to read 'Dear C'.

55. CL to William Wordsworth, [22 January 1830], Lucas, II, p. 827.

56. Patmore, *My Friends and Acquaintance*, p. 52.

57. CL to Bernard Barton, 25 July 1829, Lucas, II, p. 814.

58. Patmore, *My Friends and Acquaintance*, p. 53.

59. ibid., p. 54; my italics.

60. ibid., pp. 53–5.

61. ibid., p. 27; my italics.

62. ibid., p. 28.

63. ibid., p. 71.

64. CL to Sarah Stoddart Hazlitt, [24 May 1830], Lucas, II, p. 854.

65 CL to James Vale Asbury, [no date], Lucas, II, p. 845.

66. CL to Bernard Barton, [30 August 1830], Lucas, II, pp. 858–9.

67. CL to Edward Moxon, 12 November 1830, Lucas, II, p. 861.

68. Thomas Allsop (ed.), *Letters, Conversations and Recollections of S. T. Coleridge* (Moxon, 1836), p. 204.

69. ibid., pp. 208–9.

70. Sadler (ed.), *Diary of Henry Crabb Robinson*, II, p. 36.

71. Patmore, *My Friends and Acquaintance*, p. 22.

72. Cited by F. V. Morley, *Lamb Before Elia*, p. 233.

73. Edmund Blunden (ed.), *Charles Lamb: His Life Recorded by his Contemporaries* (Hogarth, 1934), p. 186.

74. Charles Eliot Norton (ed.), *Thomas Carlyle, Reminiscences* (J. M. Dent, 1972), p. 65.

75. Sadler (ed.), *Diary of Henry Crabb Robinson*, III, p. 11.

76. Patmore, *My Friends and Acquaintance*, pp. 45–6.

77. CL to William Wordsworth, end of May [1833], Lucas, II, p. 911.

78. CL to Sarah Stoddart Hazlitt, 31 May 1833, Lucas, II, p. 913; CL to Edward Moxon, [28 January 1834], Lucas, II, p. 927.

79. CL to B. W. Procter, 11 November 1824, Lucas, II, p. 656.

Chapter 13: Emma and the End

1. CL to Edward Moxon, [24 July 1833], Lucas, II, p. 915.

2. CL and ML to Edward and Emma Moxon, [?31 July 1833], Lucas, II, p. 916.

3. ibid.

4. Cited by Ernest Carton Ross, *Charles Lamb and Emma Isola: A survey of the evidence relevant to their personal relationship* (Charles Lamb Society, 1950), p. 37.

5. Cited by Ross, *Charles Lamb and Emma Isola*, p. 5.

6. Cited ibid., p. 4.

7. Ross, *Charles Lamb and Emma Isola*, p. 37.

8. ibid.

9. ibid., p. 9.

10. Cited by Ross, *Charles Lamb and Emma Isola*, pp. 18, 20, 22.

11. Dorothy Wordsworth to Jane Pollard Marshall, 29 September 1802, Ernest de Selincourt (ed.), *The Letters of William and Dorothy Wordsworth* (Clarendon, 1970), I, p. 377.

12. CL and ML to Edward and Emma Moxon, [?31 July 1833],

Lucas, II, p. 916, and CL to Edward Moxon, [17 October 1833], Lucas, II, p. 919.

13. CL to Mary Betham, 24 January 1834, Lucas, II, p. 927.

14. Charles Lamb to Miss Fryer, 14 February 1834, Lucas, II, pp. 928–9.

15. John Forster in Edmund Blunden (ed.), *Charles Lamb: His Life Recorded by his Contemporaries* (Hogarth, 1934), pp. 240–41.

16. CL to William Wordsworth, 20 March 1822, Lucas, II, p. 563.

17. Lucas, *Life*, II, pp. 66–7.

18. Letter from John Rickman, 24 January 1835, cited in *Charles Lamb Society Bulletin*, no. 58, April 1943.

19. Thomas Sadler (ed.), *Diary, Reminiscences and Correspondence of Henry Crabb Robinson*, 3 vols. (Macmillan, 1869), III, pp. 58–9.

20. Cited by Jane Aaron, *A Double Singleness: Gender and the Writings of Charles and Mary Lamb* (Clarendon, 1991), p. 3.

21. ibid.

22. Sadler (ed.), *Diary of Henry Crabb Robinson*, 3 December 1835, III, p. 73.

23. B. W. Procter to Thomas Talfourd, 22 June 1841, Lucas, *Life*, II, p. 285.

24. Sadler (ed.), *Diary of Henry Crabb Robinson*, III, p. 293.

25. Thomas Noon Talfourd, *Final Memorials of Charles Lamb* (Moxon, 1850), p. 360.

26. Juliet Barker, *Wordsworth: A Life* (Viking, 2000), p. 86.

27. Richard Holmes, *Coleridge: Early Visions* (Flamingo, 1999), p. 36n.

28. E. L. Griggs (ed.), *Collected Letters of Samuel Taylor Coleridge*, 6 vols. (Oxford University Press, 1956–71), I, p. 297.

Index

'C' indicates Charles Lamb; 'C&M' Charles and Mary Lamb; and 'M' Mary Lamb.

428

436